ROYAL MISTRESSES
of the House of Hanover–Windsor

SUSANNA DE VRIES

PIRGOS PRESS

© Susanna de Vries, 2012

This book is copyright. Apart from any fair dealing for the purposes of study, research, criticism, review, or as permitted under the Copyright Act, no part may be reproduced by any process printed or digital without written permission. Inquiries for reproduction by any means whatsoever should be made to the publisher. All photographs taken before 1955 are deemed under the terms of The Copyright Act to be out of copyright. The historical engravings by James Gillray are taken from originals which are the property of Pirgos Press and need their permission in order to be reproduced.

First published in May 2012, reprinted July of that year with updates.
Published by Pirgos Press, Cutty Sark Studio,
10 Matingara Street, Chapel Hill, Brisbane, 4069.
Printed and bound by Everbest, China.
Distributed in Australia by Dennis Jones & Associates Pty Ltd. Tel: 03-9762-9100.

National Library of Australia Cataloguing-in-Publication entry:
Author: De Vries, Susanna, 1935-
Title: ROYAL MISTRESSES OF THE HOUSE OF HANOVER-WINDSOR.
Editors: Marusia McCormick and Jake de Vries.

End notes with biographical details.
Includes index.
ISBN 978-0-9806216-2-4 (pbk.)

Subjects:
1) Hanover, House of–History.
2) Windsor, House of–History.
3) Mistresses–England–History.
4) Feminism–England–History.
5) Women–Sexual behaviour–Great Britain–History.
6) Favorites, Royal–England–History.

Dewey Number: 941 07

Front cover: THE MYSTERIOUS MISTRESS, unsigned nineteenth century pastel from a private collection. Photograph copyright © Pirgos Press.
Cover and book design by Jake de Vries.
Indexed by Jake de Vries.

Contents

PROLOGUE	1
CHAPTER 1 Melusine, Duchess of Kendal and Prince George Ludwig (later George I)	5
CHAPTER 2 Mary 'Perdita' Darby Robinson and George Augustus, Prince of Wales (later George IV)	25
CHAPTER 3 Maria Fitzherbert and George Augustus, Prince of Wales (later George IV)	53
CHAPTER 4 Lady Jennie Churchill and Edward, Prince of Wales (later Edward VII)	93
CHAPTER 5 Lady Daisy Brooke and Edward, Prince of Wales (later Edward VII)	137
CHAPTER 6 Alice Keppel and Edward, Prince of Wales (later Edward VII)	171
CHAPTER 7 Freda (Winifred) Dudley Ward and Edward, Prince of Wales (later Edward VIII)	213
CHAPTER 8 Lady Thelma Morgan Furness and Edward, Prince of Wales (later Edward VIII)	234
CHAPTER 9 Wallis Warfield Simpson and Edward VIII (later Duke of Windsor)	289
CHAPTER 10 Camilla, Duchess of Cornwall and Charles, Prince of Wales	359
DEDICATION AND ACKNOWLEDGEMENTS	397
ENDNOTES	398
INDEX	416

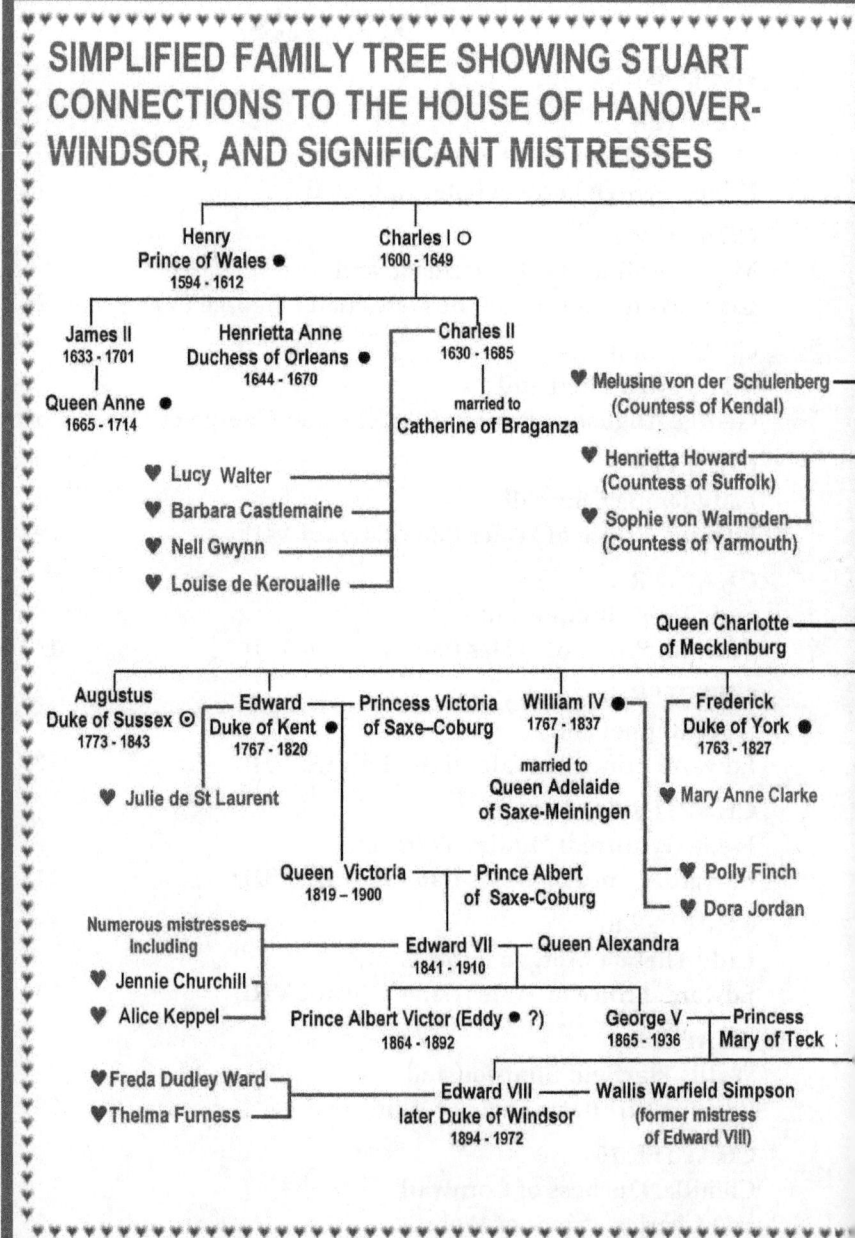

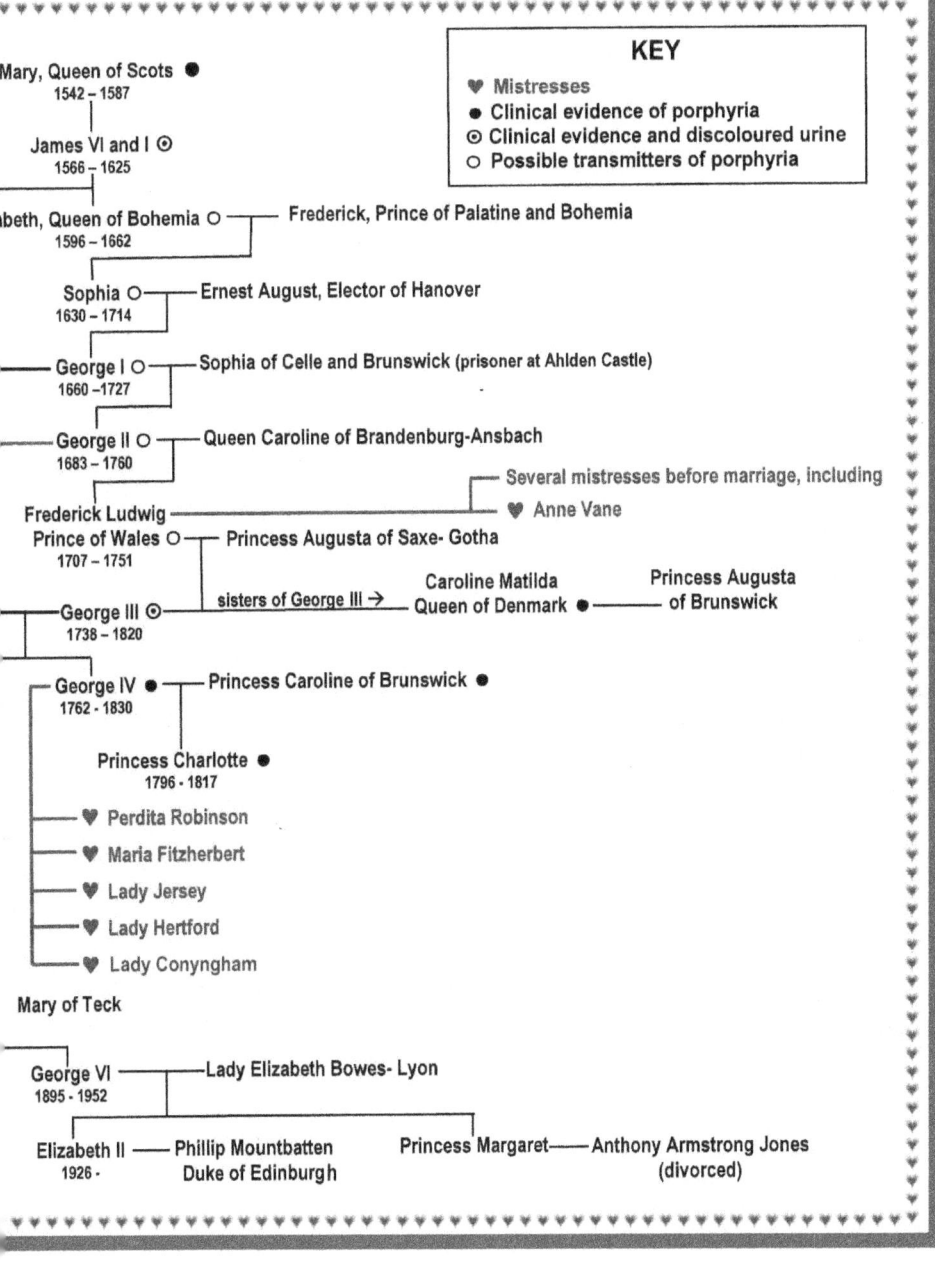

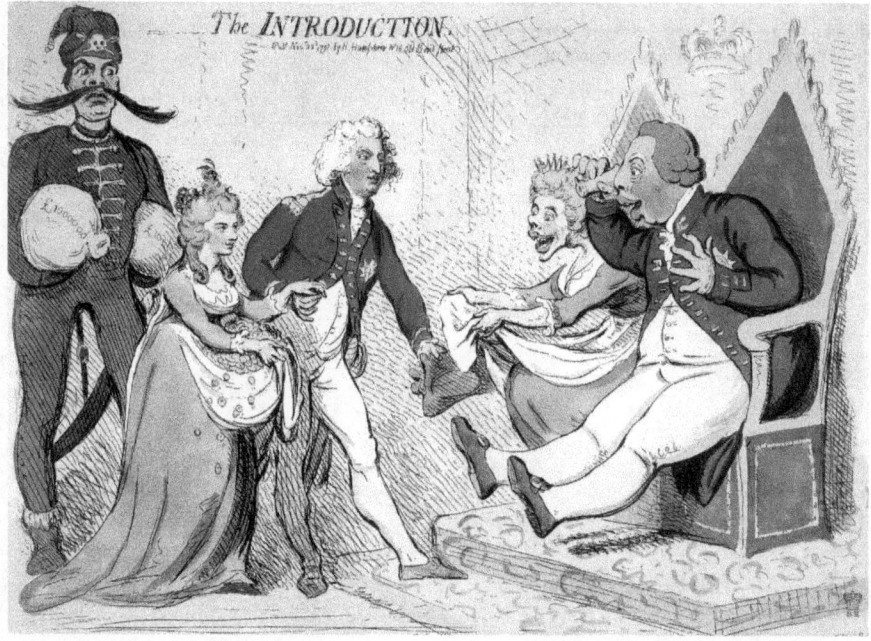

James Gillray's etching is an acid comment on the arranged marriages of the sons of George III, made for dynastic and financial reasons. Prince Frederick, father of two illegitimate sons, was made to marry the daughter of the King of Prussia. Her dowry in gold coins is carried by a Prussian soldier as the Prince introduces his wealthy German bride to his delighted parents.

AUTHOR DETAILS

Susanna de Vries was born and raised in England and now divides her time between Australia and Europe. She is the author of a dozen biographies of women and three books of art history.

As an adopted child, the product of a liaison between a married aristocrat and his married mistress, she was drawn to research this complex topic and the result was *Royal Mistresses*.

Educated at St George's Ascot, Berkshire Susanna studied art history and literature in Paris and Madrid. She undertook post-graduate study in Florence and on a Churchill Fellowship was allowed to conduct research in the Royal Library at Windsor Castle. She received an Order of Australia (AM) for 'services to art and literature' and an award for a distinguished contribution to literature by the Australian Society of Women Writers. She has retired from lecturing at university but is an approved lecturer for the Australian branch of NADFAS, the Fine and Decorative Art Society.

Susanna became interested in effects of arranged marriages between cousins, a usual practice among royal families and the genetic and psychological effects when her first husband worked in the Department of Clinical Psychiatry headed by Professor Sir Martin Roth, a respected psychiatrist consulted by several members of the royal family and came to Australia when her late husband t was appointed professor at the Medical School of the University of Queensland. A list of her publications is on line at **www.bookfinder.com**

INTRODUCTION

ARRANGED MARRIAGES LEAD TO MISTRESSES — FROM MELUSINE & WALLIS TO CAMILLA —

Every arranged marriage provides a vacancy for a mistress.
Translation of an old French proverb.

Princes of the House of Hanover made arranged marriages for political, financial and dynastic reasons. Most of them compensated for loveless arranged marriages to German cousins by taking mistresses. Royal brides had to have blue blood and be virginal to prevent any chance of a cuckoo in the royal nest, so a prince marrying his mistress was unthinkable.

The first mistress of the British branch of the German House of Hanover was Melusine von der Schulenburg. Before the coronation of her royal lover as George I, Melusine arrived in England by ship with Petronilla von Schulenburg, one of her three illegitimate daughters the future King had fathered during his time as Crown Prince of Hanover. Even though George I was divorced and had a mistress, the Archbishop of Canterbury anointed him as Defender of the Faith and nominal head of the Anglican Church, even though this Church did not allow divorce.

George I's son, the future King George II, installed Mrs Henrietta Howard as *his* mistress. When Henrietta lost her looks he gave her money to buy a house and replaced her with the much younger Sophie von Wallmoden, mother of his illegitimate son. When George II died, the avaricious Sophie returned to Hanover with a chest filled with jewels and money from the late King.

George III was faithful to his wife and keen that the royal family should epitomise family values. He and Queen Charlotte had 17 children, but his sons were spendthrifts and had many mistresses. In mid life George III was anguished by the fact that he had plenty of illegitimate grandchildren but no legitimate ones.

His eldest son, 'Prinny', the future George IV, treated his wife and his mistresses badly. His final mistress, the avaricious Lady Elizabeth Conyngham, stole jewels and valuable *objets d'art* from Windsor Castle as George IV lay on his deathbed. He was succeeded by his debt-ridden younger brother, Prince William, Duke of Clarence. Keen to produce a legitimate heir, William abandoned his devoted mistress, Dorothea Jordan, who had had born him ten illegitimate children and left her to die in poverty. As King William IV he married his cousin, Princess Adelaide of Saxe-Meiningen, hoping she would provide the nation with a legitimate heir, but each of their babies died in infancy.

In order to sire an heir for the nation, William's younger brother, Prince Edward, was ordered to jettison Julie de St Laurent, with whom he had been living happily for 27 years. Poor Julie was dismissed like an errant housemaid, so Prince Edward could make an arranged marriage to his cousin, Princess Victorine of Saxe Coburg. Their young daughter, Princess Victoria, mounted the throne after the death of William IV.

Julie de St Laurent's birth certificate and other documents about her disappeared in order that Julie could be erased from history. Queen Victoria, deeply shocked to learn that her father had taken a mistress, promised to restore morality to the monarchy but was distressed by the dissolute behaviour of her son and heir, the future Edward VII.

Royal Mistresses reveals the destruction of sexually explicit letters from princes to royal mistresses and *vice versa*. Embarrassing letters that the future George IV wrote to his actress-mistress Perdita Robinson were destroyed as were loving letters to and from Maria Fitzherbert. Sexually explicit letters Edward VII wrote to Lady Daisy Warwick were destroyed on the orders of George V, after Daisy attempted to blackmail the royal family by threatening to publish them.

Julie de St Laurent.
Rare lithograph of the 'lost' royal mistress by an unknown artist.

Introduction

As Prince of Wales, Edward VII seduced the wives of five of his friends and had hundreds of extra-marital liaisons, including many with expensive courtesans. His most fascinating mistresses were Lady Jennie Churchill and Daisy, Countess of Warwick, both married. King Edward VII's final mistress, Mrs Alice Keppel, was the great-grandmother of Camilla, Duchess of Cornwall. Camilla made history as the first royal mistress to be allowed to marry into the British royal family.

In 1910, after the death of Edward VII, his morally upright son, George V inherited the Crown, followed by Edward VIII who was the lover of the divorced Mrs Wallis Simpson.

Although the story of Edward, Prince of Wales, and Wallis Simpson is well known, this book discloses hitherto untold aspects of their relationship, including facts about Edward's deep-seated psychological and sexual problems. A diary, kept by Consuelo, elder sister of Edward's mistress Thelma Furness, reveals disturbing facts about Edward, the 'Peter Pan Prince'. New light is cast on a troubled Prince from abject letters he wrote to his first mistress, Mrs Freda Dudley Ward.

The uncrowned Edward VIII rocked the nation by abdicating in order to marry Wallis Simpson and became Duke of Windsor. Edward VIII was succeeded by his younger brother, George VI, who with his devoted wife, the former Lady Elizabeth Bowes-Lyon, inspired Britons during the London Blitz and raised wartime morale. Their hard-working daughter, Princess Elizabeth, fell in love with handsome but penniless Prince Philip of Greece. Initially her parents opposed the marriage but their love match has endured for 50 years, unlike the marriages of three of their children.

After the sad semi-arranged marriage of Prince Charles and Lady Diana Spencer, Charles was allowed to marry the woman he loved — his first mistress. Today, as the Duchess of Cornwall, Camilla is guiding Princess Catherine, the latest recruit to the royal family. The romantic and very popular marriage of the former Miss Kate Middleton has re-invigorated the monarchy.

Royal Mistresses reveals changing requirements for royal brides who are no longer required to have blue blood as well as the changed status of women today.

THE ROYAL HOUSE

OF HANOVER

CHAPTER 1

Countess Melusine von der Schulenburg, Duchess of Kendal (1667–1743)
and
King George I

Melusine, Duchess of Kendal, would have sold the King's honour for a shilling, were that the highest bid [offered] at auction. Horace Walpole, son of Robert Walpole, Chief Minister to George I.

THE CROWING OF A DIVORCED KING WITH A MISTRESS

In August 1714, the death of the childless Queen Anne left Britain in turmoil as there was no official heir. As Catholics were not allowed to rule, the late Queen's Catholic half-brother could not inherit the Crown. What the country needed was a Protestant prince with Stuart blood who was willing to move to Britain.

To prevent civil unrest and stabilise the country, Parliament offered the British Crown to 54-year-old Prince George Ludwig of Hanover, despite the fact he was divorced and spoke little English. What tipped the scale in his favour was the fact he had a married son, so the succession of a Protestant Prince of Wales was assured.

The new monarch had to be anointed as Head of the Anglican Church, but the King's sordid private life was unlikely to appeal to the Archbishop of Canterbury or to devout Anglicans. It was vital therefore that the fact their new King had sired three illegitimate children by his long-term German mistress, as well as being accused of ordering the murder of his wife's lover remain hidden.

As a young man the dissolute Prince George Ludwig had shared a mistress with his equally dissolute father. After his unhappy arranged marriage, George Ludwig formed a long-term relationship with the daughter of a Hanoverian general. The Prince's mistress bore him three daughters and was made Countess Ehrengarde Melusine von Schulenburg.

Countess Melusine agreed to come to Britain only because George Ludwig assured her they would spend much of their time in Hanover, so they could see their two married daughters frequently.

⁎⁎⁎

On a foggy day in early September 1714, a large sailing vessel anchored in the Thames Estuary. Aboard were Britain's new King, his mistress Melusine and one of their illegitimate daughters, the King's legitimate son and heir George Augustus, now Prince of Wales while his wife Caroline, Princess of Wales had still to arrive.

It was deemed wise to leave the King's mistress and their unmarried illegitimate daughter on board the sailing vessel which would take them to a secluded port in Kent where they could land while the rest of the royal party were rowed ashore by barge to Greenwich Palace.

The arrival of the new King on British soil was not a great success. George Ludwig turned red with anger when crowds lining the banks of the Thames cheered his son but ignored him. This led to a violent altercation between the new monarch and his heir as they made their way to the Painted Hall of Greenwich Palace. Father and son, who hated each other, almost came to blows.

Announced by a fanfare of silver trumpets, standing on a dais, George I and the Prince of Wales faced an excited crowd of courtiers and landowners, eager for a glimpse of their new monarch and the new Prince of Wales. What they saw was a portly middle-aged man with a florid complexion and a son who resembled him, flanked by German speaking courtiers who looked like black-robed crows.

King George I, despite inheriting the British Crown, remained the ruler of Hanover. He spoke very little English but would become the progenitor of the British House of Hanover.

SKELETONS IN THE CLOSET OF A DIVORCED KING

George Ludwig remembered his previous visit to London at the age of 22 when, as Crown Prince of Hanover, he had been ordered by his domineering mother to seek the hand of Princess Anne, England's future Queen and had been rebuffed.

Princess Anne had not been impressed by the boorish coarse Crown Prince from Hanover and rejected his offer of marriage in favour of the more handsome Prince of Denmark. After such a very public rejection, George Ludwig slunk home to his widowed mother, the Electress (ruler) of Hanover.

Only his lack of money and large gambling debts made him consider his mother's scheme he should marry a distant cousin, Princess Sophia Dorothea of Celle. Sophia was the 16-year-old daughter of the wealthy Duke of Brunswick, who lived in a castle with furniture made of solid silver with his French wife and their only child, Princess Sophia. At this time Germany before unification was a collection of separate principalities and dukedoms and the Duke of Brunswick scandalised them by marrying a pretty young governess employed in his household.

This meant that Sophia Dorothea and her mother lacked the royal blood considered vital for any royal bride. Crown Prince George Ludwig of Hanover was a crushing snob, obsessed with the idea of ancient bloodlines. He regarded marrying Princess Sophia, who was merely the daughter of a humble governess, as a marriage that was beneath his dignity. However, the Crown Prince was running short of money so he reluctantly agreed to his mother's plan for a dynastic marriage to his young cousin. By doing this George Ludwig would acquire Princess Sophia Dorothea's dowry and greatly increase his wealth. However, he had no intention of leaving Melusine von der Schulenburg, his young mistress. Melusine was one of several Maids of Honour to Prince George Ludwig's mother, the Electress Sophia.

For her part, Princess Sophia Dorothea of Celle was forced into this arranged marriage by her elderly father. The Duke had spent his money on art treasures and land and now wanted protection for Celle from soldiers of the Hanoverian Army.

In 1682, Prince George Ludwig married Princess Sophia with little enthusiasm. The wedding took place in pouring rain, which was considered a bad omen. Crown Prince George Ludwig and Princess Sophia travelled to Celle by coach.

In return for her large dowry in money and land, the Princess was provided with a suite of rooms at Herrenhausen Palace and her own ladies in waiting. The Princess also received elegant clothes, suitable for wearing at court. She was expected to appear in public with her husband and produce an heir.

After a single night of brutal sex with her husband, Princess Sophia Dorothea fell pregnant and gave birth to Prince George Augustus, heir to the principality of Hanover.

However, Prince George Ludwig did not live in the same part of the Herrenhausen Palace as his wife. Princess Sophie and her little son lived in one wing of the palace, while the Prince, when home on leave from the army, had his own rooms in his mother's wing, where he lived with his mistress.

George Ludwig's relationship with Melusine was long-term and after bearing the Prince three illegitimate daughters, his mistress was given the title of Countess von Schulenburg.

While the Crown Prince was allowed to take a mistress, as a royal wife Princess Sophia had to remain faithful to him. Adultery for the wife of the Crown Prince was regarded as treason.

Lonely, miserable and humiliated, the Princess of Celle missed her mother badly and begged to return home to Celle, but her request was refused by her stern father. Aware he had no other heir and needed the Hanoverian Army to protect him were Brunswick to be invaded, the elderly Duke of Brunswick did not want the dynastic and political alliance he had carefully engineered between the dukedom of Celle and the principality of Hanover to be broken by the whim of a silly girl. He told his daughter it was her duty to remain in Hanover. However Princess Sophie, neglected and abused by her husband, was desperate for affection and a decade after her marriage to Prince George Ludwig, Sophie threw caution to the winds and had a passionate love affair with Count Philip Christoph von Königsmarck, Captain of Dragoons at the Palace. The handsome count was son of a wealthy Swedish diplomat. Years earlier, when the Count's father had a diplomatic posting to Celle, Philip von Königsmarck and Sophie, both in their early teens, had flirted innocently with each other and declared their love.

Although both of them knew that sleeping with a married princess was treason, punishable by death, nevertheless they planned to escape from Herrenhausen Palace by night.

Melusine, who had been appointed Princess Sophia's Lady in Waiting, was instructed by George Ludwig to spy on Princess Sophia and report back to him. She was to intercept and read all his wife's correspondence. By devious means Melusine obtained a note from Count von Königsmarck to Princess Sophia. It gave the date and time he would arrive at her tower with a coach and horses to take her away to another part of Germany.

Warned by Melusine, George Ludwig gave instructions to his bodyguards to bind and gag his wife so she could not warn her lover when he arrived. When Count von Königsmarck entered the rooms of Princess Sophia, bodyguards emerged from hiding, drew their swords, killed Konigsmarck and threw his body in the river. His murder, ordered by George Ludwig, would be confirmed decades later when a former royal bodyguard confessed on his deathbed he had helped to kill Count Königsmarck.[1]

Princess Sophia Dorothea was divorced for the alleged 'desertion' of her husband, although technically she had never actually left Herrenhausen Palace.[2] Still in her early twenties, Sophia spent the rest of her life as a prisoner at Ahlden Castle, distraught that she was not allowed to see her children. Her son, Prince George Augustus, was only eleven years old at the time of the divorce. Each night he prayed his father might die so he could free his beloved mother from her prison. This twisted relationship established a pattern of filial hatred that ran all the way through the Hanoverian dynasty.

A GERMAN-SPEAKING KING AND HIS MISTRESS

Prince George Ludwig, crowned George I of Great Britain, was not as handsome as kings of the Stuart dynasty and lacked their charm. His family name was Guelph, (pronounced Gwelf) and he much preferred Hanover to England.

The coronation of the divorced monarch by the Archbishop of Canterbury took place in Westminster Abbey on 20 October 1714. The King's Hanoverian advisors felt that Countess Melusine von Schulenburg, should not attend. But among the guests in Westminster Abbey were *two* mistresses of former Stuart Kings. When George I learned of this it encouraged him to move Melusine from a country inn, where she was in hiding to the royal suite at Kensington Palace, which was the official royal residence.

When Melusine and her illegitimate daughter, Petronilla Melusina von Schulenburg, arrived at Kensington Palace, Petronilla was introduced to the courtiers as the Countess's niece, daughter of her brother, rather than her illegitimate daughter by the new King of England.

A portrait of Melusine, painted when young, shows her as raven-haired and attractive. Two decades later on her arrival in London, Countess Melusine had lost her looks and was starting to worry about the security of her position and her lack of any official income to pay for lavish court dresses required of her as a royal mistress of a king without a wife.

In her late forties, Countess Melusine's high cheek bones and dark eyes suggested she had once been a beauty but by now her complexion was badly scarred by smallpox. Being very thin, she was nicknamed 'The Maypole'. It was whispered that in his youth Prince George Ludwig had married Melusine in a morganatic marriage, so her daughters would never be eligible to rule over Britain or Hanover, but no proof of this marriage was ever found.

George I hoped the British Treasury would provide handsome allowances for his mistress. But as head of Cabinet, Sir Robert Walpole, (now virtually Prime Minister although he lacked that title) refused King George's request for Parliament to grant Melusine an annual income out of the Civil List.

Walpole sent back the terse reply, 'Paying a royal mistress for her services is tantamount to paying the wages of sin'.

The newly-crowned King was furious, remembering how in Hanover his every wish was law. Robert Walpole, aware Charles II had plundered Treasury funds to support his many mistresses with money allocated to feed and clothe British soldiers was determined this must *never* be allowed to happen again.

George I was notoriously mean and solved the tricky problem of supporting his mistress by giving Melusine Irish titles, which included many acres of farmland. In July 1716, Melusine was created Duchess of Munster, Countess of Dungannon and Baroness Dundalk. In those days Ireland was an English colony, garrisoned by British troops. The British Crown had confiscated rich farmlands from Irish landowners penalised for insisting they remain Catholic rather than converting to Protestantism. The result was that Melusine's Irish titles came to her along with acres and acres of confiscated Irish farmland.

In addition to creating new titles for his mistress, the King awarded the avaricious Melusine the right to mint Irish coins for circulation. This high-handed action infuriated Irish patriots. The Irish satirist, Dean Jonathan Swift, (author of *Gulliver's Travels*) demanded to know why the King's German mistress was profiting from a new issue of Irish coins. Incensed Irish patriots had had enough — they organised street riots in which effigies of the King's mistress were burned at the stake. Melusine hastily sold her coinage rights to a Birmingham manufacturer of saucepans and refused to visit her lands in Dungannon and Munster.

In March 1719, George I rewarded his mistress by giving her three English titles, including that of Duchess of Kendal which had fallen vacant due to the death of the previous incumbent without a heir. With the title of Duchess of Kendal came ownership of a crumbling castle and pasture land that could be rented out for grazing sheep. However, the castle was in ruins and rentals for pasturing sheep on her lands were meagre, so Melusine continued to press her royal lover for more money.

The King and Melusine's daughter was created Countess of Walsingham by her royal father. The farmland that accompanied that title was very rich, so Petronilla received much higher rents from her land than her mother did from *her* land in England.

Melusine's youngest daughter, Margaret Gertrude, known as 'Trüdchen', who married Count Albrecht von Schaumberg-Lippe, was her favourite child. Melusine and the King spent long periods visiting their beloved Trüdchen. They enjoyed staying in Hanover in the spacious elegant rooms and formal gardens of the Palace of Herrenhausen, which George I much preferred to Kensington Palace, near the quiet rural village of Kensington. Their sorrow was great when Trüdchen died in 1726 aged only 25-years-old.[3]

⁎

George I's courtiers were amused when a fat lady, years younger than Melusine, turned up at Kensington Palace with a pile of baggage. Baroness Sophie von Kielmansegg was accompanied by her elderly husband, Baron von Kielmansegg. The court assumed the plump lady must be another royal mistress and that the Baron was a complacent husband. What surprised the courtiers was the fact that Baroness Sophie and Duchess Melusine embraced each other warmly and exchanged sisterly kisses. The King's German-speaking advisors dared not explain the real reason for such a display of affection.

Baroness von Kielmansegg was *not* a rival to Melusine but a trusted friend. The baroness was the King's half sister (daughter of his late father by his mistress Clara Platen), or his illegitimate daughter. Countess Platen was a venal woman who decades earlier had been the mistress of Augustus, Elector of Hanover, George Ludwig's debauched father. Augustus had instructed his mistress to initiate his young heir into the pleasures of sex. This meant that father and son took turns to spend time with the voracious Countess.

When the Countess Platen fell pregnant as a result of this time-share arrangement, neither the father or the son were certain which of them had fathered the little girl. In her teens, Sophie was given a dowry and married off to elderly Baron von Kielmansseg.

Now Baron and Baroness von Kielmansseg had arrived in London, eager for their share of the spoils. Melusine, Duchess of Kendal, and Baroness von Kielmansegg agreed to share the jewels of the late Queen Anne. Caroline, Princess of Wales, who both of them disliked, was given only a few rings and brooches to keep her quiet.

George I, Baron and Baroness Kielmansegg and Countess Melusine made a happy foursome, always conversing in German. They enjoyed playing cards together or listening to music. On warm nights they and Petronilla Melusina boarded the royal barge at Whitehall and went upriver to Chelsea, with musicians playing in a second barge alongside them.

The cash-strapped Baron von Kielmansegg was made Master of the King's Horse, a job that commanded a high salary for doing very little. Since the Baron knew next to nothing about horses or organising ceremonial events in London, this was just as well. The fact that he was married to the King's half-sister remained a secret.

George Augustus, Prince of Wales, always keen to damage his father's reputation, told a few cronies details of the murder of Count von Königsmarck and other family scandals. Tension between the supporters of the Prince of Wales and the King ran high.

As the ancient Whitehall Palace had become dilapidated, George I preferred to live at Kensington Palace with Melusine and Baroness Sophie von Kielmansegg, and her husband.

Official entertaining was severely curtailed, which pleased George I whose command of English was limited. What he could not avoid was attending diplomatic levées at the Palace of St James at which foreign diplomats presented their credentials to him, one of the few times the King and his estranged son and heir, George Augustus, met.

While the King and his mistress lived in luxury at Kensington Palace, the Prince and Princess of Wales resided in the decaying Palace of St James with their own attendants. They had nothing good to say about the King's mistress, knowing that Melusine had spied on the King's wife and caused her downfall.

In his cups, the eyes of the Prince of Wales would fill with tears when he told friends about his mother, confined in a remote castle in Hanover. He hoped his father would die soon, so he could release his mother from captivity and banish Melusine from the court.

The London mob, aware that the King had a German-speaking mistress, covered in jewels, called her the 'foreign whore'. They jeered and threw stones at Melusine's carriage when she ventured out for a drive.

ROYAL INTRIGUES AND A NEW MISTRESS

The ageing Melusine, Duchess of Kendal, was keen the King would use his influence to marry off their daughter to a British aristocrat. Given a large dowry Petronilla married the Earl of Chesterfield, famous for statement that 'Power corrupts and absolute power corrupts absolutely. The Earl fell out with Melusine and the marriage was not a troubled one.

As Melusine aged, she feared the King might replace her by a younger mistress. Despite being ugly, George I *did* have the allure of royalty and the ability to dispense titles and jewels.

The promiscuous young Lady Anne Brett, daughter of the Countess of Macclesfield, and several other ladies of the court, competed for the monarch's affection. Finally the King succeeded in bedding Lady Anne after giving her jewels from the late Queen Anne's collection.

George I intended to keep this relationship low-key. He owed a great deal to Melusine and she could, if angered, have revealed the secret of the murder of Count von Königsmarck. George I was not by nature a kind or sensitive man, but he continued to treat Melusine much better than anyone else at court.

Lady Anne Brett had high hopes of social advancement. She was disgruntled that she remained a 'backstairs' mistress, visited in private but not created a countess or a duchess.

According to Horace Walpole, Lady Ann did receive her own suite of apartments at the Palace of St James rather than living at Kensington Palace which was Melusine's domain.

Rendered insecure by the fact she had competition and Lady Anne Brett was decades younger, Melusine spent lavishly on a new wardrobe of designer clothes, a lady's maid and her own personal hairdresser. To pay for these she let it be known in court circles that, in return for a substantial sum, she would arrange private interviews with the monarch who had the power to award lucrative posts in the Army or the Royal Household.

Melusine was running what is now called a cash-for-access scheme (similar to the one recently attempted by Sarah Ferguson). For a fat fee the Duchess of Kendal would arrange 'private interviews' with the monarch, who was able to dispense titles and honours.

Melusine's most successful cash-for-access scheme involved the affluent Henry James Brydges. Through financial acumen and hard work Brydges had risen to the post of Paymaster of the Armed Forces during the War of the Spanish Succession. He was accused of taking bribes in return for contracts to provision the army. Henry James Brydges bribed his way out of it and was never prosecuted. After leaving the Army, he invested his ill-gotten gains well and became one of England's wealthiest men and owned a magnificent baroque mansion called Cannons.

Now he needed a title — not just Lord or Viscount but something really grand. Melusine fixed that for a substantial fee.[4] In 1717, for no apparent reason, James Brydges was created Duke of Chandos by the King.

∗∗

At the christening of one of his grandchildren, the King's temper exploded and he attempted to throttle his son and heir. A fierce scuffle ensued inside the church until father and son were pulled apart by courtiers. In revenge the King ordered the Prince and

Princess of Wales and their children to be thrown out of St James Palace that very night.

The Wales' moved to Leicester House in Leicester Square and consoled themselves by planning how, when George I died, they would banish Countess Melusine and bring Princess Sophia Dorothea out of her confinement in the Castle of Ahlden and live with them in England.

During the boom years of his reign, George I wearied of his relatively modest suite of rooms in Kensington Palace, the former country house of William III. He ordered plans to be drawn up by architect Vanburgh, designer of Blenheim Palace, to enlarge Kensington Palace.

Melusine approved of Vanbrugh's grandiose schemes for Kensington Palace, but the monarch rejected the architect's scheme. The King favoured the less expensive plan drawn up William Benson, who had replaced Sir Christopher Wren's as Royal Surveyor. Passionately fond of classical music, George I commissioned a music room with a cupola. It was to be used for the concerts and chamber music which he, Melusine and his half-sister enjoyed. Another improvement was the magnificent staircase that led to their private apartments. For years Kensington Palace rang with the sounds of hammers and had stair wells blocked by ladders. The windows overlooked a chain of ponds which George I ordered to be turned into a lake, now known as the Serpentine, surrounded by landscaped gardens, today's Kensington Gardens.

The King and Melusine were happy to live quietly at the refurbished palace and eat meals in their private apartment, served to them by the King's turban-wearing Turkish servants.

Each year in August, the King hosted an elaborate garden party at Kensington Palace to celebrate the anniversary of his accession to the throne of Great Britain. A specially erected fountain ran red with claret rather than water and an expensive firework display took place. Protocol demanded that Caroline, Princess of Wales, was the official hostess, which would have been galling for Melusine.

⁂

As he aged, George I developed a painful neurological disorder. At the time the disease was undiagnosed but is now believed to have been porphyria, which affects the circulatory system, causing severe intestinal pains and swelling of the limbs. Although George I was inflicted with many of the symptoms suffered by Queen Anne, his physicians believed his agonies were caused by gout and prescribed medications, which proved of limited benefit and increased his ill-temper.

THE GREAT FINANCIAL CRASH ENRICHES MELUSINE

In 1720 Melusine, Duchess of Kendal, was heavily implicated in the greatest financial scandal in British history — the South Sea Bubble. The instigators were George Caswall, a shady financier, and John Blunt, a London stockbroker. They masterminded the establishment of the British South Seas Company during the War of the Spanish Succession.

Melusine, in return for a large bribe, persuaded the King to lend his support to the new company. At a time when trading in stocks and shares was a relatively new concept, investors were assured that, once the war ended, the South Seas Company would establish a lucrative trade in silver, spices, wool, foodstuffs and slaves between England, the British West Indies and the Spanish colonies in the Caribbean and South America. It was known that the Spanish colonies contained vast amounts of gold and silver.[5]

A prospectus, publicising the South Seas Company, created the impression that they had received permission from the King of Spain to send ships to trade with the Spanish colonies. In reality Caswell and Blunt had only received permission to send one ship per year to South America, so their prospectus was highly misleading.

In return for a large gift of shares, Melusine helped set up a series of meetings between the directors of the British South Seas Company and leading members of the British Government.

The King's mistress gave wealthy investors, including the Duke of Chandos the impression that the monarch supported the new trading company. Melusine became heavily involved in promoting the trading venture and encouraged landowners and political figures to purchase shares in this dubious enterprise.

An oil painting in the Tate Gallery depicts how South Sea Company shares were traded before the Stock Exchange was built in 1773. It shows clients of Jonathan's Coffee House near the Royal Exchange in a ferment of excitement over soaring prices displayed on placards in the street. As the placards were visible through the window of the Coffee House, people kept rushing out to buy more shares as prices rose. Encouraged by his mistress, George I had bought a large parcel of shares which inspired confidence among investors.

In 1720, the British Government agreed that the South Seas Company would buy most of the National Debt — nearly ten million pounds sterling in outstanding war debts. This encouraged speculators even further. Once it was announced that the British Government was involved and huge profits could be made by bringing gold and silver from South America, share prices in the South Seas Company soared from £100 to £1000 a share. Speculators borrowed from banks to buy more shares and prices soared to unsustainable levels.

This share-buying fever was the subject of an engraving by William Hogarth which depicted avaricious speculators on a merry-go-round.

Due to a series of small naval battles between Spain and England, the company's projected trade with the Spanish colonies in South America never eventuated. In reality the only merchandise the South Seas Company ever traded were slaves. These were sold by corrupt African chieftains to traders in return for gunpowder. The unfortunate slaves were chained up in huge slave forts like Elmina on the West African coast and shipped from West Africa to the British West Indies. Thousands died en route.

Eventually the truth leaked out. There were no ships returning to England filled with gold and silver — the South Seas Company was losing money rather than providing promised fortunes. Panic selling began — prices slumped as the 'bubble' burst and the South

Seas Company crashed, its shares no longer worth the paper they were printed on.

More than a thousand aristocrats, landed gentry, leading physicians and lawyers were ruined. The directors of the South Seas Company and the King and his mistress were vilified. Ruined investors had to sell their homes, some committed suicide, others lost their life savings, one of these being the Duke of Chandos.

The estates and property of directors of the South Seas Company were confiscated, the Chancellor of the Exchequer was sent to the Tower of London and the Postmaster-General committed suicide.

British credit abroad was damaged — Jacobite supporters clamoured for the King to be deposed and for a Catholic monarch to return to the throne. But to no avail — the House of Hanover remained on the throne of Great Britain.

Melusine's arch-enemy, Sir Robert Walpole, emerged unscathed — all along he had been wary of the South Seas Company and their promises. As Prime Minister, Walpole was called in to restore order. The financial crash was so severe it took many years for the British economy to recover.

One of the few to benefit from the stock market crash was Melusine, Duchess of Kendal, who used bribes she had received from the South Seas Company to buy jewellery and land at rock bottom prices from bankrupted investors.

Aware of Melusine's greed, Robert Walpole's son, Horace Walpole, a Member of Parliament, described the King's mistress as an 'avaricious woman of low morals who would have sold the King's honour for a shilling were that the highest bid [she] received at auction'.[6]

In December 1726, the King received the news that the Princess of Celle had died. On her deathbed Princess Sophie claimed to have seen Count von Königsmarck's ghost who accused George I of having him murdered. Shortly before her death the Princess had written a letter, cursing her ex-husband and claiming he would roast in hell.

On learning of his mother's death the Prince of Wales wept bitterly while Melusine and George I celebrated with champagne. In an angry scene the King forbade the Prince of Wales to attend his mother's funeral.

A gypsy had prophesied that George I would not outlive his wife for long, a prophecy that troubled him. So that his divorced wife could be buried with the necessary royal honours, it was necessary for George I to travel to Hanover for the funeral. He insisted that Melusine accompanied him, but they had to wait until the weather improved.

Not until 3 June 1727, did King George I and his mistress cross the English Channel, followed by a bumpy ride over rough roads in a handsome carriage bearing the royal arms.

Five days later the King reached Delden where he ate an enormous supper in the castle of a local nobleman. His host urged the couple to stay overnight, but George I was anxious to reach Osnabruck, his birthplace. As they crossed the border and entered the Principality of Hanover, the King was handed the sealed letter Princess Sophia Dorothea had written only days before her death.

Approaching Osnabruck, the King read his wife's letter. Princess Sophia told the King he would burn in hell because he had ruined her life. Stress and terror of hellfire meant veins stood out on George I's forehead and his eyes bulged more than normal. He collapsed on the floor of the carriage in what the physician described as an 'apoplectic fit' (probably a heart attack). The carriage continued bumping along the potholed road until a frantic Melusine was able to attract the attention of the coachman, who halted the galloping horses. But by the time the carriage reached Osnabruck George I was dead.

The mayor and town council of Osnabruck arranged for a temporary burial of the King until his body could be returned to London for burial in Westminster Abbey.

After George I's death, his eldest son, created Prince of Wales, succeeded him as George II. The new King hated his father for the ill treatment of Princess Sophia of Celle so refused to let the dead King's body be buried in Westminster Abbey, the traditional resting place of England's kings. Eventually, King George I's body was exhumed and taken by coach to a specially designed mausoleum in the chapel of Herrenhausen Palace.

Aware of his heir's hatred for Melusine, George I had had the foresight to give his mistress Kendal House near Isleworth, on the outskirts of London, where she could live in peace after her lover's death. The author of *Vanity Fair*, William Makepiece Thackeray, described how,

> George I's heart was always in Hanover. He was fifty-four years of age when he came among us, we took him for our King only because he served our turn. We laughed at his uncouth ways and sneered at him... Cynical and selfish as he was, he was better than a King out of Saint Germain [a suburb of Paris] — a Stuart Pretender obeying a French King's orders with a swarm of Jesuits trailing behind him.[7]

The newly-crowned George II was alleged to have attempted to burn his late father's will, aware that George I had bequeathed Melusine a very large sum of money with additional bequests to his illegitimate daughters. Melusine was also provided with a lavish Hanoverian state pension, equal to £7,500 a year.[8]

Melusine, Duchess of Kendal, did not return to Hanover but moved to Kendal House, which King George I had given her. At Kendal House, the superstitious Melusine used to keep a candle burning in her window.

Horace Walpole described how,

> George I had told his mistress that, if he could, he would appear to her after his death. Soon after that event occurred, a large and rather ugly bird flew into her room through the window. She believed the King's soul inhabited it and took the utmost care of the bird.[9]

Melusine outlived her royal lover by sixteen years. She died at Kendal House in 1743, leaving a fortune in land and jewels to the two daughters who survived her.

HENRIETTA HOWARD, THE 'BACKSTAIRS MISTRESS'

As Prince of Wales, George II had taken a 'backstairs mistress', named Henrietta Howard, a member of his wife's household, as Princess Caroline had been warned by her doctors she could die were she to bear another child.

Accordingly Princess Caroline decided she would chose her husband's mistress and the unfortunate Mrs Howard was selected to fill the role. As an orphan Henrietta had been married off young to a husband who was a violent alcoholic. She had fled from a violent marriage to serve Princess Caroline, later crowned Queen Caroline. The Princess loved her husband and did not want him to have a mistress with whom he would fall in love. She told Henrietta this was a purely practical arrangement to provide her husband with sexual relief. She made the Prince of Wales promise he would never give jewels or honours to Mrs Henrietta Howard. Henrietta remained as a Woman of the Bedchamber doing humble duties including emptying Princess Caroline's bedpan and serving at table.

The future King was allowed to visit Henrietta in her room but only for one hour a night. She found George II a very boring man and a lacklustre lover. Henrietta put up with the situation because she had been promised enough money to buy her own home once their sexual arrangement ended.

In 1723, after Henrietta had become deaf and lost her looks, George II replaced her with the young avaricious and very beautiful Sophie von Wallmoden, Duchess of Yarmouth.

However, Henrietta made certain the King kept his promise and gave her sufficient money to build Marble Hill House and fill it with splendid antiques. On a trip to take the waters in Bath, Henrietta, now the widowed Countess of Suffolk, met George Berkeley, son of an Earl who genuinely loved her and they lived happily at Marble Hill House until her death in 1767.

Melusine, Duchess of Kendal.

King George I.

Princess Sophia Dorothea.

Count Philip von Königsmarck.

Prince George Ludwig lived at Herrenhausen Palace in Hanover before becoming King George I of Britain.

Melusine's Coat of Arms.

Above: An early engraving of Kensington Palace.
Below: A recent photograph of Kensington Palace.

William Hogarth's engraving, *Harvest of Greed* is an ironic vision showing promoters and investors on a merry-go-round in the 'South Sea Bubble' disaster.

CHAPTER 2

Mary 'Perdita' Darby Robinson (1758–1800)
and
George Augustus, Prince of Wales (later George IV)

George, Prince of Wales is a spoiled, selfish beast.
Sir Charles Greville, member of the King's Privy Council.

Every event in my life has been marked by acute sensibility.
Perdita Robinson in *The Memoirs of Mary Darby Robinson,* published posthumously.

A BLEAK CHILDHOOD AND AN UNHAPPY MARRIAGE

Mary Darby was one of five children of Hester Darby, a former governess, and Captain John Darby, owner of a merchant ship engaged in trade between Bristol and northern Canada. Captain Darby made several voyages each year to the colony of Labrador where he set up a fur trading post. Mrs Darby educated her children at home. Each night she read to them from the works of Shakespeare rather than from books specially written for children. Mary had a quick brain and a good memory. From an early age she could recite from memory speeches by Shakespearean characters like Miranda from *The Tempest*, Rosalind from *As You Like It* and Juliet, heroine of *Romeo and Juliet*.

Mary's father, unknown to his wife and family, was supporting a young mistress who became pregnant. After a bitter row, Captain Darby told his wife their marriage was over — he would live in Labrador and she could have the family home in Bristol, although the title deeds were in his name. His money was needed to develop his fur trading venture further so his wife must support herself and their five children by returning to teaching.

Divorce was not an option for Hester Darby. At that time it could only be granted by the Houses of Parliament so divorce was the preserve of wealthy aristocrats. But Mrs Darby made the best of an unfortunate situation. She turned the family home into a day school for girls and earned enough money to raise her children.

At fourteen Mary was mature for her age. As she had a beautiful speaking voice and clear diction, she helped her mother by giving English and elocution lessons.

Mrs Darby, worried about the future of her children, wrote to her husband, requesting regular payments to help support their five children and contribute to dowries for the girls. A very angry Captain Darby returned to Bristol, telling his wife she had broken their agreement. He said he had another family to support and refused to give her or their children a penny. He would exercise his legal right to sell his house in which she had no right to remain.

Mrs Darby's lawyers confirmed that, as the law stood, Captain Darby was within his rights as a husband to sell the family home and keep the money. In fact, he not only sold the family home and made his wife and children homeless, he also exercised his right to the money in his wife's bank account. In the 18th century, before the passing of the Married Woman's Property Act in 1875, all money earned by a wife was deemed to be the property of the husband, so Mrs Darby could do nothing to stop him.

So without legal protection of any kind Mary her mother and her siblings descended from middle-class comfort to poverty and homelessness. They moved to London where Mrs Darby had relatives and she found teaching work. Women teachers were paid far less than male teachers, so the family had to live in a cheap lodging house. Aged fifteen, Mary had her last year of school under a teacher who encouraged her to write poetry and think about writing a novel. Publishing was seen as a masculine preserve, so it was hard for women to have books published in those days. It was deemed so unfeminine for women to write books that even Jane Austen had her first novel published anonymously and the Bronte sisters published under male names.

Mary needed to earn money to survive. A family friend took pity on the fatherless family and contacted the famous actor-manager David Garrick, telling him that Mary was an attractive girl with a beautiful speaking voice who could recite long passages from Shakespeare by heart and would be ideal for his company so the famous actor-manager agreed to audition Mary Darby. He asked her to read the part of Miranda from *The Tempest*. Garrick was so impressed by Miss Darby's talent that he offered her a place in his company, which was performing at the Theatre Royal at Covent Garden. Mary was thrilled and signed the contract.

She rushed home to tell her mother the good news, but Mrs Hester Darby was horrified. She warned Mary that actresses were often part-time courtesans and being on stage meant she had little chance of making a good marriage. Mary promised her mother she would guard her virginity until she married.

Initially, Mary was given walk-on roles but was told to understudy the leading lady.

Returning from the theatre with some play scripts, Mary dropped one of them in the street. It was picked up by a handsome young man, wearing expensive clothes, who introduced himself as Thomas Robinson. He told Mary he was a law clerk and was training with the law firm of Messrs Vernon & Elderton. Young Mr Robinson had the manners and bearing of a gentleman.

The next time they met in the street they talked at some length. Thomas Robinson invited Mary to be his guest at the Christmas party of his law firm, to be held in the home of one of the senior partners. Mary, who had just turned 16, found Thomas very attractive and was excited at the prospect of attending the party as his guest.

At first, Mary's mother refused to let her attend, but in the end Mrs Darby relented on condition she came as Mary's chaperone. Thomas Robinson said he would be delighted but, in secret, he organised Henry Wayman, a fellow law clerk, to keep Mrs Darby occupied so he could spend time alone with Mary.

At the party, held in an imposing private home, Henry Wayman had agreed to tell Mrs Darby that Thomas Robinson was heir to a wealthy childless uncle and would have a lucrative career as a lawyer once he had finished his articles. This was complete fiction. In reality Thomas Robinson was addicted to gambling and had been given a final warning that, unless he settled his debts, he would be dismissed from the law firm.

While Henry Wayman was spinning tall tales to Mrs Darby, Thomas Robinson lured Mary away from other guests, kissed her passionately under the mistletoe and assured the naïve 16-year-old he loved her and wanted to marry her.

Carried away by the excitement of her first kiss and believing the stories about Thomas's wealthy uncle, Mary agreed to became engaged to him. Thomas Robinson and Henry Wayman reassured Mrs Darby that her daughter would want for nothing once she was married. As Hester Darby believed Mr Wayman, she advised Mary to abandon her fledgling stage career and marry the young Thomas Robinson. Following her mother's advice, Mary cancelled her contract with David Garrick.

As Robinson's fiancée Mary was allowed to visit Thomas at his lodgings where he seduced her. Meanwhile, Mrs Darby heard rumours that young Robinson had been dismissed from Messrs Vernon and Elderton, so she made an appointment to see the senior partner. She learned Thomas Robinson was adopted by a childless couple who had been horrified to discover his gambling addiction. Initially they had paid his gambling debts but told him this was the last time they would do so. When he ran up more debts they disowned Thomas and he came to London, used forged references to apply for a post as an articled clerk. His gambling debts were drawn to the attention of Messrs Vernon and Elder and he received several warnings they must be paid. They had been forced to dismiss him to preserve the good name of the firm. No other legal firm would employ him, so Thomas Robinson's legal career was over.

Mrs Darby realised that it was too late for her pregnant daughter to seek a backyard abortion. In order to preserve family respectability, she insisted her daughter marry her fiancé immediately. The wedding took place very quietly on 12 April, 1774. Thomas was penniless. Mary had no proper wedding dress, there were no bridesmaids, no reception and no honeymoon. After the wedding, Mr and Mrs Robinson rented a sparsely furnished room in a run-down lodging house. Thomas's attempts to earn money by manual work failed.

Pursued by creditors, Mary borrowed money from her mother. Meanwhile, Mary and Thomas had fled to Wales to stay with Thomas's grandmother. The old lady became fond of Mary, worried about her unborn child and gave Thomas money, although she was by no means wealthy.

Back in London Thomas returned to the gambling tables and soon lost the golden guineas his mother had given him. His cronies included elderly rakes like Lord Lyttleton, who was fascinated by beautiful young Mrs Robinson, in spite of the fact she was several months pregnant.

When the owner of the gaming house demanded immediate settlement of Thomas's debts, Lord Lyttleton proposed a gentleman's agreement. He offered to pay the debts and give Thomas some extra money, provided Mary would become his mistress.

Mary was deeply shocked by her husband's dissolute attitude and furious about Lord Lyttleton's offer. She refused to be treated like a whore.

Thomas Robinson's creditors were threatening to use force to collect their debts so, once again, he and Mary fled from London to his grandmother's home in Wales. This was where their daughter Mary Elizabeth was born on 18 November 1774. Mary was thrilled with her pretty baby girl and wrote a tender poem dedicated to little Mary Elizabeth.

Finally the police traced Thomas Robinson to Wales, he was arrested, taken back to London, tried and sentenced to serve three years in the grim confines of the King's Bench Debtors' prison.

Mary's mother was furious that her daughter had brought shame on the family. She told Mary she could give her no more assistance — her priority was helping her younger children. Mary had ruined her life and must take the consequences.

Homeless and penniless Mary and her baby daughter had no option but to join her debauched husband in the King's Bench Jail.

Charles Dickens highlighted the grim conditions in debtor's prisons in his novel *Little Dorrit*. In this novel the blameless young Amy Dorrit shares her father's cell and goes out to work in the day. Mary did the same. She and her baby slept in her husband's dark damp cell. Allowed out of jail during the day, Mary found part-time work copying documents in a legal office, leaving little Mary Elizabeth to be cared for by her father. This work paid Mary enough to buy food for the three of them as debtor's prisons did not supply meals to inmates.

In prison Mary also found time to write a book of reflective poems about love and loss, titled *Captivity*. She sent the manuscript to Georgiana, Duchess of Devonshire, a wealthy patron of the arts whose name she had heard mentioned by David Garrick. The young Duchess was impressed by the pathos and sincerity of Mary's poems and paid for them to be published in a limited edition. Mary's first book was dedicated to her patron, Georgiana, Duchess of Devonshire, who felt sympathy for Mary as her own marriage was an unhappy one.

An epidemic of typhoid in the King's Bench Prison caused several deaths. Sanitation was terrible and consisted of one toilet bucket in each cell. The health of little Mary Elizabeth was at risk. Mary's husband managed to negotiate a reduction in his three year sentence by claiming his wife and baby were at risk when the inmate of the next cell died from typhoid. He was freed from jail after serving only fifteen months of his three-year sentence.

When Mary Robinson emerged from the debtor's prison she was no longer the naïve 16-year-old. She realised her best chance of supporting herself and her child was to beg David Garrick to let her rejoin his theatre company. After she wrote to him, explaining her plight, she was granted an interview by Garrick and the famous playwright Richard Brinsley Sheridan. They agreed to re-employ her for a season at the Drury Lane Theatre.

She was given a non-speaking role in Shakespeare's *Romeo and Juliet* and told she was to understudy the actress playing Juliet. Lacking money to pay someone to care for Mary Elizabeth, Mary took the adorable little girl to the theatre and her dresser agreed to mind the toddler while Mary was on stage.

In 1776, when the leading lady fell ill, Mary took on the dream role of Juliet at short notice. The public applauded the actress with the beautiful speaking voice and Mary made curtain call after curtain call. Theatre critics praised Mrs Robinson's performance. Both Garrick and Sheridan were pleased with her and the following season Mary played two major roles — Viola in *Twelfth Night* and Rosalind in *As You Like It*, for which she received excellent reviews. Mary's money now supported the couple, who were scarcely on speaking terms, and their infant daughter.

In December 1779, David Garrick gave the 22-year-old Mary Darby Robinson the testing role of Princess Perdita in Shakespeare's *A Winter's Tale*, at the Drury Lane Theatre. Critics described her performance as 'brilliant in a difficult role in a Shakespeare play that is rarely performed'.

While Mary's acting career was thriving, her private life was disastrous. She caught her husband making love with her maid and threw him out of their lodgings. From then on he hated her and took his revenge by claiming his right to all his wife's earnings. Thomas Robinson's work in a legal office had made him aware of the legal rights of husbands. Before the passing of the important Married Women's Property Act in 1875 any money a wife earned was legally the property of her husband.

Each month Thomas Robinson visited Drury Lane Theatre to collect Mary's substantial earnings, since she was now one of the stars of Garrick's company. Aware her husband spent her money on gambling and drink, Mary raged against the injustice of the legal system but to no avail. Women had no power — laws were made by men and administered by men.

Fortunately, the theatre manager liked Mary and disliked her arrogant husband and made sure Thomas did not know the full extent of her earnings. This enabled Mary to pay her rent and buy food for herself and her little daughter.

Although short of money because of her wastrel husband, 'Perdita' Robinson now had a fine reputation as successful 'classical' actress. Her superb figure, delicate complexion and mass of blonde curls made her stage presence unforgettable.

The celebrated artist John Hoppner painted a striking portrait of Mary in the role of Perdita. Her portrait was exhibited at the Royal Academy of Arts in London, which resulted in Hoppner receiving a commission for smaller versions of the portrait from admirers of the talented actress.

'PRINCE FLORIZEL' AND 'PRINCESS PERDITA'

When 18-year-old George Augustus, Prince of Wales, visited the Royal Academy's exhibition at Somerset House he admired Hoppner's portrait of 'Perdita', who was depicted in a low cut black dress, revealing her cleavage. His Royal Highness arranged to attend a charity performance of *The Winter's Tale* from the Royal Box at Drury Lane Theatre, staring Perdita Robinson.

After the play ended, the theatre manager agreed to conduct His Royal Highness backstage to congratulate the star on her performance. In her dressing room, the handsome blonde Prince raised the star's hand to his lips, kissed it and asked if Perdita would do him the honour of dining alone with him that evening.

Mary knew that the 18-year-old Prince of Wales had already a reputation as a womanizer and politely refused his invitation. However, finding the young Prince handsome she smiled and gave the impression that she might *eventually* agree to dine with him — provided others were present.

Greatly encouraged, the young Prince of Wales ordered large bouquets of flowers to be delivered to Perdita's dressing room every day. Among the hothouse blooms were passionate notes signed 'Prince Florizel' (the name of Shakespeare's character in *The Winter's Tale* who falls in love with Princess Perdita).

The passionate love notes assured 'Perdita' that her very own 'Prince Florizel' adored her. Her dresser and several fellow actors warned Mary not to trust the Prince of Wales — he was a spoiled young prince whose enthusiasms for women or friends never lasted long.[1] His mother, the pious Queen Charlotte, had born her husband 17 children, who were raised and educated by stern tutors. Neither Queen Charlotte or the dutiful King George III could understand how they had produced an irresponsible selfish heir who was deep in debt to moneylenders and leading a decadent life.

At 18, Prince George Augustus of Wales was good-looking although starting to put on weight. Self-absorbed and narcissistic he loved sitting to artists to have his portrait painted. The heir to the throne sent his most senior equerry, Lord Malden, to give Perdita a flattering miniature portrait of himself in a diamond-studded frame. The Prince of Wales had added a lock of his blond hair to the package along with a passionate letter asking for one of Perdita's golden ringlets in return.

Once again, the letter begged the star to dine with him. She wrote back, thanking him for the miniature, sent one of her blonde ringlets in return but was evasive about dining with him.

Short of money, Mary pawned the diamond-studded picture frame but kept the portrait and the Prince's passionate love letters in a tin box in her dressing room.

Unknown to Mary, the Prince of Wales had a fetish for female hair and collected ringlets or locks of hair, as well as samples of pubic hair, from woman he bedded. The collection had started as a result of the Prince's bet with gambling cronies at Brook's Club, as to which of them could collect the most samples of pubic hair from different women. From this time on, the Prince of Wales developed a fetish about female hair. Fascinated by Mary's golden curls he vowed to his gambling cronies he would possess her, no matter how much it cost. As was the custom among the young bucks at Brook's gambling club, bets were laid as to whether 'Prinny', the young Prince of Wales, would succeed.

※

While pursuing 'Perdita' with the aim of seducing her, Prinny was living recklessly, piling debt on debt. He knew that at the age of 21 he would inherit large sums from the Duchy of Cornwall revenues and had signed promissory notes to pay back the moneylenders at that time. He was spending large sums on gambling and pedigree horses. He also had grandiose schemes to renovate and redecorate the dilapidated Carlton House in Trafalgar Square, which was the former residence of George III's deceased father, Prince Frederick of Wales. Since Prince Frederick's premature death Carlton House had been empty for many years. Prinny's ambition was to turn it into an elegant residence to outshine Buckingham House (today's Buckingham Palace) where he was currently residing.

Mary, now living apart from her husband, decided that the time had come to take a lover. Aware that journalists followed her she was wary of the press.

She arranged with Lord Malden to meet the Prince of Wales and his younger brother, Prince Frederick, Duke of York, for dinner at an inn situated on remote Eel Pie Island in the River Thames between Twickenham and Richmond. The Prince suggested they all wear Venetian carnival costumes so no one could recognise them.

Mary, wearing a carnival mask and a long black cloak over her dress, paid a coachman to drive her to Twickenham. She told the coachman to wait for her and crossed the narrow footbridge that led to the island and the inn. In a private dining room she dined with the two young princes.

The Prince of Wales called Mary Robinson by her stage name of 'Perdita', which she had acquired after she played the role of Perdita in *A Winter's Tale*. After several bottles of wine Mary relaxed and told the young princes the sad story of her marriage, referring to her debt-ridden husband as a 'dipsomaniac' (as alcoholics were known in the 18th century). Unaware the Prince of Wales was also addicted to gambling for high stakes, she explained that her husband spent her earnings at the gambling tables.

Although the newspapers described her as a wealthy actress, this was not true — in fact, she had severe money worries.

The young Prince of Wales was moved by her story. Careful not to mention his own gambling addiction he assured Perdita he loved her and would take care of her financially if she would agree to live with him in a house near the theatre, he would rent for the two of the them. He had booked a room at the inn hoping that these assurances would be enough to make the beautiful actress spend the night with him in this remote spot.

As they were leaving the private dining room a journalist approached Perdita. When he began to ask her questions, Perdita fled across the footbridge to her carriage and returned to London alone.

The following morning a brief story about the Prince of Wales, dining *incognito* at Eel Pie Island with the celebrated actress, appeared in *The Morning Herald*.

Prinny, believing he had a chance of installing Perdita as his resident mistress, sent Lord Malden to negotiate an agreement under which he would rent a suitable house near the Drury Lane Theatre where he could stay with her *incognito* whenever possible. The Prince was well aware that his parents would be furious if they knew he was to live in a rented house with a married actress, rather than staying with them at Buckingham House.

Perdita was worried about her little daughter and her reaction to this new relationship and refused to be separated from Mary Elizabeth. Lord Malden cynically assured Perdita that she need have no fear — the Prince of Wales was a man of honour and would look after little Mary Elizabeth as though she were his own daughter.

Lord Malden must have known how immature and selfish the 18-year-old Prince of Wales was when he assured Perdita that he would give her daughter the best education money could buy. As a further inducement Lord Malden added that His Royal Highness was a very generous man and would provide money for a dowry so little Mary Elizabeth could make a good marriage.

Carried away by his own eloquence (or the rash promises of the amorous Prince), Lord Malden pledged that when the Prince turned 21 and accessed the revenues of the Duchy of Cornwall, he would give Perdita £25,000 — an enormous sum for that time — to buy herself an elegant London residence.

This sounded like a very generous offer, but Perdita was no longer the naïve girl who had been taken in by the grandiose promises of Thomas Robinson. She remembered the lawyer's office where she had worked copying documents and the power of contract law.

She smiled at Lord Malden and told him the Prince of Wales must get a lawyer to draw up a contract confirming that payment would be made when His Royal Highness turned 21. The contract had to be signed by His Royal Highness and witnessed by him and Mary would keep copies.

Mary's wishes were conveyed to the Prince of Wales. He was annoyed as he knew that when lawyers were involved it would take time and cost more to resolve various issues. Baulked of his desires, the Prince of Wales decided to attempt a spot of emotional blackmail. He sent back a message threatening to kill himself if Perdita did not become his mistress within a week as he could not live without her.

Perdita took advice from fellow actors who warned her again about the fickleness of princes who could not be trusted to keep their word. She insisted on having the signed contract in her possession before she moved in with the Prince of Wales and become his official mistress. Perdita flirted a little with the corpulent young Lord Malden so he would take her side and explained she was the breadwinner responsible for the welfare of her little daughter.

A few days later Perdita realised her determined stance had paid off when she received two copies of the contract or bond of payment signed by the heir to the throne with his seal affixed, promising to pay her the sum she had named when he came of age and provide a dowry for little Mary Elizabeth.

Perdita signed both copies and returned one to the Prince of Wales via the attentive Lord Malden.

The Prince ordered another equerry, Captain Jack Willett Payne, to draw cash from his account at Coutts Bank and pay a letting agent a year's rent on an unfurnished terrace house in Cork

Street and bring him the lease. The lawyers, wise to the ways of princes with women, insisted the lease agreement must have a clause, giving the Prince the right to rescind the lease at a month's notice on payment of a cancellation fee.

The Prince of Wales enjoyed buying furniture and paintings. At Mr Christie's auction rooms in King Street he purchased chairs, a sofa, a double bed and a few paintings for the rented house.

Perdita and her daughter moved into their elegant abode in Cork Street, Soho, which was within easy walking distance of Drury Lane Theatre.

To seal their agreement the Prince of Wales gave Perdita a magnificent phaeton — a type of light travelling coach — the latest in luxury private transport. The phaeton attracted attention as it was painted bright yellow with deep blue leather upholstery and

Was drawn by four magnificent thoroughbred Arab horses. In today's terms the coach was the equivalent of a Ferrari.

Perdita was deliriously happy, convinced by such a luxurious gift their love would last forever. She dashed around showing off her new transport, enjoying the excitement of driving the horses herself.[2] On 12 June 1781, the *Morning Herald* described how,

> Fortune has *certainly* smiled on Perdita. On Sunday she sported a new phaeton drawn by four chestnut-coloured ponies with a postillion and servants in blue and silver liveries. She dashed through the Hyde Park turnpike at four o'clock in the afternoon, dressed in a navy blue great-coat prettily trimmed in silver; a plume of feathers gracing her hat.

Ironic cartoons about her new position appeared in the scandal sheets. One was captioned, 'The sailing ship *Wales* has boarded the *Perdita* and is enjoying the fruits of war'.

The theatre manager was pleased with the publicity for Perdita as it resulted in increased ticket sales for her performances. She was the celebrity *du jour*, deluged with invitations to parties and balls — her hostesses expressing the hope Mrs Darby Robinson might bring the Prince of Wales with her.

Whenever the Prince of Wales did not have an official engagement or was not gambling for high stakes with cronies at Brook's Club in Pall Mall, he stayed the night with his mistress.

Perdita enjoyed the attention she received as she drove herself in her magnificent yellow carriage around Hyde Park and along Rotten Row. Thanks to the fact she was a royal mistress she had become a fashion icon, famous for her enticing semi-transparent muslin gowns with low necklines, which were widely copied and known as *'perditas'*.

In the rented house in Cork Street, she and George Augustus were waited on by servants, dressed in blue and silver livery with an embroidered crest of Prince of Wales' feathers. His Royal Highness paid for a groom to feed and care for the Arab horses that pulled Perdita's yellow carriage. Staff wages for a maid, a cook and a footman at Cork Street were paid by Captain Willet Payne on behalf of the Prince. Whenever possible he dined with Perdita at the Cork Street residence and stayed the night in her bed.

Each night when the young Prince was free he sat in the Royal Box to watch her perform, thrilled to be known as the lover of a beautiful and talented actress. He and the beautiful actress were the centre of attention. However, the vain and immature Prince of Wales became jealous if he felt people concentrated on Perdita and ignored him.

Unknown to Perdita, Prinny was sliding ever deeper into debt to moneylenders. He was paying large sums each month in interest on his loans, paying rent on the Cork Street house and wages of his staff. He had already started to collect paintings for the day when he would have his own official residence and move from Buckingham House to Carlton House in Pall Mall.

His favourite amusement was gambling and drinking with other young aristocrats and men-about-town at Brook's — a private club whose wealthy members played for very high stakes. Each member had to take a large sum in golden guineas to Brook's and keep the money in a special drawer in the gambling table so they could settle their debts immediately. Fortunes and country houses were lost overnight at Brook's Club. The Prince was one of the largest losers but could not stop gambling and was always in a bad mood when he lost.

Before long Perdita realised that Prinny was subject to severe mood swings. Moods of euphoria, in which he spent extravagantly, were followed by bouts of deep depression. Once the honeymoon period was over he displayed the violent temper of many members of the Hanoverian dynasty. When he flew into a rage Perdita either burst into tears or retaliated with a tantrum of her own.

The Prince of Wales complained she spent far too much time learning her lines and rehearsing and was never free at the times he wanted to be with her. Worried about their relationship, Perdita went to see the actor-manager, Richard Brinsley Sheridan, who was now running Drury Lane. She told Sheridan she wanted to break her contract as she needed to devote more time to the Prince and her little daughter. Sheridan, who was one of the Prince of Wales' fellow members of Brook's Club, thought it unwise to reveal that she was not the Prince's *only* love interest.

Prinny had boasted at Brook's of having slept with the courtesan, Grace Dalrymple Elliott — known as 'Dilly Dally', famous for her one-night stands. The Prince had produced several of Grace's pubic hairs and a ringlet as proof he had been her lover. Sheridan feared the 18-year-old Prince was tiring of Perdita with her demanding career and a needy small child. He knew the Prince of Wales had dropped women without a word of explanation and hoped Perdita's charms would prevent this happening.

Following Perdita's instructions Sheridan cancelled her contract. Before doing so, he warned Perdita that by backing out of her commitments at Drury Lane, she would never be offered similar parts again. Mindful that the Prince of Wales was a fellow member of Brook's Club, Sheridan kept quiet about the fact that the Prince boasted of his night with Grace Dalrymple Elliott. He was also pursuing Lady Melbourne, a married woman famous for cuckolding her elderly husband with virile young lovers.

Early in 1783, Sheridan engaged another actress to play the leading roles for the following season.

As Sheridan had suspected, the Prince of Wales' passion for Perdita was over. He now resented the money he had been forced to spend on housing her and stopped coming to the theatre. Grace Dalrymple Elliott had left London for Paris, having been paid a large sum by the Duc d'Orleans to become his resident mistress.

Prinny, who enjoyed the company of older women, now frequented the *soirees* of Lady Melbourne, an expert player of the Game of Love who enthralled the Prince of Wales with her husky voice and her promise of sexual delights.

Unaware that her royal lover was chasing Lady Melbourne, Perdita planned a surprise party for Prinny at the Cork Street house. She and her little daughter went shopping in Bond Street and on her return was horrified to find the furniture, her clothes, books and other possessions were gone. At first she thought the house had been burgled.

Neighbours advised a stunned Mrs Robinson that her trunks had been packed by a valet, wearing the livery of the Prince of Wales, and a senior figure who, from the description, must have been Captain Willett Payne. The trunks containing Perdita's possessions had been loaded into a hansom cab. The driver had been ordered to deliver Perdita's possession to Mr Robinson, who was living in a run-down area at the east end of London.

In a state of shock, Perdita contacted the letting agent who icily informed her the lease on the house had been terminated by Captain Willett Payne, on the orders of the Prince of Wales. All the furniture had been sent to auction so she was at liberty to buy it if she wished.

Perdita, now homeless, with no capital and no possessions, other than the yellow coach and horses, moved to an inn with a mews and stables behind it for her horses. She contacted the office of the Prince of Wales and was told His Royal Highness did not wish to discuss the matter and she should address her concerns to His Royal Highness in writing. However, her erstwhile lover did not answer her frantic letters and neither did Lord Malden or Captain Willet Payne.

Perdita learned from the gossip columns that the fickle Prince of Wales was pursuing the attractive husky-voiced Lady Melbourne, who had cuckolded her husband several times and whose sons were alleged to have different fathers.³

Perdita was furious at having been deceived and called Prinny, 'fickle, parsimonious and temperamental'. What made her even more angry was the fact she had thrown away her chances of several leading roles, believing the Prince of Wales was *genuinely* in love with her.

Perdita had no chance of returning to the stage as a serious actress. She realised she was now no longer the envy of London, but just another discarded royal mistress. All that remained of her romance was the ivory picture frame studded with diamonds, containing a miniature portrait of the Prince of Wales she had redeemed from the pawnbroker. She had to act now to obtain justice for herself and her daughter.

Although Perdita had been humiliated by the Prince of Wales she still had his signed bond or contract promising to pay her £25,000 when he came of age at twenty-one, so she could buy a house and provide a dowry for her daughter.⁴ Her other asset was the tin box containing Prinny's erotic love letters, worth big money to scandal sheets like the *Morning Post* and its rival *The Morning Herald*.

After the scandals associated with previous Hanoverian monarchs, George III was keen that his family be seen as devout and virtuous. So Perdita believed the King would pay to keep the doings of his sex-obsessed heir out of the papers. If the King refused to honour the bond his heir had signed, Perdita could threaten to sell the Prince's sexually explicit letters to the press or print them in a memoir. She had additional ammunition as she was privy to the secret that another son, the young Prince Frederick, had made a housemaid pregnant. The girl had been dismissed and the child had been adopted by a couple named Molloy — another scandal that the King did not want revealed.

Mary Darby Robinson wrote a very polite letter to King George III. She asked His Majesty to pay the sum cited in the contract his son had signed and she would be happy to hand over the love letters to anyone he nominated. She added a veiled threat that if His Majesty did not pay, she would have to pass the letters to the *Morning Post*. To prove the point she enclosed a note with brief extracts of the most erotic letters from the Prince of Wales and listed the dates of the other letters.

Perdita's bulky envelope was hand delivered by messenger to the King's Private Secretary at Buckingham House. The prudish George III was shocked to read about the bond his son had signed and the sexual content of his letters to the actress.

The King summoned his heir to Buckingham House. His Majesty told his wayward heir that his letters to the actress were obscene and disgusting. Were the letters to be published the public would lose all respect for a hereditary monarchy.[5]

George III added that, as his son was under age and in debt, a way must be found to get the money to buy off the wretched actress. He demanded the Prince of Wales marry a Protestant princess, one or other of his many German cousins. The dowry he would receive should be used to pay his debts.

The Prince of Wales was horrified. He told his father his German cousins were either very plain or downright ugly. Having had experience of acting from his time with Perdita, he played the role of penitent son, burst into tears and promised to change his ways, although he had no intention of doing so.

Lord Malden was sent to negotiate with Perdita. He told her she would never receive the full amount of the promised bond, because the Prince of Wales was in debt and most of the revenues he would receive on his coming-of-age were *already* allocated. Eventually, worn down by arguing and in dire need of cash, Perdita agreed to take a mere £1,000 pounds in return for handing over a dozen of the Prince's most sexually explicit letters, with the promise of more money in a few months time for *more* letters, provided she did not go to the press.

George III did not have much cash available as Parliament kept him short of money. He had to ask the Chancellor of the Exchequer, Lord John North, for money to buy off the woman he referred to as that 'wretched actress'. Lord North argued that it was not the British government's responsibility to pay off a wronged mistress of the Prince of Wales. Eventually some repayment was arranged but it was nothing like the amount cited in the bond the Prince of Wales had signed.

The lovesick Lord Malden felt guilty over his role in the matter. As Perdita was getting the worst of the deal, he tried to help her. Perdita used the first instalment to repay her debtors while awaiting the second one. Lord Malden politely asked His Majesty to pay off the balance of the bond, but his request was completely ignored.

Only after the intervention of the wily lawyer-turned-politician, Charles James Fox (who like Lord Malden lusted after Perdita), was a settlement negotiated. The amount outstanding was bargained down so far that Perdita would never be able to buy the handsome home of her dreams. While flirting with Perdita and trying to seduce her, Charles James Fox did his best to reduce the amount of compensation she would accept. As a result, the final instalment was less than a quarter of what she should have received, paid very reluctantly by George III. On receipt of this amount Perdita handed over the love letters to Charles James Fox, who was entrusted with burning them.

Perdita had learned another lesson — it was hard to negotiate with a clever lawyer. On Fox's legal advice a discretionary clause was inserted into Perdita's deed of settlement under which she was forbidden to discuss the contents of the letters with *anyone,* or name how much money she had received for them.

In lieu of the outstanding monies Fox negotiated an annuity of £500 a year and a further £250 for little Mary Elizabeth, to be paid annually for the rest of her life. Fox made it clear he expected Perdita to show her gratitude to him in the traditional way.

Charles James Fox was swarthy, plump and short in stature, a gambler and drinker but he was witty and amusing. Both he and Lord Malden were after Perdita as a bed companion. But Fox was far better company than the tongue-tied corpulent Lord Malden, who continued to insist to Perdita that he loved her.

The wily Charles James Fox managed to laugh his way into Perdita's bed. Briefly, he was her lover, until he returned to the arms of his mistress, the former courtesan Lizzie Armistead.

Perdita then sought the protection of Lord Maldon but found him a disappointing lover.

With the money she received, Perdita was able to fulfil her childhood dream and become a published author under her real name of Mary Darby Robinson.

Perdita was under no illusions that she loved Lord Malden, aware he had been responsible for presenting her with a false impression of the Prince of Wales. Nevertheless, she accepted his offer of help and moved with her little daughter into Lord Malden's London residence. His servants protected Perdita from Thomas Robinson, the husband to whom she was shackled for life. Robinson was now living on the streets and, from time to time, he appeared on Lord Malden's doorstep — an unwashed vagrant demanding money — and was ejected by footmen. Eventually, Thomas Robinson died destitute and was buried in a pauper's communal grave.

※

The Prince of Wales had one of Perdita's ringlets and snippets of her pubic hair as proof she had been his mistress. He also wanted a portrait of his ex-mistress to hang on one of the walls of Carlton House, which would soon become his official residence. He was excited by the idea of owning his own home and commissioned several artworks for it. Late in the year 1781, the Prince of Wales commissioned a portrait of his former mistress, regretting he had not bought John Hoppner's sensual portrait of Perdita when he first saw it in the Royal Academy or one of the smaller versions.

The Prince, who had a good eye for art, selected Thomas Gainsborough to paint Perdita. Hoppner had painted her wearing a black dress ornamented with red bows and a plunging neckline showing off her cleavage, her delicate features and pale complexion, shown against a dark background.

Gainsborough was determined to produce a different version of the famous actress. He posed Perdita sitting on a mossy bank against a painted backdrop of trees. The artist specialised in painting the texture of silk and in this portrait Perdita wears an elegant gauzy silk dress. Beside her is her Pomeranian terrier, dogs being considered an symbol of faithfulness in art, perhaps a subtle reproach to the Prince of Wales for the ill-treatment of his mistress. In her left hand Perdita holds the oval portrait miniature of the Prince of Wales in its diamond-studded frame. She looks wistful, dreamy and vulnerable. Clearly this was not the vision of the actress-mistress the Prince had hoped for. He wanted a 'trophy' portrait with a suggestion of his mistress's fabulous cleavage which is *not* shown by Gainsborough. The second portrait presents Perdita as what she became — a leading woman author of novels, non-fiction and poetry, who the poet Samuel Taylor Coleridge called 'a woman with a well-stocked mind'.

In mid-life, when the Carlton House renovations sent the Prince of Wales once more into debt, he sold Gainsborough's portrait of Perdita to a friend and fellow art collector, his contemporary Lord Hertford. The portrait of Perdita remained in the Hertford family. This portrait (shown in the colour section of this book) has become one of the treasures of London's Wallace Collection in Manchester House, Manchester Square, near London's Oxford Street.[6]

CAPTAIN TARLETON, WAR HERO AND MAN OF ACTION

Perdita's first meeting with Captain Tarleton took place when Lord Malden took her to the theatre. In the interval Lord Malden introduced her to his friend, the tall, lean and tanned Captain Banestre (Ban) Tarleton, a much-decorated hero of the American wars of Independence. Lord Malden told Perdita that Captain Tarleton, now on half pay, was writing a history of the war. Fascinated by writers and bored by Lord Malden, Perdita found Captain Tarleton interesting and flirted with the attractive captain.

Several evenings later, over a game of cards at Brook's Club, Captain Tarleton wagered Lord Malden he could seduce Perdita who he claimed was little better than a whore. Flushed with drink, Lord Malden bet Captain Tarleton a thousand guineas that his mistress would remain faithful to him, no matter *what* inducements Tarleton offered her.

After being wined and dined several times by Tarleton, the handsome war hero spent the night with Perdita and made the same request as the Prince of Wales — he asked her for a golden ringlet and a few of her pubic hairs as proof he had slept with her. Perdita obliged.

Back at Brook's Club a triumphant Captain Tarleton claimed he had won the wager and produced samples of Perdita's hair as proof. When Perdita learned the men had laid bets on her having sex with Tarleton, she was furious. So was Lord Malden who felt betrayed and humiliated. He wrote Perdita a note, telling her he refused to have anything more to do with her.

Perdita climbed into her yellow phaeton and drove her horses to Lord Malden's residence in an attempt to smooth things over between them. She was driving too fast and the coach overturned with Perdita inside it.

It was not Lord Malden but the resourceful Captain Tarleton who came to her rescue. Perdita had already been trapped under the overturned phaeton for more than an hour. Tarleton organised men to lift up the coach and when they finally released Perdita, he found her deathly pale and trembling with delayed shock.

One of the horses had its leg broken by the fall and had to be shot, which reduced Perdita to hysterics. Captain Tarleton took pity on her, drove her home in his carriage and invited her to stay the night. As they started to talk, Tarleton realised with surprise he had totally misjudged Perdita. He discovered that she was highly intelligent, sensitive and better educated than he was. Both of them wanted to write professionally so they had a great deal in common. The result was that Captain Tarleton became the lover and writing partner of Mrs Robinson.

Members of the Captain's family were Anglo-Irish gentry, proud of their ancient name. Horrified that their son was living with the infamous Perdita, a 'scarlet woman' and former mistress of the Prince of Wales, the Tarletons agreed to pay off his major debts on condition he left for France — *alone*.

His creditors were demanding payment and Captain Tarleton was still on half pay from the Army at a time of financial stringency. By going to France he could escape from minor creditors who might not find it worthwhile to take him to court. He had no wish to be sent to a debtor's prison and regretted that his family were forcing him and Perdita apart. He loved her but the risk of ending up in a debtor's prison forced him obey his parents.

On 24 July 1783, Ban Tarleton left a letter addressed to Mary Robinson, explaining that he loved her but had no option but to leave for France or he would be jailed. Mary was aware her lover had debts he could not pay. She was expecting his child, but did not want to tell him the news until she had managed to raise enough money for the baby's birth. Mary received financial help from wealthy friends and she persuaded the same friends to pay off her lover's debts. Carrying letters in which she was promised a sum of money, she followed Ban Tarleton to Dover in her yellow phaeton to tell him she was carrying his child and still loved him, and that she had obtained the money to pay off his debts.

Bumping over rough roads brought on a miscarriage. A rural midwife was called and Mary went into labour in the midwife's primitive cottage and lost Tarleton's baby. Due to the unhealthy conditions of the cottage, Mary caught an infection which turned into rheumatic fever. She suffered severe pain as the valves of her heart were affected and she was bedridden for months.

Finally, Mary returned to London where prolonged treatment in spa baths brought some relief rather than a total cure. From France, Captain Tarleton heard his mistress had lost a baby and realised she had been carrying his child. Distraught by this discovery, Ban Tarleton returned to England, told Mary he loved her and they must move to France where the cost of living was far cheaper than in England.

Living in France, Mary helped her lover finish the manuscript of his war book, *The History of the American Campaigns*. It had many chapters written by Mary Darby Robinson, who stylistically was the better writer of the two. However, so ingrained was the prejudice against women authors, writing anything other than romantic novels, the London publishers *refused* to acknowledge Mary Darby Robinson as co-author on the title page, claiming it was impossible a woman could have written a military history. They also knew that if male critics sighted a female name on the title page they would damn the book completely.

The war book was a *success d'estime* for Captain Tarleton but had only a small but influential circulation so did not make him rich. Fortunately, he was promoted to the rank of Colonel, which was an honour but he remained an officer on half pay.

Eventually Mary and her lover returned to London where Colonel Tarleton became a Member of Parliament, which was then an honorary (unpaid) post. Mary Robinson wrote her lovers' speeches as well as a volume of poems about love and loss. Samuel Taylor Coleridge, author of *The Ancient Mariner* and *Kubla Khan*, read Mary's love poems and praised them.[7]

For the next fifteen years, Mary and Colonel Tarleton, MP lived in Clarges Street, Mayfair, working on a series of historical novels and non-fiction books. Mary's health improved but she never fully recovered the use of her legs.

Mary was now incapable of childbearing, but Ban Tarleton was being pressured by his ageing parents to give them a grandson to carry on the Tarleton name. Unknown to Mary, her lover proposed marriage to a young woman he scarcely knew and was accepted. Her name was Susan Bertie and she was the illegitimate daughter of the Duke of Ancaster. Formerly Miss Bertie had been spurned for her illegitimacy, but since the Duke had left her a large bequest in his will, she was now wooed by fortune hunters like Ban Tarleton.

Colonel Tarleton was still a good looking man and charmed Miss Bertie into agreeing to marry him. The first thing Mary knew about her partner's engagement to Miss Bertie was reading about it in *The Times* over breakfast. So great was the shock, she almost fainted, bitterly hurt that the man she had adored and worked so hard for over the years could behave so badly to her. Mary's bitter experiences proved how totally different standards applied to men and women in the 18th century. Ban Tarleton was a serial seducer and adulterer, but was able to marry a virginal heiress, while Mary Robinson was seen as an outcast and a 'scarlet woman'.

Having had her life changed by a father who sold the family home over her head, been deceived by three men she had loved, the now semi-paralysed Mary took her revenge. She wrote an important novel called *The False Friend* which, like Jane Austen's *Northanger Abbey*, mocked the whole genre of the romantic novel. Mary's female characters in the novel were deceived by men who manipulated the idea of romance for their own ends to gain possession of women's dowries. She warned female readers to beware of the whole concept of romance, which never lasted very long and was used by men for their own ends.

Once the press realised that Mary Darby Robinson and the actress Perdita Robinson were the same person, they gave *The False Friend* a great deal of publicity — a former royal mistress, disillusioned by another faithless lover, writing a novel. Critics and readers eagerly discussed *The False Friend*. The first edition sold out. A second edition followed and sold out as well.

Mary, often in pain from her damaged heart, was encouraged by the support of women readers like the feminist author Mary Wollstonecraft. Both these clever women, way in advance of their era, felt strongly that the law was biased against women. The only hope was for women to make their voices heard, so they could gain independence and the right to *keep* money they earned.

Under the name Mary Robinson, she became the author of six historical novels and several books of poetry. In hindsight, her most important publication was *A Letter To The Women Of England on the Injustice of Mental Subordination.* This daring book demanded justice for women in a male-dominated world. From her wheelchair, Mary advised women to read widely, learn the art of public speaking and argue for laws that held women back to be changed. She described how men denied girls a good education and then called them 'brainless'. It was men who controlled the legal system, the divorce courts, politics and the church.

A Letter To The Women Of England caused outrage among male readers that a mere woman had *dared* to express such radical views. The book was published in 1799, the same year that the dissolute Prince of Wales sired George Crole, yet another royal bastard. George Crole was his illegitimate son by Elizabeth Crole to whom the Prince of Wales behaved in the same callous way as he had done to Perdita. The fickle Prince promised Elizabeth Crole an annuity and a house in London if she became his mistress. Once he tired of her and money lenders were pressing him he cancelled the lease on the house and the promised annuity. But it seems that Elizabeth Crole managed to blackmail him into providing an annuity of £500 for herself and her child.[8]

When George III became insane, the Prince of Wales, now forced into a marriage with a wealthy German princess he loathed, became Prince Regent. His legal advisors heard that Mrs Robinson was writing her memoirs even though she had signed a confidentiality clause over the contents of his love letters to her. Royal advisors still feared that *anything* Mrs Robinson might publish about her affair could damage the Prince Regent. He was unpopular and mocked unmercifully in cartoons by Gillray for his scandal-prone life and poor treatment of the German princess he had been forced to marry for her dowry.

Clearly under the terms of her agreement Mrs Robinson could not publish the contents of the Prince's love letters, which had long since been destroyed. But living with the future King and sharing his bed she had been privy to many royal secrets. There was too much at stake to risk Mrs Robinson writing about broken promises and royal bastards. Republicanism was in the air in France — it must not be allowed to spread to England. While the French shrugged off sexual scandals, English church goers would be shocked to learn scandalous details about their future King who would eventually be anointed Head of the Anglican Church in Westminster Abbey. Aware Mrs Robinson was living in reduced circumstances and could not afford high legal costs, the King's lawyers threatened to take out an injunction against her for libel, should she publish *anything at all* about the Prince of Wales.

Nursed by her unmarried daughter, Mary Elizabeth Robinson, Mary Darby Robinson died in 1800.

The Memoirs of Mrs Robinson, published posthumously, was printed in an extremely small edition circulated among friends and relatives. Mary's memoir was never sold in bookshops and copies of it became very valuable.

George Augustus, Prince of Wales. Lithograph after a portrait by H.P. Bome, 1805. (Original in the Ashmolean Museum)

Portrait of Perdita. Artist impression after a detail from a painting by Gainsborough.

Drury Lane Theatre, where Perdita frequently performed.

Buckingham House, which would later be extended and known as Buckingham Palace.

Perdita from an engraving by Birch after a painting by Sir John Reynolds.

Captain Tarleton. Mezzotint after a painting by Sir Joshua Reynolds.

CHAPTER 3

Maria Fitzherbert (Smythe-Weld) (1756–1837) and George Augustus, Prince of Wales (King George IV)

The virtuous Mrs Fitzherbert is far more dangerous to the Prince of Wales than all the women of ill repute he has taken and abandoned. Charles James Fox, lawyer and politician.

Once you learn the truth about royalty you will no longer reverence it. Mystery is its life. Walter Bagehot, *The English Constitution*, 1867.

FROM FAIRY-TALE BRIDE TO GRIEVING WIDOW

In July 1775, straight from a convent school in France, sweet natured Maria Smythe, eldest daughter of a large Catholic family, had a romantic wedding to the owner of a castle overlooking the sea. Maria had two weddings, an official Protestant one followed by a private Catholic ceremony in the private chapel of Lulworth Castle, her new home. Catholic priests were forbidden to celebrate mass or officiate at public weddings or baptisms which was why old Catholic families had their private chapels.

Maria's wedding portrait shows as an 18-year-old beauty with a mass of shoulder-length blonde curls.[1]

Three months later Edward Weld was fatally injured in a riding accident. His young wife nursed him devotedly until his painful death. Maria had married for love, knew nothing of the world outside her convent and naively believed her husband's family would behave generously towards her. When she was nursing her husband she did not ask him if he had signed a new will which bequeathed their home and its contents to her. Under the existing will, everything Edward Weld owned went to his younger brother, who refused to give Maria even a small portion of her late husband's estate.

The grief-stricken young widow returned to her family home, Brambridge House, Colden Common, near Winchester with only her clothes and a few wedding presents. Mary returned to Brambridge House and nursed her paralysed father who had suffered a heart attack.

Maria's mother, the former Mary Errington, was a staunch Catholic. Her sister, Isabella, Maria's aunt had turned Protestant in order to marry the wealthy Earl of Sefton.

Lady Sefton felt that her niece should not remain hidden away in rural Hampshire, acting as an unpaid nurse and governess. This was the Jane Austen era when matchmaking was one of the main occupations of the wives of the landed gentry. To help Maria, who lacked a dowry, find a new husband, it was agreed she was to spend four months at Sefton House in London with Lady Sefton who would chaperone her favourite niece.

The Earl of Sefton, who owned agricultural estates in the north of England, thought Thomas Fitzherbert, a recently widowed Catholic landowner in Staffordshire, might be an ideal husband for his widowed niece. Thomas Fitzherbert owned Swynnerton Hall and a town residence in Mayfair. The Fitzherberts of Swynnerton Hall were one of England's oldest Catholic dynasties. They and the Smythes of Brambridge clung fiercely to the faith of their Catholic forbears, but suffered severe discrimination for doing so.

At Brambridge House, an upstairs room was used as a chapel, while at Swynnerton Hall the Fitzherberts had their own Catholic chapel in the grounds with a priest-confessor who lived with them.

Lady Sefton gave an elegant dinner party at Sefton House and placed tall personable Thomas Fitzherbert next to her beautiful niece. He was impressed by Maria's natural charm and unspoiled beauty and the fact she did not follow the latest fashion for powdering her hair white and wearing it in a towering pyramid as so many society ladies did. Maria defied the custom and wore blonde curls which framed her beautiful face.

After talking to Maria all evening, Thomas Fitzherbert believed she would make an excellent wife. The next day he wrote to Lady Sefton, requesting permission to woo her niece, indicating he was prepared to overlook the fact her ward lacked a dowry.

Maria was cautious by nature and wanted time to get to know Thomas Fitzherbert, who was ten years her senior. However, she soon realised what a fine and honourable man he was and fell in love for the second time.

On 24 June 1778, 22-year-old Maria married Thomas Fitzherbert in a legal ceremony at the Anglican Church of St Mary in Swynnerton village. They had a second secret Catholic ceremony for the family only in the small vaulted Catholic chapel in the grounds of Swynnerton Hall.[2]

Six months later the couple were thrilled to learn Maria was pregnant, but she miscarried and lost a much wanted baby boy. Worried about his young wife, in the spring of 1780 her husband took her south for a holiday to his Mayfair residence. He hoped that sight-seeing in London would take her mind off the tragic loss of their baby.

While on holiday, Mr and Mrs Fitzherbert were being driven in their coach through Hyde Park's Rotten Row, where fashionable Londoners paraded on horseback. A fair-haired young man on a chestnut horse rode beside their carriage for almost half a mile, staring fixedly through the window at Mrs Fitzherbert.

Maria ignored the stranger's impudent behaviour and looked straight ahead without acknowledging the presence of the young man. As the coachman turned right into Hyde Park Gate the man raised his hat in a gesture of farewell and smiled at her. Maria did not respond.

Once the carriage was out of earshot, Thomas told his wife her young admirer was none other than His Royal Highness, George Augustus, Prince of Wales.

Back at their Park Street residence, Maria related the incident to her married sister, Lady Frances Haggerston, who lived nearby and knew all the latest London gossip. Frances told Maria that the Prince of Wales had a bad reputation. He seemed to prefer women older than himself and his name had been linked to that of several married women, so Maria must be careful not to give him the *least* encouragement.

In 1778, the Papists Act, which reduced discrimination against Catholics, was passed by the British Parliament. Soon after the enactment there was talk of a petition against the Act and Thomas Fitzherbert, a staunch Catholic, feared there could be riots.

On 2 June 1780, a Protestant backlash was led by the bigoted Protestant Lord George Gordon. He led a march on Westminster, calling for the repeal of the Papists Act and for even sterner measures to be implemented against Catholics. His followers were a mixed bunch who included thugs and tramps. When drunk, some of the protesters set fire to Catholic homes along their route to Westminster and the Houses of Parliament.

The night sky was red with flames when Maria's brother-in-law arrived, asking Thomas to accompany him to save Catholic homes which were being burned and looted. At that time, London had no police force and the King had as yet not called out the Army to help.

Thomas embraced his wife and left the house with his brother-in-law to help Catholic citizens. Maria was desperately worried and spent a sleepless night.[3]

Dawn was breaking when Thomas returned, his face and hands black with soot and his clothes badly charred. Maria helped her exhausted husband undress and put him to bed. As he developed a fever and coughed continually, Maria sent for the doctor, who diagnosed that her husband's lungs had been badly damaged by inhaling smoke. Should he fail to improve, Maria was advised to take Thomas to the South of France where in a warmer climate he had a better chance to recover.

Maria, having attended a French convent, spoke fluent French. She rented a vacant villa in Nice and with her ailing husband on a stretcher crossed the English Channel by ferry. At Calais they hired a coach and horses to take them south to Nice.

However, Thomas's damaged lungs did not improve and every breath he drew became more painful. Realising he was dying, Thomas summoned his lawyer from London and he instructed him to prepare a new will. In it he bequeathed the Mayfair residence to Maria together with sufficient capital to provide her with a generous annual income for the rest of her life. He bequeathed his agricultural estates in Staffordshire and Derbyshire and Swynnerton Hall to his brother.

On 7 May 1781, after spending months fighting for breath, Thomas Fitzherbert died. He was only 37-years-old. It was not possible to ship his body back to England so the funeral service and burial was held in Nice.

Exhausted by the events of the last six months, Maria made a retreat to the convent near Paris where she had once been a pupil. Emerging with her faith strengthened, Maria stayed with a former school friends and did some travelling in France, praying that time would heal the pain caused by the loss of her second husband.

Early in 1783, Maria received a letter from her Aunt Isabella Sefton, warning her that France was sliding into revolution and it was high time she came home. Maria returned to London and opened up the Park Street Mayfair residence which was now her property. She was dismayed to read that her return to London was featured in the social pages of London's *Morning Herald* and *Daily Advertiser*.

On 27 July 1784, the *Herald* noted 'Mrs Fitzherbert has returned to us and her wealth and beauty ensure there will be many suitors for her hand'. Maria, still in mourning for husband, was outraged. Marriage was the last thing on her mind.

Worried that her favourite niece was always at home, still grieving over the loss of her husband, Lady Sefton invited her young brother, Henry Errington, and Mary to join her and her husband in the Sefton's box at Covent Garden.

Escorted by link boys, Maria went by sedan chair to the opera house, wearing a fashionable black lace off-the-shoulder evening gown. As a respectable widow she covered her long blonde hair and her face with a black lace veil. Inside the privacy of the Earl of Sefton's box Maria pushed back the veil, allowing her luxuriant blonde curls to fall to her shoulders. Her fashionably low cut French gown showed off her magnificent bosom and creamy complexion to good advantage.

Peering through opera glasses the 21-year old Prince of Wales spotted the beautiful lady seated beside his friend, Henry Errington. Like the Prince of Wales, Henry Errington and the Earl of Sefton were all members of Brook's Club, the fashionable Pall Mall all-male institution where the wealthy dined and gambled for high stakes and where fortunes were lost and won on a single throw of the dice.[4]

The Prince realised that the young woman with the mass of blonde curls in the Sefton's box was the beauty whose carriage he had followed in Rotten Row several years earlier.

After the curtain descended the audience streamed towards the exits. The Prince of Wales jumped up from his seat, caught up with the Seftons and Henry Errington and asked to be introduced to the beautiful lady. With reluctance Maria's uncle presented the philandering Prince to his virtuous niece.

Maria dropped the Prince a curtsey. The Prince of Wales, a handsome youth, six years younger than Maria, took her hand, raised it to his lips and expressed the hope they would meet again soon. For her part, Maria remembered how the young Prince had ogled her in front of her husband and quickly made her escape to the Earl of Sefton's carriage.

After leaving Covent Garden, the Prince of Wales attended an gambling session at a private house at which he met his good friend, Georgiana, Duchess of Devonshire and confided to her he was intrigued by Mrs Fitzherbert. He asked the Duchess to invite the beautiful widow to a luncheon at Devonshire House and seat him next to her.

The childless Duchess Georgiana had made an arranged marriage to the Duke but the two of them led separate lives. The Duchess of Devonshire filled her time with parties, matchmaking and political intrigue and was delighted to organise a luncheon party. As requested, she seated the besotted young Prince of Wales beside Mrs Fitzherbert at the best table.

Maria wore black to indicate she was still in mourning. With her fair complexion, blonde hair and cornflower blue eyes, black suited her. She said only a few words to the Prince. There was much joking and laughing about gambling and references to large sums lost and won at the faro tables. As Maria disapproved of gambling she saw the Prince of Wales as an irresponsible young man with more money than sense.

The Duchess of Devonshire was celebrated for her wit. She found Maria boring and did not take to her, probably because she realised that the young widow was even better looking than herself.

The witty young Duchess was a gambling addict who had borrowed money from the Prince to pay off her gambling debts, which she dared not admit to her husband. Under those circumstances the Duchess was prepared to put herself out in order to be agreeable to Mrs Fitzherbert, the new *inamorata* of the amorous Prince of Wales.

When Lady Sefton learned that Maria had lunched with the Duchess of Devonshire and the Prince of Wales she echoed the warning of Maria's sister, Lady Haggerston, telling her niece the Prince of Wales was a rake and she must be careful or the gossips would have a field day. Maria would lose her reputation and throw away any chance of making a third marriage to a respectable man. Although Mary felt that her good name was important, she assured her aunt she had no wish to remarry.

The following day, Mrs Fitzherbert received a magnificent bouquet of flowers and a velvet-lined box containing a gold bracelet with a card saying they came from George Augustus, Prince of Wales. Unwilling to be compromised, Maria returned the bracelet with a note saying that, although she liked the Prince's flowers, she regretted she was unable to accept jewels.

This reply and the fact the widow returned his gift told the amorous Prince that Mrs Fitzherbert was totally uninterested in becoming his mistress. Accustomed to easy conquests, the Prince was now even more intrigued by Mrs Fitzherbert. He refused to be put off and arranged for her to be invited to more functions at the homes of mutual friends.

Seated beside the Prince at luncheons and dinners Maria found that he was cleverer than she had first thought and knew a great deal about French art, a topic that interested her.

The fact that Maria had been educated in France and the Prince of Wales was enthusiastic about everything French, made Mrs Fitzherbert even more attractive in his eyes. He was renovating and redecorating Carlton House, his new residence in Pall Mall, in the French neo-classical style. He enjoyed talking to Mrs Fitzherbert about French architecture and art and it was clear to Maria that the Prince had a serious interest in these subjects.

Maria had a good sense of humour and laughed at the Prince's amusing accounts of attending Mr Christie's auctions, bidding and outwitting crafty art dealers on major paintings for his collection. Encouraged by her interest in art, Prinny sent Mrs Fitzherbert a miniature portrait of himself in an ivory locket studded with diamonds (a smaller version of the portrait he had given Perdita Robinson several years earlier). Maria wore the miniature on a black velvet ribbon round her neck, which set off her creamy skin to advantage. It features in her portrait painted by Richard Cosway who made several copies of this particular portrait for the Prince of Wales and relatives of Maria.

During a gambling session at Brook's Club, the Prince, at a loss as to how he could seduce a religious widow, sought the help of an old friend, Charles James Fox, a well-known rake. Fox, who was a relative of the Duchess of Devonshire, admitted he had no idea how to proceed — Mrs Fitzherbert was independently wealthy and had everything she needed already.

SWEET LASS OF RICHMOND HILL

Maria wanted to avoid the amorous advances of the young Prince of Wales and told her confessor of her problems.

The priest advised her to move away from Mayfair where it was easy for the Prince to follow her and move to the country. Maria went to the riverside town of Richmond and rented Marble Hill House, which was owned by the niece of the late Countess of Suffolk. Maria decided to restore the large neglected garden of Marble Hill House, which took up much of her time. As a strange coincidence, Marble Hill's original owner was Henrietta Howard, Countess of Suffolk, who had been the 'backstairs' mistress of George II.

Undeterred by the distance between London and Richmond the Prince of Wales drove out to visit Maria in his elegant phaeton, drawn by chestnut horses, bringing with him a necklace of sapphires and diamonds and a matching set of earrings. Once again Maria refused to accept these expensive presents.

The Prince of Wales' visits sparked rumours he intended to marry a Catholic, which meant he would have to renounce the Crown. Errand boys sung a popular ballad 'Sweet lass of Richmond Hill' which was supposed to contain the Prince's sentiments, 'I'd crowns resign to call thee mine, sweet lass of Richmond Hill.'

James Gillray, who disliked Catholics nearly as much as he disliked the House of Hanover, had great success with a saucy etching showing the Prince of Wales in bed, dreaming Mrs Fitzherbert was sleeping beside him. The suggestion she had yielded to the blandishments of young Prinny upset Maria.

To protect her reputation as a virtuous widow, Maria engaged Isobel Piggott, daughter of a retired Admiral, as her resident chaperone and companion. She insisted that the middle-aged Isobel be present whenever the Prince of Wales called on her at Marble Hill House.

With Miss Piggot in attendance the three of them spent delightful afternoons talking of politics and the improvements Maria had made to the house and garden at Marble Hill. They discussed Dutch and French paintings, coming up for auction, which the Prince hoped to buy for his growing art collection. He sought Maria's opinions over projected alterations and colour schemes for Carlton House on which he was working with the architect Henry Holland and brought her samples of materials for curtains and upholstery.

The Prince found Mrs Fitzherbert was fluency in French very useful in negotiating his purchases of paintings from French refugees now arriving in London. It was clear to Maria that the Prince had an exceptionally good eye for art.

Slowly Maria became fond of the handsome but self-absorbed young Prince although she felt that, at times, he behaved more like a spoiled petulant child than a future King of England.

Each time the Prince visited Maria at Richmond he fell more in love, convinced that he had at last found the perfect woman with whom to share his life. He realised that Maria's weak spot was her compassion, so the Prince worked hard to make soft-hearted Maria feel sympathetic towards him. He told her about his loveless boyhood, when his mother was so preoccupied by his father's bouts of illness she had little time to spare for her children.

The Prince now freely admitted he had made mistakes by falling for the wrong type of women. He claimed that with Maria by his side he was capable of doing great things. Maria whose happy childhood had been spent in a loving family atmosphere felt sorry for the Prince but still refused his amorous advances.

The heir to the throne, unable to make Mrs Fitzherbert his mistress, played his trump card. He threatened to kill himself if Maria refused to live with him, assuring her that his life lacked meaning without her. As a devout Catholic suicide was reprehensible to Maria, but becoming the Prince's mistress was out of the question.

The Prince of Wales now talked of marriage and appealed to Maria's religious instincts, telling her she was his only hope of salvation and once he was King he would repeal all discrimination against Catholics. Maria reminded the Prince of the laws preventing the heir to the throne marrying a Catholic. If the Prince lost his head and married her, he would forfeit the Crown. The Bill of Rights, designed to prevent a Catholic taking the throne, strictly forbade marriage of any member of the royal family to a Catholic, as did the Act of Settlement of 1701. The Royal Marriage Act of 1772 was even more specific and gave George III the right to select spouses for all his children.

Should the Prince of Wales be foolish enough to marry Mrs Fitzherbert in a secret ceremony George III could disinherit him in favour of the heir presumptive, his second son, Prince Frederick.

Not that Prince Frederick was a model son. He had sired at least four bastards who had to be supported from the royal purse. In spite of these transgressions the King and Queen preferred the hard-working Prince Frederick to the vain, self-absorbed indolent Prince of Wales.

It seemed that any marriage between the Prince of Wales and Mrs Fitzherbert would have to be a secret one. When Maria told her confessor about her dilemma, he was alarmed at talk of a clandestine marriage and advised her to return to the safety of the nuns in her French convent.

Maria told the Prince the situation had got out of hand and she was returning to France, chaperoned by her friend Lady Anne Lindesay. Maria admitted she loved the Prince, but the situation had become far too dangerous for both of them — there was no way he could have a serious relationship with a Catholic or his father would disinherit him.

The Prince of Wales was excited by Maria's admission that she *did* love him but was terrified she would leave for France. He could not follow her without the King's permission, which he knew would not be granted. The more the Prince thought about the situation the more desperate he became.

Georgina, Duchess of Devonshire, a good friend to the Prince of Wales who often referred to her as a sister, described how the Prince,

> ...has been like a madman. He was ill last Wednesday and took three pints of brandy which half killed him and he was confined three days to his bed. I fancy he made himself worse than he was, in hopes to prevent the departure of a certain lady [Maria Fitzherbert] who goes abroad on Wednesday.[5]

EMOTIONAL BLACKMAIL AND A WEDDING RING FOR MARIA

On 8 July 1784, the Prince of Wales made a feeble attempt at suicide in an effort to prevent Maria Fitzherbert leaving for France. Maria received a note from Mr Keate, the Prince's personal barber surgeon, who used to bleed the Prince when suffering what were known as his 'nervous attacks'. Mr Keate's note explained that the Prince of Wales had tried to commit suicide by falling on his sword. This was a gross exaggeration. The Prince had stabbed himself in the chest with a small ornamental dagger, just badly enough to make it bleed. He ordered Keate to bandage the wound with previously bloodstained bandages to make the injury appear more impressive.

While Maria was packing for her departure to France, the Prince sent his carriage to Maria's home with three members of his household — Lord Southampton, Lord Onslow and Mr Keate. They claimed that His Royal Highness's life was in danger and it was vital Mrs Fitzherbert visit him at Carlton House.

Although she could hardly refuse, Maria was worried she was being lured to the Prince's residence to have sex with him against her will. As Miss Piggott was away, Maria insisted she needed someone to replace her as a chaperone. Lord Onslow reassured her that they were going to Devonshire House to collect the young Duchess of Devonshire who would accompany them to Carlton House.

When the women arrived at Carlton House, Maria found the Prince of Wales lying on a crimson velvet sofa swathed in blood-stained bandages, looking deathly pale. The Prince told Maria how much he loved her and asked her to kiss him. The heir to the throne murmured that the only thing that would make him want to get better was if Maria would promise to marry him. He would pledge his word with a ring.

The Duchess of Devonshire slipped a valuable ring off her finger and gave it to the Prince who placed it on Maria's finger and declared she was now his wife. The surgeon intervened, claiming his patient must rest. The Prince begged Maria for one last kiss.

Maria and the Duchess of Devonshire were escorted out of the room.[6] As they descended the steps of Carlton House, Lord Southampton ran after them saying the Prince insisted on seeing a signed deposition that Maria would marry him. The document must be witnessed by Lord Southampton and Lord Onslow. Unless the Prince sighted it he could not sleep and sleep was vital for his recovery.

The Duchess of Devonshire suggested they go back to Devonshire House and draw up a pledge. Mrs Fitzherbert must sign the document which would be returned to Carlton House by carriage, so the Prince could see it and sleep soundly.

Maria fell into the trap the Prince and his friends had set for her. She signed the document, which was witnessed and taken to Carlton House. She returned to her Mayfair home where she spent a sleepless night. The more she considered what had happened, the more worried she became, fearing she had been tricked into signing. She was in a precarious position. Breaking the law by agreeing to marry the heir to the throne without the permission of the King was punishable.

The next morning Maria wrote to Lord Southampton, informing him she had been trapped into signing the document and under the circumstances a wedding would be invalid.

Several newspapers, tipped off by the Prince's servants, claimed that Mrs Fitzherbert had visited Carlton House at night and made a secret marriage to the Prince of Wales. Others claimed Mrs Fitzherbert had crossed the Channel and married the Prince in a Catholic church in France.

The satirical artist, James Gillray, convinced a secret marriage had taken place between the couple in a French cathedral, made an etching of the event, titled *Wife or No Wife*.

A second Gillray etching, *The Morning After Marriage*, showed Maria Fitzherbert lying on a rumpled bed, her breasts and thighs exposed. A drooping candle suggests the bridegroom's post-coital exhaustion.

Maria was horrified by these etchings and all the crude jokes that resulted. She decided to follow her original plan and leave for France, accompanied by her friend Lady Anne Lindesay, daughter of the Earl of Balcarres. Maria left no forwarding address and hoped that in her absence the furore would die down.

When Prinny heard the news that his beloved Maria had left for France he begged his father to let him follow her. As the heir to the throne, he needed the King's permission to leave the country. The King refused, hoping his son's passion for Mrs Fitzherbert would fizzle out like so many of his previous short-lived passions for women. He gave the Prince a stern lecture about the need to pay off his huge debts, urging him to marry a wealthy princess and use her dowry to settle his debts.

Obsessed with finding Maria, the Prince did not listen. With the help of his French friend, the Duke of Orleans, he managed to trace her in France.

Prinny bombarded Maria with emotional letters, including an 18-page missive in which he implored his beloved to return to England and signed it 'Your most affectionate lover and tenderest [sic] of husbands.'

But these tender affectionate sentiments did not prevent the fickle Prince, unknown to Maria, consoling himself in the arms of a paid courtesan, alleged to have born him an illegitimate son.

The Prince of Wales' debts were now so large, money lenders were camping outside Carlton House hoping to serve writs on him. George III declared he would only pay off the Prince of Wales' debts if he agreed to marry a Protestant princess. The Prince agreed, yet another promise he did not intend to keep.

On 3 November 1785, the Prince of Wales sent a 42-page letter to Maria, calling her 'Dearest of wives.' By now Maria was homesick for family and friends. Absence had made the heart grow fonder. Maria truly believed she did love the Prince of Wales and was prepared to overlook the fact that he was six years her junior.

Maria's Catholic conscience was soothed by the idea of a secret wedding — she would not be a royal mistress but a morganatic wife. Several Catholic friends supported the idea of this secret marriage as they hoped that once the Prince became King he would end all discrimination against Catholics. This marriage was illegal under civil law but Anglican and Catholic church law recognised it, so Maria agreed to marry again, believing she could take the sacrament at mass which was what really mattered to her.

On 15 December 1785, 18 months after she had been introduced to the heir to the throne at Covent Garden, Maria returned to London and agreed to marry the Prince of Wales in a secret Anglican ceremony. Two of Maria's relatives agreed to risk a jail sentence by acting as witnesses — her uncle, Henry Errington, and her brother, John Smythe.

What proved harder to find than witnesses was an Anglican clergyman willing to risk the wrath of the King by performing this illegal marriage. Under the 1772 Royal Marriage Act the Prince of Wales was underage so could *not* marry without his father's consent. The Act stated that no members of the Royal family could marry before the age of 25 without the written consent of the King.

Under British law the marriage of a Catholic to the heir to the throne was illegal for several reasons. The Act of Succession laid down that 'anyone who professes the Popish religion or marries a Papist' be excluded from succeeding to the throne'. However, this secret wedding was legal under *ecclesiastical* law (both Anglican and Catholic) but illegal under *civil* law. The King had the right to declare the marriage null and void if he sighted the wedding certificate. His Majesty could also disinherit and punish his heir for disobedience and replace the Prince of Wales, with Prince Frederick, Duke of York, who was second in line to the throne.

This secret wedding was intended to soothe Mrs Fitzherbert's conscience about having sex with the Prince of Wales so she could attend mass with fellow Catholics, confess her sins and be forgiven.

Eventually, the Reverend Robert Burke agreed to marry 28-years-old Maria Fitzherbert to the 22-year-old Prince of Wales. Aware that he was to conduct an illegal ceremony, the Revd Burke struck a hard bargain with the Prince of Wales and charged £500 (roughly $95,000 in today's money) for his services. In addition to this extortionate fee the Revd Burke insisted he be appointed one of the Prince of Wales' chaplains and, once the Prince became King, be rewarded with the title of bishop.[7]

In December 1785, the Anglican ceremony took place by candlelight in Maria's sitting room in her Mayfair house. The Prince's friend, Lord Orlando Bridgeman, kept guard outside the front door so no one could enter — the press must not learn that an illegal wedding, rumoured for so long, had finally taken place.

Once the brief ceremony was over, the Prince of Wales wrote out his own wedding certificate, signed by Maria and witnessed by John Smythe and Henry Errington. Maria's previous marriages to Catholic landowners had been celebrated with Anglican ceremonies followed by illicit Catholic ceremonies, so she was no stranger to illegal weddings.

The couple enjoyed a brief honeymoon at Richmond where the marriage was consummated. Two weeks after the wedding, rumours of a secret royal marriage were featured in the press and questions were raised in Parliament about the Prince of Wales and Mrs Fitzherbert. It placed the heir to the throne in a very tricky position indeed. Had he admitted they were true, it was likely he would have lost his right to the Crown. However, denying there had been a secret wedding meant labelling Maria his mistress rather than his morganatic wife she believed she was in the eyes of God.

The Prince asked his friend, the devious Parliamentarian, Charles James Fox, to deny he had made a secret wedding. Fox indicated to the fellow members of the House of Commons that Mrs Fitzherbert was *only* a mistress. Maria never forgave Fox for impugning her honour and claimed he had treated her like a streetwalker.

The Pope's emissary, Cardinal Weld — a member of the family who had behaved so badly to Maria when Edward Weld died — was sent to reassure her that her secret wedding *was* legal in the eyes of Catholics.

It would take the Pope several more years to make a direct communication to Maria confirming that her secret marriage was legal under Catholic law. Fearing the King would disinherit his eldest son, Maria behaved unselfishly and hid all evidence of their marriage. Doing this meant she was treated by many people as though she *were* the Prince of Wales' mistress. In order to prevent her brother and her favourite uncle from being jailed for acting as witnesses, Maria took a pair of embroidery scissors and snipped their names out of the wedding certificate. For safety Maria hid the certificate in a vaults of Coutt's Bank, terrified what might happen to the Prince of Wales should it reach King George III.

Proud of her good name, Maria could not defend herself by producing her wedding certificate or the King could have disinherited his heir.

Charles James Fox produced in Parliament a letter from the Prince of Wales in which he stated he had *never* married Mrs Fitzherbert. The letter and Fox's statement that the Prince of Wales and Mrs Fitzherbert were *definitely* not married made headlines. Fox's disclaimer reassured Parliament. They voted money to help pay off the Prince of Wales' soaring debts, which now amounted to almost £30,000,000 in today's money. The King was so relieved he granted his heir an additional £60,000 a year to help him complete the restoration of Carlton House as his official residence. George III also demanded his heir marry a Protestant princess and sire an heir. Parliament echoed the King's wishes.

The two-faced Prince of Wales wrote an affectionate letter of thanks to Charles James Fox, with not one single word of reproach for having blackened the name and character of the lady he allegedly loved.

Various lewd cartoons suggested Mrs Fitzherbert was pregnant by the Prince. Things became so embarrassing for Maria she retired to Richmond and refused to see the Prince of Wales for months. However, time healed her wounds. The Prince wrote abject letters of apology and eventually Maria came to believe the denial of a secret wedding ceremony was entirely the fault of Fox, who, as a loyal friend, had only done this to prevent the Prince of Wales being disinherited by his father.

DAYS OF WINE AND ROSES

After many months the Prince and Maria were reunited and their sexual relationship resumed. His Royal Highness promised Maria an entertaining allowance and paid several instalments but then had to cease the arrangement as debt collectors were again after him.

The Prince of Wales allowed Maria to pay for lavish dinner parties for his younger brothers and gambling cronies from Brook's Club.

With Maria as his official hostess, the Prince of Wales' lavish spending continued. (Several psychiatrists see his bouts of manic spending, followed by periods of depression as symptomatic of the manic-depressive illness, now referred to as bi-polar disorder.)

During his manic 'highs' the Prince of Wales bought scores of pedigree horses and expensive paintings. In the 'low' or depressive phases he also spent money to cheer himself up. When the King demanded he cease spending, the manipulative Prince of Wales threatened suicide whereupon Mrs Fitzherbert would talk him out of his plan.

The Prince and Maria enjoyed hosting lavish entertainments at Carlton House. Guests marvelled at the large ornate rooms in the Prince's official residence. They had been decorated in the French neo-classical style with their elaborate ceilings, pure silk curtains, French crystal chandeliers and superb French and English paintings (many of which are now in the Royal Collection). The Prince of Wales had excellent taste in art and was determined to buy back works from the art collection accumulated by Charles I. These paintings had been sold by Cromwell after the execution of Charles I. Prinny enjoyed finding new and significant artists to add to his growing art collection.

Maria, became caught up in the Prince's passion for entertaining. She sold her Park Street home and leased a much grander house in St James's Square from a member of the peerage, where she gave elegant dinner parties for Prinny's younger brother, Prince William, Duke of Clarence and his mistress, Dorothea Jordan. Mrs Jordan, the famous actress, was the mother of William's ten illegitimate children, who were known as the young Fitzclarences.

At Carlton House and in Maria's home in St James's Square entertaining continued for the future King with Maria as the official hostess. Hordes of liveried flunkeys in blue and gold with powdered wigs and white gloves served platters heaped with food while an orchestra played Prinny's favourite music. Amid the elegant décor the Prince of Wales wandered around with Maria on his arm, conversing with guests who included foreign royalty. The

Prince of Wales was establishing a rival court to that of his father on borrowed money, promising to repay the moneylenders once he wore the Crown.

The King and Queen, known for a more modest style of living at Buckingham House, were furious at hearing accounts of their eldest son's lavish spending. They refused to meet Mrs Fitzherbert and pretended she did not exist. The Prince of Wales' dowdy young sisters eventually met Mrs Fitzherbert and they reported that 'Fitz', as the Prince lovingly called Maria, was a good influence on their 'difficult' brother.

Prinny continued purchasing major artworks by Dutch and French artists even though debt collectors were picketing Carlton House, hoping to shame the high-spending Prince of Wales into settling outstanding accounts. The heir to the throne ignored them and claimed they would be paid when his father died and he became King.

By 1786 the Prince of Wales' debts were so large, he decided to move to Brighton where he and Maria could live more cheaply than in the centre of London. He instructed his servants to close Carlton House and place the exquisite furnishings under dust sheets. He dismissed all but a skeleton staff and booked himself a cheap seat on the public coach to Brighton. By doing this, the Prince tried to convince his father and Parliament he was economising. It was agreed Maria would follow him to Brighton as soon as he had found a suitable house for her, as they could not live openly together without causing a major scandal.

When Maria arrived at Brighton she loved its clean sea air and developed a great affection for the seaside village that would soon become an elegant resort. Initially she lived in a rented house, now demolished, in a street near the Prince's residence. Maria had incurred heavy debts by entertaining the Prince and his friends in such grand style— now she was able to clear her debts from of her annual income bequeathed to her by her late husband, by living far more cheaply than in London.

The Prince purchased an old farmhouse with extensive grounds near the seafront. With the aid of the architect Henry Holland he renovated and extended the building. adding a large portico to it.

Decades later the building would be redeveloped in the style of an Indian palace.

The new pastime of bathing from 'bathing machines' — wooden changing cabins on wheels drawn by horses to the edge of the sea — was something both the Prince and Maria loved. At Brighton the couple lived quietly, enjoying drives in their carriage along the Sussex coast, walking over the Downs or strolling arm in arm along the sea front. Maria was happy — unlike most other royal mistresses, she genuinely loved Prince George Augustus and was not after his money or gifts of jewels. Observers noticed that the Prince of Wales was drinking and gambling less, which they attributed to Mrs Fitzherbert's good influence on him.

The Prince had promised to buy Maria a house in Brighton, but like many of his promises, this one did not eventuate. Selfish as ever, Prinny was busy with schemes to build himself a grand residence in Brighton, which would eventually become the well known Brighton Pavilion.

For the sake of her reputation, Maria never lived with the Prince of Wales. In 1804 she employed architect William Pordon to build Steine House for her and paid for the building of the house herself.[8] Steine House originally had a private Catholic chapel incorporated into its design, as Maria was still very devout.

When their seaside idyll ended, Prinny and Maria returned to London to find rumours of 'Catholic plots' in the papers. Covent Garden opera house and Drury Lane Theatre had been set on fire by arsonists, who, it was alleged, had been encouraged to do this by the Pope. As anti-Catholic hysteria mounted, Mrs Fitzherbert, easily recognisable from all the cartoons and satirical etchings that featured her, ran the risk of being attacked as she drove around central London in her carriage.

Cartoons featuring the Prince's Catholic mistress became even more cruel but Maria steadfastly refused to change her religion.

THE REGENCY CRISIS 1788–1789

The loss of the American colonies depressed George III almost as much as the wild conduct and the debts of his heir.

However, by October 1788 it became clear that the King's mind was wandering. The royal physicians reported George III was suffering from headaches, deafness, internal pains and badly swollen legs.[9] The King was in pain with cramps in his lower and upper limbs and suffered periods of severe mental disorder.

On 31 October 1788, *The Morning Post* claimed the King was suffering from an unusual form of dropsy, the disease that physicians believed had killed Queen Anne.

On 5 November 1788, the Prince of Wales was summoned by his mother, who was worried about the King's mysterious illness. Half-way through dinner George III, provoked by a remark from his heir, jumped out of his chair, gripped his heir by the throat and tried to throttle him. With manic energy his father dragged the Prince of Wales towards a wall and smashed his head against it. For several moments everyone was so stunned they remained frozen. Finally the Vice-Chamberlain and several footmen managed to separate the King and his heir.[10]

Eventually, George III calmed down and allowed himself to be led away and put to bed by servants.

The Prince of Wales, believing he would be King should his father be declared insane or die, imagined himself dismissing ministers he disliked and dispensing honours to old friends.

Prime Minister William Pitt, fearing what would happen if this vain and impulsive Prince were placed in charge as Prince Regent, delayed appointing him to that position.

At Carlton House the Prince of Wales was in his element, receiving visits from those wishing to be on good terms with him and obtain favours should he receive the powers of Regent.

But this did not happen yet. Eventually, George III was able to have a long sleep and when he awoke his confused mental state had greatly improved, so the proposed Regency Bill was shelved. The King's recovery dashed any hope that the Prince of Wales would gain power. He slunk back to Brighton with Maria and resumed his former way of life. Mrs Fitzherbert was now in a very difficult situation. The Prince's manic depressive moods, his uncontrolled passion for gambling and for buying expensive antiques and paintings was driving the normally placid Maria to despair.

Prince Charming's good looks were declining as the result of a life of excess. Georgiana, Duchess of Devonshire, in a secret journal she never expected to be read during her own lifetime, claimed the Prince of Wales was becoming coarser in looks and conducts. The Duchess still disliked the fact that Mrs Fitzherbert was better looking (though not as clever or witty) as she was and claimed in her secret account of the life of the Prince of Wales that he

> ...is inclined to be too fat and looks like a woman in men's clothes... His face is still handsome...His person, dress and the admiration he meets from women take up his thoughts to a large degree. He is good natured but extravagant. By some shabby traits to his mistresses one would imagine him more inclined to extravagance than generosity. [11]

The summer of 1792 saw the Prince and Mrs Fitzherbert in residence in Brighton, where, due to the worsening political situation, French aristocrats fleeing from the guillotine were arriving by boat. New arrivals included the Princesse de Lamballe, head of Queen Marie-Antoinette's household, who stayed with Maria at Steine House. Later the princess returned to Paris to be with the Queen Marie-Antoinette and both of them perished at the hands of the mob.

While revolution raged in France refugees arrived in England, many short of funds. The Prince of Wales enjoyed himself buying *objets d'art* from refugees who had brought portable valuables, jewels and small paintings with them to finance their stay in England. In January 1793, King Louis XIV of France was guillotined and the Republican Government declared war on Britain. The shock of the French King's execution caused George III and Queen Charlotte to worry about their own safety, as Britain prepared for war. The Prince of Wales was thrilled to be appointed Honorary Colonel of the Tenth Royal Hussars and spent large sums on hand-tailored uniforms, covered in gold braid and a luxurious tent.

⁂

Perdita Robinson, portrait in oils commissioned by George Augustus, Prince of Wales, from Thomas Gainsborough. The painting is now held in the Wallace Collection, London.

Maria Fitzherbert, aquatint by R. Ackerman of Bond Street after the original portrait by Richard Cosway.

Sir Thomas Lawrence, George Augustus, Prince of Wales, as an officer in the Tenth Royal Hussars. There are 4 versions of this portrait, one was sold at auction by Sotheby's, London two are in private collections. The best known, version dated 1815, is in London's National Portrait Gallery and in it the Prince of Wales wears a blue ribbon across his chest.

Hand-coloured engraving of Carlton House, Pall Mall, official
London residence of the Prince of Wales (now demolished).

The Rose Satin Drawing Room, Carlton House.
Acquatint from a private collection.

Brighton Pavilion, home of the Prince of Wales. The architect John Nash based his design on Indian temples. From *Views of the Royal Pavilion*, London, 1826.

The Banqueting Hall, Brighton Royal Pavilion, Brighton where the Prince of Wales, aided by Mrs Fitzherbert entertained. Design by John Nash. Taken from Nash's book, *Views of the Royal Pavilion*, published 1826.

Wife or no Wife by James Gillray, shows the Prince of Wales and Maria Fitzherbert in an illegal Catholic ceremony in France.

The Morning after the Marriage, etched by James Gillray, shows the Prince of Wales and Maria Fitzherbert emerging from bed with the Prince clearly the worse for drink.

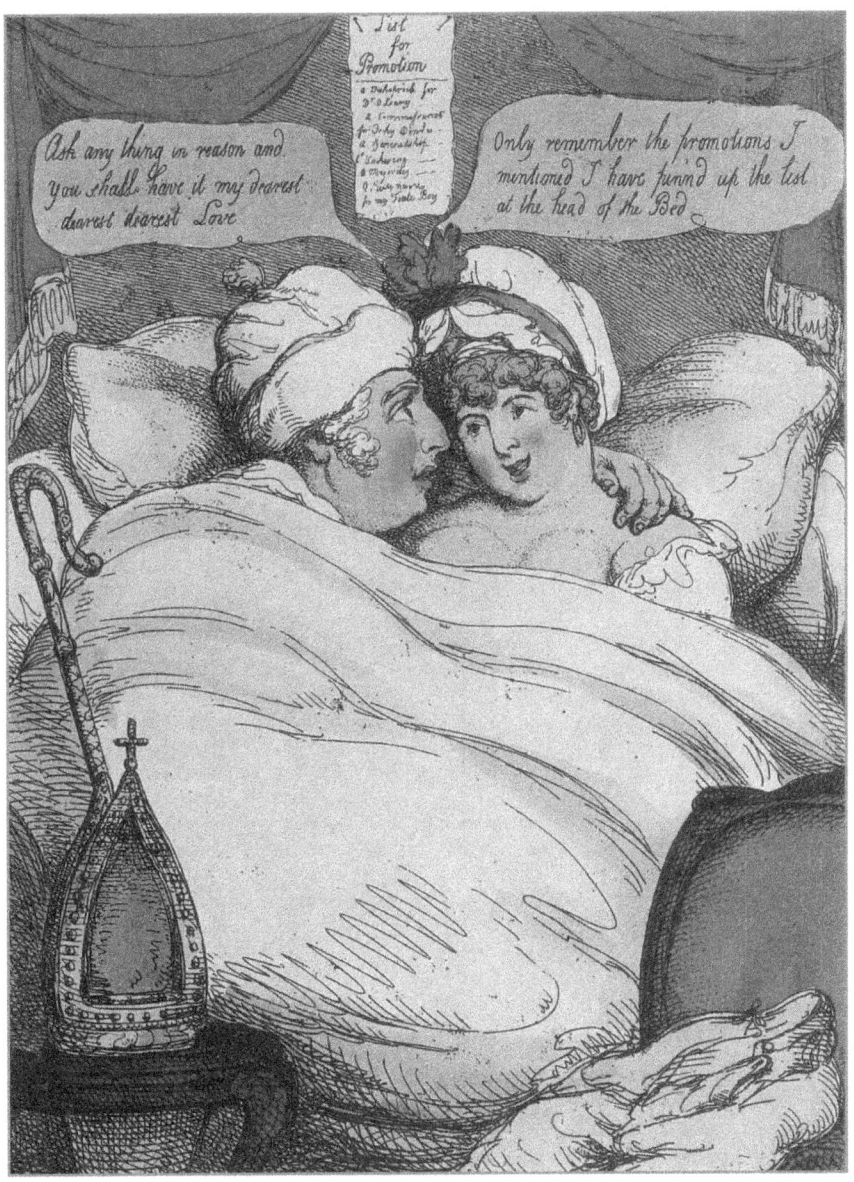

James Gillray's satirical engraving shows Mary Anne Clarke and her royal lover, Prince Frederick, Duke of York who was the Commander-in-Chief of the British Army. A list of men who had paid Mary Anne for military promotions is pinned above the bed. Engraving in the collection of the author.

Lady Randolph Churchill. This superb portrait in oils was painted by the Viennese artist and sculptor Emil Fuchs who worked in London between 1897-1911. Fuchs also received commissions from Edward VII and was impressed by Jennie's beauty and her lively personality. Private collection.

The Prince's debts were now so high that Thomas Coutts, the Royal banker, refused to lend him any more money. In response to another request for financial help, the King insisted his son must marry one of his wealthy German cousins. The large dowry could be used to settle his debts. The King did not think that his heir's invalid 'marriage' to Mrs Fitzherbert was worth mentioning — to him she was nothing more than a mistress and expendable. His son must do the right thing and marry a princess.

In 1793, while spending the summer with the Prince of Wales in Brighton, Maria seemed unaware that her alleged husband's freedom was soon to be curtailed.

Prinny's sickly younger brother, Prince Augustus, Duke of Sussex, returned from Italy where he had been convalescing. Prince Augustus shocked his parents by telling them how in Italy he had married the Hon Augusta Murray, daughter of Lord Dunmore, who was ten years *older* than himself. She was an aristocrat all right, but in the eyes of the King lacked the vital blood-royal necessary for a royal bride.

This marriage infuriated George III whose sons had broken the rules he laid down for them that he should chose their wives and had Prince Augustus' marriage annulled by the Court of Privileges. The fact that a marriage to the daughter of a Protestant aristocrat could be annulled, made Maria realise that there would be no acceptance of her morganatic marriage with the Prince of Wales while the King was still alive.

Queen Charlotte, worried by the whole situation, enlisted the aid of two of her ladies-in-waiting, Lady Hertford and Lady Jersey, to lure the foolish heir to the throne away from Mrs Fitzherbert. Initially the motherly Lady Hertford failed to make an impression. It was Lady Frances Jersey, razor-slim, clever as a serpent and bored by her elderly husband, who managed to lure the young Prince of Wales into her bed. Keen to win the Queen's approval and gain influence over the Prince of Wales, the future King, Lady Jersey did her best to turn Prinny against Mrs Fitzherbert. Telling him that Maria was fat had no effect — clearly the Prince liked his beloved Fitz as she was.

Lady Jersey tried a different tack. She warned the Prince of Wales he was becoming very unpopular over his association with a Catholic. He should renounce Maria and marry a Protestant princess and his wife's dowry would settle his debts and Parliament would increase his annual allowance. Lady Jersey promised to help the Prince choose the most attractive of the two wealthy German princesses his parents had selected. Both had large dowries — Princess Caroline of Brunswick was a niece of the King, the other princess was a niece of the Queen.

AN ARRANGED MARRIAGE CAUSES THE WAR OF THE WALES

Lady Jersey knew that Princess Caroline of Brunswick rarely washed and suffered from body odour — she would *not* be a good partner for the fastidious, foppish Prince of Wales. The Duke of Wellington claimed that Lady Jersey urged the Prince of Wales to chose a wife of

> ...indifferent character and not very inviting appearance, in the hope that disgust with his wife would secure constancy to his mistress.

Flattering engagement portraits were exchanged, commissioned on the understanding court artists would favour their sitters. In her engagement portrait the homely features, potato nose and beady eyes of Princess Caroline were almost hidden by a huge beribboned bonnet which covered the upper part of her face. However, her low cut Empire line dress drew attention to her ample bust, an attribute the Prince of Wales could never resist.

In her time alone with her princely lover, Lady Frances Jersey made it quite clear that he *must* abandon Mrs Fitzherbert in order to make his arranged marriage work. He agreed, happy in the knowledge Parliament were to increase his annual allowance once he was married.

Inconsistent as ever, the Prince wrote Maria an affectionate note in which he said nothing about his impending marriage to 26-year-old Princess Caroline, now en route from Brunswick to England. On the day Maria received this note from the Prince she was about to have diner with his younger brother, Prince William, Duke of Clarence and William's long term mistress, Mrs Jordan.

Dorothea Jordan, a well-known actress, was the mother of William's ten illegitimate children. She had invested a great deal of money in her relationship with Prince William from her earnings as an actress.

What neither Maria nor Dorothea Jordan realised at that time was that Prince William was also being urged to jettison his long term mistress, marry a virginal blue-blooded heiress and sire a legitimate son who, should the Prince of Wales' arranged marriage fail to produce an heir, could become a future monarch.

Dining with Prince William and Mrs Jordan at Bushey House, Maria was surprised to receive a second note brought to her by a special messenger, Captain Jack Willett-Payne, the Prince's hatchet man. In this brusque note the Prince of Wales, too cowardly to face Maria and tell her the news, informed her of his arranged marriage with Princess Caroline of Brunswick-Wolfenbuttel. He added that he was sorry but he would be unable to see Maria ever again.

The shock was so profound Maria almost fainted. Eventually, she was calm enough to return home to find London filled with rejoicing at the impending royal marriage.

Maria went to stay with friends in Margate on the Kent coast. In spite of the shameful way she had been treated she was still genuinely concerned about the Prince of Wales. Being a kind and generous woman, she kept the certificate of their wedding hidden in the vaults of Coutts Bank, rather than sending it to the press or to the King.

George III knew there had been talk of some sort of marriage between his heir and Mrs Fitzherbert. However, under the Royal Marriage Act such a marriage was automatically invalid so there was no need for *any* annulment.

Maria was in a difficult position — regarded as another discarded royal mistress, she was unable to explain her position and defend herself in public.

Lady Jersey had managed to persuade the Prince of Wales to appoint her as Lady-in-Waiting to Princess Caroline. She went by coach to Dover to meet the bride as she landed, taking with her a full-skirted dress in a hideous shade of greenish-yellow. She knew it would not flatter the bride who was short and stocky with plump arms. The cunning Lady Jersey lied to Princess Caroline and told her the Prince of Wales had personally selected this dress because greenish-yellow was his favourite colour, so she must wear it for their first meeting.

When the foppish Prince of Wales arrived at St James' Palace and saw the woman he was to marry and with whom he was expected to create an heir, the horror of the situation made him perspire. The Prince was repelled by his bride's body odour, her looks and that hideous outfit.

The Prince's equerry, Lord Harris Malmesbury, had taken the trouble to warn Princess Caroline that the Prince was fastidious about personal hygiene and used to bathe and change his linen each day. Princess Caroline, as self-absorbed as the Prince of Wales, had not bothered to heed his advice.

At the sight of his bride, the Prince turned to his equerry and said, 'Harris, I'm not well, pray fetch me a glass of brandy'. After gulping down the brandy the Prince left the room.

Princess Caroline complained to Lord Malmesbury in her strong German accent, 'I find ze Prince fat. He is nozzing like as handsome as in his portrait.'

The pre-wedding dinner was a farce. The Prince of Wales sat next to Lady Jersey, drank a great deal of champagne and fondled her breasts between each course. His mistress teased and flattered the Prince and fed him choice morsels from her fork like a spoiled child. His bride was determined to show she did not care that the groom had a mistress. By now Princess Caroline must have realised she had been tricked by Lady Jersey into wearing that dreadful dress. To disguise her hurt feelings, the Princess told jokes so crude everyone seated near her was embarrassed.

On 8 April 1795, the morning of his marriage to Princess Caroline in the Chapel Royal at St James's Palace, the bridegroom sent Maria Fitzherbert a note telling her that she was the only woman he had loved. Whether Maria believed him or not is another matter.

Weeping into a huge red handkerchief, the Prince managed to get through the wedding ceremony. At the reception he drank so much he needed help to propel him into the bridal chamber where he slumped semi-comatose on the floor. During the night, he managed to stagger to the marital bed and consummate the marriage before rolling off the bed and passing out in the fireplace.

Later he told Lord Malmesbury he suspected his wife was not a virgin. Princess Caroline of Wales tried to dismiss the scheming Lady Frances Jersey and after violent scenes, in June 1795 Lady Jersey was made to resign as Princess Caroline's Lady-in-Waiting.

The Prince and Princess of Wales occupied separate wings of Carlton House and only communicated through notes delivered by liveried footmen. The Prince wrote to his wife, informing her that he did not intend having sexual relations with her again. He consoled himself for a loveless marriage with the thought that his wife's dowry and an increased allowance from Parliament had settled his debts and improved his financial position. Eventually he fell out with Lady Jersey.

The new Princess of Wales did her best to upstage her husband and become the 'people's princess'. London crowds cheered Princess Caroline's coach but jeered at the coach of the Prince of Wales and were delighted to learn that the Princess of Wales was pregnant.

Nine months after their arranged wedding, on 7 January 1796, Princess Caroline bore a daughter who was christened Princess Charlotte after Queen Charlotte, the baby's grandmother.

In one of his moods of depression, aware the public preferred his wife to him and missing Maria, the Prince of Wales made a new will in which he left all his property to 'my Maria Fitzherbert, the wife of my heart and soul.'

The Prince wrote to Maria, imploring her to come back to him, but Maria ignored his letters. The Prince's sisters also wrote to 'dear Fitz' urging her to return to their brother. But Maria was wary of what she regarded as the Prince's betrayal and refused. She bought herself a house in Ealing, then a peaceful rural neighbourhood, and lived there quietly with Miss Piggott.

Not until the summer of 1800 did Maria Fitzherbert take pity on the Prince of Wales. She had received written assurance from the Papal Court in Rome that her Anglican wedding was legal. Satisfied with their approval, Maria resumed contact with the Prince of Wales, but on *her* terms rather than his and made it quite clear that their reconciliation was on a sisterly basis. In June 1800, her reunion with the Prince of Wales was celebrated with a lavish 'public breakfast', attended by 400 people.

In 1802, Maria returned to Steine House in Brighton, as the second phase of the Prince of Wales new Oriental style residence with its beautiful new dining room was ready for him.

'We live like brother and sister', Maria wrote to her friend Lady Anne Barnard, explaining the new turn their relationship had taken. Maria enjoyed acting as hostess at parties given by the Prince of Wales in the new dining room with a conservatory attached, both designed for him in the office of Henry Holland.

THE WAR OF THE WALES

In 1801, Princess Caroline and her little daughter moved to Montagu House at Blackheath, a rural area to the south-east of London where her widowed mother, Princess Augusta, was living. Pretty little Princess Charlotte was a subject of great interest to the populace — the only legal grandchild of the King and Queen and heir to the throne should anything happen to her father. In 1806, a secret commission, known as the 'Delicate Investigation', was set up to see if the Prince of Wales had grounds to divorce his wife, but nothing could be proved.

In 1811, the Prince of Wales was appointed Regent and high society took his side against Princess Caroline, who was denied access to her daughter.

In 1814, the War of the Wales had reached such a point that the Princess of Wales was offered a large annual allowance if she would leave the country. She accepted the offer and toured Italy. Princess Caroline purchased the beautiful Villa d'Este on the shores of Lake Como and lived there, amid scandal she was having an affair with her Italian 'Chamberlain' who had awarded himself the title of 'Baron' Bartolemeo Pergami. Together the couple made an extensive tour of Italy, but the Prince of Wales could not obtain the necessary evidence of adultery in order to divorce his wife.

Due to inflation caused by the Napolenic wars, Maria's large legacy from her second husband was depreciating, so she sold the Ealing house to Prinny's youngest brother, Prince Edward, Duke of Kent, who lived there with his mistress, Julie de St Laurent, until they were given a suite of rooms in Kensington Palace.

Summering in the Royal Pavilion at Brighton, the Prince of Wales fell ill with a mysterious fever. Maria was so concerned she left her house on the Steine, moved into the Royal Pavilion and nursed the Prince devotedly until he recovered.

Maria remained the heir to the throne's ideal woman, but meanwhile the fickle Prince had brief sexual relationships with actresses and courtesans, including Anna Maria Crouch and Lucy Howard. He also fathered an illegitimate son by a Mrs Cole, the former mistress of Lord Egremont, and paid her maintenance for his child.

Always in the background was the faithful Mrs Fitzherbert, who was now more like the Prince's surrogate mother than his mistress and was treated by him and his brothers with great affection.

Several years earlier, out of the kindness of her heart, Maria had offered to take care of little Mary Georgina Seymour, known as Minnie, whose dead parents had been good friends of the Prince of Wales. Lady Anne Horatia Seymour and her husband, Lord Hugh Seymour, were part of the wealthy Hertford dynasty.

Maria had hoped to adopt Minnie but there were objections to this as Maria was a devout Catholic and the Seymour and Hertford families were Protestants. Therefore the guardianship of orphaned Minnie Seymour had been given to the second Marquis of Hertford. But as a confirmed bachelor the Marquis had no wish to keep the little girl and entrusted her to the care of Mrs Fitzherbert, who had been very fond of pretty little Minnie when her parents were still alive. Gossip spread that Minnie Seymour had been fathered by the Prince of Wales, but the rumours were clearly untrue.

A few years later Maria took charge of a second little girl, Marianne Smythe, allegedly the daughter of John Smythe, Maria's unmarried brother. More false rumours started that Marianne was Maria's child by the Prince of Wales.[12]

The adoption of Minnie Seymour, of whom the Prince became very fond, had a bad outcome for Mrs Fitzherbert, because it led to a much closer friendship between the Prince of Wales and middle-aged Lady Isabella Hertford.

The Hertfords owned Hertford House in central London as well as Manchester House and a country estate, called Ragley Hall. Their magnificent collection of paintings had been bought from the proceeds of coal mines which were opened up on their land. Lady Isabella had born her husband thirteen children and had a blameless reputation.

One of Lady Isabella Hertford's sons, Lord Yarmouth, and the Prince of Wales were good friends and fellow art collectors, attending viewings and auctions at James Christie's auction rooms.[13]

Although Prinny had known Lady Isabella for years as the mother of his friend, he now developed a veritable obsession with her. Through his friendship with Lord Yarmouth, the Prince knew when Lady Isabella's husband was away from home. He visited her at Hertford House and Ragley Hall and they would talk about his art collection and possible new purchases.

As part of the Prince's obsession with his new 'surrogate mother', who seemed intent on replacing Mrs Fitzherbert in that role, His Royal Highness gave Lady Hertford expensive presents, including rolls of specially imported hand-painted Chinese wallpaper. Lady Isabella's family maintained this was a purely platonic relationship but Maria was jealous and did not believe them.

The Prince enjoyed staying as a guest at Lady Isabella's country house where he was treated like one of her children. Maria heard gossip about the Prince of Wales' infatuation with the glamorous grandmother, which led to jealous rows between them.

In 1811, due to the King's mysterious illness and his madness, the Prince of Wales was created Prince Regent and threw a big party at Carlton House to celebrate his elevated status.

Maria was not consulted about the preparations for this important celebration — instead the Prince took the advice of Lady Hertford. Maria had expected to be seated beside the Prince Regent in her usual place at the top table. Instead Maria found herself seated at far end of the room at a table of guests seen as of little importance, while Lady Hertford was seated next to the Prince in the position of honour.

Lady Hertford did what the Prince always enjoyed —she fed him with choice morsels from her own plate as if he were a child. The sight of another woman sitting in her place and taking over her role was too much for Maria — she rose from her chair and went home. Her *rapprochement* with the heir to the throne was over. She never talked to the Prince of Wales again .

Meanwhile, Princess Caroline had written several letters of complaint to the Editor of *The Times* about her treatment by the Prince of Wales, ensuring many people took her side. Princess Charlotte Augusta, the only legal grandchild of the King and heir to the throne, lived with her grandparents at Windsor Castle, rarely seeing her mother but having some contact with her father.

The Prince Regent continued to live at Carlton House. By now he had lost his boyish looks and put on a great deal of weight. His corpulent appearance was caricatured in James Gillray's etching *A Voluptuary under the horrors of Digestion*. It shows the Prince's face reddened with drink smoking a cigar, with half-empty flasks of claret on the table, a chamber pot behind him and an alleged cure for syphilis on the floor on his right. The Prince Regent was clearly not in good health.

His father, George III, now in his eighties, was very ill and suffering severe pains from undiagnosed porphyria. The King lived in a twilight world of blindness and senile decay.

THE SAD END OF PRINCESS CHARLOTTE

The reputation of the House of Hanover had never been lower. By far the most popular member of royal family was the attractive but temperamental Princess Charlotte who was cheered and adored by large crowds whenever she made a public appearance. In May 1816, her arranged marriage to Prince Leopold of Saxe-Coburg was celebrated all over the country. Unlike the troubled marriage of her parents, Princess Charlotte's marriage turned out well. Early in 1817, it was announced that the Princess was pregnant and the birth of an heir for the nation was eagerly anticipated and huge celebrations were planned.

After being in labour for 50 hours (as her doctor refused to use forceps) Princess Charlotte delivered a stillborn son and died from a *post-partum* haemorrhage. Her doctor was blamed for the tragedy and committed suicide. Princess Charlotte's death was mourned with a similar fervour to the death of Diana, Princess of Wales.

Due to the fact that Prince Frederick, Prince William and Prince Edward had long-term mistresses but no wives, George III had numerous illegitimate grandchildren but no legitimate ones. George IV's second son, Prince Frederick, Duke of York, was the next in line to the throne after the now childless Prince Regent.

Debt-laden Prince Frederick obeyed his parents and went to Prussia where he made a dynastic marriage to the wealthy Princess Frederica Charlotte, daughter of the King of Prussia. (Illustrated in the frontispiece by James Gillray 'The Introduction' on page vi).

Princess Frederica, possibly lesbian, refused all sexual contact with her husband and they lived apart. Prince Frederick could not divorce his Prussian wife for fear of upsetting the dynastic alliance between Britain and the powerful King of Prussia.

Living alone in London, Prince Frederick was appointed Commander of the British Army. Somewhat unwisely the Prince took an ambitious journalist named Mrs Mary Anne Clarke, as his resident mistress. Mary Anne, clever, witty and ambitious, had grown up in the slums. She had endured an abusive marriage, had left her alcoholic husband and was trying to educate three children on very little money. Prince Frederick failed to supply funds for

Mary Anne to live in style as he had become a gambling addict and was in debt. Mary Anne Clarke devised a clever but illegal scheme to support herself and her children by selling commissions to those men who wished to become officers in prestigious Army regiments. Each week she gave Prince Frederick a list of names of those who had bribed her and he ensured they would be gazetted as officers. The scheme worked well for Mary Anne until a member of Prince Frederick's staff complained of corruption. Mary Anne and the Prince were summoned to appear before a Select Committee of the House of Commons. As Mary Anne looked extremely attractive and flirted with her investigators she was not prosecuted.

However, the scandal was so great the Duke of York had to resign as Commander-in-Chief of the Army. He and Mary Anne separated and she received money from her ex-lover on condition she did not publish Prince Frederick's love letters in a proposed memoir. Instead she published a novel called The Two Princes, which told a great deal of the story.

Mary Anne Clark. Engraving after an unnamed artist.

Mary Anne foolishly libelled a powerful former lover, who had become the Chancellor of the Irish Exchequer. She was tried, found guilty and jailed under harsh conditions, designed to silence her. Her health was ruined and Mary Anne and her children went to live in France where she died in poverty.[14]

The premature death of Princess Charlotte in 1817 had Parliament worried. Second in line after the Prince Regent was Prince Frederick, but his premature death in 1827 meant that there was no *legitimate* second-generation heir. Prince William, Duke of Clarence, and Prince Edward, Duke of Kent, were urged to abandon their long-term mistresses, marry blue-blooded brides and produce heirs for the nation. The continuation of the House of Hanover depended on these two princes.

Now he was second in succession to the throne, Prince William callously rid himself of Dorothea Jordan, his long term and faithful mistress who had devoted the best years of her life to caring from him and who had supported him from her earnings.

Dorothea (Dora) had born Prince William ten healthy children and expected to spend the rest of her life with her royal lover. Prince William was too cowardly to face Dora and tell her she must leave as he needed to marry a virginal princess. Instead, he sent a member of his staff with the message that it was impossible for someone so close to the throne to live with an actress. Mrs Jordan must leave. Bitterly hurt she departed and short of money she died alone and in poverty at St Cloud, near Paris.

In 1820, King George III, now a tragic figure, deaf, blind and raving mad, died lacking *legitimate* grandchildren. The question of the hour was whether the separated Princess Caroline of Wales should be crowned beside George IV. A proposed Pains and Penalties Bill, intended to depose Princess Caroline and dissolve the marriage, passed the House of Lords, but the Bill was not submitted to the House of Commons as there was little chance the Commons would pass it.

When Princess Caroline asked Lord Liverpool what style of dress she should wear at her coronation, he told her she was not to attend. Princess Caroline informed the press and there was an outcry. The carriage of the adulterous King George IV was stoned on the way to Westminster Abbey and several of its windows were broken.

On 19 July 1821, Princess Caroline, wearing coronation robes and a coronet, presented herself first at the East and then at the West doors of Westminster Abbey. But the new King's officials had deliberately provided the wrong time for the coronation ceremony and when Caroline arrived, guests were already installed inside the Abbey. Pages of the Royal Household, aided by a group of prize fighters employed by George IV, had slammed the heavy doors shut. In vain Princess Caroline's liveried footmen shouted,

'Open up in the name of the Queen' and pounded with their fists on the doors, but the door to the Abbey remained barred.

Instead of being crowned beside her husband a desperately unhappy Princess Caroline was forced to return to her home at Blackheath. The stress and public humiliation took its toll. The following evening the uncrowned Queen of England collapsed. A doctor was summoned but with the limited resources available in those days he could not help her. Caroline, in great pain and preparing for death, burned her private papers.

On 7 August 1821, the uncrowned Queen Caroline died amid rumours she had been poisoned. Today it is believed she died from cancer or from a ruptured bowel. Many members of the public were angered by her death, believing that, even if she had not been poisoned, her life had been shortened by the appalling conduct of her husband. Street riots took place as Caroline's coffin passed through London. It was taken to Harwich, placed on a warship and taken back to Brunswick. On Caroline's coffin was a brass plaque engraved with the words, 'Caroline of Brunswick, the injured Queen of England'.

LADY ELIZABETH CONYNGHAM, THE FINAL MISTRESS

In 1820, George IV met avaricious Lady Elizabeth Conyngham on a visit to Ireland and became besotted by her. The ambitious raven-haired Miss Elizabeth Dennison had married elderly Lord Conyngham for his money and social advancement as he owned Slane Castle, high on a hill to the north of Dublin.

The new Lady Elizabeth Conyngham soon realised that her husband's estate was riddled with debt. Keen to acquire jewels (the traditional reward of royal mistresses) Lady Conyngham seduced George IV when he was on a State visit in Ireland. As the monarch was now ailing and lonely, Lady Conyngham and her complacent husband were invited by the lonely and elderly monarch to live with him at Windsor Castle. Elizabeth's husband was created High Steward of Windsor Castle, a sinecure with a large salary and few duties, and elevated to the rank of Marquis.

The King's staff were nauseated by the sight of the ageing monarch pawing Lady Conyngham's breasts as she dined with the King while the newly promoted Marquis of Conyngham turned a blind eye and got drunk on the King's best claret. Young Lady Conyngham was happy to live with her husband at Windsor free of charge and receive expensive jewels from a besotted monarch. A satirical cartoon shows Lady Conyngham 'fishing for jewels' with the King at Virginia Water, near Windsor Castle.

George IV suffered the same health problems as his father. To alleviate the pains in his limbs, Lady Elizabeth Conyngham gave him doses of laudanum. As the king became progressively worse he was confined to his bed which left Lady Conyngham and her husband ideally placed to steal valuable *objets d'art* from Windsor Castle, load them onto a cart and sell them for cash in London. The wife of the Russian Ambassador to London, Princess Dorothea von Lieven, in secret intelligence reports to General Alexander von Benckendorf, her brother in Russia, described the avaricious Lady Elizabeth Conyngham, mistress of the monarch as

> ...vulgar and foolish. Not an idea in her head, not a word to say for herself, nothing but a hand to accept pearls and diamonds and an enormous balcony [her bust] on which to wear them. [Lady Conyngham] only stays with the king because of his diamonds, pearls and good dinners.[15]

Lady Conyngham ensured the ailing King took larger and larger doses of laudanum, aware that in his drowsy state he would not notice how much she was purloining.

In one of his rare moment of clarity, King George IV begged to be buried with one of his many miniature portrait of 'my Maria, the only woman I ever loved' in his coffin.

Hearing that the King was dying, Mrs Fitzherbert wrote him an affectionate note, assuring George IV how fond she had been of him in happier days. The dying King, almost blind and too ill to hold a pen, read Maria's loving letter, burst into tears and placed the letter under his pillow.

On 26 June 1830, after George IV was dead, Mrs Fitzherbert's letter was found under the King's pillow, stained with his tears.

Years earlier, George IV had issued instructions, 'Bury me with the picture of my beloved wife, my Maria Fitzherbert, suspended round my neck by a ribbon, as I used to wear it... Place it upon my heart.'

Isabella Piggott, Mrs Fitzherbert's lady companion, recorded that, when Maria was told that these wishes had been followed and George IV had been buried holding one of her portrait miniatures, she burst into tears.

The Duke of Wellington, who was Prime Minister at the time, acted as executor of the childless King. With Mrs Fitzherbert's permission he destroyed all her letters to the former Prince of Wales. The Duke of Wellington also destroyed George IV's macabre collection of women's ringlets and snippets of pubic hair, held in envelopes marked with the name of each lady who had provided the sample of her hair. He had found the collection in the King's suite of rooms at Windsor Castle. Under the circumstances, the Iron Duke felt it wiser to burn the entire collection, so no report could reach the press. He described this gross discovery in a letter to Lady Harriet Arbuthnot, written a week after the death of George IV. His successor, King William IV, formerly in the navy, had a bawdy sense of humour and told his Admiralty cronies about his brother's macabre collection and joked that George IV had left 'enough female pubic hair to stuff a mattress' were current in male circles in London.

William IV came to the throne because his elder brother, Prince Frederick, Duke of York, second-in-line to the throne, had died in 1827 with at least three illegitimate sons but no legal heir. With ten illegitimate children who lived with him, William IV was crowned beside his German wife, Queen Adelaide. William's ten children by Dora Jordan were in the front row at his coronation and his eldest son rode beside him in the coronation coach. Dorothea Jordan, their loving and loyal mother having been abandoned to die in poverty.

George III's fourth son, Prince Edward, Duke of Kent, was next in line to the throne as William had no legitimate children.

Prince Edward had a *most* inconvenient mistress who was jettisoned and deliberately erased from history. Julie de St Laurent had not known that her long-term partner was betrothed to a wealthy widowed German princess until she saw the notice of his engagement in *The Times*. Julie was so shocked at the news she vomited and fainted. So that Prince Edward could make an arranged marriage and sire a legal heir, the unfortunate Julie de St Laurent had to leave Kensington Palace where she and her lover had happily shared an apartment for over two decades.

Free of an inconvenient long term mistress, Prince Edward, Duke of Kent married his distant cousin, Princess Victoria of Saxe-Coburg-Saalfeld and gave Britain a legal heir to keep the House of Hanover in business. Prince Edward died in 1820, leaving his young daughter, Princess Victoria, in Kensington Palace, aware that her destiny was to reign after William IV, as he and Queen Adelaide had no living children. Victoria, taught by her widowed mother to venerate her late father's memory, was shocked to learn he had lived with a mistress for over two decades before making an arranged marriage to her German mother.

It remains an intriguing mystery how all documentation on Julie de St Laurent vanished, thereby erasing her name from the history books. Allegedly, their destruction was carried out by household staff instructed by Queen Victoria. And so Julie de St Laurent's place and date of birth, her parentage, any possible children by Prince Edward, and her fate after being ejected from Kensington Palace has vanished without trace.

In March 1837, Maria Fitzherbert died in her own home in Brighton. Maria was very popular there as she and the Prince Regent had been responsible for turning a poverty-stricken fishing village into an elegant Regency resort. In accordance with Maria's wishes she was buried in the Catholic Church of St John the Baptist, at Bristol Road, East Brighton. A memorial shows her wearing three wedding rings — one for each husband.[16]

Above:
Swynnerton Hall, the residence of Mr and Mrs Fitzherbert.

Left:
Steine House at 55 Old Steine, Brighton, where Mrs Fitzherbert lived from 1804 until her death in 1837.

Cosway painted several versions of this miniature on ivory of Maria Fitzherbert, one example was buried with George IV.

Engraving of Lady Isabella Hertford when young. As a glamorous grandmother she replaced Maria Fitzherbert.

A King-fisher. A satirical engraving of Lady Conyngham fishing (for jewels) from George IV at Virginia Water near Windsor.

CHAPTER 4

Lady Jennie Churchill (née Jerome) (1854–1921) and Albert Edward (Bertie), Prince of Wales, later Edward VII

Lady Randolph Churchill was like a marvellous diamond — a host of facets seemed to sparkle all at once. Daisy, Countess of Warwick, *Afterthoughts*, London, 1931

JENNIE JEROME, DAUGHTER OF 'THE KING OF NEW YORK'

Jennie Jerome was born with a silver spoon in her mouth. Her father, Leonard Jerome, was a stockbroker who made millions by investing in railroad stock. Young Leonard had studied law at New York's Princeton university, but as share prices soared during America's Golden Age he decided to embrace the exciting life of speculating in stock and shares

In April 1849, Leonard married Clarissa Hall, who gave him two beautiful daughters, Clara and Jeanette — their second daughter would always be known as Jennie.[1] Within a few months of Jennie's birth share prices crashed and Leonard lost a great deal of money but still had enough to take himself, his wife and their small daughters to Paris for a two-month holiday.

Leonard Jerome did extremely well and earned a second fortune in a subsequent stock market boom which left him worth the equivalent of US$500 million in today's money.

The now fabulously wealthy Leonard Jerome, known by journalists as 'The King of New York', had a third daughter named Camille, who died in infancy. To house his growing family he built a magnificent mansion on Madison Avenue with a summer villa on the sea front at newly fashionable Newport.[2] Leonard, a man of wide interests, became a director of *The New York Times* in 1860 and wrote some of its editorials.

Jennie was six when the family left Brooklyn for an even more opulent life on Madison Avenue. Their New York residence boasted a handsome ballroom and a concert hall large enough to seat 600 people. Leonard Jerome was a flamboyant character who enjoyed taking risks and, like his daughter Jennie, the one who most closely resembled him, believed in living life to the full. He bought land in the Bronx, developed New York's Jerome Park racecourse and purchased race horses. He also purchased an ocean-going yacht and won races with it.[3]

Clarissa Jerome bore Leonard a fourth daughter they named Leonie. The girls were looked after by nannies and governesses. Surrounded by all the luxury money could buy, they learned to speak French and German, to play the piano extremely well and become accomplished and fearless horsewomen.

However, there was one problem for the attractive Jerome girls — their prospects of marrying into America's high society were limited. The doyenne of New York society, Mrs Caroline Astor, found Leonard Jerome too flamboyant and *nouveau riche* to include the Jeromes in her list of America's Top Four Hundred families whose daughters were invited to the annual ball she gave for the debutantes of that season.

Leonard Jerome was a great lover of music and organised recitals in his private concert hall for aspiring young singers in return for sexual favours. Eventually, Clarissa Jerome had enough of her husband flaunting his mistresses. In 1867 she decided to return to Paris, the city she loved, and took her three beautiful daughters with her to finish their education in Europe before making their debut at the court of Emperor Napoleon III.

Each summer Leonard rejoined his family for a long holiday in Paris, a city he also loved. By now Jennie had become totally bilingual from attending her French private school. Those formative years in Paris had a profound influence on her development and her character and for the rest of her life her speech and letters were filled with French phrases. She became very knowledgeable about French food, French music and French literature. She learned the art of dressing elegantly, buying couture gowns from the salons of Charles Worth, the leading Paris designer. She was also typically French in her acceptance of extra marital sex. In France it was accepted that most upper-class men had a mistress but would never leave their wives.

Presented at the court of Emperor Napoleon III and Empress Eugenie, Jennie, tall and slender with lustrous black hair and a curvaceous figure, was acknowledged as one of the most beautiful debutantes of the season. It seemed likely that she would receive proposals from several French aristocrats. But in the midst of the season of 1870, elegant dinner parties and balls ceased as the Prussian army crossed the border and invaded Paris.

Napoleon III, Empress Eugenie and their courtiers fled to England. The three Jerome girls and their mother managed to catch the last train from Paris for London before the Prussian Army took over the city. Soon after Leonard Jerome arrived in London, they travelled to Cowes, a small yachting town on the Isle of Wight, where the French court were in residence. There, Leonard rented the Villa Rosetta for his family. The place had resonance for Leonard as his distant ancestors (the Jerrams or Jeromes) had farmed at Cowes before emigrating to America in the eighteenth century.

Due to her father's wealth and connections, the 19-year-old Miss Jennie Jerome and her elder sister were invited to a ball on board a British warship to celebrate the engagement of a younger brother of the Prince of Wales to a daughter of the Tsar of Russia. The deck was hung with Chinese lanterns while an orchestra played romantic Strauss waltzes. Jennie looked stunning in an off-the-shoulder white tulle gown and long white kid gloves.

The Prince of Wales opened the dancing by waltzing decorously with Princess Alexandra of Denmark, to whom he had been married for nine years. His interest was aroused by the dark-haired American girl whose Parisian elegance intrigued him. He requested the pleasure of the next dance with Miss Jeanette Jerome. This honour would secure Jennie's entrée into the privileged world of British high society. Had Princess Alexandra not been present, the 32-year-old Prince would have monopolised the fascinating Miss Jerome for the rest of the evening. But this was impossible.

Once the music ceased, the heir to the throne handed the beautiful Miss Jerome to the next partner on her dance card. This happened to be the Prince's 23-year-old friend, Lord Randolph Churchill, a younger son of the Duke and Duchess of Marlborough. Lord Randolph, expensively educated at Eton and Oxford, was the third son of the Duke of Marlborough. Keen to impress this beautiful young woman and aware he was a better talker than a dancer, Lord Randolph asked Miss Jerome if they could sit out the next dance. In the romantic twilight they talked for hours, discovering they loved horses and hunting, both were avid readers, both of them spoke French fluently and admired French culture.

On learning that Lord Randolph was due to leave Cowes in two days time, Jennie begged her mother to invite him to dine the following evening.

The dinner at the Villa Rosita was a great success. Jennie and her blonde elder sister Clara, played duets at the piano in an impromptu after-dinner concert. Jennie and Lord Randolph remained in the candlelit music room to talk, both convinced they had found a soul mate. Lord Randolph, now head over heels in love, extended his stay in Cowes and confided to the Prince of Wales that he was going to marry Miss Jerome. Within three days he and Jennie were secretly engaged.

Jennie, bubbling with excitement, told her mother she was to marry the son of a duke. But Mrs Jerome was far from delighted — as a younger son Lord Randolph was *not* a great catch.

The *real* catch had been Randolph's elder brother, Lord George Blandford, whose arranged marriage had taken place years earlier to Lady Bertha Hamilton, daughter of the Duke of Abercorn, an Anglo-Irish peer. Under the laws of primogeniture it was the wayward Lord George Blandford who would inherit Blenheim Palace and the title of duke — Lord Randolph could expect very little and it was hoped he would marry money.

When Randolph told his parents he wished to marry the daughter of a New York speculator, the Duke and Duchess of Marlborough and Lord Blandford were horrified. The Duchess had hoped her favourite son would marry an aristocratic English heiress and regarded Miss Jerome as an American adventuress in search of a title. Lord Randolph assured his mother that Miss Jerome was an exceptional young woman, far better educated than most English girls. She spoke fluent French and German and was a brilliant pianist of concert standard. The Duchess of Marlborough remained unimpressed.

In contrast Bertie — as Lord Randolph and other close friends were allowed to call the Prince of Wales — approved of the beautiful Miss Jerome and encouraged Randolph to pursue his courtship.

On making enquiries about Leonard Jerome in New York, the Duke of Marlborough was appalled to learn Jennie's father had lost a fortune through unwise speculation and was suffering heavy losses on the stock market. The Jerome mansion was heavily mortgaged and Leonard's debts were piling up.[4]

Hearing about Leonard's mistresses and the apparent fragility of the Jerome fortune, the Duke was determined to delay this unsuitable marriage, hoping his son would come to his senses and break off the engagement. The Duke warned Randolph that Miss Jerome's father was in debt and could not be trusted to behave properly over his daughter's marriage settlement.

On learning of the Duke's insulting comments, Jennie defended her father vehemently and even threatened to break off the engagement. She pointed out that her father was a distinguished man. He was a founding member of the American Jockey Club, part owner of the *New York Times* and had inaugurated the Transatlantic Yacht Race.

⁂

Jennie was aware that Blenheim Palace was one of England's grandest stately homes, donated by a grateful nation to General John Churchill, victor of the battle of Blenheim against the French Army. She was not aware that the Marlborough fortune had been eroded by centuries of extravagance and the high costs of maintaining Blenheim Palace. While Randolph's elder brother, Lord Blandford, was a drunken womaniser who had been expelled from Eton, the Duke had hopes that clever young Randolph would enter Parliament. Lord Randolph promised his father he would try to do so, but on one condition — he was allowed to marry Miss Jennie Jerome. The Duke of Marlborough finally gave in.

Consequently, Lord Randolph stood for Parliament and was elected Member for Woodstock, his local constituency. The Duke was delighted. He settled Randolph's debts and bought the couple a short lease on a house in Charles Street, Mayfair. However, he became angry when Jennie's father refused to hand over the full amount of her dowry. Leonard Jerome insisted it was customary for American brides to retain half their dowries for their personal use and demanded this be done in the case of his favourite daughter.

The Duke, aware that Members of Parliament were unpaid and Randolph would not earn a salary unless he became a Cabinet Minister, felt he must protect his son's interests. Negotiations over the marriage settlement became so acrimonious that plans for a white wedding in London were shelved.

By now the Prussian Army had left Paris. It was therefore deemed safe for Mrs Jerome and her daughters to leave the Isle of Wight and return to their rented house near the Boulevard Haussman. Randolph paid several visits to Paris to see Jennie, but although the couple were engaged, Mrs Jerome chaperoned her daughter strictly, as negotiations over the marriage settlement had stalled. She was not happy with the match but had no wish for her daughter's reputation to be compromised should the marriage never eventuate. Like her father, Jennie enjoyed taking risks. Somehow or other she managed to give her mother the slip and visit Randolph in his Paris hotel. Letters from Jennie to Randolph refer to the fact she spent time alone with her fiancé in the bedroom of his hotel in the Rue de Rivoli. [5]

Eventually, Jennie must have confessed to her mother she was pregnant. This is born out by the fact that suddenly Mrs Jerome dropped her objections to the match and made preparations for a quiet wedding in Paris. Under normal circumstances marriage for the son of a Duke would have meant a very large society wedding.

In April 1874, the Duke and Duchess of Marlborough showed their displeasure over Randolph's marriage by refusing to attend a wedding of which they did not approve. However, they did agree to come to Paris to meet Jennie a few weeks before the small ceremony which was to be held at the British Embassy in Paris (but for some reason never recorded there). Leonard Jerome arrived in Paris to give his daughter away and a second ceremony was held in the chapel of the American Legation which *was* recorded.

After a brief honeymoon in France, Lord Randolph and his bride crossed the Channel by ferry and drove their carriage to Blenheim Palace. Jennie, always the proud American, was unimpressed by one of Britain's grandest stately homes, finding Blenheim Palace with its huge rooms and lack of heating most uncomfortable. The Duchess was not exactly welcoming, convinced that Jennie was a scheming girl who had trapped her son into marriage by getting pregnant and Lord Blandford was quite hostile to her.[6]

In polite society it was customary that in the final months of her pregnancy the future mother must remain at home or stay with relatives. Jennie and Randolph spent time at Blenheim where the Duchess was still chilly and forbidding, although sometimes concerned about the approaching birth of her grandson.

On 30 November 1874, seven and a half months after their wedding, Winston Leonard Spencer Churchill was born at Blenheim Palace. Jennie had intended to have her baby in London but, after going out with a shooting party into the grounds of Blenheim, suffered a bad fall. The London gynaecologist could not arrive in time. Lady Randolph gave birth to her first child in a tiny little bedroom on the ground floor of Blenheim Palace, attended by the local country doctor.[7]

In a desperate effort to save face, a great deal of effort was expended to claim that Winston's birth was premature. Relations between Jennie and her mother-in-law, the Duchess of Marlborough remained strained. Jennie's biographer, Anne Sebba, postulates that Winston was not premature — in fact, he was a fine healthy baby conceived in Paris before Jennie and Randolph married.

Having spent her childhood in a New York mansion with central heating and the latest innovations in plumbing, Jennie found the vast unheated rooms of Blenheim Palace cold and cheerless, particularly in winter. Used to excellent cuisine in France, Jennie disliked what she regarded as stodgy English food.

Randolph's circle of amusing London friends, many of whom were members of the Prince of Wales' 'Marlborough House set', was more to Jennie's taste. Dressed in the latest elegant Parisian gowns and her diamond star (a gift from her mother) glittering in her dark hair, Lady Randolph took London by storm, attending grand balls and dinner parties, with the Prince of Wales as one of her keenest admirers. Having visited America years earlier, Bertie liked American women, finding them more amusing and better educated than their English counterparts.

Princess Alexandra of Denmark and Jennie Jerome, who had both grown up outside England, became good friends. In Royal Ascot week the Prince of Wales personally escorted Lady Randolph Churchill to a private lunch hosted by Lord Hartington, eldest son of the Duke of Devonshire.

The approval of the Prince of Wales and his wife opened the doors of London's leading hostesses to young Lady Churchill. She was the first American to set a fashion for the sons of British aristocrats to marry American wives, exchanging American money for titles and crumbling stately homes which needed vast sums spent on their upkeep. There was only one problem — unlike the wealthy American debutantes who followed her example and married cash-strapped aristocrats, Jennie did *not* have vast sums of money at her disposal.

This was unfortunate for Lord Randolph who entered politics out of a sense of duty and obligation to this father. He would not receive payment for all his work for his local constituency until finally he was made a Cabinet Minister. The fact that neither Jennie or Randolph had any idea of budgeting and both of them were spendthrifts contributed to the rift that developed in what had begun as a love-match.

As a superb pianist, specialising in Beethoven sonatas and the works of Chopin, Lady Randolph Churchill was in demand when she could be prevailed upon to perform after dinner in the mansions and stately homes of Randolph's friends. Her stunning looks and French elegance made her a popular member of the 'Marlborough House set'.

Lord and Lady Randolph continued to live at 47 Charles Street, Mayfair, the house whose lease the Duke had kindly purchased for them. When Lord Randolph made his maiden speech in Parliament, Jennie Churchill began her career as a political hostess with the Prince of Wales and the Prime Minister as her guests of honour.

Initially Jennie and her husband were happy, although as strong characters they did have arguments. However, in the second year of their marriage Lord Randolph began to exhibit symptoms of a mysterious disease. His illness resulted in severe headaches and savage outbursts of rage, usually directed at his wife. To Jennie's distress, Randolph became far less affectionate and their arguments over money and her extravagance became fierce. To compensate for her husband's bouts of rage and the weeks he scarcely spoke a word to her, Jennie threw herself into London's hectic social life, acquiring a reputation as an excellent political hostess as well as a witty and cultured young woman.

THE AYLESFORD SCANDAL AND ITS OUTCOME

In 1875, the Prince of Wales made a tour of India where an obliging maharajah organised a tiger shoot for the Prince and his friends. The Prince's party included the Earl of Aylesford, whose wife, Lady Edith Aylesford, had enjoyed a brief affair with the Prince of Wales.

In India the Earl of Aylesford received a letter from Lady Aylesford announcing she was leaving him for Lord Blandford (Jennie's brother-in-law). They would defy convention and live together in Paris. Lady Edith Aylesford, seeing life through rose-coloured spectacles, did not realise that Lord Blandford was even more dissolute than her alcoholic husband.

The Earl of Aylesford left India for London, intending to divorce his wife, citing Blandford as the guilty party. The Prince of Wales, his vanity piqued that Lady Aylesford had replaced him so quickly with Lord Blandford, supported Lord Aylesford in his demand for a divorce, in spite of the scandal.

The elderly Duke of Marlborough, appalled by the prospect of his heir caught up in a sordid divorce, begged Lord Randolph to seek the help of Princess Alexandra to prevent a divorce which would disgrace all of them. Somehow or other, Randolph found the love letters the Prince of Wales had written to Lady Aylesford, which could be used in court to claim Lady Aylesford was an immoral woman. Should the Prince of Wales be named in court, he would be disinherited by Queen Victoria, who felt divorce was a sin in the eyes of God.

The Queen despaired of her wayward heir and his association with women of dubious virtue. She warned her eldest son that, were he to be even mentioned in a divorce case, he would 'never sit on the throne of England'.[8]

In an attempt to prevent Lord Blandford's divorce, which would plunge them *all* in disgrace, Lord Randolph foolishly showed Princess Alexandra the Prince of Wales' love letters to Lady Edith Aylesford, hoping the princess would get her husband to stop supporting Lord Aylesford's wish for a divorce. Greatly distressed Princess Alexandra cabled her husband.

From India the Prince of Wales cabled back, protesting his relationship with Lady Aylesford was merely a flirtation, nothing more. He implored the support of his wife to prevent being disinherited by his mother.

Furious that Lord Randolph had intervened, the Prince ordered his friend Lord Charles Beresford to act as his second in the duel he intended to fight with Lord Randolph in France, where duelling was still legal.

As requested, Princess Alexandra met her erring husband at Southampton docks and staged a 'happy family reunion' in front of journalists, although they had lived separate lives for years. To preserve their image as a devoted couple, the Prince and Princess of Wales drove through London in an open carriage, waving to the cheering crowds. That evening Princess Alexandra accompanied her adulterous husband to Covent Garden and were seen holding hands in the royal box. This effectively killed any speculation by journalists about a split in the royal marriage.

The Prince of Wales still insisted he would fight a duel with Lord Randolph. To protect His Royal Highness from his own folly, Prime Minister Disraeli persuaded Lord Aylesford to drop the idea of a divorce and remove himself to Texas where he owned a cattle ranch.

Disraeli ordered Lord Randolph to apologise to the Prince of Wales and arranged for the compromising love letters to Lady Aylesford to be retrieved and burned. Lord Randolph, his brain and his judgement affected by his mysterious illness, wrote a most ungracious letter of apology to the Prince of Wales. The Prince retaliated by refusing to meet *any* member of the Churchill family or go to *any* house where they were received.[9] As the leader of London society, His Royal Highness insisted that Lord Randolph and his family were to be shunned by 'polite' society.

Jennie Churchill, with her marriage under stress, hated the fact she had become a virtual outcast. She decided it was a good time for her and Randolph to visit her father and see something of America and Canada. Accompanied by two members of Randolph's staff the Churchills visited Niagara Falls, Newport and

New York to see Jennie's father before making a scenic tour of Canada.

Returning from America, Jennie learned her father-in-law had been urged by the Prime Minister to accept the post of Viceroy of Ireland, since he was ostracised from society by the heir to the throne which was awkward for everyone. The Duke of Marlborough had previously turned down the role of Viceroy of Ireland as it required a huge expenditure of his own money to carry out all the entertaining required in this British colony. Jennie and Randolph were also to base themselves in Ireland until the scandal had blown over.

Lord Randolph, no doubt feeling guilty for the havoc he had caused, accepted an unpaid post of Private Secretary to his father in addition to his Parliamentary duties in Britain. He had to divide his time between Dublin and London whenever the House of Commons was sitting. His illness was treated by Dr Thomas Buzzard who diagnosed syphilis.[10] With no effective form of treatment in those days for this fatal disease it fell to Dr Buzzard to warn the Churchills of the risks involved in sexual intercourse.

At first Jennie was lonely in Dublin. Randolph was either at the House of Commons or travelling with his father in Ireland. Randolph incurred heavy gambling losses and had to borrow from the bank, while Jennie consoled herself by spending extravagantly. Her annual allowance from her father had not been paid, which was a cause of friction. Jennie had to live with her in-laws in Dublin's Vice-regal residence. On the occasions when she did see Randolph his temper was worse and his doctor's bills were mounting.

Eventually, the young Churchills were given a smaller house in Phoenix Park by which time it was claimed that all marital relations had ceased. Syphilis was not always easy to diagnose as the Wasserman blood test for the disease had not yet been invented. Doctors knew the final or tertiary stage meant insanity and total paralysis could take many years to develop.[11]

Hunting, a popular sport in horse-mad Ireland, became Lady Randolph's distraction from her problems. Like Daisy Warwick, Jennie enjoyed the thrills and risks of the hunting field. If bad weather made hunting impossible she rode alone in Phoenix Park, where Jennie's striking good looks attracted the attention of a number of men and innocent flirtations sometimes developed into passionate but brief romances.

Doctors discouraged Jennie from having sexual relations with her ailing husband, which meant that she felt no compunction about taking lovers during the three years she spent in Ireland.[12]

Her second son, John Strange Spencer Churchill, (known as Jack), was born in Dublin in February 1880, shortly before Jennie and her in-laws returned to London. It is possible he was fathered by Lord Randolph as some family members believe. Other sources suggest Jack's father was the 55-year-old Colonel John Strange Jocelyn, Earl of Roden, who acted as Jack's godfather. Another likely candidate was the much younger 'Star' Falmouth, seventh Viscount Falmouth, who served as military secretary to the Duke of Marlborough in Ireland. Viscount Falmouth, tall, handsome and muscular, was a brilliant horseman and a great admirer of Lady Churchill. Lord d'Abernon, a future British ambassador and admirer, and probably another of Jennie's lovers, was bowled over by her beauty as well as her personality. He made a memorable description of Lady Randolph as

> ...more of a panther than a woman, but with a cultivated intelligence unknown in the jungle. Her desire to please and her delight in life make her the centre of a devoted circle.[13]

In 1880, the Duke and Duchess of Marlborough, Jennie and her two sons left Ireland as a general election had seen a change of government in Britain. The Tory Party under Disraeli was beaten, ending the Duke of Marlborough's Vice-regal appointment. Winston was five-years-old and Jack still a baby. Randolph was already in London and he and Jennie rented a larger house in St James Place. Randolph was busy forming and then leading what became known as the Fourth Party: Jennie's literary skills became useful in vetting her husband's speeches and entertaining for him.

Jennie hoped that the Prince of Wales would lift his ban on both of them, so they could enjoy the social life of the Marlborough House set as part of the London season. To Jennie's intense disappointment they were *still* excluded by the Prince from the most prestigious dinner parties and balls. Jennie compensated for this lack of social life by entertaining Randolph's friends and political colleagues at their home.

At one elegant party, to which the Churchills managed to obtain an invitation, the Prince of Wales was the guest of honour. He smiled broadly at Jennie but pointedly ignored Randolph.

In remission from his 'mystery illness', Lord Randolph threw himself with renewed vigour into politics. His period of travelling around Ireland with his father had given him first-hand knowledge of the country at a time when the question of Home Rule for Ireland — under which Ireland would be given more say in how it was governed — was a hot topic. Lord Randolph's well informed and impassioned speeches in Parliament on 'the Irish question' led to him being spoken of as a rising star in a future government — a Cabinet Minister or even a future Prime Minister.

Jennie was heartened by the improvement in Randolph's career. With her usual energy she threw herself into renewing friendships to help Randolph achieve his hopes of attaining a Cabinet post. She attended meetings, speaking to women's groups and electioneering on his behalf. As yet she did not advocate women's suffrage and would not support this until later. Women did not receive the vote in Britain until 1920, along with their American counterparts. Australian women were the first British subjects to receive the vote in 1900 as a spin-off from Federation.

To help her husband Jennie founded the influential Primrose League, a grass-roots Tory group which would eventually have over a million members. Randolph's Fourth Party stood for 'Tory democracy' and offered itself as an alternative to the Conservative and the Irish Parties. His long term aim was to reform the Conservative Party, which in the public mind was associated with the aristocracy and landed gentry, and widen its electoral appeal to the middle-class and working people. Jennie's Primrose League echoed these ambitions.

Unfortunately, at this critical time in his career, Randolph's symptoms reappeared, causing him to suffer splitting headaches and bad tempers, which made him difficult to work or live with. Randolph and his violent tempers alienated political colleagues and close friends who noted with concern how rude he was to Jennie.

To compensate for her loveless stressful marriage, Jennie, who craved affection, used shopping as a substitute. She spent extravagantly on clothes from Paris, hot-house flowers, expensive foods and beautiful things for the home to cheer herself up in moods of misery.

Randolph was often prostrate with exhaustion. He and Jennie could not afford a country house where he could have escaped the stress of political life and the smog and smoke-laden atmosphere of Victorian London. Randolph spent many weekends at Blenheim Palace, which to Jennie's despair he continued to regard as his home.

In the cold winter of 1881, after spending an unhappy month at Blenheim Palace, Jennie wrote to her mother confessing that no matter how hard she tried to help Randolph, her mother-in-law was determined to undermine her. The Duchess disliked Winston and Jennie hated staying at chilly Blenheim Palace.[14]

In 1882, at the age of seven, Winston was packed off to St George's Ascot.[15] This preparatory school for boys had a sadistic headmaster who enjoyed caning Winston and others in his charge so savagely that some terrified boys soiled themselves. Lord Randolph, often ill and preoccupied with his political career, was angry at receiving his eldest son's poor school reports. Winston's letters to Jennie from St George's School are heartbreaking, pleading with her to visit him.

Jennie, preoccupied with Randolph's illness and his political aspirations, rarely visited Winston. She left young Jack to the care of Nanny Everest who also took care of Winston during the school holidays and he remained devoted to her.

Lack of money was still a problem for Jennie and Randolph who were living way beyond their means. Randolph was convinced he would soon manage to gain a place in Cabinet and receive a salary. The Duke of Marlborough was unable to provide financial help to his second son as his income had been substantially reduced by the agricultural downturn.

Leonard Jerome sent his favourite daughter money whenever he could spare it. However, he was also experiencing financial difficulties. Jennie's father managed to retain his Madison Avenue mansion for a few more years but eventually had to sell out, having been affected by the stock market crash of 1873 and the bank crashes of the 1880s. Leonard Jerome also had to find marriage portions for Jennie's sisters, Leonie and Clara, both of whom married younger sons of aristocrats with small incomes in an era when 'gentlemen' did not soil their hands by working in offices or entering the professions.

In 1882, Jennie and Randolph moved to a larger house in Connaught Place, near Hyde Park, one of the first in London to be fitted with electric lighting. With enthusiasm Jennie threw herself into redecorating their new home and painted a mural on her bedroom ceiling herself. As a child, she had been taught to paint and this plus her writing and her music would be some consolation for an unhappy marriage.

In December 1882, Jennie fell ill and for weeks had a raging fever. When she recovered, her doctors told her she had been suffering from typhoid, widespread at a time when many London homes had poor plumbing and drainage. Randolph was away, taking a cure at a French health spa, and did not return to London to see his wife, even when she was very ill indeed.

However, once her husband did return he seemed slightly better. Once more he threw himself into the political fray. The Duchess of Marlborough, Jennie and one of her sisters-in-law were urged by Randolph to take an active part in his campaign, even though they did not have the vote themselves.

For the next few years Jennie was politically active on Randolph's behalf. He attributed his next victory in a Woodstock by-election to his wife's efforts. Jennie re-wrote some of her husband's speeches and spoke of his political aims at social gatherings and became an inspiring public speaker.

In July 1883, the Duke of Marlborough died unexpectedly. After the enormous funeral, the reading of the Duke's will saw some money left to the cash-strapped Randolph. Blandford, Randolph's elder brother, inherited the bulk of his father's estate and the title of Duke of Marlborough.

After the Duke's death, Randolph's relations with his elder brother worsened. When Lord Randolph married Miss Jerome, Blandford had been scathing that an American was entering this ancient British family. However, having deserted Lady Aylesford and the illegitimate son he fathered with her, Blandford abandoned his principles and married Lilian Hammersley, a wealthy American widow, who became the eighth Duchess of Marlborough. Jennie thought Blandford's marriage to a fellow American ironic in view of his very scathing comments about her marrying into a noble English family. Fortunately, she liked the new American Duchess Lilian and appreciated the fact her money helped pay for the upkeep of Blenheim Palace.

Randolph was absent from home a great deal. When abroad, he wrote Jennie affectionate letters but was downright hostile on the rare occasions they were alone together and seemed to have a split personality. Most of the time Randolph was busy in the House of Commons which often sat till late into the night. Jennie continued to give dinner parties for her husband, keeping up the pretence they were a devoted couple.

Randolph frequently took holidays with male friends, a habit that raised a few eyebrows. He was still blacklisted by the Prince of Wales. Jennie, bi-lingual in French and speaking good German, accepted invitations to parties at foreign embassies and enjoyed the chance to use her knowledge of these languages.

※

In 1883, at a diplomatic reception, Jennie met the handsome Count Charles (Karl) Rudolf Ferdinand Andreas Kinsky, son of an Austrian Prince and the Princess of Lichtenstein, both of them

Catholic.[16] Count Kinsky was in great demand by London hostesses for his good looks, charm and personal fortune. Kinsky, a diplomat at the Austro-Hungarian Embassy at the Court of St James, was Jennie's *beau ideal* of a Renaissance man — tall, athletic, a talented linguist and an excellent pianist, able to play duets with Jennie as well as ride to hounds with her. He acquired hero status in Britain when, as an amateur jockey, he won the 1883 Grand National on Zoedone, the chestnut horse he had trained himself.

As a handsome bachelor, Count Kinsky was very popular and had several brief affairs, but it was Lady Randolph Churchill whom he preferred. Strangely enough, Randolph did not seem to mind Jennie's new relationship. Lord Randolph liked Count Kinsky so much he accepted an invitation to Vienna to see the Count's family estate.

Lord Randolph worked hard, spending a great deal of time at the House of Commons, touring the country making speeches and hoping to gain control of a revitalised Tory Party.

Meanwhile Jennie's elder sister Clara had married the handsome but improvident Moreton Frewen. They lived in a crumbling mansion in Sussex and often invited Jennie and Count Kinsky to spend weekends with them.

Randolph seemed to be in remission from his illness and was either hard at work in the House of Commons or absent abroad, so Count Kinsky became a regular guest in the Churchill's London home. He became like a favourite uncle to young Winston, who hero-worshipped the dashing horseman.

Winston was now a boarder at Harrow and had difficulty passing exams. One day he arrived back from boarding school unexpectedly and found Jennie and Count Kinsky breakfasting together. It was then that the truth dawned on Winston — his mother and Kinsky were lovers.

While Count Kinsky was a diversion from a marriage that had gone very wrong, Jennie knew his Catholic family would never countenance him marrying her as a Protestant with children from a previous marriage. Nevertheless, he was a shoulder to lean on in a time of trouble, though not a very faithful lover. Jennie, who lacked strong religious beliefs, was very French in her matter-of-fact attitude to sex and neither gave fidelity to her lovers or demanded it from them.

LINGERING LUNCHES WITH A SEX-ADDICTED PRINCE

By 1884, Lord Randolph Churchill was a prominent figure in the Conservative Party. The Prince of Wales decided it was time to lift his ban on Lord Randolph and re-instate him and his stunningly attractive wife as part of his Marlborough House set.

On 18 March 1884, the Prince and Princess of Wales attended a dinner organised by Lord Randolph's friend, Sir Henry James, the Attorney General, to which Randolph and Jennie were guests.[17] This dinner included Prime Minister Gladstone and ended eight years of ostracism by the Prince of Wales.

A few months later, on 2 June 1884, the Prince of Wales and Lord and Lady Randolph dined together at the fashionable Paris restaurant, the Café des Anglais on the Boulevard des Italiens. This historic restaurant with its mahogany and walnut panelling and huge gilded mirrors was frequented by European royalty, divas from Garnier's Paris opera and famous writers of the calibre of Marcel Proust and Oscar Wilde. Jennie, who had just turned thirty, was at her sparkling best. She was delighted to be back in Paris, a city which held so many happy memories for her.

Queen Victoria made no secret of the fact she felt her heir would prove a disaster as king. She had never loved Bertie who, as a child, had suffered from attention deficit syndrome and had problems in concentrating on his lessons. Bertie's reports from his tutors were so poor he had little confidence in himself. His mother constantly belittled him and refused to give him any official responsibilities. Psychiatrists claim lack of maternal love as a reason why some men have multiple sexual relationships. It is alleged Bertie had many hundreds of extra-marital relationships, at a time when this was dangerous as syphilis was widespread. In today's terminology, Bertie was a sex addict. Sex addiction is regarded as an obsessive-compulsive form of behaviour. Bertie did his best to assuage his sense of maternal rejection by acquiring a large number of desirable sexual partners to boost his self-esteem.[18]

In the 1880s and 1890s, Bertie was a regular visitor at the luxurious Paris brothel Le Chabanais and paid for sessions with a large number of 'ladies of the night'. At his favourite Paris brothel Bertie's visits were recorded by the Prefecture of Police, whose job it was to follow him. ensuring his safety.[19]

Each suite at Le Chabanais was decorated in a different style. Bertie's favourite suite (also favoured by the artist Henri de Toulouse-Lautrec), was decorated to resemble a Moorish palace. It had a large copper tub in which the Prince of Wales liked to bathe naked with several prostitutes at a time. Extra-marital sex with beautiful women, who flattered his vanity, was Bertie's consolation for what had become a sexless marriage as well as the validation of his masculinity. But this was not enough. Bertie needed to parade his upper-class female conquests in public and escorted stunningly beautiful ladies to the races and other public places. His high society mistresses included Lady Jennie Churchill and Daisy, Countess of Warwick. During the latter years of his life Mrs Alice Keppel — a society beauty almost young enough to be his daughter — was his constant companion.

The Prince of Wales had been attracted to Jennie since their first meeting at Cowes. On their return to London he renewed his interest in Lady Churchill and was determined to possess her. It was now known that she and Lord Randolph Churchill spent most of their time apart.

Lady Jennie Churchill was in her thirties and at the height of her beauty. Bertie, who had wanted her for years, was aware that Jennie had taken lovers, so she could scarcely plead wifely virtue if he tried to win her. Jennie had learned by painful experience what could happen to those who offended the heir to the throne and that he could cast his former friends into social limbo.

The failure of her love match, largely due to Randolph's illness, made Jennie feel she was absolved from her marital vows of fidelity.

She continued to act as Randolph's political hostess but, apparently, felt no sense of guilt about taking lovers.

The Prince of Wales had a trump card when persuading her to become his mistress. He controlled high society, the milieu Jennie loved and where she shone so brilliantly at dinners, dances or playing the piano in the home of friends. It had taken her eight years to regain a place in polite society. She had no wish to become an outcast again by refusing the advances of the heir to the throne.

With her husband abroad, Count Kinsky back in Vienna and Princess Alexandra away in Denmark, Jennie and the Prince of Wales crossed the boundary between friendship and a sexual relationship. *Cache ton jeu* (play your cards close to your chest) was Jennie's motto, so she tactfully called Bertie her *ami intime*.

However, sex changed little in their relationship — the Prince and Jennie, even after becoming lovers, saw each other just as friends. There were no sentimental love letters, only brief notes requesting Jennie to entertain Bertie at times when he knew her husband was absent.

Jennie's letters about her visits to Sandringham are deliberately superficial. They describe what she wore for morning walks, lunches and dinners with the Prince. Bertie, a very accomplished seducer, probably explained to Jennie that his marital relations with Princess Alexandra had ended after the painful births of her two last children. His wife's doctors had warned her not to have another child.

AIDED BY THE DUCHESS OF DUKE STREET

The Prince of Wales sent Jennie brief notes from 1887 onwards, asking if he could call on Lady Churchill at home, sometimes for lunch and at other times in the late afternoon. One hand-written note says that the Prince has to sit on a Royal Commission but he hopes to be able to leave by 3 pm, will come directly to her house and is longing to see her.

In the days before telephones Bertie sent notes, setting a time of arrival at the homes of several married ladies with whom he dallied when their husband were away. One of them was his final mistress, Mrs Alice Keppel.

The Prince of Wales used to arrive at Lady Churchill's house in a inconspicuous horse-drawn green brougham used for his amorous assignations. Bertie's coachman would park in the street close to the home of the lady the Prince was honouring with his attentions and drove him back to Marlborough House once the visit was over.

Jennie's tact and discretion meant that very few people even realised she and the Prince were more than friends. Queen Victoria even received Lady Churchill at Buckingham Palace, believing her to be a good influence on her wayward son. Some of Bertie's notes to Jennie are addressed to *Ma chère Ami*, which in French denotes a degree of intimacy. As old friends, the Prince was able to tease Jennie about the number of men in love with her — in return, Jennie teased him affectionately about *his* conquests without the slightest hint of jealousy.

To ensure no one on her staff would tell the press about her intimate luncheons with the Prince of Wales, Jennie employed Rosa Lewis, a woman she could trust and would not talk to the press. The Prince liked Rosa for her good plain cooking as well as her discretion. Rosa Lewis knew the sort of food Bertie liked — his favourite dish was boiled ham previously soaked in champagne. He hated heavy sauces, which might splash the front of his clothes.

Rosa, born in poverty, had risen from scullery maid to undercook and then to head cook. For special guests at intimate lunches Rosa and a loyal *sous chef* prepared and served the food at the table, which avoided the need for other servants to be present. Jennie and the Prince of Wales swapped stories of the latest *amours* of members of the Marlborough House set — a topic of endless interest to the Prince.

One of Rosa's favourite sayings was 'No names, no lawyers, no pack drill'. Her discretion would eventually be rewarded when Bertie became King. He loaned Rosa Lewis enough money at a low rate of interest to buy the lease of a building at the corner of Duke and Jermyn Streets. There Rosa ran the famous Cavendish Hotel with private rooms for gentlemen who wished to lunch or dine alone with ladies to whom they were *not* married. A special entrance and lift were installed so the Prince of Wales could come and go at will.

His Royal Highness followed his usual *modus operandi* with Lady Randolph. He wrote to his *chère ami,* 'Would it be very indiscreet if I proposed myself as a guest to luncheon?' The Prince would arrive at the Churchill residence in his green brougham, often bringing French champagne with him. Bertie hated corsets and in several of his notes asked Jennie to change into a free flowing tea gown or a Japanese kimono *before* he arrived, which seems suggestive. Corsets did not need to be worn under a kimono so Jennie did not need a maid to help unlace them.

Jennie's replies to these notes are held in the Royal Archives at Windsor Castle. It seems significant that requests to inspect them by the respected biographers, Anita Leslie and Shane Leslie, who were both related of Jennie Churchill by marriage, were denied.[20] Withholding Jennie's replies to notes from the Prince of Wales suggests *something* reflect badly on the monarchy and needs to remain concealed.

Bertie's request to Jennie Churchill to wear a kimono or a tea gown is significant. Lady Daisy Brooke was famous for her house parties at Easton Lodge, where ladies wore loose tea gowns, flirted with their lovers and went to a bedroom or a cottage in the grounds, built specially for lovers' trysts. Tea gowns were made from voile or silk tulle, fastened by a belt with a jewelled clasp, easily undone by an impatient lover. No underclothes or corsets were worn. Corsets left marks on the lady's body and as they took a long time to unlace were regarded as 'passion killers'.

The Prince of Wales liked 'his' favourites to be the centre of attraction at any social function he attended. He himself was a leader of fashion with an interest in elegant clothes and military uniforms of which he had a large collection. Now that he was involved with Lady Churchill, the Prince of Wales insisted Lord

Randolph buy his wife a new evening gown for the annual Sandringham Ball so that she would dazzle everyone.

Jennie's ball gowns were always extravagant, even when she and Randolph were short of money. She commissioned the House of Worth in Paris to design hand-embroidered or jewelled ball gowns, one of which cost far more than an average working man earned in an entire year. One ball gown, which won Jennie great admiration, had a bodice trimmed with the shimmering green wings of beetles.

Being suitably dressed was a major preoccupation for female guests at Sandringham. A simple gown was worn for breakfast, a fitted jacket and a long woollen skirt was worn on country walks or watching the Prince of Wales shoot grouse. The female guests had a change of clothes for luncheon and a long gown for afternoons that did not need a corset. The ladies changed for dinner into off-the-shoulder long evening gowns when expensive jewellery could be worn. Name cards were placed on bedroom doors and willing wives who slept apart from their husbands would leave their doors unlocked.

***

As a political hostess Lady Randolph Churchill was acknowledged as one of the most influential women in London. When her husband was well enough, she used to give successful dinner parties to further his career. She also found time to give superb piano recitals for various charities.

Randolph was wrapped up in his demanding career or took holidays abroad. Neither of the Churchills had much time for their young sons. Although Winston adored his mother, it was faithful loving Nanny Everest who comforted and cared for the Churchill boys.

Eventually Randolph and Jennie's debts were so great that she had to dismiss their servants and rent out their London home. Lord Randolph went to live at his club, while Jennie had to move in with her disapproving mother-in-law, the Dowager Duchess of Marlborough, which was not easy for her.

In October 1884, Jennie's younger sister Leonie married Jack Leslie, a younger son of the Irish landowner Sir John Leslie. The marriage took place in Manhattan. The Leslie family owned large estates scattered around Ireland, including Castle Leslie at Glaslough in County Monaghan, which was full of art treasures and where Jennie became a frequent visitor.

LORD RANDOLPH'S RISE AND FALL

Randolph was away in India from December 1884 till March 1885 and his letters were full of stories about elephant and tiger hunts. But this trip had a more serious side. Randolph obtained extensive first hand knowledge of the country so that he was the best informed member of Parliament on India. Consequently, three months later Randolph was appointed Secretary of State for India in a caretaker government until a new election could be held. This paid appointment was welcome as Randolph and his wife had serious financial problems.

After his return to Britain, Lord Randolph had to fight a by-election for Woodstock, the seat he had held for the last ten years. His wife and sister helped canvas on his behalf. When Randolph won the seat, many credited Jennie's appeal and glamour for his success.

Jennie knew it was vital to hide Randolph's bouts of ill health and depression from his colleagues. In remission from his illness, he was a hard worker. Jennie was ambitious for her husband to become Chancellor of the Exchequer and he was regarded as a possible future Prime Minister. But by the end of 1885, Randolph had become seriously ill with repeated bouts of headaches, congestion of the lungs, a chronic cough and a heart murmur.

In January 1886, Randolph lost his job and his salary when the Conservative Government under Lord Salisbury was defeated. He and Jennie were now in even worse financial trouble but their extravagance did not stop. Jennie shopped with fervour, while Randolph gambled away money he did not have and was depressed by his losses. Bitter rows threatened to remove even the façade of a happy marriage.

In June 1886, Randolph was appointed Chancellor of the Exchequer at the age of 37. He was the youngest politician ever to have held that high position, which gave him a salary of £5,000 per annum. Recognising Randolph's political importance, the Prince of Wales had diner with him and Jennie at their residence in Connaught Place.

However, Randolph's respite from money worries was short lived. His erratic behaviour at home and in Parliament was noted by his friends and political colleagues.

A few days before Christmas, Lord Randolph's resignation as Chancellor of the Exchequer was announced on the front page of *The Times*. He had not discussed his intention to resign with anyone, not even with Jennie. What was worse, Lord Randolph had not extended the courtesy of first submitting his resignation to Queen Victoria or the Prime Minister.

As Chancellor of the Exchequer, Randolph had proposed a reformist budget which would spread the tax more fairly but would penalise the landed gentry and the prosperous middle-class, who objected fiercely to his proposed reforms. Prime Minister Salisbury and the Secretary of State for War, whose budget for the Navy and the Army were also badly affected, refused to back Randolph's proposed budget. Randolph's gamble that the Prime Minister would ask him to reconsider his resignation, take him back into Cabinet and pass his budget, failed. Lord Salisbury, tired of being threatened by Randolph accepted his resignation.

Jennie was appalled. Her husband was once again without a salary and their debts were soaring. Relations between the couple were icy and there was speculation in the press that Lord and Lady Randolph were to divorce. But by January 1887 Jennie and Randolph abandoned any idea of a divorce, realising the consequences would be ostracism from society again. This would end any hope Randolph could resurrect his blighted political career. It was obvious that Jennie and Randolph had problems when they did not spend Christmas together.

As Lord Randolph's 'mystery illness' progressed, he became even more difficult to live with and the couple spent more time apart. One of his treatments involved taking mercury by mouth, which slowed the progress of syphilis rather than curing it.[10]

In spite of the couple's soaring debts, Jennie seemed unable to stop spending huge sums on gowns from the House of Worth and other Paris couturiers, out-of-season delicacies and hothouse flowers.

Jennie appealed to her good friend, the Prince of Wales, for financial help. He gave Jennie a generous gift of money to tide her over and much needed emotional support. She always knew he was a good friend in whom she could confide.

By the spring of 1894, Randolph, who was still a Member of Parliament, though no longer in Cabinet, was very ill indeed. Colleagues in the House of Commons noticed his loss of hair (due to Dr Buzzard's prescription of mercury) and trembling hands. Randolph's speeches became rambling and incoherent, and friends and relatives were embarrassed by his irrational behaviour. He had the shuffling gait of a syphilitic but may also have had a slow growing brain tumour. Concerned friends persuaded him to retire from the House of Commons.

Through all the anguish Jennie suffered, the Prince of Wales remained sympathetic and supportive.

In June 1894, Jennie took Randolph on a world cruise, accompanied by medical specialist Dr Thomas Keith. She grieved as she watched her brilliant husband turn into a semi-paralysed wreck. When they reached Hong Kong, Jennie received a telegram telling her that Count Charles Kinsky was making an arranged marriage to Countess Elizabeth Metternich, a young Catholic aristocrat. Count Kinsky's parents, Prince and Princess Kinsky, were strict Catholics and wanted grandchildren. Once they were told Lady Randolph Churchill's husband was dying, they worried that Jennie and their son might marry, so they arranged his marriage to a Catholic princess.

In letters to her sisters Jennie admitted that Kinsky had not been her lover exclusively, but she would have loved to marry him, so his marriage to a much younger woman was a bitter blow. Jennie believed Randolph's fatal illness and Kinsky's marriage had paid her back for her 'iniquities' as she described her extra-marital affairs in letters to her sisters.

On the latter stages of that nightmare voyage, Randolph's mania had become so violent that he had to be confined in a straight jacket in their cabin. Jennie endured the pain of witnessing his terrible end. Her future looked bleak. She was in her forties, Randolph's life was ending in scenes of horror and madness and their debts were soaring.

Lady Churchill and her dying husband returned to the Duchess of Marlborough's chilly London house on Christmas Eve and spent a grim Christmas there. Randolph's agony lasted another month — almost blind and progressively more and more paralysed, he groaned and screamed in torment as the morphine prescribed for him lost its effectiveness.

Showing great courage, Jennie took over the nursing of her husband in his last days. She scarcely slept or ate and was totally exhausted by the time he died on 24 January 1895. His death certificate, signed by a doctor, stated the cause of death as 'General Paralysis of the Insane', the medical terminology for crippling paralysis caused by tertiary syphilis.

Naturally, the real cause of Randolph's death was kept from the press. His funeral took place in Westminster Abbey. After the ceremony his body was taken by train back to Blenheim and he was buried beside his ancestors in the little churchyard at Bladon.

On learning of Randolph's death, Bertie wrote to Jennie immediately and sent the letter in his carriage from Marlborough House telling his adored Jennie that,

> The sad news reached me this morning that all was over and I felt for his and our sakes it was best so. There was a cloud in our friendship but I am glad to think it has long been forgotten by both of us.[21]

It took Jennie two years to recover completely from grief and depression and regain her former zest for life. She was now 43 but looked much younger.

With Jennie, Bertie behaved far better than with many of his former mistresses (although he had continued to be supportive to

Lillie Langtry when she went on the stage). Bertie was understanding and offered support when Jennie confided her financial problems to him. He arranged for his main financial advisor Sir Ernest Cassel to help Jennie sort out her tangled financial affairs. Unfortunately, Jennie, who had no head for finance, disregarded Sir Ernest's Cassel's advice to live within her means.

Urged by the Prince of Wales to help Lady Churchill, Sir Ernest employed Jack Churchill in his office. Jack had hoped to become an officer in a prestigious regiment, but buying a commission would have cost money — working for Sir Ernest was not his preferred career. Jennie had already spent the money Randolph had left for her and his sons, so there was no money for Jack to buy a commission or to send Winston to university. To compensate her elder son for not being able to attend university, Jennie sent him lists of books that he should read in order to improve his style as a writer. Her advice and encouragement would help Winston in his career as an author, a war correspondent and in his political speeches.

The sexual aspect of the Prince of Wales' relationship with Jennie (unlike many of his affairs with other mistresses) was only a very small part of their lasting friendship. Letters from Jennie's sisters Clara and Leonie make it clear they were aware of their sister's 'indiscretions' by which they meant her extra-marital relationships.

In *Royal Mistresses and Bastards* Anthony Camp lists many of Edward VII's mistresses, complete with their dates of their relationships. The long list includes Lady Jennie Churchill, Lady Daisy Brooke, Lady Edith Aylesford, Lady Susan Vane Tempest Stuart, several French courtesans, the actress-courtesan Sarah Bernhardt and Rosie Boote, an English chorus girl, raised in poverty. After spending a few nights with the Prince of Wales, the voluptuous Rosie amazed everyone by marrying into the peerage and becoming a Marchioness.

In his list Anthony Camp states that Jennie Churchill was the mistress of Prince of Wales from 1886-1889, other sources tend to suggest their relationship lasted slightly longer.

LADY RANDOLPH CHURCHILL IN LOVE AGAIN

When Princess Alexandra was away in Denmark, Jennie often organised parties for Bertie. She was acquainted with his friends, familiar with his habits, likes and dislikes and knew how to amuse him and how to tease him affectionately. In return the Prince of Wales gave Lady Churchill beautiful gifts and remained a loyal friend. Jennie was now a widow with two sons to support and Winston had just entered Sandhurst, intending to make a career in the Army.

The Prince of Wales made it abundantly clear that Lady Churchill would always have a very special place in his life and in his heart. She was even liked by Queen Victoria who disapproved of most of her eldest son's friends as raffish and extravagant. Jennie was one of the very few people who had access to the gardens of Buckingham Palace via a private entrance.

In 1898, Lady Randolph Churchill amazed her friends when they learned that she was head over heels in love with young Captain Caryl Harry Ramsden, who was years younger than herself. Headstrong and impulsive, Jennie boarded a ship and followed the handsome officer to Egypt, where they enjoyed a trip up the Nile together on a house boat. Jennie returned to Cairo with Captain Ramsden, who, no doubt, vowed eternal love and loyalty. Jennie, due to depart by ship from Alexandria was waved goodbye by her virile lover.

On learning that the ship had engine trouble and would not leave for at least another 24 hours, Jennie returned to their hotel. She was furious to find the fickle Captain Ramsden in the arms of the wife of another officer. Jennie told Captain Ramsden what she thought of him and departed.

When Jennie returned to London the Prince of Wales, having heard the story from a friend in Cairo, wrote Jennie a teasing letter. He said she should have remained faithful to *him*, pointing out 'Old friends are *best!*'

In spite of her soaring debts Jennie kept on ordering more expensive Paris gowns from Jacques Doucet and the House of Charles Worth. She had to find more money to pay off loans she had taken from insurance offices to clear the most pressing of her debts.[16] Like her father, she lived dangerously, piling debt upon debt. By now, Leonard Jerome was also in debt and had lost financial control of the race track he had developed, so was unable to help his daughter.

Once again, the Prince of Wales came to her rescue — not with a loan but a *gift* of money. The prince found Jennie so amusing and attractive he always forgave her for her extravagances, probably because he too was living on money, borrowed from his Jewish friends. Jennie was fortunate to have a good friend in Alfred Rothschild, who had a soft spot for her and loaned her money. Alfred Rothschild was a great music lover, so in return he asked Jennie to give private concerts for his friends at his country house.

By June 1898, Jennie was invited by Daisy, Countess of Warwick, to stay at Warwick Castle where one of Daisy's famous fancy dress balls was being held. One of her guest was the Prince of Wales. Daisy, knowing Jennie could cajole the Prince out of a bad mood, placed her next to the heir to the throne. Also seated at the Prince's table was George Cornwallis-West, a handsome young officer in the Scots Guards who fell head over heels in love with Jennie. George was a superb dancer and Jennie loved dancing.[22]

According to George's memoirs, Jennie Churchill looked about 30 and only later did he learn from his mother, Patsy Cornwallis-West, that Jennie was 43 while George was still in his early twenties — the same age as her son Winston.

The past was coming back to haunt members of the Marlborough set, who had practiced free love so assiduously. Twenty years previously, the Prince of Wales, as a house guest of Colonel and Mrs Cornwall-West, had enjoyed a brief sexual fling with George's mother, Patsy Cornwallis-West, a famous society beauty. Nine months later Patsy Cornwallis-West gave birth to a boy named George. A local newspaper ran the story that a farm labourer had seen the Prince of Wales and Mrs Cornwallis-West making love in the woods, so gossips claimed the Prince of Wales was young George's father. Colonel Cornwallis-West sued for libel and won his case. However, suspicions lingered that the farm worker had been right.

In a letter to Daisy, Countess of Warwick, Jennie referring to rumours she was going to marry George Cornwallis-West wrote,' 'Dearest Daisy, I am NOT going to marry anyone. If a perfect DARLING with at least £40,000 a year wants me *very much* I might consider it.[23]

The devil-may-care young George Cornwallis-West would have trouble finding £400 a year, let alone £40,000. But Jennie did not care — she had lost her heart to George, which was a risky thing to do. But Jennie always enjoyed taking risks.

When Lady Churchill confided to her sisters that she was marrying a man twenty years younger than herself (only sixteen days older than Winston) and that her fiancé had no money, Clara and Leonie told her she must be crazy.[24]

Jennie retorted that George was the heir to Ruthin Castle in Wales and 10,000 acres of land. She omitted to tell her sisters that the castle was crumbling and the land around it unsuitable for farming. On hearing that Jennie and George Cornwallis-West were to be married the Prince of Wales was furious. There were no advantages for him in Jennie making a love match to George and becoming unavailable to him.[25]

The Prince of Wales would have understood if Jennie had married an elderly man for money, but for her to lose her head and marry an irresponsible young man was crazy. He could hardly admit to a former mistress that George Cornwallis-West might be *his* son. The Prince pointed out she was the widow of a distinguished politician, a member of the Churchill family and leader of Anglo-American society in London. She must be careful of her reputation.[26] He added gently that her passion for the immature George was unsuitable due to their age difference.

Meanwhile, George, as Jennie's fiancé, was writing Jennie passionate letters with hearts at the top of every page, professing his undying love.

Bertie, worried about Jennie's future, decided a man-to-man approach was best. He invited George aboard the royal yacht

Britannia and issued a stern warning about marrying a woman much older than himself. George, deeply in love, refused to listen. Bertie did not like to tell him that he had once been his mother's lover and might even be George's father. Bertie pointed out that George was a poorly paid lieutenant in the Scots Guards and could not support the expensive tastes of Lady Randolph Churchill. But Jennie appealed to Bertie to help George and, as he could never resist her, he did help.

Colonel and Mrs Cornwallis-West were appalled at the thought of Jennie Churchill marrying their son and foretold disaster. Jennie was not much younger than George's mother and they believed far too old to be able to give them grandchildren. Winston kept quiet, convinced that young George would bow to family pressure and the projected marriage would not take place.

The Prince, who prophesied the marriage would be a disaster, had a quiet word with the right people. Lieutenant Cornwallis-West was promoted to the rank of captain and appointed aide-de-camp to Lord Methuen, scheduled to accompany his commanding officer to South Africa. In 1899, the newly promoted Captain Cornwallis-West left for South Africa on the outbreak of the Boer War. At the same time both Lady Churchill's sons were also off to South Africa — Winston as war correspondent for the *Morning Post* while Jack was going there to fight.

※

Lady Randolph Churchill threw herself enthusiastically into raising funds to equip a converted ocean liner, called *The Maine*, as a hospital ship. It was to sail to South Africa and care for the wounded. She threw herself into fund-raising with her usual energy. The necessary money was raised and the former passenger liner was fitted with berths for 300 wounded man, an operating theatre and on board had four doctors, five nurses and a seagoing crew. Jennie set off for Durban on 23 December 1899.

The Prince of Wales was very proud of Lady Churchill. She acted as a volunteer nurse and organiser of concerts on board ship, intending to raise staff morale. The Prince wrote Jennie a letter, congratulating her on her wartime work and her courage.

A few weeks later, Jennie received a cable saying George was ill and being shipped back to England. He was annoyed to find he was returning to England while Jennie was on her way to South Africa aboard the hospital ship she had helped to fund. This left Jennie in a tricky position. She could scarcely back out of the project when the country was in a fervour of patriotism. Her worries increased when she learned that Winston had been captured by the Boers.

In January 1900, Jennie arrived at Durban and learned that Winston had made a dramatic escape and become a war hero after writing up his adventures in the press. Jack Churchill had been wounded during the relief of Ladysmith. When Jack came on board the hospital ship, Jennie saw her son's wounds were properly treated and could soon return to active service.

Jennie made a journey into the interior to see Winston. She passed the burned-out train wreck from which Winston had made a dramatic escape a few weeks earlier.

Eventually Jennie returned to Britain aboard the *Maine*. After their six month's separation George was still desperate to marry Jennie, but she was beginning to waver. However young George managed to persuade Jennie he loved her so much they *must* marry.

Against bitter opposition from George's parents and his siblings, Jennie married her young lover on 28 July 1900 in a quiet wedding at St Paul's Church, Knightsbridge, wearing a pale blue dress. As Mrs Cornwallis-West, Jennie left the wedding ceremony under an arch of crossed swords held by George's brother officers. None of George's family were present, a similar situation as at her first wedding in Paris.

The Prince of Wales was away on a royal tour so could not attend Jennie's second wedding. However, he called on her before she went on honeymoon to give her a belated wedding present. He kissed Jennie and congratulated her, although privately he believed that the marriage was crazy and bound to end in tears.

Jennie's second marriage was troubled by the couple's lack of money. George's family were so upset they refused to give Jennie heirloom jewels that should have gone to George's wife. The couple could not afford to buy anywhere to live and rented a large house in the country where George pursued several money-making schemes that failed.

Jennie was 50 and had lines around her eyes, grey streaks in her hair and had gained weight. George looked younger than his 30 years. After a few years of marriage Jennie was dismayed to find her husband calling her 'dear old pussy cat' rather than 'darling'. This did not please Jennie, who was accustomed to being the most beautiful woman in the room.

Jennie's friendship with the Prince of Wales obtained various opportunities of employment for her husband. Bertie was still very fond of Jennie, even though she annoyed him by chiding him over taking Alice Keppel — who was almost young enough to be his daughter — as his mistress. Perhaps she said this in return for Bertie telling her that George was young enough to be her son.

Winston had been forced to abandon the idea of going to university as Jennie had already spent the money left in Lord Randolph's will for his sons' education. Jennie, aware that her elder son had a talent for public speaking and debating, aided his education as well as she could. She advised Winston what books he should read in an intensive reading course of English literature and history. With his mother's help Winston did become an excellent writer.

It was at this time that Jennie started to write her memoir, *The Remniscences of Lady Randolph Churchill*, on which she hoped to make money, but the memoir conceals as much as it reveals.[27]

While married to George, Jennie had her portrait painted by Emil Fuchs, a Viennese artist and sculptor working in London. Fuchs had been commissioned to design a medal commemorating the coronation of King Edward VII. The artist found Jennie fascinating and painted a superb portrait, describing Lady Jennie Churchill as,

> ...striking and distinguished in appearance with black hair and piercing dark eyes [Lady Churchill] had remarkable feminine

charm... She had dimples in her cheeks when she laughed and one in her chin.[28].

Jennie became determined that Winston must achieve an even higher post in government than his father. She wrote to former lovers, including the Prince of Wales, asking them to help Winston achieve his aims. Bertie explained to his *'chere amie'* that, in his position, he could not take sides in party politics, but wished Winston luck in the forthcoming Odham election.

Winston Churchill was elected, largely thanks to his mother's support and her highly professional campaigning on his behalf. It was thanks to his mother that Winston acquired an unshakeable faith in his own destiny.

※

Queen Victoria died on 22 January 1901. Bertie succeeded to the throne as Edward VII, unwilling to take his dead father's name.

Jennie received an amusing letter from Winston, wondering if being King would revolutionise Bertie's way of life. Would the new King `sell his horses and scatter his Jews' (a dig at wealthy Sir Ernest Cassel, Reuben Sassoon and the Rothschilds). `Will he continue to be friendly to you? Will "la Keppel" be appointed First Lady of the Bedchamber?'

As one of the King's favourites, Jennie received an official invitation to attend the coronation, seated with other mistresses in a special reserved area in Westminster Abbey. Naturally, Jennie accepted the invitation. She looked magnificent, wearing one of the Marlborough family tiaras, and coronation robes trimmed with ermine. She sat beside her younger sister, Leonie Leslie, who was by now the secret mistress of the King's younger brother, the Duke of Connaught. Jennie's friend, Daisy, Countess of Warwick, who was wearing the Warwick diamonds, sat beside her husband in the main part of the Abbey.

Winston, who normally chose to ignore gossip about his mother's lovers found it amusing that Jennie was seated with the new King's *inamoratas:* Alice Keppel, Sarah Bernhardt, the former

Duchess di Carioccolo, Lillie Langtry and many others in what some courtiers humorously termed 'The King's Loose Box'.

In recognition of Jennie's work in raising funds for a hospital ship in wartime, the newly-crowned King invested her with the Order of the Royal Red Cross and made her a Lady of Grace of St John of Jerusalem.

In May 1907, Jennie gave a large house party with King Edward VII and his current mistress, Mrs Alice Keppel, on the glittering guest list. By now, Edward VII had become so stout that he could no longer manage to climb the stairs and he and Alice Keppel were given ground floor rooms.

Jennie was working hard as editor of her own literary magazine, *The Anglo-Saxon Review*, a beautiful transatlantic journal which was expensive to produce. In fact, it was too expensive for the market and folded after only ten issues.

In September 1908, young Winston pleased his mother when he married a beautiful, sensible, but penniless young lady called Clementine Hozier. The wedding took place at St Margaret's, Westminster. Clementine (Clemmie) was the daughter of Jennie's friend, the divorced Lady Blanche Hozier, but Clementine did not know the name of her father, as her mother had had many lovers. Clemmie was the god-daughter of Leonie's husband, Jack Leslie. Jennie was delighted by this genuine love match, saying, 'Winston is not easy. He is very difficult indeed and she (Clemmie) is just right'.[29]

As the reign of Edward VII drew to a close, Jennie's marriage to George Cornwallis-West was foundering. George was often away hunting or shooting grouse with male cronies. Jennie had time on her hands, and kept busy by writing a play called *His Borrowed Plumes*. The plot concerned a lady who lost her husband to a younger woman. This was ironic as it was what was about to happen to Jennie.

For the leading role, Jennie had chosen an attractive actress, a Boer War widow, Mrs Pat Campbell. Jennie was so busy organising a huge gala premiere she failed to spot that George was spending his afternoons at her leading lady's London house. The actress's dalliances with Jennie's husband led to the break up of Jennie's marriage. Bertie had been right when he warned her that the age difference between her and George was too great for any marriage to survive.

Jennie showed generosity of spirit when she wrote to her disapproving mother-in-law, Mrs Patsy Cornwallis-West, saying that George was free to marry Mrs Patrick Campbell or anyone else he liked. She bore no grudges against him and hoped they could be friends. She reverted to her former name of Lady Randolph Churchill by deed poll and obtained a divorce from George in 1914, two years after their separation.

Once again Lady Randolph was tireless in her charity work, renovating houses to bring in money and playing the piano at the houses of friends or at charity concerts.

King Edward VII died in May 1910. In her letter of condolence to Queen Alexandra, Jennie expressed her view that the late Edward VII had been a great King and a loveable man. She also had some sympathy for the lady she had criticised, Alice Keppel, the King's final mistress. Knowing that this was a sad time for Mrs Keppel, Jennie called to pay her respects in person, something many members of London society did not do.

The pleasure-loving Bertie was succeeded by his prudish son George V and the equally straight-laced Queen Mary. Mistresses were now out of favour at Buckingham Palace.

LADY RANDOLPH CHURCHILL'S LAST LOVE

Jennie had to deal with Winston's disgrace over the failed Dardanelles campaign and the slaughter of thousands of Anzacs at Gallipoli. Appointed First Lord of the Admiralty in 1911, he had taken on an enormous work load. His badly executed plan, to attack Constantinople via landings of Anzac and British forces on beaches below Gallipoli's steep cliffs, would haunt him for the rest of his life. As a result Winston was removed from office. He was given a ministerial post without portfolio as Chancellor the Duchy of Lancaster.

Denied entry to the War Cabinet Winston resigned and, like

Jack, now a major in the Hussars, enlisted as major in the Oxfordshire Yeomanry and left for France. Winston's mother still believed he had it in him to do great things. Jennie, who derived comfort from painting as well as writing and music, encouraged Winston to paint as a way to ward off the depression that dogged him.

Jennie raised funds for the American Women's War Relief Fund and chaired its Executive Committee. The fund provided motorised ambulances and female drivers for the front. They also provided famine relief for Belgians whose homes had been torched by the invading Germans and orphanages and clothing for the many homeless Belgian children. Her sister Leonie Leslie ran a camp in Ireland for Belgian refugees whose homes and livelihoods had been destroyed by the Germans.

Lady Randolph Churchill found love again at the age of 54 when she met a young colonial officer on leave from Nigeria. Montagu Porch, known as Porchy, looked distinguished and adored Jennie. He was slightly younger than George Cornwallis-West, but was more mature than Jennie's ex-husband.

At their 1918 wedding Jennie was described as blooming again, looking attractive and younger than her years. She bought a small house in London and continued to improve and decorate houses and re-sell them at a profit. Her new husband realised that Jennie was extravagant and nothing would change her. Porchy felt their best chance of a happy marriage was for him to return to Nigeria and establish himself in an import-export business to pay the mortgage on Jennie's house and her debts. Once this was accomplished he would return to London and live there with Jennie as he could not see her living happily in Africa, away from her family and friends.

Jeanie was happy with the idea of living with Porchy after his return from Nigeria. She took a holiday and went to stay with a titled female friend in Rome. Being Jennie, she went shopping for beautiful clothes, elegant shoes, bibelots and antiques which she arranged to be shipped back to London.

Back home, she paid a visit to Lady Francis Horner in Somerset. Wearing a new pair of Italian high-heeled shoes, Jennie rushed down the stairs to avoid being late for dinner, slipped and fell, breaking several bones. After the doctor had examined her leg she returned to London by ambulance. Initially her condition did not seem serious, but two weeks later gangrene set in. At that time there were no antibiotics to stop infection and Jennie's leg had to be amputated above the knee. Porchy, who was still in Africa, sent loving telegrams and her sisters arrived to be with her.

On 29 June, an artery above the amputation haemorrhaged, Jennie fainted and never regained consciousness. Winston came rushing around in his pyjamas but was too late — his adored mother was dead. The news made headlines in the London press.

Lady Randolph was buried at Bladon beside Randolph on 2 July 1921, her grave lined with the flowers she had loved — white roses and pale mauve orchids. A memorial service was held for Lady Churchill in Westminster Abbey.

Jennie had died intestate with a mountain of debts. She never saw the son — whose future she was certain would be brilliant — become the Prime Minister who saved Britain in its darkest hour in World War Two.

Jennie Churchill had been right to believe in Winston's genius. His words would inspire British families to face Nazi bombs and the miseries of food rationing. Jennie Jerome became a legend as the mother of Winston — arguably Britain's greatest Prime Minister.

Coat of Arms of
Edward, Prince of Wales
(later Edward VII)

The Jerome Mansion, Madison Avenue, New York, Jennie's childhood home.

Lady Jennie Churchill

Lord Randolph Churchill

Blenheim Palace, ancestral home of the Dukes of Marlborough and birthplace of Winston Churchill.

Lady Randolph Churchill with her sons Jack and Winston (right).

During the Boer War, the American Ladies' Hospital Ship Society, led by the widowed Jennie Churchill, used a converted liner, the *S.S. Maine*, to bring wounded British soldiers from Durban back to Britain.

Wearing the uniform of a nurse, Jennie Churchill beside her wounded son Jack on the hospital ship *S.S. Maine*. He had been shot through the leg but recovered.

Pre-wedding portrait of Lady Churchill at the age of sixty-four. The inset shows her third and much younger husband, Montagu Phippen Porch.

In 1895 at the age of 21, Winston Churchill was commissioned as a lieutenant in the 4th (Queen's Own) Hussars and presented a photo in uniform to his mother.

CHAPTER 5

Lady Frances 'Daisy' Brooke (née Maynard) later Countess of Warwick (1861–1938) and Albert Edward (Bertie), Prince of Wales, later Edward VII

'Daisy Brooke... the loveliest woman in England, of high rank, ample riches and great intelligence.'
Elinor Glynn, novelist and neighbour of Lady Daisy in rural Essex.

BRITAIN'S WEALTHIEST HEIRESS

Frances Evelyn 'Daisy' Maynard, was born in Mayfair's Berkeley Square, an elegant part of central London. After her father died, her mother, Blanche Fitzroy Maynard, took the adorable three year old to visit her elderly grandfather, Viscount Maynard, at his country estate near Dunmow in Essex. From an early age Daisy was a natural coquette. Her grandfather was charmed by little Daisy when she climbed on his lap and put her arms around his neck. Within a few days, the elderly Viscount Maynard became so fond of his little granddaughter that he altered his will, leaving her his vast estates and all his possession.

Viscount Maynard died only a few months after changing his will. When family members assembled for the reading of the will they were enraged to learn that they received nothing. It was little Daisy who would inherit the Maynard millions, a country estate in Essex, farmland in Leicestershire and a collection of Old Master paintings.

It took time for Viscount Maynard's will to be probated but at the age of four Daisy Maynard became England's wealthiest heiress. Lacking a father, the little girl was made a ward in chancery so her large inheritance was under the control of the Lord Chancellor's office. Daisy was unable to touch her fortune until she came of age at twenty-one.

After spending two years in mourning, Daisy's mother married again. Her second husband, the Earl of Rosslyn, was a member of the Royal Household, so Daisy became accustomed to visiting Windsor Castle and meeting the widowed Queen and her family.

Lady Rosslyn ensured her clever daughter had an excellent governess who taught her to speak fluent German and French and gave her a thorough grounding in literature, geography and history. In her teens, Daisy became a fearless horsewomen, enjoying the thrill of jumping fences and taking risks on the hunting field. She was one of the first young women to take up the new sport of bicycling, believing it brought new freedom to women.

At eighteen, the Hon Daisy Maynard was a poised intelligent young lady, deemed to be ready for marriage. Her coming-out ball was an important event, attended by members of the royal family, including the Prince and Princess of Wales and Prince Leopold, Queen Victoria's favourite son. Prince Leopold was dazzled by Daisy Maynard with her shapely figure, deep blue eyes. creamy complexion and lively personality. Unfortunately, like two of his deceased younger brothers, Prince Leopold suffered from haemophilia and had to be extremely careful and abstain from sporting or strenuous activities. Should the young Prince cut himself he would bleed to death.

In 1880, encouraged by Queen Victoria and Prime Minister Disraeli, Prince Leopold invited Daisy to a weekend house party at his country residence. Young Lord Francis Greville Brooke, heir to the Earl of Warwick, was one of the Prince's guests'. Daisy was introduced to the athletic Francis Brooke and after only a brief acquaintance fell in love with him.

Lord Francis was fascinated by the stunningly beautiful young woman and he asked her to marry him. Daisy, only seventeen and straight out of the schoolroom, scarcely knew the pleasant young man everyone called 'Brookie'. Nevertheless, she accepted his proposal of marriage.

The next day, the ailing Prince Leopold also made advances to Daisy and plucked up courage to ask her to marry him. Daisy declined and politely explained she had already accepted a proposal of marriage from his friend, Lord Francis Brooke.

Lady Rosslyn was mortified to learn that her daughter had rejected a proposal from royalty in favour of a young man who had done little other than shoot grouse and stalk deer.

The Earl of Warwick, Brookie's father, owned Warwick Castle, a historic edifice in need of a great deal of money to restore it to its former glory. Lady Rosslyn feared Daisy's fortune would be spent on maintaining this crumbling castle.

Brookie was *genuinely* in love with Daisy, dazzled by her good looks, boundless energy and high spirits but was a tongue-tied suitor. He confessed in a letter to Daisy that, like most Englishman, he was bad at expressing his feelings.

Lady Rosslyn did not want this match to go ahead and refused to let her daughter receive any more letters from Lord Brooke. She hoped that Daisy might change her mind and agree to marry Prince Leopold if she stopped hearing from Lord Brooke.

Absence often makes the heart grow fonder. Daisy felt she loved Brookie more every day and was desolate that her mother banned her from seeing him.[1] Daisy, ever the romantic, was in love with the *idea* of love. She invested Brookie, who was pleasant but neither handsome nor very clever, with romantic qualities he did not possess. Ultimately she was bound to be disappointed.

Eventually, Daisy wore down her mother's opposition to the match. Her engagement to Lord Francis Brooke was announced at a ball at Grosvenor House in June 1880. However, Lady Rosslyn insisted her daughter wait a year before marrying Lord Brooke.

Lord Rosslyn, Daisy's stepfather, wrote to Prime Minister Disraeli claiming that he approved of Lord Brooke as a 'steady and domestic young man, who gives promise of making a true and loving husband'.[2]

Unfortunately, 'steady and domestic' were not the qualities Daisy was looking for. She wanted a husband who would sweep her off her feet, enchant her with poems praising her beauty before making passionate love. She did not want him to discuss the finer points of fly fishing and shooting grouse, his pet topics.

During prolonged negotiations over the marriage settlement it was agreed that the bridal pair would take over Easton Lodge and Lord and Lady Rosslyn and their children would move out.

In the 1880s, before the passing of the Married Women's Property Act, a husband automatically assumed control of his wife's dowry as well as any property she had inherited. In Daisy's case, lawyers acting for Lady Rosslyn, ensured that her wealthy daughter retained control of a large portion of the Maynard millions. Should Daisy die without heirs, the entire estate and fortune would revert to Lady Rosslyn or *her* heirs rather than to Lord Brooke. This clause in the pre-wedding agreement did not please the Earl of Warwick. He had hoped that his son would control the Maynard fortune in its entirety.

Her unusual marriage settlement left Daisy in control of her own fortune once she reached the age of 21 and ceased being a ward of the Lord Chancellor. The fact that Daisy would eventually control her own fortune gave her unusual power and freedom in an era when wives were subservient to their husbands. Strong-willed Lady Daisy Brooke, when she came of age would have the upper hand in this marriage.

Queen Victoria, in perpetual mourning for Prince Albert, had been invited to the wedding but declined to attend. She asked

Lord Brooke and his wife-to-be to Windsor Castle. Daisy was instructed to bring her wedding dress with her so the Queen could see it. By now Queen Victoria realised that Daisy would not have been the right wife for the sickly Prince Leopold and was planning his marriage to a German princess.

While Queen Victoria adored clever young Prince Leopold, she disliked and distrusted her eldest son, the wayward Albert Edward (Bertie), Prince of Wales, but felt sorry for Bertie's wife, Princess Alexandra. Bertie had been made to marry the sweet-natured Danish princess in order to end what his prudish parents regarded as a scandalous liaison with a young actress called Nellie Clifden. He was fond of Princess Alexandra but was no longer in love with her. The Prince of Wales had been given no responsibilities by Queen Victoria. He devoted his life to shooting game, eating huge meals and having affairs with bored aristocratic wives or bedding expensive courtesans and prostitutes.

***

On 30 April 1881, the cream of British society, including the Prince and Princess of Wales, were at Westminster Abbey to see England's wealthiest heiress marry Lord Francis Greville Brooke, whose title dated to the days of the Wars of the Roses. The 18-year-old bride wore her Paris-made trousseau and the Warwick diamonds. Daisy was thrilled to have her portrait in the society magazines.

The newly-weds honeymooned in a house on the River Thames loaned them as a wedding present by the Duke of Buccleuch. Daisy had hoped Brookie would take her to Italy on their honeymoon and show her the wonders of Italian architecture, but he preferred to teach his new wife the art of fly fishing. Daisy found fishing extremely boring and soon gave up.

In 1882, Daisy bore her husband a male heir who they named Leopold Guy and would always be called by his second name. Daisy, young and carefree, employed a nursemaid and a nanny to look after her son and was soon back in the saddle, jumping fences with reckless abandon.

By now, Brookie had entered Parliament. When not sitting in the House of Commons he was shooting grouse and stalking deer, pastimes Daisy disliked. Brookie liked going on African safaris, bagging lions, elephants and zebra, which took him away from Easton Lodge for long periods. But Daisy had had enough. She declined invitations to shooting parties, leaving Brookie to go by himself and developed interests of her own and entertained her own friends.

Daisy was an avid reader and a keen gardener. She created a walled garden at Easton Lodge in which there was a specimen of every plant mentioned in the plays and sonnets of Shakespeare.

The marriage of Lady Brooke and her husband drifted apart with surprising speed. They had not known each other well before their wedding and soon discovered they had few shared interests. It is impossible to tell if there were sexual problems in their relationship as nothing about the intimate side of their marriage was put in writing by either spouse.

By the mid 1880s, Lord and Lady Brooke were leading separate lives but had no intention of suffering the public disgrace of a divorce.

In 1884, the ailing Prince Leopold died as a result of haemophilia, known as the 'royal disease', passed on by Victoria's children to several European royal families.

THE 'GAME OF LOVE' AT EASTON LODGE

Daisy was a great flirt as well as a passionate romantic. In her memoirs, *My Life's Ebb and Flow*, she explained gaily 'My husband seemed to accept the inevitability of my having a train of admirers, I could not help it. It was all a great game'.[3]

It was understood in the aristocrat circles in which Daisy moved that after producing a male heir the wife could take a lover, provided she was discreet about it. Bed-hopping amongst aristocrats took place all the time at country house parties with the Prince of Wales as the chief bed-hopper. However, double standards prevailed. Aristocrats could do as they pleased as long as they were not involved in a divorce, but housemaids were sacked on the spot if caught *in flagrante* with a guest, a member of the male staff or even the son of the house.

While her husband was away shooting various animals, Daisy entertained her own circle of friends at Easton Lodge. She gave large house parties, which were attended by people she found interesting in the world of the arts and in politics. Well-known names in Lady Brooke's visitors' book included various Cabinet Ministers, Lord Randolph Churchill and his American wife, Jennie, as well as famous writers and the occasional artist.

Among her guests were handsome men of action including Lord Charles Beresford, a hero decorated for his bravery in rescuing General Gordon from Khartoum. He was accompanied by his plain but wealthy wife, Lady Minna Beresford. Tall, muscular and amusing, Lord Charles came from a cash-strapped aristocratic Anglo-Irish family. He had married the well-connected Lady Minna for her money when he was an impecunious naval lieutenant. Later, his wife's money would help him to rise to the rank of Admiral.

Daisy was head over heels in love with the handsome and charismatic Lord Charles Beresford. Lady Minna was jealous of the way her husband looked at the beautiful Lady Brooke and made certain they did not attend any more of Daisy's parties. However, Lord Charles Beresford and Lady Brooke contrived to meet at house parties in stately homes owned by mutual friends and they became lovers.

Whenever Lord Charles returned from a long sea voyage, the couple would meet at Easton Lodge or another grand country house. At night Daisy would leave the door of her bedroom unlocked waiting for Lord Charles to join her once the other guests were asleep.

One night, Lord Charles threw open the door crying 'Cock a doodle doo' and with a large erection jumped onto the bed. There was a cry of alarm — then the lights came on. Lord Charles found himself in bed with the wife of the Bishop of Chester, with the angry Bishop beside her.

An embarrassed Lord Charles left the house the next morning before breakfast so he did not have to face the Bishop and his wife.

Daisy's first child, Guy, was her husband's son, but her second child, little Marjorie, (known as Queenie), born in October 1884, had been fathered by Lord Charles. Brookie raised Marjorie and loved her, unaware that her father was Lord Charles Beresford.[4]

In addition to producing a male heir in the first four years of her marriage, Daisy bore a child each subsequent year. Marjorie thrived but a second son named Charles (probably after his birth father) died in infancy. Little Charles was also fathered by Lord Charles Beresford.

Daisy, who adored Lord Charles Beresford, mistook his lust for love and foolishly believed he would leave his wife to marry her. Her passion was such she was prepared to let Brookie divorce her if her lover would obtain a divorce and marry her. She liked the idea that little Marjorie would be raised by her birth father.

However, Lord Charles had no intention of divorcing his wife and becoming involved in a scandal which would wreck his career. In a moment of passion he may have told Daisy he loved her, but as Lady Beresford had supported him faithfully he had no intention of deserting her and marrying Daisy Brooke.

Although Lord Charles found Daisy a passionate and intellectually stimulating mistress and was gratified that such a beautiful woman loved him, he remained married to Lady Minna. But Daisy did not give up that easily.

Lady Minna was childless and Daisy may have thought that her lover's wife was past childbearing age. At Christmas 1887, Daisy was furious to hear that Lady Minna was pregnant. Carried away by jealousy, she wrote an angry letter to Lord Charles, reminding him of his promise not to have sex with *anyone* else, pointing out that Marjorie had been fathered by him. Daisy insisted that Lord Charles cease sexual relations with his wife and be faithful to her as she had been faithful to him, which implied that she had not had sex with Brookie for some years.

When Lord Charles went away to sea he had asked his wife to open his mail. The pregnant Lady Minna read Daisy's letter and was incandescent with rage to read that Lady Brooke had born her husband's child.

Lady Minna Beresford sent Daisy's highly compromising letter to George Lewis, the most feared lawyer in London, who specialised in high profile divorces. Minna instructed the solicitor to contact Lady Brooke and tell her she must withdraw from London society for at least a year and refrain from meeting or contacting her husband. If Lady Brooke did not comply the lawyer was to send Lady Brooke's compromising letter to Lord Brooke.

The request was relayed by George Lewis to Lady Brooke with the demand she desist from harassing his client's husband, otherwise a copy of her letter would be sent to the editor of *The Times*. This threat scared Daisy, aware the press would love this salacious story which would ruin her reputation.

Daisy was now in a very tricky situation indeed. As Brookie and Lord Beresford were friends of the Prince of Wales, Daisy hoped that the Prince could help her. She knew from pillow talk with Lord Charles that the Prince of Wales had been involved in the divorce cases of several angry husbands — surely he would know how to solve her problem. The Prince could put pressure on Lady Minna's lawyer so the compromising letter (which she now regretted having written) could be returned to her. Daisy requested a meeting with the Prince of Wales at Marlborough House.

Wearing her most alluring ensemble Daisy smiled at Bertie under downcast lashes, admitted that she had been foolish and asked for his help in getting the divorce lawyer to return her letter. Daisy described how the Prince responded.

> ...I saw him looking at me in a way all women understand. He hoped his friendship would make up for my sailor lover's loss. I knew I had won so asked him to tea.[5]

Bertie, his hopes aroused by Daisy's flirtatious manner, accepted the invitation to visit her at her home. He agreed to do his best to retrieve Daisy's compromising letter.

Following his visit to Easton Lodge, the Prince of Wales paid a personal visit to the home of Lady Minna's solicitor to avoid gossip that he had been seen visiting the office of a famous divorce lawyer. He was extremely annoyed when the lawyer refused to hand over Lady Brooke's offending letter.

As Lady Daisy's champion, the Prince next visited Lady Minna in her London home at Eaton Square and asked her to withdraw any legal action against Lady Brooke. His Royal Highness promised Lady Minna Beresford on his honour that Lady Daisy Brooke would never trouble her or her husband again, hoping Lady Brooke would become *his* mistress. But Lady Minna refused to comply with Bertie's polite request.

Lord Charles was summoned home by his distraught wife, who was furious with his friend for interfering in his personal affairs. When Lord Charles met the Prince of Wales at a social function, he threatened to expose what he knew of the Prince's love life to the press. The two almost came to blows and had to be separated by shocked guests. In revenge the Prince of Wales did what he had done with the Churchills and declared the Beresfords *persona non grata*, in society.

As Prime Minister, Lord Salisbury intervened to prevent scandal and the Prince and Lord Charles agreed to bury the hatchet but their years of close friendship were over.

※

The Prince of Wales' attempts to head off what could have been a scandalous divorce brought him and Lady Daisy closer. The Prince of Wales expected Lady Brooke to show her gratitude in the traditional way. Bertie was offered more than tea and cake the next time he paid a visit to Easton Lodge. Daisy had created a romantic 'Garden of Love' where secret trysts between lovers took place — now the Prince of Wales became one of her lovers.

From that time onwards, the Prince became a regular visitor to Daisy's lavish house parties. Entertaining the Prince of Wales was seen as the acme of social success. Daisy threw herself into her new role and spent lavishly on entertaining her royal lover. She never gave a thought to how much it cost, having always taken her inherited fortune for granted.

The novelist Elinor Glyn, still a regular guest at Easton Lodge, described Daisy as 'the loveliest woman in England, of high rank, ample riches and great intelligence. Her immense prestige made every invitation to Easton Lodge a great honour.'[6]

A weekend party at Easton Lodge meant 20 or more guests arrived around four pm on a Saturday. Many guests brought their personal maids and valets, who would be accommodated in the servants' hall. Guests were greeted by the major domo who was in control. Footmen carried the luggage of guests to the appropriate room, each of which had a name card on the door so assignations could be arranged. Rarely did married couples share a room.

Lady Brooke would greet her guest at an elaborate high tea, set out on a large round table. There were muffins, crumpets, sandwiches, scones with jam and cream. The Prince of Wales was known for his prodigious appetite and consumed large meals throughout the day. Naturally Princess Alexandra never attended these house parties and spent more and more time with her parents and her sisters in Denmark.

Female guests wore exquisite ankle-length gowns of velvet, silk or lace. Each of the male guests would cast an eye around the room and decide which lady interested them and make himself agreeable to her. No introductions were made by the hostess. In aristocratic circles it was assumed they all knew each other already or would be informally introduced by other guests.

Once tea was over, the ladies retired upstairs to dress in formal attire for dinner and their maids were kept busy fastening corsets and styling the ladies' hair. Daisy's little son Guy would arrive at their rooms with a spray of gardenias or orchids from the greenhouses. Serious overtures were made at dinner.

The Prince had his own suite near that of Daisy. There was a great deal of corridor creeping in the night. In the morning a gong was rung so guests could return to their own rooms before the ladies' maids and valets arrived to attend to their employers' needs.

***

As well as entertaining guests at Easton Lodge, a few years earlier Daisy had purchased a beautiful Mediterranean villa on the French Riviera at Beaulieu (French for 'beautiful place'). This picturesque fishing harbour was situated between Nice and Monte Carlo and had an international flavour. Russian Grand Dukes and British aristocrats escaped Europe's chilly winters at Beaulieu. Brookie rarely visited his wife's Mediterranean villa. While her husband was on safari, Daisy invited the Prince of Wales to stay and in these romantic surroundings their affair blossomed.

Daisy was now 29 and at the height of her beauty. She found the Prince of Wales, twenty years older than herself, charming and was flattered by his attentions. She was less discreet than her friend, Lady Jennie Churchill, who never admitted that the Prince of Wales had been her lover. Many years later Daisy Brooke revealed to her son-in-law that the heir to the throne was

> ...a very perfect, gentle lover. He had good manners and was very considerate... I think *anyone* would have been won over by him.

Although Daisy found Bertie boring when he discoursed at length on grouse shooting, she enjoyed the social cachet of being his mistress *en titre*.

For his part the middle-aged Prince of Wales was besotted with Lady Brooke, his latest conquest. On his return from a romantic holiday at her villa at Beaulieu he wrote Daisy Brooke a series of passionate letters, calling her 'My own Daisy darling wife.' He gave her a gold ring, originally donated to him by his mother and father, with the inscription 'To Bertie from his affectionate parents A. & V.R. (Albert & Victoria Regina)' dated July 1860.

Daisy enjoyed boasting about her new relationship. To her closest female friends she spoke frankly about her royal lover and described the Prince of Wales as very good in bed. What she did not know was that the Prince had been taught by experts, included the courtesan Catherine Walters to whom he paid a annual retainer for her sexual services. Another of the Prince's costly courtesans was Cora Pearl, reputed to have the most beautiful breasts in Paris.

One incident involving the Prince of Wales nearly lost him the throne. The event took place in 1890, shortly after the drama with Lady Minna Beresford and became famous as the Tranby Croft affair. It began at a country house party where baccarat (at the time an illegal game in England) was played for high stakes among members of the Prince's Marlborough House set. The house party was held at a country mansion in the north of England called Tranby Croft and the host was Sir Arthur Wilson, a wealthy ship owner.

The Prince and a group of his friends were house guests at Tranby Croft for the 1890 Doncaster Races. Lord and Lady Brooke had also been invited, but they had to cancel their visit to Tranby Croft at the last minute. Daisy's step-father, Lord Rosslyn, had died unexpectedly and the Brookes had to go to Scotland for his funeral. They arranged to dine with the Prince of Wales in York on their way back from Scotland.

Over dinner, Bertie told the Brookes about an unfortunate incident that had taken place at the Tranby Croft house party. Sir William Gordon-Cummings of the Scots Guards had been accused of cheating at baccarat. The Prince of Wales and five of his friends had signed a statement to the effect that they had seen Sir William cheating and insisted he must never play for money again. Sir William agreed as long as they swore to keep the incident secret.

A few days later the story was reported in the press, which was very serious as playing baccarat was against the law. It was Daisy who had told her friends the secret and one of them had talked to the press who printed the story.

Sir William Gordon-Cummings was furious and sued for slander. The Prince of Wales was forced to appear as a witness in the court case which took place in June, 1891. His Royal Highness was censured in the press and by Sir Edward Clarke, the Solicitor-General for taking part in an illegal gambling session. The scandal cast a murky shadow on the Prince of Wales and the circles in which he moved.

Queen Victoria, who had read about her son's illegal gambling activities in the press, summoned him to Windsor Castle. She gave him a severe reprimand, threatening to disinherit him in favour of one of his younger brothers should Bertie be involved in any more scandals.

As a result Princess Alexandra never forgave Daisy Brooke for disclosing the Tranby Croft affair and the illegal baccarat game, as her husband nearly lost his right to inherit the throne and her children would also have been disinherited.

Daisy Brooke was named 'Babbling Brooke' in an anonymous pamphlet, titled *Lady River*. The pamphlet found its way into society drawing rooms and specifically named Daisy Brooke as the Prince of Wales' replacement for his previous high profile mistress, Mrs Lillie Langtry.

Lady River contained an extract from Daisy's foolish letter sent to her lover, Lord Charles and intercepted by Lady Beresford. For weeks this scandalous pamphlet was the talk of the town.

Rumours circulated that Lord Brooke was very angry about his wife's affairs and might seek a divorce. But this did not happen. Somehow Daisy managed to keep her hold over her husband. She continued her affair with the Prince of Wales while staying on reasonably good terms with her husband.

Eventually, the secret leaked out as to who *were* the authors of the malicious pamphlet — Mrs Gerald Paget and her sister, Lady Minna Beresford. The ladies had taken their revenge on Lady Brooke for the unhappiness her foolish actions had brought to Lady Beresford.

Princess Alexandra had read a copy of *Lady River* which referred to Daisy as the 'Babbling Brooke'. From now on the Princess of Wales referred to Daisy by this name and refused to be in the same room with her.

In 1899, Brookie succeeded his father and became Earl of Warwick. He inherited the upkeep of Warwick Castle and a pile of debts. Daisy's fortune was used to make Warwick Castle more comfortable so they could entertain there on the grand scale, but the couple's main residence remained Easton Lodge. Daisy had paid Harold Peto to redesign the gardens at Easton Lodge, which now included a Japanese water garden and an Italian Renaissance-style garden.

At Warwick Castle, Daisy paid for a generator to be installed in a disused corn mill in the castle grounds to supply it with electricity so that lighting and central heating could be fitted in the bedrooms. She installed bathrooms and toilets and paid for a special suite with a painted ceiling for her lover, the Prince of

Wales. She also paid for the construction of a private railway station on the London line near Warwick Castle so the Prince of Wales could visit her more easily.

Bertie enjoyed occupying the luxurious suite next to that of his 'darling Daisy-wife', the term he used in his amorous letters to her. Brookie had a smaller suite in another part of the castle. Daisy's boudoir, decorated in her favourite colour blue, was used for amorous assignations with the Prince of Wales.

In the Great Dining Hall at Warwick Castle, Daisy hosted a series of magnificent banquets with the Prince of Wales beside her as guest of honour. Distinguished guests were looked down on by hunting trophies, the stuffed heads of lions, cheetahs and tigers.

The Prince continued to write loving letters, many of which ended with the message 'God bless you my own adored little Daisy wife.' He signed them 'Your only love'.[7]

Daisy described in her memoirs how the Prince of Wales 'wrote me a letter twice or three times a week, telling me everything that happed to him. He expected me to write frequently.'

Both Daisy and the Prince of Wales were spending money at a great rate. Several wealthy Jewish financiers and stockbrokers loaned large sums of money to the Prince of Wales and became his financial advisors. The Rothschilds and Sir Ernest Cassel (eventually knighted by Bertie) were treated as friends and entertained at Marlborough House or at shooting parties at Sandringham. A new wing of Sandringham House was paid for with money borrowed from the Rothschilds.[8]

The Prince of Wales and Alfred Rothschild had been friends since their days at Trinity College, Cambridge. The young Alfred Rothschild became the first Jewish Director of the Bank of England. These financiers basked in the Prince of Wales' friendship, built large country houses to entertain him and his mistresses and loaned him money at a low rate of interest. Their loans made it possible for Bertie to have his new royal yacht *The Britannia* built for him. Jewish financiers gave him stock market tips and invested his money so he was able to live in great luxury and lend or give money to Lady Churchill and to the mistress who would replace Daisy Warwick, Mrs Alice Keppel.

Bertie's fascination with Daisy Warwick and her presence at his side at social events and race meetings annoyed and humiliated Princess Alexandra. She felt that Daisy Warwick flaunted her relationship with her husband. Unlike his previous mistress, Lillie Langtry, Daisy was never awed by being in royal circles. She regarded it as normal as with her stepfather, Lord Rosslyn, a member of the Royal Household, Daisy had known Queen Victoria and her family since her childhood. Princess Alexandra detested Daisy so much she did not attend her husband's fiftieth birthday celebrations because Daisy, Countess of Warwick was in attendance and was the focus of the Prince of Wales' social and emotional life.

The Prince wrote to Daisy frequently, sent her cards for Christmas and anniversaries as well as delightful presents. Daisy had learned German from her governess. Bertie, like all members of a royal family, was bi-lingual in German and English. He and Daisy would often talk in German in front of her servants so they could not understand what was being said.

Daisy enjoyed sailing on large ocean-going yachts with Bertie at Cowes, wearing a fetching white suit with a long white skirt and a straw boater hat. But Princess Alexandra resented the Countess of Warwick accompanying her husband to Cowes Week.

Daisy also attended Royal Ascot with the Prince and the St Ledger and Newmarket races. With her complacent husband in tow, she attended balls at Marlborough House. But Brookie, now the Earl of Warwick, was often away for months at a time, probably the only way he could endure this situation.

Daisy and the Prince of Wales spent time in Paris together but travelled there separately. His Royal Highness stayed at the Hotel Bristol while Daisy, observing the proprieties, stayed at an adjoining hotel and was sculpted by Rodin. She also invited the famous American artist John Singer Sergeant to come to Easton Lodge and paint her portrait — years later he did.

Bertie, who loved elegant clothes, accompanied Daisy when she visited the fashion houses of couturiers Charles Worth and

Jacques Doucet to order new ball gowns. Very daringly, they dined together in public at some of the best restaurants.

In February 1895, Daisy, Countess of Warwick, was at the height of her social power. She gave a grand fancy dress ball or *bal poudré* at Warwick Castle as a delayed celebration for the fact Brookie had inherited the title of Earl of Warwick. For her ball, the Countess of Warwick ordered special trains and imported two dozen of London's leading hairdressers to organise powdered wigs and special hairdos for her guests. She employed over a hundred temporary staff from Warwick and surrounding villages, where there was a great deal of poverty. Amid the winter snow huge torches burned outside the walls of the castle as the guests arrived.

The Great Hall was lit by over five thousand large wax candles. Gilt-edged invitations had asked guests to dress as though they were attending a ball held by Louis XIV and Marie Antoinette at Versailles. Daisy went as Queen Marie Antoinette, wearing a tall white wig and a dress of rose-pink brocade woven with gold thread. A sapphire-blue train, secured by diamond clips, fell in folds from her shoulders. Brookie was Louise XIV wearing a wig and a red velvet costume trimmed with gold lace. Daisy's eldest daughter, Lady Marjorie, and one of her friends were maids of honour dressed in white.

Mrs Alice Keppel, the young beauty who would soon replace Daisy in the affections of the Prince of Wales, was present at the ball along with hundreds of other guests. Alice wore a dress of antique brocade, a tall white wig and pink satin shoes with diamond buckles. They were not introduced. Alice was with her husband and a group of friends from Scotland and Bertie only had eyes for his hostess.

Among the guests was Joseph Laycock, who was soon to play a significant part in Daisy's life. Laycock, a confirmed bachelor, was a millionaire playboy who had considerable success with women. He attended the ball looking dark and dashing, dressed as an Indian rajah. Dancing took place in the Cedar Drawing Room, hung with family portraits, and the ball continued till dawn. Joe Laycock only had one dance with his hostess.

At midnight a buffet dinner was served by candlelight in the Great Hall where 40 tables had been set out for the guests. Gossip writers, covering the event, were dined and wined — they described Lady Warwick's embroidered and bejewelled costume in detail. In contrast a radical socialist magazine, called *The Clarion*, attacked Lady Warwick for selfishly wasting thousands of pounds on what they scathingly referred to as

> a silly masquerade, men and women strutting before each other's envious eyes. So much money has been spent on entertainment while hundreds of thousands of working men and women and gaunt and ragged children were living in grinding poverty.[9]

A NEW LIFE FOR DAISY WARWICK

Daisy, was pleased with the flattering press coverage her party received in the gossip columns. What upset her was reading harsh criticisms of her extravagance in radical socialist papers.

She visited Robert Blatchford, the editor of the socialist publication *The Clarion* at his dingy London office, trying to defend herself against charges of extravagance at a time when poverty-stricken families could not afford to put food on the table.

The Countess of Warwick, wearing an expensive costume by Charles Worth of Paris and a mink stole claimed to the radical young editor that by holding a ball in her castle and employing temporary staff she was giving work to those who needed it. Indignantly she pointed out that she had established a school for needlework on her estate to provide work for local village girls. They earned money making costumes for her fancy dress balls and embroidering lingerie for her friends. She was also a trustee of the Warwick workhouse and donated funds for its upkeep.

Robert Blatchford asked Lady Warwick to sit down. He explained the differences between productive and unproductive labour and talked to her at length about Socialist economic and political theory.

Later at a dinner party, given by Jennie Churchill's sister Clara and her husband Moreton Frewen, Daisy met the media tycoon,

William T. Stead, publisher of the influential *Review of Reviews*, and other journals. Stead owned the building in Norfolk Street where *The Clarion* had its offices and knew Robert Blatchford, but was more tactful than Blatchford.

William Stead was wealthy, high principled and influential. His father had been a clergyman in a poor parish and he was an advocate of social reforms. He published cheap versions of the classics, so working men and women could read them. He did not lecture Lady Warwick, as Blatchford had done, but instead inspired her to help the poor and under privileged in practical ways. Stead was a believer in free education for all children up to the age of sixteen.

Lady Warwick's conversation with William Stead was her catalyst to fight for free education for the poor. At that time the government did not supply free secondary education, with the result that many children of the poor were working in terrible conditions as cheap labour in factories and mines.

As a result of her admiration for Stead, whose enthusiasm she found infectious, Daisy's attitude on the responsibilities of the rich to the poor changed. She horrified many of her aristocratic friends who regarded it as natural that they should live in luxury while the poor lived in squalor, lacking access to education or any form of unemployment benefit.

As part of Daisy's conversion to Socialism, she improved the workers' cottages on the Warwick Castle estate. She also refused to let her husband's bailiff evict tenants who were unable to pay their rents. In addition, Daisy provided money for free secondary education for the children of the workers on the estate.

For years Daisy continued to correspond with William Stead and lunched with him at regular intervals. They became close friends and eventually she confided in him her intimate relationship with the Prince of Wales. She also told him that Lady Majorie was the child of Lord Charles Beresford.

Rather than being shocked, Stead, the great moral crusader, was not at all censorious. He told Daisy he hoped to have a chance to talk to the Prince about Socialist theories and educational opportunities for working-class people.

Daisy promised William Stead to arrange a meeting with the Prince of Wales. In December 1896, she invited the Prince to lunch at her London residence in South Audley Street to meet William Stead. After being lectured by Daisy, the Prince reluctantly agreed to meet the crusading media tycoon but remained unconvinced by Stead's Socialist ideas.

Bertie became resentful of Daisy's espousal of socialist theories. He claimed he found it incongruous to be lectured about helping the poor by a lady sipping French champagne from a crystal glass who had spent the annual wages of a working man on one single Paris ball gown. In fact, Daisy's political theories were still very muddled and bore no relation to her luxurious lifestyle.

It would be another ten years before Daisy joined the Socialist Party. However, she was interested in meeting Fabian Socialists, intellectuals and writers like George Bernard Shaw, Beatrice and Sydney Webb and H.G. Wells. She invited Wells, a socialist and advocate of free love, to live rent-free in a house on the Easton Lodge estate.

Daisy financed the establishment of a co-educational boarding school for disadvantaged children in rural Essex. This was a revolutionary idea as most aristocrats felt that the working-class should not get ideas above their station. She expended much time and effort on the project and discussed it with the Prince of Wales. He showed polite interest but no more.

It was Joe Laycock, the man who had looked so handsome as a mahajah at the fancy dress ball at Warwick Castle, who supported her educational scheme enthusiastically.

※

It was not long before Joe Laycock replaced the Prince of Wales as Daisy's favourite lover. Their romance flourished when he and Daisy hunted with the Quorn in the winter season of 1894–95. Daisy, reckless as always, enjoyed the thrill of a new love affair while still spending the occasional afternoon in her boudoir with the portly Prince of Wales.

Joe Laycock was a wealthy bachelor who had inherited several estates. He was younger, fitter and more attractive than the Prince of Wales and more interested in Daisy's plans for her school for the children of estate workers. At Daisy's request Joe provided three scholarships for the sons of tenants on his Durham and Nottinghamshire estates, while the Prince of Wales showed scant interest in her scheme. But after eight years of receiving passionate love letters and gifts from the Prince of Wales it was difficult to tell him she liked him as a friend but no longer wanted a sexual relationship without wounding his ego.

In the summer of 1897 the Prince of Wales's horse Persimmon won the Ascot Gold Cup. Daisy Warwick was in the Royal Enclosure elegantly dressed to congratulate the Prince on his win and celebrate with champagne.

The following day, 17 June 1897, Bertie wrote to Daisy saying he enjoyed seeing her at Ascot and was happy that she had seen his horse win. Bertie addressed his letter to 'My own lovely little Daisy'. He wrote, 'It was nice seeing just a little of you – my sweet love' and added 'Don't forget my darling to expect me from five on Sunday next'. He ended the letter, 'Goodnight and God keep you, my own adored little Daisy wife'.[10]

However, differences in their political views were starting to drive a wedge between Lady Warwick and the Prince of Wales. A further issue for conflicts was the fact that Daisy was expecting a baby and, as the date did not fit, the Prince of Wales could not have been responsible for it.

Clearly, it was Joe Laycock who had made Daisy pregnant. With Brookie away for months at a time, she had been spending weeks with Joe Laycock on his estate at Wiseton in Nottinghamshire. Once Daisy realised she was pregnant she wanted Joe to be involved with what she knew was his love-child. Only Brookie was aware of the truth and, amazingly enough, forgave her.[11]

After having a clandestine affair with Joe Laycock for three years, she decided to drop the portly middle-aged Prince for her younger and leaner lover. She wrote a tactful letter to the Prince of Wales, telling him untruthfully that she was pregnant by her husband and their affair must end. She hoped they would remain friends forever.

In his reply, Bertie showed a nice side to his character, or, maybe, he was keen to end the affair, finding Daisy's political lectures hard to take. He wrote her a very charming letter.

> How could you, my love for a moment imagine that I should withdraw my friendship from you. On the contrary, I wish to befriend you more than ever. You cannot prevent me giving you the same love as the friendship I have always felt for you. ...we have that sentimental feeling of affinity which cannot be eradicated by time.[12]

Not wishing Princess Alexandra to think she was bearing her husband's child Daisy wrote her a placatory letter. She lied and told the Princess the relationship with her husband had ended a long time ago. She expressed the hope they would remain good friends and work together on committees for charities that both of them supported.

Princess Alexandra took Daisy Warwick's conciliatory letter with a pinch of salt, aware that she was a blabbermouth who had almost cost her husband his throne. Princess Alexandra informed her eldest son, the future King George V, about Daisy Warwick. Prince George told his wife, 'If Lady Warwick asks you to become president of any charity of hers, *refuse*'.

On 29 March 1898, Daisy gave birth to a son named Maynard Greville, (Maynard being Daisy's family name). Daisy would be launched onto a roller coast ride of love and jealousy in her affair with Joe Laycock.

It was a blow to the Prince's pride when he discovered that the much younger Joe Laycock had replaced him. There were angry scenes as he suspected that little Maynard had been fathered by Laycock. In the end Bertie overcame his resentment at being replaced and insisted once more he wanted to remain friends with Daisy.

***

At the aged of 39, Daisy experienced great sadness when on his return from the Boer War Captain Laycock dropped her in favour of a married aristocrat named Kitty Downshire, who was a decade younger than Daisy and had already had a string of lovers. This time the Game of Love was Daisy's undoing.

In 1901, after the death of Queen Victoria, the Prince of Wales was crowned as King Edward VII. That same year Daisy had a brief reunion with Captain Laycock, but long enough for her to become pregnant. Joe resented her pregnancy so much that Daisy decided to have an abortion, which nearly cost her life.

In 1903, Daisy and Joe Laycock had a much longer reconciliation. Once again Daisy fell pregnant, but this time she insisted on having the baby. Joe was furious and refused to meet with Daisy again saying it was too harrowing for all three of them

Brookie forgave his wife when she gave birth to a daughter named Mercy. Daisy adored the little girl and was distressed that Joe showed no interest in Mercy or his illegitimate son Maynard. Daisy realised she had lost the man she loved so passionately.

From 1907 onward, Daisy's inherited fortune was gradually being eroded by inflation and a marked fall in wheat prices on the farms she owned. As her mother had predicted, maintenance of Warwick Castle was costing Daisy more than she could afford.

The Earl of Warwick had made bad investments in timber and gold and lost much of his money. There was a danger the Earl and Countess of Warwick could go bankrupt unless they could sell off Warwick Castle, which proved impossible.

In spite of everything that had happened in this troubled marriage and having raised three children who were not his, Brookie remained fond of Daisy. He had once declared he would rather be married to his fascinating wife 'with all her peccadilloes' than to any other woman in the world.[13]

LADY WARWICK — AUTHOR AND BLACKMAILER

On 6 May 1910, after only nine years on the throne, King Edward VII died at the age of 68 and was succeeded by George V.

By now Daisy was in serious need of money, something she had never thought could happen to her. Fortunately, she had literary skills and made money from popular books and newspaper articles.

Between 1898-1934, the Countess of Warwick wrote twelve books with some help from editors and ghost writers. They included a history of Warwick Castle and a book on garden design, on which she had considerable expertise, having designed two rose gardens and a Shakespearean garden with a specimen of every plant the bard had mentioned in his plays and sonnets. Daisy also wrote several pamphlets and books on Socialism, a short biography of William Morris, leader of the Arts and Crafts Movement, and a book on cats, her favourite pets.

Daisy Warwick had a great love of animals and worked tirelessly for the RSPCA as a branch president. She visited her local slaughterhouse and was horrified to see animals killed by having their heads chopped off with a pole-axe (an axe at the end of a long stick). Daisy did her best to have the law amended. Eventually the law was passed, so pole axes were banned and animals in Britain's slaughter houses were killed with a bolt pistol.

In 1912, Daisy Warwick sailed to America to give lectures to women's clubs about Warwick Castle and planned to give talks on Socialism. She found her audience far more interested in her castle and her haute couture outfits than the Socialist theories she wished to discuss.

***

By 1914, Lady Warwick's creditors were pressing for repayment. It was then that Daisy remembered the late King's love letters, locked away in a deed box in her boudoir. The threat to publish the sexually explicit ones, might help raise money through a spot of genteel blackmail on King George V. She knew that the prudish George V was keen to keep stories of his father's mistresses out of the press, determined to base his reign on the family values espoused by his grandmother, Queen Victoria.

Daisy decided that the *threat* of writing a kiss-and-tell memoir could be used to extract cash from George V to pay off her debts. She contacted Frank Harris, a raffish writer and editor aware Harris had had success in America. She asked him what sort of money she might earn if she wrote a frank memoir, giving details of her royal love affair and suggested she might retain Harris as a ghost writer. Frank Harris assured the Countess of Warwick that, if she included some of the late King's love letters, her book would be a best seller in America and in Britain. Were Edward VII's love letters to be excluded, sales would be *much* smaller.

Daisy kept this project from her husband, whose health was declining, aware he would not approve. She selected Arthur de Cros, a wealthy industrialist who had founded the Dunlop Rubber Company to act as her negotiator at Buckingham Palace. Daisy outlined her plan to him. Should she receive 'compensation' (a euphemism for blackmail money) for omitting the late King's love letters from her memoirs, Arthur du Cros would have the debt she owed him repaid in full.

So that George V had some idea of the salacious contents of some of the love letters written by his late father, Edward VII, Daisy attached a copy of a particularly sexy letter to her request for 'compensation' for omitting the love letters from her memoirs. In this particular letter her royal lover had named intimate portions of Daisy's anatomy that gave him pleasure.

Lord Stamfordham, the King's Private Secretary, showed the Countess of Warwick's letter to George V. The prudish King was horrified. He wanted to know how much money Lady Warwick was asking to refrain from publishing intimate royal love letters from his father to the Countess of Warwick. Arthur du Cros suggested that £85,000 (a large sum in 1914) would induce the Countess of Warwick to refrain from doing so.

George V was prudish but he was no fool. On the advice of Lord Stamfordham he consulted lawyers. They explained that, under the Copyright Act, as his father's heir, the King held the copyright to his father's letters, *not* the Countess of Warwick. Legally Lady Warwick could not publish these letters without the permission of the King.[14] Should she do so King George V could sue her. While equerries kept Arthur du Cros busy with fictitious negotiations, George V's lawyers were drawing up an injunction to prevent Daisy from publishing the love letters. Daisy, Arthur du Cros and the raffish Frank Harris, convinced they were on a winning streak, suggested raising the asking price of the letters from £85,000 to a £125,000, aware a deal was being set up by Frank Harris to sell the letters for a great deal more in America.[15]

Meanwhile Belgian neutrality, which had been guaranteed by Britain, was violated by Germany and the Cabinet were discussing going to war. In the midst of chaos caused by declaring war on Germany, George V, incensed that the price of the letters had been raised by Lady Warwick, decided to sue her if she published his father's letters.

On 3 August 1914, the royal lawyers informed the Countess of Warwick that, under existing copyright laws, she could *not* publish her letters from the late King or His Majesty King George V would sue her. Dumbfounded Daisy considered what to do about it.

To save money, Daisy left Warwick Castle for Easton Lodge. Meanwhile, Frank Harris had left for America and, without Daisy's permission, had taken some of the letters with him. Lord Stamfordham visited Easton Lodge to interrogate Lady Warwick and find out which letters Frank Harris had taken to America.

As Britain was at war, Lord Stamfordham saw the salacious letters as documents which could reflect badly on the image of the monarchy. The role of the monarchy was to inspire men to die for their country, so its image must not be damaged in any way.

Daisy, Countess of Warwick, requested a private interview with George V, which the King granted. But she was offended by the monarch's censorious attitude to what she regarded as her romantic love affair with his father. George V who had always been faithful to his wife had a very different point of view and saw nothing romantic in the relationship. The King made it clear to Daisy that, if she did not hand over the letters, she would be treated as a traitor.

Daisy did her best to put a positive spin on events. She duly handed over her love letters except for those which Frank Harris had stolen. According to her accompanying note she showed,

> ...splendid generosity in handing over the letters King Edward wrote me of his great love, and which belong absolutely to me... I am innocent of all charges brought against me which I resent deeply and shall never forget or forgive.[16]

The matter was hushed up for fifty years. The person who did best from the attempt at blackmail was Arthur du Cros. In 1916 he was created a baronet by royal command in the New Year Honours. It was Sir Arthur's reward for his silence about the 'Darling Daisy' letters from Edward VII. These letters (minus those taken by Frank Harris) were eventually destroyed by someone in the Royal Household, the fate of many love letters from princes and kings to their mistresses and *vice versa*.

Sir Arthur's title was also his reward for funding two motorised ambulances to be used in war time France and for 'services to the Crown', a blanket phrase which could mean anything. The newly created Baron du Cros was so delighted by his title he forgave Lady Warwick her debt.

Lord Stamfordham was a man of vision. Long before King George V did, he realised that having a King with the German name of Saxe-Coburg-Gotha, presented a problem as Britain was at war with Germany. It took Lord Stamfordham several years to persuade George V that the House of Saxe-Coburg-Gotha must change its name to Windsor. In the third year of the war (not the first as stated incorrectly in some history books) the family name was changed to 'House of Windsor', a solid English name which the public loved.

After the British Government had declared war on Germany, the patriotic Earl of Warwick and his heir were among the first to volunteer to fight for King and country. Footmen, grooms and gardeners from Warwick Castle and Easton Lodge enlisted, leaving only very old men still working. Many of these young men would die in the forthcoming war and life would never be the same for the British aristocracy.

Daisy Warwick volunteered for duties with the Red Cross, organised the re-housing of Belgian war refugees on her estate and supervised the running of the trade school for working-class children that she had funded.

Maynard Greville, Joe Laycock's son and Daisy's favourite child, enlisted in the Royal Flying Corps. As Maynard was under age he was not yet allowed to fly, so he trained as a mechanic.

In the 1920s Daisy's depleted fortune suffered even more. In wartime she had lost much of her invested income from mines in the Belgian Congo and Brookie had made a series of disastrous investments. Daisy earned some money (aided by ghost writer S.L Bensusan) writing articles on a variety of topics for the American press. She still had problems with Frank Harris who was pressuring her to honour their agreement and pay him for the draft memoir he had written for her. But Daisy disliked what he had written and refused to pay him. The dispute rumbled on for years and eventually Harris returned a few but not *all* the letters he had removed from Easton Lodge without Daisy's permission.

During World War One, Daisy received a visit from the beautiful and witty Lillie Langtry, who had been the mistress of Edward, Prince of Wales from 1887-1880.

As Lillie's husband, Edward Langtry, was threatened with bankruptcy, she became a subject of scandal. The Prince, fearing he could be named in Lillie's sordid divorce from her husband, dropped her with a flimsy excuse.

After bearing an illegitimate daughter, sired by a Prince of the House of Battenberg, Lillie defied convention, went on the stage and had great success in America. With her own money she bought herself a villa in Monte Carlo. Having broken the bank by gambling at the casino, Lillie had become a great deal wealthier than Daisy Warwick. Determined to look young, Lillie dyed her hair, wore tight corsets and a great deal of make-up, while Daisy favoured the natural look, had put on weight and let her hair go white. Daisy had lost her fortune but was much happier than the the now weathy Lillie who complained of loneliness. Lillie had quarrelled with her only daughter and her much younger second husband, the aristocratic debt-ridden Hugo de Bathe from whom she had separated in order to avoid settling his gambling debts.[17]

On 22 February 1918, the Tudor wing of Easton Lodge was ravaged by fire. The elderly Lady Warwick escaped, carrying her favourite parrot on her shoulder. Brookie, who had serious health problems, was led to safety by a nurse and, wrapped in a blanket, watched as their house was burning. The Old Master paintings were saved but the Tudor wing was ruined. It transpired that the fire had been started by Daisy's pet monkey and she had to pay to restore the burned-out part of the house. As the villa at Beaulieu had already been sold she was desperate for money.

Over the next decade Daisy sold hundreds of acres of freehold land at Easton and from Maynard estates in Leicestershire to tenant farmers (rather than to developers) and paid off her debts.

As she aged, Daisy put on weight and had changed from the heedless flirt into a far more serious woman. Her belief in secondary education for all children and other social welfare issues persuaded the Countess of Warwick to enter politics.

In 1924, four years after English women finally received the vote, 'Red Daisy' stood as Labour candidate for Westminster against the Conservative candidate, the dapper Anthony Eden. Daisy appeared on the hustings in an elegant Paris suit, a picture hat and her pearls looking every inch the *grande dame*. Not surprisingly, she failed to win the support of most Labour voters who refused to vote for a 'toff'.

That same year Brookie died after a long illness. He and Daisy had been married for almost half a century and their eldest son Guy inherited Warwick Castle. Guy had risen to the rank of Major-General in World War One, but he suffered severe psychological damage caused by the carnage of trench warfare and became an alcoholic. Eventually Guy was deemed incapable of administering Warwick Castle. Guy predeceased his mother, an distressing experience for her.

In 1929 the first volume of Daisy's memoirs, titled *Life's Ebb and Flow*, was published very successfully. However, the details of her complex extra-marital love life had to be omitted from the book which concentrated on descriptions of her fancy dress balls and expensive hand embroidered dresses. All mention that Joe Laycock, the great love of Daisy's life and the father of two of her children, had to be omitted from the two volumes of her memoirs. The second volume, *Afterthoughts*, can be read as a fascinating record of the leisured way of life of the British aristocracy, the same world portrayed so well in *Downton Abbey* which vanished after World War One.[18] Both volumes were written with the aid of an editor and ghost writer, S.L. Bensusan.

Still deeply convinced of the values of Socialism, Daisy tried to donate her mansion to be used as a conference centre for the Labour Party but they soon discovered they lacked the money for the upkeep of such a grand house. After a trial period the Labour Party abandoned the idea and declined her gift. Daisy moved to a smaller house in the grounds designed by an architect friend and turned the grounds into a bird and animal sanctuary.[19]

Daisy claimed that she 'meant to make old age the happiest period in my life'. She cared for stray dogs and cats in special kennels and purchased a troop of adorable Shetland ponies, discarded from a circus that had gone broke. When Daisy found the miniature ponies, they were about to be consigned to the local slaughterhouse to be turned into cat food. The Shetland ponies loved Daisy and arrived each morning at the side of her small architect designed house to be hand-fed. The thought she had saved their lives made Daisy happy.

Daisy, surrounded by her favourite books and much loved animals, was determined to enjoy the final years of her life with reading and frequent visits from her children and grandchildren.

In 1938 Daisy died of cancer and was buried at Easton beside her amiable husband. But long before death claimed Lady Daisy Warwick she had written to her close friend, Lady Jennie Churchill, 'We have both lived our lives to the full and gathered more experiences than most women.'[20] This could serve as an epitaph for all three of these talented but complex Edwardian ladies.

Above: Daisy, Countess of Warwick, whose hair had gone darker in mid-life.

Left: The newly wed, Lady Daisy Brooke in one of her Paris ball gowns.

Below: Romantic Warwick Castle, costly to maintain.

Daisy with her favourite son Maynard, born in March 1898. The adorable Maynard was *not* the child of the Earl of Warwick but of Daisy's new lover, wealthy landowner Joe Laycock. Maynard's arrival precipitated the end of Daisy's eight-year love affair with the Prince of Wales.

The entrance hall of Easton Lodge, Daisy's ancestral home.

Daisy with Maynard and Mercy

'Brookie', Earl of Warwick, who remained loyal to his wife

Daisy at Easton Lodge in the 1930s, feeding her beloved Shetland ponies who she had saved from the slaughter-house.

Easton Lodge and the Italianate part of the magnificent gardens redesigned by Harold Peto and paid for by Daisy. These gardens are now open to the public.

CHAPTER 6

Alice Keppel (1869–1947) and Edward VII

The role of a royal mistress is to curtsey and jump into bed. Alice Keppel.

It would have been difficult to find any other lady who would have filled the part of friend to King Edward VII with the same loyalty and discretion. Baron Hardinge of Penshurst, referring to Alice Keppel.

'A WOMAN WHO ERRED WITH A CERTAIN MAGNIFICENCE'

Among members of the aristocracy, Edward VII's beautiful young mistress, Alice Keppel, was referred to as 'the second Queen of England' as she spent more time with the King than the long-suffering Queen Alexandra.

Mrs Keppel's critics claimed she had the morals of an alley cat. However, Alice Keppel was *not* indiscriminate like an alley cat. She was highly selective in her choice of lovers — choosing them for their wealth, social standing and generosity. A love match to a handsome former Army officer with limited prospects of an inheritance, meant Alice had to be the one who brought in money. Alice flattered, cosseted and entertained a few wealthy men in her boudoir and accepted gifts of money and jewels from them. She kept her marriage together at a time when divorce was social suicide for women. Like Daisy, Countess of Warwick, who became a royal mistress for the social kudos, Alice, who enjoyed the social prestige of being a royal mistress, made certain that everyone knew that she too had the blood of Kings of Scotland in her veins.

The eighth child of Sir William and Lady Edmonstone, Alice was proud of her long pedigree. Her ancestral home was Duntreath Castle, overlooking Loch Lomond, an estate granted to Alice's distant ancestors by a King of Scotland, whose daughter married an Edmonstone. Her family tree went back to Robert the Bruce and included several medieval kings of Scotland.

The central keep or sandstone tower, built around 1452, consisted of three floors and an attic with a narrow stair, easy to defend by a single swordsman. George IV was said to have slept here on his 1822 visit to Scotland. The castle was extended during the reign of Queen Victoria, when the Edmonstones had made money on property in Ireland and added pepper-pot towers and a baronial hall. By the time Alice was born, the castle was so large and imposing that the building and its gardens needed a large staff to maintain them.[1]

Alice and her siblings (seven elder sisters and a brother) grew up surrounded by loyal family retainers. In addition to the baronial hall, Duntreath Castle had a billiard room, library, drawing room and breakfast room. The main rooms were filled with flowers from the gardens. Flagged passageways led to a large antiquated kitchen with an open hearth where meat was roasted. There were sculleries, a larder, a room for hanging game, a laundry and drying room, a sitting room for the housekeeper and a pantry. Stables and a dairy were housed in the outbuildings and the former dungeons had been converted into wine cellars.

In the magnificent grounds peacocks preened beside the lake and deer grazed on acres of parkland. Grouse moors provided excellent shooting. Since labour was still relatively cheap in the wilds of Scotland, Sir William and Lady Edmonstone employed a head cook and an assistant, a scullery maid and housemaids, a lady's maid for Lady Edmonstone, a nanny, nursemaids and governesses, several footmen, a cellarman and a boot boy as well as an army of gardeners, gamekeepers and ghillies.

Lady Edmonstone found Alice, her strong-minded youngest daughter, more difficult to raise than her other children.[2] For her part Alice was bored with her dutiful elder sisters, most of whom had married young, but adored her brother Archie. The two of them remained close as twins all their lives.

At 16 Alice had long shining chestnut hair, and blue-green eyes under long dark lashes. She was the acknowledged beauty of the family and as such was expected to make a brilliant marriage.

As a single girl Alice slept in one of the turret rooms of Duntreath Castle, which had 40 cm thick stone walls. There was no such thing as running water so jugs of hot water had to be carried by maids up a spiral stair to the turret, so Alice could wash or take a hip bath. In the Scottish winter, the water froze solid in the basin in Alice's bedroom.

The Edmonstone girls were taught by a series of governesses in the schoolroom. Alice felt it was unfair that money was spent on sending her brother Archie away to boarding school while she had to stay home with a governess. As was the custom, Alice remained in the schoolroom until she had her coming-out season in London.

Upper-crust girls entered society after being presented at court once they reached marriageable age. During their London season mothers or aunts chaperoned the debutantes to balls and dinners, where they were expected to find wealthy husbands.

Marriage to a complacent husband — when most upper-class men had mistresses — meant upper-class wives, once they had born a male heir and a replacement, could do virtually what they liked, as long as they were discreet about it. Divorce was unforgivable.

Lady Edmonstone had trained Alice to be an excellent manager of a large establishment and an accomplished hostess. In those days of plentiful staff it was not necessary for girls of Alice's background to know how to cook, wash or iron clothes — maids took care of such mundane tasks. Alice could arrange flowers beautifully but 'ladies' did not sully their delicate hands with manual work.

Alice adored her elderly father, Sir William Edmonstone, a retired Admiral of the Fleet, who died in 1886. Still devastated by the death of her father, Alice was deemed old enough to leave the schoolroom, put up her long hair in an elaborate coiffeure and 'come out' into society. But her London debut with a presentation ceremony at Buckingham Palace was not nearly as grand as Lady Edmonstone had originally planned. With the death of Sir William Edmonstone, young Archie had become the laird of Duntreath during the agricultural downturn of the 1880s. The annual income from the estate had shrunk substantially, so Alice Edmonstone did not make her debut into society at a grand 'coming out' ball, as by now her widowed mother and Archie had financial worries.

In the year that Alice had her 'season', London was invaded by American heiresses and their mothers. Armed with newly acquired money from railroads, property and meat packing works the American 'buccaneers' were hunting for titled husbands — heirs to dukedoms, earldoms and stately homes — just the category of husband Lady Edmonstone intended to secure for Alice.

The London season was a marriage market, riddled by snobbery, jealousies and avarice. Aristocratic mothers of eligible sons knew *exactly* how much each debutante's dowry was worth. Alice's dowry was not a large one, but it was apparent she was a highly intelligent young woman with a mind of her own. Formidable mothers carefully steered eligible sons away from the beautiful but far from rich Miss Edmonstone towards more pliant and wealthier girls as potential daughters-in-law.

At the end of the season, Alice Edmonstone, unwilling to settle for second best, returned to Duntreath Castle. She spent several years at home helping her mother and attended Highland balls and other social events.

Not until Alice was twenty-two (when most girls were safely married) did Alice finally accept a proposal of marriage.

The Hon George Keppel was the third son of the Earl of Albermarle, whose family had served successive monarchs for generations. George graduated from the Royal Military College and became an officer in the historic Scottish regiment, the Gordon Highlanders. George was tall, broad-shouldered and handsome with a fashionably curled moustache. His family was staunchly monarchist and owned a large estate at Quidenham in Norfolk, but as a younger son he would inherit very little except aristocratic attitudes.

The Keppel family claimed descent from Joost van Keppel, a handsome young Dutchman who had arrived in England with King William III. The King had given his favourite the extinct title of Earl of Albemarle, together with land in Norfolk and several other estates. However, Joost van Keppel's descendants gambled away most of the family assets until only Quidenham and its grouse moors remained in its possession. They dropped the 'van' from their name and called themselves Keppel.

In June 1891, when Alice, dressed in white, walked up the aisle to marry the Hon George Keppel, wedding guest commented on what a handsome couple they made. But the couple's finances were limited. Army Officers in prestigious regiments could not live on their pay alone, which was just sufficient to meet the costs of their mess bills — they were expected to have a private income. George's wealthy aunt had promised to 'look after him financially' once he was married. Alice's brother settled £15,000 on his beloved sister while George's aunt promised to put up £5,000 in trust. In the eyes of the world Alice had married for love rather than made a brilliant match.

George Keppel's father was Household Treasurer to Queen Victoria and a Keppel uncle also worked for the Queen. Perhaps when the Hon George Keppel decided to sell his Army commission a year after marrying Alice and move to London, he hoped that a suitable post would be found for him in the Royal Household. But like the allowance from his aunt, such a post did not materialise. Using the dowry provided by Alice's brother and money from the sale of George's Army commission, the newly-weds paid for their move to London and the lease on a small but pretty house at the far end of Belgravia's elegant Wilton Crescent.

Victorian London was an expensive place to live. In those days a vast gulf yawned between wealthy aristocrats and the working-classes. Aristocrats employed an army of servants in their grand London homes and held elaborate dinner parties with at least eight courses as well as an after-dinner concert or other entertainment. The Hon George and Alice Keppel expected to enjoy a similar life with aristocratic friends, to which they were convinced their birth and rank entitled them.

However, money was tight in the Keppel household and Alice's husband was not trained for any kind of work apart from soldiering. George Keppel had a small income, but thanks to Alice's boudoir activities he managed to employ a valet to shave him, trim and curl his luxuriant moustache, care for his clothes and his shooting and fishing gear. Gentlemen like the Hon George Keppel might have trouble paying their tailors and wine merchants, but they did not work at anything as vulgar as trade or commerce. It was demeaning for aristocrats to work — the professions, trade and commerce were the occupations of the middle-class.

It was left to the resourceful Alice, the daughter of a Baronet, to support the household. As a member of the aristocracy, her options for earning an income outside the home were limited.

Alice realised there was one way a good-looking young woman could make money. She knew several aristocratic wives with complacent husbands and wealthy lovers who gave them jewels, expensive paintings and property. Everyone knew that Lady Sackville of Knole House — England's magnificent Elizabethan mansion near Sevenoaks which cost a fortune to maintain — was given valuable antiques and jewels by an elderly admirer. Her cash-strapped husband, Lionel Sackville, did not object since he had installed *his* mistress in one of the 365 rooms at Knole House.

Once it was clear that George's rich aunt would do nothing more for them, Alice selected a wealthy widower as her 'afternoon' lover. Who better than William Beckett, a merchant banker, to become the friend and 'protector' of a young woman with a limited allowance and expensive tastes?

William Beckett had two small children and may have fathered Alice's eldest daughter, Violet. He would inherit the title of Baron Grimthorpe and become senior partner in Beckett's Bank. He was well-travelled, well-read and able to grant bank loans at low rates of interest, something Alice found extremely appealing.

In order to enjoy languorous afternoons in her rose-scented boudoir with William Beckett, Alice made certain her husband was busy elsewhere. George visited the Keppel estate at Quidenham for shooting parties, joined the Norfolk Artillery in 1894 and was made a member of a gentleman's club in St James', which ensured Alice was free to entertain in her boudoir in the afternoons.

Like many aristocratic couples the Keppels did not ask each other awkward questions about love affairs. The Hon George Keppel had sexual relations with his wife when it suited her. He behaved like many husbands in the Victorian and Edwardian eras and engaged in discreet sexual relationships with working-class girls. Many people regarded George Keppel as an upper-crust ninny who had no idea what went on in his home. Others claimed that he was sexually 'cold'. This seems unlikely. It is possible that he fathered Sonia Keppel but not Violet Keppel, Alice's eldest daughter.

Sonia Keppel, in her carefully sanitised but entertaining memoir with its ambivalent title, *Edwardian Daughter*, was careful to avoid any mention of family problems. She ignored her mother's lovers, the scandal over Violet's lesbian affair with Vita Sackville West and the fact her marriage was not a success and ended in divorce and claimed her parents enjoyed a 'marriage of love and laughter'. While Sonia's memoir is enjoyable, it conceals as much as it reveals.

Sonia remained silent about the way her mother acquired enough money to live in grand style, how she obtained loans from a wealthy banker as well as shares and valuable jewels. However, Sonia did admit, tongue in cheek, that her mother 'was very fond' of bankers.

A year after Mrs Keppel's *affaire* with William Beckett began she gave birth to a pretty little girl, christened Violet, who was alleged to have 'the Beckett nose'. Violet inherited her mother's good looks, was clever and precocious, and had a talent for writing. Violet was spoiled and indulged by her mother though not by George Keppel. It was Violet's younger sister, Sonia, who George adored and it was likely she was George's daughter or, probably, the daughter of Edward VII. George's dislike of Violet

Keppel affected the dynamics of the family and caused a life-long feud between the sisters. The claim that Sonia was Edward VII's daughter made Violet even more jealous of her younger sister. Against all reason, Violet insisted that King Edward VII (by this time Alice's lover rather than William Beckett) had fathered her. This was impossible as at the time of Violet's conception Alice had yet to meet Edward. All their lives Violet and Sonia competed fiercely for their mother's attention.

Of course, a society 'beauty' with a strong personality, like Mrs Keppel, would always attract gossip. Lady Mary Curzon, detained by ill health from accompanying her husband to India (where he served as Viceroy), wrote him long gossipy letters from London. She claimed that, apart from William Beckett, Alice Keppel's lovers included the wealthy bachelor Lord Henry Alington and the handsome but married Lord Stavordale, (who later succeeded to the title of Earl of Ilchester).

Lady Mary Curzon and others in her set knew that the Hon George Keppel had no job and only a small private income. It was Alice's boudoir activities that made it possible for the Keppels to employ a cook, a butler and several maids and pay all their household expenses. The Keppels were always delightful guests and significantly, never argued in public. Due, mainly to Alice's beauty and her lively conversation, their mantelpiece was always overflowing with invitations to dinner parties and society balls.

***

Alice met the Prince of Wales at a fortuitous time. His *affaire* with the married heiress Daisy, Countess of Warwick, was ending as he was tired of Daisy's socialist views and constant lectures about the poor and needy. He was in the market for a younger, less demanding mistress.

There are various accounts of the first meeting between the heir to the throne and Mrs Keppel. The most widely accepted has the corpulent middle-aged Prince of Wales introduced to the 29-year-old Alice in the summer of 1898. This was seven years after her marriage by which time she had a small daughter named Violet by a previous lover. Sir John Leslie of Castle Leslie, a relation by marriage of Lady Jennie Churchill, claimed he introduced his friend Bertie, the Prince of Wales, to Mrs Keppel at the races, but there are other claimants to this honour. King Edward VII's biographer, Giles St Aubyn, claims they met at a dinner party which changed the Prince of Wales life 'as he had found the most perfect mistress in the history of royal infidelity'.[3]

Bertie admired Alice's chestnut-brown hair, sparkling blue eyes and curvaceous figure, accentuated by the wasp-waisted gowns that were the current fashion. He already knew a great deal about Mrs Keppel and her obliging husband, because Colonel F.C. Keppel, George's uncle, had in the past worked for the Prince of Wales as an equerry.

The Prince and Mrs Keppel exchanged polite conversation. Alice admitted that she adored playing bridge, which interested the Prince of Wales who, bored by whist, was searching for a regular bridge partner. This newly fashionable card game would supply a socially acceptable reason for the Prince of Wales and the Hon Mrs George Keppel to spend a great deal of time together.

When Alice first became the mistress of His Royal Highness, the Prince of Wales was fifty seven years old and weighed 110 kilograms (sixteen stone). Due to the size of his paunch, the Prince's nickname was 'Tum-Tum'. His breath reeked of tobacco as a result of smoking twenty Turkish cigarettes and up to a dozen cigars each day. Alice made the smell of stale tobacco bearable by taking up smoking herself, using an elegant ivory holder. 'Tum-Tum's' vast girth had given him heart and digestive problems and possibly diabetes. His genital-urinary problems would eventually lead to sexual problems including erectile dysfunction.

Catherine Walters (Skittles), the courtesan provided with an annual retainer by Bertie, told her other long-term lover,

A cartoon of the Prince of Wales, known as 'Tum-Tum'

Wilfred Scawen Blunt, that the Prince of Wales had been impotent since 1895 — three years *before* he met Mrs Keppel. Perhaps she exaggerated but certainly in the final years of their relationship Alice was more of a nurse-companion than a mistress. But initially the prospect of sexual relations with a beautiful young woman inspired and invigorated the ageing roué who set about wooing the beautiful and flirtatious Mrs Keppel.

Each afternoon the Prince of Wales' horse-drawn brougham would make its way from Marlborough House to Wilton Crescent. The coachman dropped him at Mrs Keppel's door and waited outside until his employer re-appeared.

For Alice it was important that her lovers were her friends. She became genuinely fond of Bertie who was a man of great charm. His generosity to her was legendary. She regarded him as her 'sugar daddy' and was happy to 'curtsey and jump into bed' with the ageing prince — but on *her* terms. The besotted Prince of Wales, thrilled by the conquest of a beautiful young woman, roughly the same age as his eldest daughter, showered Alice with expensive jewels.[4]

Bertie, christened Albert Edward after his father Prince Albert, chose to reign as Edward VII. Like most kings-in-waiting, Bertie had no work to keep himself occupied, as Queen Victoria distrusted him and refused to allow him to examine state papers.

To befitted his exalted status as Prince of Wales, Bertie felt his new *'maitresse'* should have a luxurious residence where she could entertain him and selected friends. The problem was how could George Keppel, who had no job and a very small private income, afford a larger house to entertain his sovereign?

The Prince of Wales consulted his financial advisor, Sir Ernest Cassel, who arranged a loan at a low rate of interest for the Keppels. This made it possible for Alice and her husband to move from their small house in Wilton Crescent to a far more imposing six-storey house in Portman Square. An important advantage of the larger house was the fact it offered far more privacy than their former cramped terrace house.

The Hon Mr Keppel and his beautiful wife now had the luxury of separate bedroom suites, each with its own bathroom and dressing room, complete with running hot and cold water. The house also had that wonderful new invention — electric light.

Thanks to the generosity of the Prince of Wales, Alice could employ a larger household, including a lady's maid to lace up her corsets and style her hair, two housemaids, a cook, a well-trained butler, named Rolfe, who ran the establishment, and a boot boy. George's valet continued to lay out his clothes and run his bath. The Keppel girls had a nanny and a nursemaid and in due course a French governess. Eventually, they would attend the most fashionable private schools in London.

Portman Square, with its large and handsome houses, offered another advantage. Alice's former lover, Lord Alington, had a mansion on the far side of the square, so it would have been easy to entertain him in the afternoons. Whether this happened or not, Mrs Keppel did not keep a diary and was careful not to write any compromising letters about her afternoon activities.

Alice had few illusions about the way her family lived comfortably on money provided by wealthy lovers. In a memorable exchange, Alice advised Clementine Churchill, wife of the impecunious Winston, to acquire a wealthy generous lover. When Alice offered to find a lover for her, Winston, who disliked any mention of the role wealthy lovers played in his mother's life, angrily claimed that Alice Keppel was 'an avaricious bitch'.[5]

With the expert advice of Bertie's financial advisor, Sir Ernest Cassel, Alice played the London Stock Exchange during the peaceful years of the *belle époque* in a stock market and property boom. She proved to be a shrewd investor and, as a result, she and her husband were able to spend the rest of their lives in luxury, living in the Ritz Hotel or in a villa in Tuscany on invested capital.

Alice Keppel was known for her tact and discretion and, it was claimed, never said anything unpleasant about anyone. But why *would* she? She was too intelligent and socially adept to make powerful enemies in high places. Unlike her friend Daisy, Countess of Warwick, whose enemies included Queen Alexandra, Alice charmed those she met (other than Lord Esher). She soothed and calmed a petulant monarch-in-waiting so that he could not imagine life without her.

Among hostesses who refused to receive Mrs Keppel was Lady Sackville, doyenne of Knole House, who was no angel of virtue, having been the recipient of very expensive gifts from a wealthy bachelor who lived much of the time at Knole. In 1897, Lady Sackville invited the Prince and Princess of Wales to a reception at Knole. The heir to the throne accepted but said Princess Alexandra would not attend and instead he would bring Mrs Keppel and his old friend, Daisy Warwick. Lady Sackville (whose past included a bevy of lovers) was affronted that the Prince of Wales was diminishing the tone of 'her' reception by proposing to bring *two* mistresses rather than enhancing it by bringing the Princess of Wales.

Lady Sackville replied tactfully claiming that she would prefer to invite 'county ladies' from Kent to meet the Prince of Wales rather than have other guests ensuring Daisy, Countess of Warwick and Mrs Keppel did not attend her reception.[6]

In May 1899, Alice gave birth to her second daughter, alleged by some to have been sired by the Prince of Wales. Bertie inundated Alice with flowers after Sonia's arrival into the world was announced. It seems that the ever tactful Alice allowed both Bertie *and* George Keppel to believe they were Sonia's father.

Princess Alexandra spent most of that summer with her family in Denmark so Alice and the Prince of Wales frequently spent evenings at Marlborough House. This was where the Prince of Wales had a contraption rigged up, modelled on the apparatus used for mating stallions with mares in the royal stables — a suspended harness with footholds. This apparatus was a source of ribald humour among the Prince's male cronies.

***

In January 1901, on the death of Queen Victoria, the Prince of Wales succeeded to the throne as Edward VII and invited to his coronation many mistresses, past and present — Alice Keppel, Lady Randolph Churchill, Sarah Bernhardt, Catherine Walters and the Duchess de Cariocollo — brought together for the first and last time by Bertie to witness the historic occasion at which he was anointed King and Defender of the Anglican Church.

An area of Westminster Abbey was roped off for the King's lady friends. Lord Esher, a member of the Royal Household, jokingly dubbed the area 'The King's Loosebox' (a stall for horses and in this case, specially for mares).

Alice watched her lover being crowned. With his formidable mother dead and the Crown on his head, Bertie was free to acknowledge Alice's role in his life more openly. It was then that journalists started referring to Mrs Keppel, who now sported a series of ever larger picture hats, as 'the King's devoted companion' or his 'favourite bridge partner'.

With Bertie on the throne, Mrs Keppel's influence became more apparent. Her adored brother, Archie Edmonstone, was soon appointed to the prestigious position of Groom-in-Waiting to the Royal Household. Paid work, which was not too taxing, was found for the Hon George Keppel. The King's friend, the millionaire yachtsman and tea magnate, Sir Thomas Lipton, offered George a job in his London office. No doubt, this pleased everyone as it kept George Keppel occupied all day. As King Edward VII, Bertie remained good friends with the amiable George Keppel and often invited him to shooting parties at Sandringham, which he accepted as his due.

The King did not behave as Winston Churchill had predicted and drop Mrs Keppel and take Queen Alexandra to official functions. Instead it was Alice who accompanied the King to the races, to Cowes week and on long holidays to the Continent. The King and Queen led lives that were increasingly separate. Out of respect for Edward VII, who became a very popular King, the newspapers refrained from mentioning he had a mistress.

Although unhappy about her husband's infidelity with Daisy Warwick, Queen Alexandra accepted the situation with the discreet Mrs George Keppel, for which her husband was truly thankful. He always treated Queen Alexandra with great respect and courtesy in public. Although he had not shared his wife's bed for years, divorce was never on the cards for this royal couple or, for that matter, for Mr and Mrs Keppel, and appearances had to be maintained that the royal marriage was a devoted one. However, Edward VII respected his loyal wife and was very fond of her. The trouble was that Queen Alexandra bored him. In contrast he was fascinated by Alice, soothed by her when the stress of kingship became too much and stimulated by her lively conversation.

On one afternoon the King's green brougham was standing outside the Keppel's house with its driver when Vita Sackville-West arrived to have tea with Alice's eldest daughter Violet. The Keppel's butler made both young girls wait in a secluded corner of the hall where they could not be seen until a stout bearded man, reeking of cigar smoke descended the stairs. After the front door closed behind him, Vita realised that the bearded man was the King of England, who had clearly been inside Mrs Keppel's boudoir.[7]

Victoria Sackville-West and Violet Keppel had a passionate friendship and both of them hoped one day to become published authors. Unaware their friendship was more than platonic Alice sent the precocious Violet to Italy with Vita Sackville-West and her governess and failed to notice how her daughter had what amounted to a teenage crush on Vita.

Alice's second daughter, Sonia became a writer in later life. In Sonia's book *Edwardian Daughter* (a deliberately ambiguous title in view of the fact it was alleged in certain quarters she was the daughter of Edward VII) Sonia recorded how, when she was a toddler, her nanny brought her to have tea with her mother's lover. She described how his check trousers and white or lemon coloured spats made him look like Mr Toad of Toad Hall. On occasions she let her buttered toast slide down his immaculate trousers and King Edward VII did not object.

The Keppels had become very important fixtures on the social scene, invited everywhere as it was recognized that the best way of ensuring the King's acceptance of an invitation was to invite the Keppels.

So that Alice could maintain her position as a leader of fashion, Bertie settled Alice's astronomically expensive dress bills at the Parisian House of Worth. Catherine Walters the courtesan who worked under the name of Skittles received an annual retainer from Edward for her services. Catherine told Wilfred Blunt that a single one of Alice's embroidered ball gowns from the House of Worth cost over a thousand pounds (the entire annual wage of a working man). She also claimed Edward's virility was failing.[8]

To counteract rumours about the King's private life and his young mistress, stories about the 'devoted' royal couple were given to the press by the Doans (father and son), a family who had held the post of Court Newsmen for generations. The Doans were paid to ensure his subjects believed that Edward VII and Queen Alexandra, as guardians of the nation's morals, led a happily married life.

While those in aristocratic circles knew all about Mrs George Keppel and her relationship with Edward VII, it was vital that the working-classes, taught to venerate the King and Queen, did not learn Mrs Keppel was his mistress. And it was unthinkable they should learn that Edward VII frequented a Parisian brothel called Le Chabannais on his diplomatic trips to Paris. All his visits were noted in records kept by the Paris police who provided his security. Issuing an invitation to the King posed a tricky question for society hostesses as to whether to invite His Majesty to dinner or a grand ball with the Queen and risk he would not accept, or invite Mrs Keppel and have more chance of securing the King as a guest.

The Hon George and Mrs Alice Keppel were included in invitations to house parties in Britain's grandest houses when the King was a guest. After 'Harty-Tarty', (erstwhile lover of 'Skittles') had succeeded his father as Duke of Devonshire, Queen Alexandra, Edward VII and the Keppels were all guests at Chatsworth, the Duke's stately home in Derbyshire in the summer of 1904.

Chatsworth, the Devonshire's mansion, was so vast that even with a royal wife and royal mistress as house guests, their paths would rarely cross. Separate after-dinner entertainments were provided for Queen Alexandra and Alice Keppel. Chatsworth's landscaped gardens were large enough for both the Queen's circle and Alice's friends to enjoy separately without any risk of them meeting during the day, while the Duke of Devonshire, Edward VII, George Keppel and other guests went out shooting. There were no unpleasant incidents between the Queen and the royal mistress at any time and the royal visit to Chatsworth was deemed a great success.

There were also lavish house parties at the home of the widowed Mrs Ronald Greville at Polesden Lacey near Dorking. Maggie Greville, the illegitimate daughter of a wealthy Edinburgh brewer, Sir William McEwan, a man of humble antecedents had 'bought' his knighthood by making donations to charities and the right political parties. Maggie inherited Sir William's beer fortune and married the Hon Ronnie Greville, a close friend of the Hon George Keppel.

Maggie Greville used her inherited millions to maintain a grand London house in Charles Street, Mayfair, and a superb country house, named Polesden Lacy, on the Dorking Downs, which she had purchased in 1906.[9] The house had a vast dining room and two drawing rooms. One drawing room was specially kept for the bridge games the King and Alice loved to play for high stakes. The other drawing room contained gilded panelling removed from a decaying Venetian *palazzo* and re-installed at Polesden Lacey. Maggie Greville employed the same firm of interior designers who had decorated the Ritz Hotel in London, one of Alice's favourite haunts.

Maggie Greville's fortune and generosity were attractive to Alice, coupled with the fact that Maggie, being short and stout, presented no competition. Alice, like Jennie Churchill, preferred to be the most beautiful woman in the room. Maggie Greville always wore black adorned with emeralds the size of pigeon's eggs or long ropes of pearls. She employed one of the best French chefs in England and was besotted by royalty. Entertaining Alice and her royal lover was for Maggie Greville the acme of social success.

Alice accompanied her royal lover to a lavish shooting party at Duntreath, hosted by her brother Archie. For breakfast Bertie ate a whole haddock, two poached eggs, several rashers of bacon and half a chicken, as well as porridge, toast and marmalade. This was followed by a huge lunch and a ten course dinner with wines, and champagne plus brandy after dinner.

By the time Alice reached mid-life, the once slim lithe beauty had turned into an elegant mature woman who had put on weight.

The willowy Queen Alexandra was greatly amused on seeing her portly husband and his mistress squeeze into a hansom cab together.[10] However, Alice *did* worry about Bertie's weight and tried to persuade him to eat and smoke less. Alice and a team of six employees of the King often read his despatch boxes and make a précis of things the King needed to know to save him time.

As Edward VII, the once wayward Prince of Wales, became the most popular King of England, as well as a skilful diplomat at a time when Europe's monarchs conducted diplomat relations among themselves.

Horse racing, which Queen Victoria had considered Bertie's vice, was now approved of by the people of Britain. The King's horses often won and working men enjoyed putting 'a bob each way' on the monarch's horses. Alice enjoyed going to the races with the King and cheering on his horses. At the races she would always wear a new and magnificent outfit from Paris and one of her trademark picture hats. Bertie, who loved changing his clothes and being at the height of fashion, demanded his mistress be as well or even better dressed than his wife.

Alice revelled in the special treatment extended to her as the Kings 'constant companion'. But she also had to bear with Bertie's 'gnashes' or violent temper which affected so many males in the House of Hanover. The King's bellows of rage were dreaded by his courtiers and they were very grateful for Mrs Keppel's ability to charm the King out of his black moods.

Sonia Keppel later claimed in her memoir *Edwardian Daughter*, 'Mama could have persuaded Florence Nightingale to become a ballet dancer'. Those close to the King praised Alice's tact and charm. They welcomed the fact that the King's temper was far pleasanter whenever Mrs Keppel was with him. (Alice's great-granddaughter, Camilla, Duchess of Cornwall, has a similar capacity to soothe and calm a sometimes petulant Prince Charles, boost his ego and create a pleasant atmosphere.)

Queen Alexandra acknowledged that Mrs Keppel was a good influence on her husband. She found this particular mistress preferable to the detestable Daisy Warwick. For her part Alice strove to create the impression that the Queen approved of her relationship with the King, which was not exactly true. But by this time the long-suffering Queen of Great Britain had resigned herself to the fact that her husband would *always* have a mistress and Alice was better than many others.

Behind the scene Mrs Keppel worked to keep herself *au courant*. She read the King savoury tit-bits from the gossip columns, embroidering the stories to make them more interesting for her lover. That Alice was known as an amusing conversationalist infuriated her daughter Violet, a keen reader, as she knew her mother only skimmed through the latest novels to be able to discuss them at the dinner table. Bertie enjoyed gossip about other people's sex lives, so Alice's conversation included the latest scandals as well as political intrigues. She also kept up with the latest prices of stocks and shares. In contrast to the famously unpunctual Queen Alexandra, Alice Keppel always arrived on time.

'It would have been difficult,' said Lord Harding (one of the King's Private Secretaries), 'to have found another lady who would have filled the part of friend to King Edward with the same loyalty and discretion'.[11]

As a conduit to the monarch, Mrs Keppel was viewed with approval by politicians, Prime Ministers and diplomats. Foreign ambassadors whispered secrets in her ear and knew their views were transmitted to the King.

※

During the reigns of Queen Victoria and Edward VII, British society underwent considerable social and economic changes, brought about by the Industrial Revolution. A new very wealthy class consisting of industrialists and financiers, who had made money from the development of industries, railways and shipping, now had considerable power. At the same time, many aristocrats, including Alice's family, were suffering from declining earnings with a sharp fall in their income from agricultural lands. When he was Prince of Wales, Bertie shocked his mother by entertaining the *noveau riche*. His friends came from a wider social strata, albeit a wealthy one, which could afford to entertain him.

Wealthy Jewish financiers like Ernest Cassel and the Rothschilds, manufacturers of powdered soap like the Leverholmes and wealthy brewers, entertained the King and his mistress and were honoured guests at Mrs Keppel's dinners for the King. Alice knew that these clever Jewish financiers provided the King with large sums of money and she also benefited from their largesse and financial expertise.

Lord Esher claimed, 'When she (Alice Keppel) came into the King's life, twelve years earlier, she was bankrupt'. Reginald Brett, 2nd Viscount Esher, made no secret of his dislike for Alice Keppel, who he regarded as a gold digger. In fact, Alice was *not* bankrupt, because her first lover, the banker William Beckett, had granted the Keppels several low interest bank loans.

Sir Ernest Cassel was the King's main financial advisor. He had earned his knighthood for doubling the King's money and with his help Alice managed to multiply her capital many times over. Using royal contacts to pick up stock market tips Alice became an astute investor and acquired wealth by buying stocks and shares in American railroads, shipping companies and African diamond mines. She and George watched with glee as their investments soared in value. Of course, there were the occasional financial setbacks like an investment in Argentine railways which were nationalised causing Alice to lose money. But she was a cool clever investor who kept her nerve and recouped her losses.

The King caused amusement among his male friends when he gave Alice a parcel of shares in a rubber company. Condoms made of vulcanised rubber were just starting to be used by married couples — previously they had been the preserve of prostitutes (from whom Bertie learned about condoms on visits to Parisian bordellos). Over the years Mrs Keppel's shares in rubber companies were supposed to have earned her fifty thousand pounds, a huge sum for the time.

✯

Prone to bronchitis, Edward VII was advised by his physicians to spend winter and early spring in the South of France. He took an annual three weeks holiday in Biarritz from late March to mid

April. Alice joined him there and sometimes took little Sonia with her. She would cross the Channel, go first to Paris and then travelled south by sleeper to Biarritz with its elegant hotels. Mrs Keppel was treated like royalty by French authorities who, unlike the British, were not at all shocked that royalty had mistresses. Alice took with her numerous trunks and valises, so she would always have the right outfit for each occasion as the King did not like her wearing the same outfit twice.

Edward VII travelled separately to Paris, ostensibly for reasons of diplomacy to strengthen the *entente cordiale* between the British and French Government, but also to see previous mistresses, including the Princesse de Sagan and Sarah Bernhardt, who were now just good friends. The King attended the theatre and visited (under an alias) his favourite brothel where the *madame* kept a chair specially designed for Bertie and other portly clients to help them achieve orgasms. He enjoyed *la specialite de la maison* — naked women having sex with each other. After his appetite for 'rough trade' had been satisfied, Bertie took the train south from Paris to Biarritz to join Mrs Keppel for a spring holiday.

To preserve appearances, Alice did not stay in the same hotel as the King but was given an entire floor to herself in Sir Ernest Cassel's handsome *Villa Eugenie*.

By the time the King was in his sixties his sexual potency was affected and Alice was virtually a nurse-companion. After years of eating gargantuan meals, Bertie had severe digestive problems, prostate and other uro-genital problems and possibly late onset diabetes. Alice worried about the King's health, chided him, talked to his doctor and tried to persuade him to moderate his meals and his smoking.

The couple had a well established routine during their holiday. They breakfasted separately and met up later in the morning when the two would take a walk along the promenade like an old married couple. They were accompanied by the King's wire-haired fox terrier on a lead. They lunched together in the Royal Suite of the sumptuous Hotel du Palais or were driven to a secluded picnic spot where servants unpacked their picnic basket. Alice, careful not to spoil her lily-white complexion, sat under a lace parasol during the picnic. Occasionally they drove across the border into northern Spain to watch the exciting Basque game of *pelota*, played with a wicker basket strapped to the player's hands.

Although Catherine Walters claimed that in his final years Edward VII was impotent, some form of mild sexual activity took place in the late afternoon before the royal mistress *en titre* returned to Sir Ernest's villa to change for dinner.

Alice and the King would meet again at 8.15 for the evening meal and play a few hands of bridge with friends. Later Mrs Keppel returned to her suite at the *Villa Eugenie* while the King spent the night in his hotel.

In the spring of 1910, the King and Mrs Keppel set off separately for Biarritz for the last holiday they would spend together. Bertie's bronchitis had been so bad that winter that Queen Alexandra tried unsuccessfully to persuade him to accompany her on a Mediterranean cruise on the royal yacht. The Queen, who had boarded the royal yacht, was annoyed by the hold Mrs Keppel had developed over her husband.

By the time Alice met the King at Biarritz he had developed a chest infection. He dismissed it as nothing more than a cold and insisted they spend their afternoons at the Golf Club or at the races. But his condition worsened and they visited Lourdes just in case the waters might help his wheezing chest. Alice was worried and insisted they take things quietly. She was somewhat reassured by the apparent improvement in the King.

After seven happy weeks together — the longest time they would ever spend in each other's company — Edward VII returned to Buckingham Palace on 27 April 1910. Queen Alexandra was still in Corfu as a guest of her brother, the newly created King of Greece. Determined to show her annoyance with her husband she did not return, so Bertie went alone to chilly Sandringham.

Returning separately to London from Biarritz, Alice had stopped off in Paris where she visited the House of Worth to buy several very expensive embroidered ball gowns for herself and Violet. She then took the train from Paris to London and returned to Portman Square.

On the evening of 2 May, the King dined and played a hand of bridge with Alice Keppel, Agnes Keyser (allegedly another of his mistresses although she was more like a nurse) and Agnes's younger sister.[12]

King Edward VII, pale and racked by bouts of coughing, returned alone to Buckingham Palace. As his condition continued to deteriorate over the following week, his doctors telegraphed Queen Alexandra, who on 5 May 1910 hurriedly returned to London.

The King rallied and was able to attend a performance of *Rigoletto* at Covent Garden, the last public engagement he would undertake.

THE DEATH OF A KING

By Friday 6 May 1910, the King, while protesting there was nothing wrong with him, suffered a series of mild heart attacks. Newspaper headlines proclaimed that the King was ill.

From Portman Square a worried Alice spread the story that the Queen had sent for her, the implication being that Queen Alexandra acknowledged her relationship with the King. According to Lord Esher and the royal physician, Sir Francis Laking, Alice had previously attempted to gain entry to Buckingham Palace but Queen Alexandra had refused to allow her to see the monarch and Alice had returned to Portman Square in tears.

Alice was desperate to say goodbye to the King. It was alleged she had been advised by Sir Ernest Cassel that the dying monarch had a substantial gift of cash for her — to be given in person. The previous day, Sir Ernest had taken £10,000 in banknotes to the King, which were profits from some share trading he had carried out for him.[13]

Lord Esher related that Mrs Keppel finally 'wheedled' her way into Buckingham Palace. According to Lord Esher and Sir Francis Laking, Alice sent a special messenger with a signed letter from Bertie, which Alice had carefully guarded for emergencies, to Queen Alexandra.

In fact, this letter had been written in 1901 when the King was about to undergo surgery for appendicitis. He had written that if he were dying he wanted to see Mrs Keppel to 'say farewell' and was 'convinced that all those who have any affection for me will carry out the wishes which I have expressed in these lines'.[14]

Queen Alexandra could scarcely refuse a written request from her husband, so Alice was admitted to the King's suite where he lay dying.

The royal mistress curtseyed to the Queen who greeted her coldly and observed stiffly, 'I'm sure you had a good influence on him'. Queen Alexandra positioned herself as far away as possible from her husband's mistress, looking out of the window. Alice sat quietly by the bedside of the King.

According to Alice Keppel's unreliable version of the story, it was the *Queen* who had sent for her so she could say goodbye to her lover. The King, only half conscious, had asked his wife and his mistress to kiss each other in friendship.

Lord Esher, who detested Alice, had his own version of the story and the royal physician, Sir Francis Laking, had a third. Both men described the King as being comatose and that he did not recognise Mrs Keppel, who lost control and had hysterics.[15] According to Lord Esher, the Queen hissed 'Get that woman away from here' and ordered Mrs Keppel to be removed from the room.

Sir Ernest Cassel had informed Alice she would receive a large sum of money from the hands of the dying King. Lord Esher's interpretation was that Mrs Keppel's hysterics were caused by her realisation she would not receive that money. Between sobs she cried out, 'I never did any harm — what is to become of *me?*' In his published *Journals and Letters,* Lord Esher claimed he was shocked that Mrs Keppel showed concern for her own future while Edward VII was dying.

After receiving a fatal injection of morphine from Sir Francis Laking, the royal physician — euthanasia apparently legal for royalty but forbidden for ordinary people — the King ceased breathing. According to Sir Francis Laking's much kinder version of the deathbed scene this was when Mrs Keppel had hysterics. Queen Alexandra, under stress, revealed the depth of her feelings about the intrusion of her husband's mistress and ordered, 'Get *that woman* away from here'.[16] This story was reported by both Laking and Lord Esher.

However, Lord Esher in *Journals and Letters* claimed *he* was the one who led the hysterical Mrs Keppel from the King's chamber into a side room to recover her composure.

The King in Love, Edward VII's Mistresses, by biographer Theo Aronson, has Sir Francis, the royal physician, lead the sobbing Mrs Keppel out of the bed chamber of the dead King, leaving Queen Alexandra alone with her husband's corpse. The version of the deathbed story related by Alice's daughter years later differs from both these accounts and naturally omits Alice's hysterics.

***

Back home at Portman Square, Alice's little daughter Sonia always remembered how her mother lay grief-stricken in bed with the blinds drawn, refusing to talk to anyone for days. Alice was genuinely fond of Edward VII. But what she could not reveal to her daughter was that the drawer of the King's bedside table contained £10,000, a fortune at the time. According to Sir Ernest Cassel, the King had planned to hand this money over to his mistress as his final gift aware she would be ostracised by his son once he was dead.

Lady Knollys, the Queen's Lady in Waiting, burned Queen Alexandra's diary and other papers after the Queen's death, so the question of what happened with Edward VII's farewell gift to his mistress in the drawer by the bedside remains unanswered.

While arrangements were made for the King's lying-in-State, his dead body lay in his bedroom for over a week. Just before the King was placed in his coffin, the Queen called Lord Esher so he could say goodbye to the King he had served so loyally. Lord Esher recorded in his diary that 'The Queen talked to me with a tenderness which betrayed the love in her soul... She had at last got all to herself the man who was the love of her youth'.

At the reading of the King's will it was revealed that he had left Mrs Keppel a large bequest. Her enemies spread the story that she had behaved badly at the King's deathbed.

Alice realised that remaining in London was impossible. King George V and Queen Mary, detested her and even refused to allow her to sign the condolence book for the late King. His lying-in-state was visited by thousands of loyal subjects, many of them in tears. Alice was given a private viewing and ushered in at night by a side door, dignified as a queen she wore black with a long veil that covered her from head to toe.

The writer Wilfred Blunt recorded from his 'pillow talk' with the courtesan Catherine Walters, one time sexual partner and confidante of the King, that Edward was impotent in his final years. On reading the fulsome obituaries, praising Edward VII for his virtues, aware that he had been an enthusiastic adulterer, Blunt sardonically observed in his diary,

> ...the [late} King has been praised as though he were St Francis of Assisi. Not a single newspaper or clergyman referred to Mrs Keppel or any of the 110 ladies he has loved or to his gambling... According to strict theology the King is most certainly burning in hell. Yet, bishops and priests, Catholic, Protestant and Non-conformist, join together in giving him a glorious place in heaven![17]

However, over half a million people turned out for the funeral procession as Edward VII was greatly loved.

Edward VII's son, George V, loathed Mrs Keppel and thought her an evil woman. Alice knew that she would be *persona non grata* at court, shunned by those who clustered around the new King. George V was concerned about the existence of indiscreet letters Edward VII may have written to Alice. He was already facing blackmail demands from Daisy, Countess of Warwick, who was short of money. But blackmail was not what Alice had in mind — if she had received indiscreet letters from the King she burned them. What Alice wanted was respectability and presentation at court for her daughters so they could make good marriages.

When Edward VII died, Alice was only 41. It was the end of the Edwardian age, an era of high living and low morals.

Alice continued to live with 'a certain magnificence.' She thought it was wise to remove herself from London.[18] Fortuitously, she received an invitation from Bertie's old friend, Sir Thomas

Lipton, to stay at one of Lipton's many tea plantations. Alice travelled to Ceylon accompanied by Violet and Sonia, a nanny, a French governess for Violet and her brother Archie and his wife. George Keppel remained in London and continued working for Sir Thomas Lipton.

After a year spent with their mother and their aunt and uncle in the humid heat of Ceylon, Violet and Sonia were sent to Germany with their governess. By this time Violet's deep seated jealousy of Sonia and antagonism with her mother was noticeable.

Alice accompanied her brother and sister-in-law to China where she bought superb Chinese antiques and Oriental porcelains. Sonia noted that by the time Alice returned to London her hair had turned white and her mother used a flattering silvery grey rinse which suited her skin tones.

***

Mrs Keppel had great talent for making money. She proceeded to increase her fortune and make provision for her own future and that of her daughters. She used the late King's bequest to purchase a large run-down house in Grosvenor Street which had been subdivided into apartments. Alice redecorated the four apartments, kept one for herself; gave one to George, one to young Sonia and the fourth one to Violet.[19] She also purchased an investment house in the handsome avenue called Queensgate in South Kensington, near the Science Museum. Alice renovated the investment house and resold it at a good profit.

MRS KEPPEL'S DAUGHTERS – VIOLET AND SONIA

Years earlier, when Violet was ten, Alice had sent her on a holiday to Florence with Vita Sackville-West, accompanied by their respective governesses. Unknown to Alice, the precocious Violet had given Vita a ring (that had once belonged to a Venetian Doge) and declared that she loved Vita. While heterosexual affairs and adultery were socially acceptable in aristocratic circles, lesbianism was seen as scandalous and depraved.

On learning that Vita had become engaged to Harold Nicholson, Violet felt betrayed. She refused to attend Vita's wedding, which took place in October 1913. Vita and Harold Nicholson's marriage was unconventional — they loved each other but at the same time both of them pursued other romances.

Alice refused to believe there could be any *genuine* love between Violet and Vita. She had planned Violet's debutante season and coming-out ball, hoping her eldest daughter would accept a proposal of marriage. Alice warned Violet to forget her love for Vita as, if it became public knowledge, the scandal would ruin Sonia's marriage prospects. Violet stubbornly refused to cooperate with Alice's extravagant plans for her debutante season.

In the summer of 1914 the Keppels holidayed at Clingendaal House near The Hague, owned by a Dutch relative, Daisy, Baroness de Brienen. Violet was still furious with Vita for marrying Harold Nicholson but insisted on inviting both of them to Clingendaal House. Harold, himself a closet homosexual, was wary of Violet and refused to attend. The Keppels' house party at Clingendaal was cut short when the Kaiser's troops invaded Belgium. Alice and her family caught the next boat back to Harwich. Alice was given two cabins because of her 'quasi-royal' status.

The Keppels arrived back in Mayfair to find England at war with Germany. All the banks were closed and their Grosvenor Street house was deserted as the servants had been given a holiday. As neither Alice nor her daughters could even boil an egg they took all their meals at The Ritz.

A few days later, George Keppel, aged 49, rejoined his old regiment and acquitted himself bravely in the trenches of France. When home on brief leave, George's shoulders and back ached from the weeks he had spent crouched in the trenches.

During London's zeppelin raids, Alice and her daughters slept on camp beds in the drawing room among Alice's Louis XV *fauteuils*, Chippendale furniture and gilt mirrors.

Subsequently, Alice went to northern France to work in a volunteer hospital at Etaples run by her friend, Lady Sarah Wilson, a Churchill relative. She managed to wangle herself a train trip to

Paris in order to buy designer clothes from the House of Worth before returning to London as the heroine of the hour.

On 11 November 1918, World War One ended and two weeks later Vita and Violet eloped to France.[20] Alice was horrified — she had no objection to adultery but lesbian love was something she could not tolerate. She was terrified by the harm it would do to both Violet's and Sonia's marriage prospects. Alice knew that few aristocratic families would want their son and heir to marry the daughter of the King's mistress.

After spending four happy months working on their novel and living *la vie de Boheme* in France, Vita finally returned to her sons and her Kentish home, because her nanny, hired to look after young Ben and Nigel, had given notice. Violet, who lived on an allowance provided by Alice, had little choice but to return to Grosvenor Square, where Alice insisted she get married.

Violet was very attractive and soon found a suitor. Major Denys Trefusis, a war hero who had been awarded a Military Cross, hoped that once the war was over he would become a writer. Even Vita approved of Denys, and described him as a crusader. He spoke fluent Russian and French, had fought bravely at Ypres and on the Somme and spent two months in a field hospital recovering from mustard gas poisoning. He dreamed of marrying Violet, settling down in a quiet cottage and writing books.

Alice had insisted Violet marry Denys or she would cut off her daughter's allowance. Violet agreed, provided she did not have to consummate the marriage.[21] Alice, desperate to avert a scandal, promised to buy Denys and Violet a country cottage and pay Dennis an annual income so he could concentrate on writing without having to worry about money.

The Hon George and Mrs Keppel sent out invitations for Violet's lavish white wedding for 16 June 1919. Alice engaged Dame Nellie Melba to sing Gounod's 'Ave Maria' at the ceremony, determined to put on a good show.

Meanwhile Vita and Violet had made a secret pact. Violet's marriage to Denys would provide them with an ideal cover to *continue* their lesbian relationship. Violet nursed the irrational hope that Vita would rescue her from her 'arranged' marriage —

they would run away together and live in the south of France where as girls they had spent happy holidays. Since both had extravagant tastes and little money of their own, this was pure fantasy on Violet's part.

On the morning of 16 June 1919, a distraught Violet Keppel waited in vain for Vita to appear and sent her a reproachful note saying her heart was broken at the idea of leaving Vita.

Violet put on the expensive wedding gown of Florentine silk Alice had paid for. On her father's arm she walked up the aisle of St George's Church in Hanover Square to marry Denys Trefusis, vowing she would never forgive her mother for forcing her to marry. Denys Trefusis had no idea Violet and Vita had been in a lesbian relationship. He believed his wife's talk of non-consummation was due to the fact she was scared of sex and was certain he would be able to deal with this once they were married.

The Trefusis-Keppel honeymoon was spent at the Ritz Hotel in Paris. In the honeymoon suite Violet refused to consummate her marriage and to Denys's surprise Vita appeared. Vita icily informed Denys that she and Violet had loved each other for years, explained they were lesbian and provided details about the ways they made love.

Denys almost fainted from shock but recovered himself. Furious he had been tricked into marriage, he telephoned Alice in London saying he never wanted to see Violet again. He demanded Alice come to Paris and take Violet home, saying he wanted nothing more to do with any of them.[22]

Alice was desperate to prevent the story reaching the newspapers, fearing it would affect Sonia's chances of making a good marriage. Eventually, Violet returned to her husband and Denys kept quiet about his unconsummated marriage.

***

Sonia Keppel was presented to King George and Queen Mary at Buckingham Palace. Alice accompanied her daughter, wearing a valuable necklace of diamonds that had once belonged to Queen

Marie Antoinette to give herself confidence. Queen Mary still disapproved of her as a former royal mistress but could no longer ban her from court to present her daughter.

Sonia's London season was a success. She received a proposal from the eligible young Rolie Cubitt, heir of the pious and wealthy Lord Ashcombe. Rolie was the Ashmore's eldest surviving son. As his two elder brothers had been killed in World War One, Rolie would inherit the Ashcombe title and the prosperous building firm of Thomas Cubitt.

Alice's main worry was that Lord and Lady Ashcombe, who were devout church goers, might hear about Violet and Vita's lesbian affair and refuse to let their heir marry Sonia.

Lord Ashcombe was far from delighted with this marriage. He found himself having to negotiate the marriage settlement with Alice rather than with George Keppel. Alice, a talented card player, proved herself to be an equally shrewd negotiator. She named the handsome sum of money she was prepared to settle on Sonia, smiled charmingly and asked Lord Ashcombe to match it.

Unnerved by having to negotiate with a woman, Lord Ashcombe hastily agreed. After signing the marriage agreement and paying more than he had intended, Lord Ashcombe observed that he hoped such an expensive marriage would endure.

'My dear Lord Ashcombe' said Alice in her husky voice, 'Neither you nor I can legislate for the future'.[23]

On 17 November 1920, the Hon Roland Cubitt married Sonia Keppel at the Guards Chapel, Wellington Barracks (the same chapel in which Sonia's granddaughter Camilla Shand would marry Andrew Parker Bowles). At this autumn wedding Sonia wore a gown of brocade velvet and carried a bouquet of lilies.[24] The bride was terrified that her nervousness would precipitate one of her asthma attacks, but her fears were groundless.

Mr and Mrs Denys Trefusis attended Sonia's wedding. Denys was under considerable stress and smoked far too much. After the reception he and Violet quarrelled again. Violet accused her husband of being her 'jailor' and declared she still loved Vita. In despair at how his life had turned out, Denys told Alice Keppel he wanted the sham marriage annulled.

To Alice, annulment on grounds of non-consummation spelt disaster for Sonia, marooned among the pious Ashcombes and members of Hampshire's hunting, shooting and fishing set. Alice threatened to disinherit Violet should she leave her husband. Violet was trapped and so this unhappy travesty of a marriage dragged on for another nine years.

Vita's and Violet's dislike for their respective mothers led both of them to write thinly disguised novels about married upper-class women who profited from sex with wealthy men. Vita's novel *The Edwardians* depicts Alice as an adulterous snob named Mrs Romola Cheyne.[25] Violet's novel, *Broderie Anglaise*, published in 1935, deals with the hypocrisy of arranged marriages. Violet depicted her mother as a character named Lady Shorne, a snobbish, money-hungry former 'beauty' with silvery blue hair. Violet's cruel satire wounded Alice as she had always regarded her adulteries as a means of securing her family's financial future.

Violet rejected any notion of 'sacrifice', claiming 'Lady Shorne' was mercenary to the core and valued her antique furniture more than she valued her daughters, using her beauty to obtain money and jewels from men. Violet also took revenge on her younger sister Sonia in another satirical novel titled *Tandem*, (1933) in which the clever elder sister is involved in 'the whirl of the literary life of Paris', while the dull younger sister remains 'stuck in the immovable respectability of the English hunting circle'.

Violet's thirst for revenge ran deep. She blamed Sonia for having ruined her chances of a perfect relationship with Vita (which was a distortion of the facts). She was determined that Sonia would never inherit her tower at St Loup in France and threatened to leave it to Vita Sackville-West.

Meanwhile, Sonia and Roland Cubitt were members of the horse-mad landed gentry in rural Hampshire, raising three children – Rosalind, Henry and Jeremy. Rosalind Cubitt, born in 1921, married Major Bruce Shand and their eldest child, Camilla, was born just before Alice died.

TUSCAN INTERLUDE – VILLA DELL'OMBRELLINO.

In 1924, with the profits from successful property deals – the sale of her renovated Grosvenor Street mansion and her Queensgate property – Alice bought herself an imposing villa estate in Bellosguardo, a quiet enclave on the outskirts of Florence[26]. The three storey Villa dell'Ombrellino had once been home to the great astronomer Galileo and had a superb view over Florence[27]. The American author, Henry James, claimed this view as the most beautiful in the world.

Violet described her mother as being amused by 'turning a house that was practically a lost cause into a thing of beauty'. Alice soon realised that modernising and furnishing a fourteenth century Tuscan villa was very different to renovating houses in London. Osbert Sitwell and other British friends helped Alice buy oak chests and *cassone* or marriage chests, which were in keeping with the villa, as well as huge mirrors and gilded chairs that resembled thrones.

Alice enjoyed buying oil paintings and antiques and having them restored. But her inability to speak Italian became something of a joke. All she could tell the head gardener was *'Bisogna begonia'* or 'I need begonias', so the garden of the Villa dell'Ombrellino was filled with these small pink flowers.[28]

Alice invested the rest of her money in foreign banks for security and settled down to enjoy life in Florence, a city that had an English library, an English pharmacy and English bookshops due to its large expatriate British and American community.

George enjoyed the art museums of Florence and wrote a guide book about them in English. Alice was not interested in museums. She was a collector and enjoyed bargaining for antiques and paintings. Eventually, she learned enough Italian to deal with her cook and army of housemaids. She enjoyed hosting superb lunch and dinner parties, sometimes inviting as many as forty or sixty guests. Among them were European royalty, English friends on holiday and titled Italians. Alice's guests included Prince Alexander Karageorge of Serbia, Prince Paul of Greece, several

Romanian princesses, nine English and French duchesses and a clutch of assorted European ambassadors.

Sir Harold Acton, the acknowledged expert on Tuscan villas on which he was writing a book, had initially been wary of becoming friendly with the late King's mistress, but Alice's wit and charm won him over. He was soon claiming that Mrs Keppel had 'cleverness, vivacity and a generous heart'. Harold Acton advised Alice to remove all the ugly nineteenth century additions from the front façade and the tatty palms which tended to drop huge leaves on guests' heads. According to him palm trees were out of place in a traditional Renaissance *parterre* garden.

Before World War Two and the onset of mass tourism to Tuscany, servants cost very little. 'Chips' Channon, when visiting the Keppels in 1934, described Alice as 'living in a super luxurious villa full of treasures, white haired, magnificent and young in spirit.'[29]

Along the Via Tornabuoni, Mrs Keppel became one of the sights of Florence, seen sipping tea in Donney's tea rooms or buying English newspapers at Sieber's bookshop.

By 1937, Violet, wanting a reconciliation with her mother, visited the Villa dell'Ombrellino. While Alice planned grand lunches and dinners, Violet, now in her late forties, flirted with young bisexual men. George Keppel sped around the narrow streets of Florence in a little red sports car Alice had bought him. He would take English and American girls (who he called his 'cuties' to museums or invite them to pose naked in a studio he rented in town. It seems likely George Keppel — often derided as London's most famous cuckold — had been chasing young women for years while Alice was occupied with her lovers.

Mr and Mrs Keppel made frequent trips to London where they stayed at the Ritz. They were staying there at the time of the abdication crisis when Edward VIII abandoned the throne in order to marry his divorced mistress, Mrs Wallis Simpson. Alice heard Edward's Abdication Speech broadcast in the dining room of the hotel and was overheard to claim disapprovingly, 'Things were done *far* better in my day'.

In August 1939, Mr and Mrs Keppel returned to England to attend their 18-year old grand-daughter, Rosalind Cubitt's coming-out-ball at Holland House, the London home of Alice's former lover Lord Stavordale.

Because of all the talk of war with Germany, Alice worried about her money held in banks in Monte Carlo and Florence and about Violet, now living in an apartment in Paris. In spite of the danger that Mussolini would arrest and intern British citizens, Alice and George returned to the Villa dell'Ombrellino.

Alice had the forethought to place her most valuable items of furniture and paintings in storage in Florence. When Mussolini declared war on England, Biarritz, where Alice had spent so many holidays with Edward VII, seemed the logical place to board a ship for England. She sent a telegram to Violet urging her to join them there, but the problem of actually obtaining berths when so many expatriates were trying to return to England had to be solved.

Fortunately, Alice still had friends in high places. The Keppels were offered berths on board a British destroyer leaving St Jean de Luz, a small port and holiday resort near Biarritz.

As their car approached the quayside they saw a dense mass of people burdened with luggage surging towards a counter where officials were inspecting their passports. The long queue of expatriate Britons, desperate to escape from the Nazis, stretched for hundreds of metres.

Mr and Mrs Keppel and their daughter, accompanied by Alice's French maid carrying her jewellery cases, were escorted through the crowd and up the gangplank. Meanwhile several burly sailors were ordered to carry on board Mrs Keppel's trunks filled with elegant clothes.

The captain kissed Mrs Keppel's hand, and said he was delighted to lend her his cabin. The rest of the passengers were furious — they had to spend the night sitting on hard benches or on the deck and many were not allowed to bring any luggage.

MRS KEPPEL — EMPRESS OF THE RITZ

Mrs Keppel was spared the distressing sight of German tanks and lorries rumbling over the Ponte Vecchio, along the road to Bellosguardo and Nazi officers billeting at her beloved Villa dell' Ombrellino.

Arriving back in England the Keppels went to stay with Sonia Cubbitt at her home, Hall Place in the Hampshire village of West Meon. Alice complained that her grandsons were noisy and undisciplined and the house was cold. In wartime Britain all coal and coke was rationed, Sonia's marriage was collapsing and tempers fraying badly.

Alice and George moved to Polesden Lacy, home of the ever hospitable Maggie Greville, who was able to obtain splendid food through black market connections in spite of wartime rationing. But even Maggie Greville became irritated, hearing Alice recount again and again the story of her escape from the Nazis. Mrs Greville commented dryly, 'To hear Alice talk about her escape, one would think she had *swum* the Channel holding her maid between her teeth.'[30]

In his seventies George had the aches and pains of old age but Alice seemed ageless, although overweight. Confessing to 'Chips' Channon she preferred 'bombs to boredom', Alice refused to return to West Meon to stay with Sonia. She booked herself and George into a suite at The Ritz, with a view over Green Park. When Alice told her daughter what she was planning, Sonia asked plaintively, 'Don't you *like* nature?'

'Yes', replied Alice, 'The nature of The Ritz'.

The Ritz had been constructed with a steel frame, so was deemed the safest place in London during the Blitz. The hotel, overlooking Green Park, hosted the *crème de la crème* of European and British society. The Polish Prime Minister in exile had his suite at the Ritz as did the exiled King Carol and his mistress, Magda Lupescu. Every night there was a private party in someone's suite. Alice was in her element, having managed to bring her French *couturier* clothes and jewels back with her, delighted that she was better dressed than most exiled royalty.

Wartime meals were limited to two courses. However, Alice ordered her guests the finest French champagne to compensate and entertained so lavishly the staff referred to her as the 'Empress of the Ritz'. Hitler's bombs did not worry the fearless Mrs Keppel. 'Chips' Channon described her as looking magnificent, her silver-grey hair immaculate; although she 'sometimes tippled' too much and repeated the same stories again and again.

In 1945, Nazi Germany was defeated. The British Government, laden with debt, instituted a strict limit of £55 on currency taken out of England. But Alice, most of whose fortune was held in banks in Monte Carlo and Italy, was not affected. She was able to return to her beloved Villa dell'Ombrellino and found Florence had suffered badly with bridges and buildings destroyed by the retreating German Army. The Germans had even blown up the Ponte Santa Trinita with the Michelangelo statues on its parapets.

Alice Keppel was 76 years old when she returned to the Villa dell'Ombrellino. Many of her former servants were dead, the parquet floors had been damaged by the hob-nailed boots of German soldiers. Food was scarce and the black market was flourishing. The practical Sonia Cubitt brought tinned food for her Tuscan holiday while Violet Trefusis brought books and ball gowns.

World War Two had changed everything. Maids and cooks, once so cheap to employ had vanished. Wealthy villa owners, who scarcely knew their way round their kitchens, were forced to cook their own meals and stoke large coke boilers themselves. This was not Alice's idea of gracious living. She returned to the luxury of the Ritz and became its *grande dame*. Alice's last visit to the Villa dell'Ombrellino took place in 1947, the year Sonia and Rolie Cubitt divorced. Alice was not pleased. Rolie had by now inherited the title of Baron Ashmore and Alice always loved a title.

On learning from her doctors she was suffering from cirrhosis of the liver, Alice decided she preferred to die at the Villa dell'Ombrellino. Violet left Paris for Florence to be with her mother, who had lost a great deal of weight and had trouble eating.

On 17 July 1947, Alice's granddaughter, Rosalind Cubitt, who had married Major Bruce Shand, gave birth to a pretty little daughter named Camilla Rosemary.

On 11 September 1947, Alice Keppel died at the Villa dell'-Ombrellino, aged 78. Her husband was heartbroken and died shortly after. The Keppels were buried side by side in Florence's English cemetery.

A memorial service for Mrs Keppel was held in London at St Mark's, Audley Street in Mayfair. The service was attended by relatives and close friends. Alice's obituary in *The Times* discreetly referred to her long friendship with King Edward and Queen Alexandra. Omitting the fact that Alice had been the King's mistress meant the proprieties were observed.

Sonia Keppel's divorce was made absolute the same year her parents died.

On Sonia's death, among other bequests, she left a quarter of a million pounds to her married granddaughter, Camilla Parker Bowles, who followed family tradition, became a royal mistress and *married* her lover, the Prince of Wales. The differences between her story and that of Alice Keppel proves how times have changed and how the royal family has adapted to changes in society.

Top: Duntreath Castle, Alice Edmonstone's ancestral home.

Above: Alice as a young woman.

Left: Alice's husband, the Hon George Keppel.

Left:
Alice Keppel with her daughter Violet.

Below:
Chatsworth, where the Prince and Princess of Wales, as well as Alice Keppel, were house guests of the Duke and Duchess of Devonshire.

Alice Keppel when she was King Edward VII's mistress.

King Edward VII, considerably older than Alice.

Interior of Polesden Lacey near Dorking as decorated and furnished by Maggie Greville where Alice Keppel and the Prince of Wales were frequent houseguests and where Mr and Mrs Keppel stayed in World War Two.

Above:
Villa dell'Ombrellino at Bellosguardo on the outskirts of Florence, sold after Alice's death. Part of the villa is now a function centre specialising in weddings.

Right:
Alice Keppel as a *grande dame* in old age, on holiday with one of her daughters.

THE ROYAL HOUSE

OF WINDSOR

CHAPTER 7

Freda (Winifred) Dudley Ward (1891–1983)
and
Edward David, Prince of Wales
(King Edward VIII, later Duke of Windsor)

The Prince of Wales made himself the slave of whoever he loved... a masochist, he liked being humbled and degraded... Unfortunately, pity is not an emotion conducive to love'. Freda Dudley Ward, discussing her intimate relationship with Edward, Prince of Wales.

The Prince is half man, half child... as though some cells in his brain remained entirely undeveloped. Sir Alan Lascelles, private secretary to Edward, Prince of Wales.

A ROMANTIC ENCOUNTER WITH THE PRINCE OF WALES

In February 1918, Freda Dudley Ward and Edward, Prince of Wales, met by chance.

Freda, wife of the Rt. Hon Dudley Ward, had been out dancing with her young admirer, 'Buster' Dominguez. World War One was raging and German Zeppelins made raids on London. Walking home through Belgrave Square, Freda and her escort heard the sound of an air raid siren, so they took shelter under the porch of the nearest house. It happened to be the residence of the wealthy socialite Mrs Maude Kerr-Smiley, the elder sister of Ernest Simpson (the first husband of Wallis, Duchess of Windsor).

Mrs Kerr-Smiley noticed a good-looking young couple in evening dress sheltering under her portico. Worried for their safety in the air raid she invited Freda and Buster Dominguez inside. As they entered, Mrs Kerr-Smiley told them she was giving a dinner dance, but her guests had left the ballroom to shelter from the raid in the basement.

Freda and her escort went down the stone stairs to join the guests, seated on wooden benches in the basement, next door to the wine cellar. They were surprised to see that the Prince of Wales was one of the guests.

Prince Edward observed Freda in the shimmering light of one of the candles and was delighted that such an attractive young woman took the empty seat next to him. It was not long before he and Freda became involved in conversation. The Prince told Freda that he was an officer in the Grenadier Guards and was on leave from northern France.

Freda and Edward chatted away in the candlelit basement and shared a bottle of wine, loosening the shy Prince's tongue. The warm candlelight encouraged confidences and soon Freda and the young Prince of Wales felt like old friends.

Buster Dominguez got the message that his company was no longer wanted and disappeared.

Freda asked the Prince to call her 'Fredie', as she was known by that name by her family and friends. In return Edward asked 'Fredie' to call him 'David', the name used by *his* family. The handsome Prince learned that Freda was 23, a few month older than himself, and discovered that she was a sophisticated and witty young woman. Like the Prince, she enjoyed the good things of life — they both loved dancing and as Freda's husband had a senior position in the Royal Household they had mutual friends.

When the 'all clear' sounded and the lights came on, Freda and Edward could finally see each other properly. The Prince of Wales found Freda beautiful with her slim, boyish figure, her heart-shaped face, framed by shining dark hair, and her doe-like eyes. For her part, Freda realised that the young Prince was even more handsome in real life than in his photographs.

The Prince of Wales was convinced he had found a soul mate. Since he was sensitive about his lack of height, the fact that Freda was petite made her doubly desirable. Before they said goodbye, the Prince asked for her address, aware that she and her husband lived separate lives.

The following morning Freda received a bouquet of flowers and a handwritten note of thanks. In the note the Prince of Wales asked Freda whether he could visit her at her home.

THE FLAWED 'PETER PAN' PRINCE

Until the age of three, Edward and his younger brother Bertie were cared for by Nanny Green. Queen Mary rarely visited her young sons in the nursery, so they were deprived of their mother's love. Nanny Green, who had lost her own child *and* her marriage, was a highly disturbed woman. Edward, who resembled her dead son, was her favourite, but the way she treated him caused serious damage to his personality. She often spanked the little boy in anger and when he started to cry, kissed him and fondled his genitals to give him pleasure, a practice that became imprinted on little Edward's mind. What Nanny Green did to him had a bizarre effects on him — all his life the Prince associated the acts of spanking and spoiling with sex and demanded this kind of treatment from his mistresses in order to obtain sexual satisfaction.[1]

In 1911, when young Edward, Prince of Wales, was a cadet at Dartmouth Royal Naval College, he suffered a severe attack of mumps. This fact was recorded by *The Lancet*, but the medical journal did *not* mention that the Prince suffered from mumps orchitis, which has often serious consequences in adolescent boys.

As a result, Prince Edward suffered from severe and painful testicular inflammation, which caused a lack of testosterone and sperm production as well as erectile dysfunction. In Edward's case it also arrested his mental and physical development.[2]

As a Crown Prince, whose duty was to sire an heir for the nation, Edward's sexual problems were causing him considerable anxiety. His parents could not understand why he was so reluctant to marry a virginal princess.

King George and Queen Mary never discussed sex or other intimate or emotional topics. Queen Mary believed the most important thing in life was to maintain royal dignity and 'keep a stiff upper lip'. She had no idea her eldest son was experiencing sexual problems as such things were never mentioned in the royal family.

※

As a naval cadet, the Prince of Wales was usually bottom of his class. He was often teased in the communal dormitory and the washroom about his puny stature, shrivelled testicles and small penis. His younger brother Bertie, the future King George VI, was teased about his stammer. Edward hated the Royal Naval College and after bitter arguments with his father was withdrawn from it and sent to France to improve his French. Then came six happy months in Germany, staying with various cousins and speaking German with them.

When war broke out in 1914, the young Prince of Wales joined the Grenadier Guards as a junior officer and was posted to France. He was not sent to the trenches as he had hoped, but was given an administrative post behind the front line for fear he would be captured. All his requests to serve in the front line were refused.

In France the Prince of Wales insisted he was driven close to the front line. Once there, he was horrified by the sight of limbless corpses protruding from shell craters and men and horses stuck deep in the mud. When his driver refused to take him any closer to the front line the Prince of Wales commandeered a bicycle and rode to a casualty clearing station. The horrific sights of men with missing limbs and faces shot away gave him nightmares.

Billeted in a French town where soldiers from the trenches came for rest and recreation, Prince Edward, like other young men of his age, had his first crude sexual encounters with French prostitutes, whose painted faces and dyed hair repelled yet excited him.

At the age of 21, the Prince received a large sum of accrued royalties from the lands and properties owned by the Duchy of

Cornwall. As Duke of Cornwall, he continued to receive annual royalties from the Duchy.

FREDA, THE MOTHER-MISTRESS

Freda Dudley Ward was born into a wealthy family. Her father, Colonel Charles Wilfred Birkin CMG, owned a profitable lace factory in Nottingham. He was also a large landowner.

Freda adored her father who provided her with a private allowance, which gave her a degree of financial independence, a privilege most women lacked. Freda's relationship with her American mother was cold and disappointing.

At the time Freda met Prince Edward, she had been married for five years to the Rt. Hon William Dudley Ward, the former Chief Whip of the Liberal Party. William Dudley Ward was a nephew of the Earl of Dudley and a grandson of Lord Esher, who was Lieutenant-Governor of Windsor Castle and a member of the King's Privy Council, as was Dudley Ward. Freda was 16 years younger than her husband.

Freda and her elderly husband realised that their marriage had been a mistake, but for the sake of their children, the Dudley Wards decided to stay together and have an 'open' marriage. A divorce in that era was so scandalous that it could have ruined the political career of Freda's husband. As her marriage was failing, Freda, who had a high sex drive, had a few casual affairs with young upper-class men.

After that first meeting in the candlelit basement, Freda and Edward, Prince of Wales, met at regular intervals and soon became lovers. The Prince desired Freda as a surrogate mother as well as a mistress. He liked the fact that Freda was a very loving mother to her little daughters, Angela (Angie) and Penelope (Pempie). The way she kissed and cuddled her daughters made Edward aware of how much he had missed in a childhood, deprived of maternal love. The immature Prince of Wales fell passionately in love with Freda.

Back in France, Edward missed Freda desperately and wrote to her almost every day. In long rambling immature letters, he told his mistress how much he loved her. His letters were filled with exclamation marks, boyish jokes, sexual innuendo and expressed the deep-seated anger he felt for his father.

Edward's letters to Freda are those of an adoring son to his mother or a teenager with a crush on a film star. Over 250 revealing letters between Edward and Freda were discovered among a stamp collection in Canada, edited and published in book form in 1988.[3] Readers of the letters were amazed by the childlike fashion of the Prince's writing, his immaturity, his keenness to avoid the responsibilities of adult life and the way he clung to Freda. The letters reveal the Prince's juvenile personality. He invented his own lisping baby language — 'pleath' stands for please, 'vewwy' for 'very' and 'Freda' becomes 'Fredie Wedie'. He also uses infantile phrases such as 'My vewy vewy own precious darling' or 'I'm tewwwibly thleepy'.

In one of his letters Edward wrote, 'I don't feel I can even exist, let alone try to live much longer without you, my precious darling beloved little Mummie'. He made abject apologies to his 'darling Fredie' for his 'naughty feelings' and his inadequate sexual performance.

Unfortunately, Freda's replies have disappeared, so she remains a shadowy figure in the story of the Peter Pan Prince. It seems significant that the Prince signed many of his letters to Freda 'your *little* David' and referred to himself in the third person as a 'naughty little boy'. His *paraphilia* (imprinting of the love object in childhood on sexual development) gave him a craving to be spanked and humiliated, as Nanny Green had done before kissing and cuddling him.

※

In 1919, the Prince left the British Army. From that time onwards he phoned Freda every day or visited her at her matrimonial home near Regent's Park, usually arriving there at about 5 pm. He played with her daughters until it was time for their evening meal. Freda employed staff so they had a choice — Edward would either stay at her home for dinner or invite Freda to dine at a restaurant. Sometimes they went to a night club where they enjoyed dancing together and made an eye-catching couple on the dance floor.

The bachelor Prince loved visiting Freda's home, aware that her husband worked until late at night and there was no chance he could appear. Eventually, William Dudley Ward realised the real situation between the Prince and his wife, but turned a blind eye.

With his mistress and her little daughters Edward enjoyed simple family pleasures, such as a plate of sandwiches and a quiet drink beside the fire on winter evenings — enjoyments he had never experienced at Buckingham Palace or Windsor Castle.

Some afternoons Edward put the song *The Teddy Bear's Picnic* on the gramophone or played games with Freda's two little girls and their teddy bears. Freda was surprised to discover how pleased Edward was to be treated like one of her children. Sometimes she found it necessary to scold him for arriving on her doorstep at inconvenient times.

The Prince retreated from his problems into an infantile affair with his mistress. As he had rarely experienced maternal love, he became more dependent on Freda as a mother figure than as a mistress. Freda felt flattered that the Prince put so much trust in her. Edward encouraged her to humiliate and degrade him before they made love together, which had alarmed her the first time it happened. Later she told a relative that 'The Prince *enjoyed* being humbled and humiliated — in fact, he positively begged for it.'

Their bizarre relationship was aided by the fact that Freda was very understanding and, although not in love with the Prince, was fond of him in a maternal way. She felt sympathy for his sexual problems and hoped that with sound advice he would be a good king. Freda had studied Freud's theories on child development in an effort to understand her own children and was perceptive enough to understand that the immature Prince of Wales had severe sexual and emotional problems. She realised that the lack of motherly love and the bizarre treatment of the abusive Nanny Green had damaged her royal lover and tried to help him. With a mixture of tact, warmth and humour Freda did her best to build up the Prince's ego. She tried to alleviate his sexual problems and prepare him for the major role he must undertake in years to come.

Edward was always very generous at Christmas and birthdays with gifts of jewellery for his mistress and her daughters. Freda was independently wealthy, so she was not desperate for couture clothes or jewels. She was neither insecure nor avaricious and did not need expensive gifts. One Christmas Prince Edward gave Freda and her little daughters a gigantic teddy bear made from a tree that had been specially trimmed by a topiary expert into this shape. (The tree was moved to the river bank at Sunbury-on-Thames and serves as reminder of Edward's love of playing with teddy bears with Freda's children.)

Freda was fond of Edward but was never 'in love' with him — to her he was the 'little Prince' who had never grown up. Owing to his erectile problems their sexual relationship grew more difficult, but Freda did her best to build up Edward's self-esteem, impeded by his father's low opinion of his capabilities. She tried to convince the heir to the throne to smoke less and moderate his drinking.

George V had given his eldest son Fort Belvedere, located near Sunningdale on the edge of Windsor Great Park. Fort Belvedere, known as 'The Fort', had been unoccupied for some time and was in a bad state of repair. Freda helped the Prince to transform it into an attractive home by decorating and furnishing it, convinced that the old building with its octagonal sitting room could be an attractive weekend retreat. It was quick to reach by road from London and the Prince could relax there, with or without Freda, away from the chilly formality of life at Buckingham Palace.

The straight-laced King and Queen saw Freda as an unhappy married woman corrupting their son. They failed to understand that she was trying to help an emotionally confused young Prince with problems and getting scant thanks for it.

Eventually, Freda became disturbed about the fact that Edward always wanted to be 'mothered' by her. She had two children of her own and did not want a lover who behaved like a child. She was fond of the troubled Prince, but found their relationship far too time-consuming. Freda craved to go dancing and meet other friends — she wanted to escape from looking after two little girls and having to cope with an elderly grumpy husband.

✷

In 1919, the Prince went on an exhausting nationwide tour of Canada by train and visited camps for lumberjacks. He was entranced by the magnificent scenery and managed to stay on a bucking bronco.

Carried away by excitement, Edward bought a ranch in Alberta with some of his Duchy of Cornwall revenues, thinking it might be convenient if he wanted to run away from his responsibilities. He hoped the beauty of the scenery at the ranch might tempt Freda to leave England and her husband and live in Canada with him. He also hoped to find oil on his land.

The heir to the throne fantasised about running away with Freda, marrying her and escaping from what he called 'this ghastly official existence'. It was all very impractical and when Edward suggested the idea to Freda, she did not take him seriously.

The Prince ended his Canadian tour with a brief visit to America, which he loved. He visited private homes on Long Island which he found far more comfortable than chilly Buckingham Palace or Windsor Castle and was enormously attracted by the warmth and spontaneity of Americans. His American visit made him wish he was not the heir to the throne and was just an ordinary person.

On his return to London, Freda told Edward he must dismiss the idea of renouncing his position and running away with her — he was destined to become a much-loved King. Freda saw her role as propping up the fragile ego of an immature young Prince and helping him to take over the role life had marked out for him.

In letters to Freda and in discussions with his aides, the Prince of Wales revealed how much he detested the kind of life he was leading. On several occasions he talked of suicide as a away out, which worried Freda a great deal. In a disturbing letter, dated 7 November 1919, he wrote to her, 'My darling, I want to die young. How divine if we could die together. There's nothing I wish for more.'

ROMANCE WITH AN AUSTRALIAN BEAUTY.

George V and Queen Mary realised that their son's feelings for Freda were increasing in intensity and that he had become more and more dependent on his mistress. He wrote Freda passionate letters from 'Buck House' telling her he was her 'devoted little boy' although by now Edward was 25. His letters were those of a schoolboy in which he thanked 'Fredie Wedie' for her love, which was all he asked for.

To protect the heir to the throne from the influence of Mrs Dudley Ward, the King decided to send his heir, accompanied by his cousin, Lord Louis (Dickie) Mountbatten, on a round-the-world tour to the Antipodes, returning via the West Indies and California. King George V hoped that almost a year's absence from Mrs Dudley Ward would break his son's slavish dependence on a married woman whose husband he knew very well. The Rt. Hon William Dudley Ward had served as Treasurer of the Royal Household and now had the even more responsible position of Vice-Chamberlain of the Royal Household.

Officially the Prince of Wales' tour was intended to strengthen Commonwealth ties to the Mother Country and to thank the Anzacs for their sacrifices in the recent war. For that reason the Prince would have to make harrowing visits to limbless men in veterans' hospitals and homes for wounded diggers.

As a farewell gift Freda gave Edward a gold locket with one of her curls in it and a gold-rimmed seal for him to seal his letters to her which he was to send to England in the diplomatic bag. The Prince gave Freda a solid silver cigarette case inscribed *'I love you more than yesterday but less than tomorrow.'*

On the battleship *HMS Renown* Prince Edward first sailed to New Zealand and made an official tour from Auckland to Invercargill.

In mid-April 1920, the Prince of Wales left New Zealand for Australia and arrived at Melbourne's St Kilda Pier in a late summer heat wave. He was driven to Government House in an open car through crowded streets under the blazing sun. That afternoon there was a royal walkabout, but there were no security guards for crowd control. The handsome young Prince, surrounded by thousands of people, was prodded and poked by excited well-wishers.

In a letter written that night to Freda, the Prince claimed he had been left bruised and battered — his right hand and arm sore from shaking many hundreds of hands.

Every day the Prince of Wales met several hundreds of people and had to try and remember the names of those who were organising his tour. He had to make numerous speeches. At the end of each day he had just enough strength to write a long letter to Freda telling her how much he missed her and how eagerly he looked forward to receiving a letter from her. This was what gave him the strength to continue. He confided to Freda how much he wished to give up the job of 'princeing' and run away to Canada with her.

> This ghastly existence of mine really seems to get more intolerably strenuous and difficult each day... I just don't see how I'm going to avoid a nervous breakdown.

The Prince's boyish charm won him many admirers. Women wept with emotion as he appeared on platforms and tried to touch his coat when he walked through a crowd. Some who shook his hand refused to wash *their* hand for weeks afterwards. No one realised how stressful and tiring were these public appearances. Surrounded by huge crowds the Prince of Wales had to smile, shake hands and keep removing his hat in salutation for hours at a time.

In his letters to Freda he wrote how bored he was by opening dozens of factories and civic centres, planting trees, cutting ribbons, meeting self-important mayors and civic dignitaries and trying to remember their names. He revealed his fears of having a nervous breakdown. the Prince suffered from periods of depression and suicide became a recurrent threat in his letters.

Once again, the Prince suggested in his nightly letters to Freda they run away to his newly acquired ranch in the wilds of Alberta, bought on his Canadian tour. He told Freda that it would not be fair to give her the 'awful responsibility' of being Queen, aware she was bound to hate life in the royal goldfish bowl as much as he did. It became clear the Prince of Wales was seriously considering handing over his role to one of his younger brothers.

⁂

A sudden cold change gave Prince Edward a bad cough and Lord Mountbatten, worried Edward was overtired, insisted he had a day off. In letters to Freda he kept repeating his wish to escape the duties of royalty, which he called 'princeing' or 'stunting'. Once he wrote to Freda, 'Sometimes my tired little brain seems to snap and I feel I'm going mad, so perhaps an escape is necessary.'

From Melbourne HMS *Renown* ploughed through heavy seas with a seasick Prince on board to Perth for more official banquets and handshaking. From Perth he boarded a train heading for the south-west of Western Australia. Heavy rains had made the ground so wet that the rails had sunk into the mud. Fifteen kilometres from Bridgetown the royal carriage tipped over on its side, skidded along the track with its wheels in the air, injuring several passengers. As there was no sign of the Prince, railway personnel were frantic, fearing he was dead.

At long last, the Prince of Wales emerged from the carriage, cool as a cucumber, waving a cocktail shaker to show that he was unharmed. The Prince explained that he had stayed behind in the compartment to gather up private papers — obviously, letters from Freda he did not want anyone to find and read. The waiting crowd cheered itself hoarse when the Prince thanked his hosts for arranging such an interesting diversion for his journey. On the night of the accident, Edward wrote to Freda to assure her he was unharmed but missing her very much. Lacking Freda's restraining influence, the Prince drank and smoked far too much, hating his royal role but performing well to the crowds who greeted him.

His Royal Highness was cheered by workers who called him 'The People's Prince' or 'The Digger Prince.' His good looks and charm won him many friends. Although tired, he did his best to fulfil his gruelling schedule, which included awarding prizes for wood chopping, watching sheep-sheering and drinking beer with gold miners. He boarded the Trans-Australian Express to Cook Siding in the Nullabor to watch Aborigines dance and throw boomerangs and laid the foundation stones in the brand new capital of Canberra and for the new Brisbane City Hall.

In Sydney, everyone and his dog wanted to meet the Prince of Wales. Once again, he was prodded and pushed and surrounded by cheering crowds. The Prince wrote to Freda sending his sealed letters through the diplomatic bag, describing his visit to Randwick veterans' hospital.

> I had to shake hands with over thousand wounded men and there were over 200 amputation cases, which was vewy twying [very trying] as one has to have a short yarn with each and I returned here vewy exhausted and dazed.

On 18 June the Prince of Wales attended a public reception in Sydney's Town Hall. People queued all night in what the *Sydney Morning Herald* called 'the longest queue ever seen in Australia'. There, over a period of three hours over, 50,000 people filed past the Prince who had to smile and shake hands with as many of them as possible which he found exhausting. Edward had been asked by his friends Lord Loughborough and his Australian wife to look out for a young lady, called Mollee Little, who would be at the Town Hall reception. He managed to find Mollee and attempted to talk to her amid the crush that surrounded him, the Prince was jostled and accidentally stepped on one of Mollee's silk-toed shoes. He blushed and apologised.

'Sire, please don't apologise,' said quick-witted Mollee. 'Just tread on the *other* foot, it's jealous!'

The Prince was entranced by the dimples in Mollee's cheeks and her beautiful deep blue eyes. He was pleased to learn that Mollee was invited to a dinner given for him to be held at Government House the following evening. Previously, the Prince of Wales had shown little interest in single girls, it was married woman who were sexually experienced who he hoped might be able to cure his sexual problems. However he was fascinated by Mollee. He had been told by Lady Shiela Loughborogh that her brother, Roy Chisholm, was in love with Mollee but she was impervious to his protestations of love which lent a certain spice to their flirtation.

On a free day, when the Prince was scheduled to go riding at Randwick, he invited Mollee to join him and Dickie Mountbatten. Mollee proved to be an excellent horsewoman who looked elegant in a white silk shirt, jodhpurs and gleaming riding boots. She could ride as well as a man, change into a long dress and dance the night away in a glamorous ball gown. Elegance was very important to the Prince of Wales and Mollee made an great impression. He monopolised her at a ball at Government House, to the annoyance of the Governor's wife, who had made a list of ladies with whom he was expected to dance. The Prince and Mollee ended the evening by doing a wild conga around Government House, which made the Governor's wife even more annoyed.

In his nightly 20-page letter to Freda complaining how tired he was Edward mentioned in a letter now held by the Mitchell Library that,

> Dickie Mountbatten is very smitten with Moll, though he doesn't often get her to himself as she is my friend and I couldn't have another little 'bit' [bit of skirt slang for girl] other than my Fredie... She [Mollee] has so much in her that is of our atmosphere and ideas... Dickie and I monopolise her at parties.

On 19 August 1920, as the HMS *Renown* made a final tour of Sydney Harbour and cheering crowds lined the waterfront to bid goodbye to the Prince of Wales. Mollee and a few other pretty girls attended a farewell party on board the ship. Edward told his side of the story to Freda, fearing she might hear about his flirtation with the fascinating Mollee from other sources.

> We took quite a party out with us as far as the Heads.... Mollee Little and 8 or 9 other girls... we danced for an hour after lunch and then everyone took his 'bit' into his cabin except for me, angel, who only took Mollee there for a final talk as she isn't my bit at all!! I've got a terrible haunting feeling that all I've said about Moll might make you thulky — though I like you to be thulky... We may have got ourselves talked about a little in Sydney, beloved. Moll is the only woman I've got to know at all well on this trip.[4]

The Prince of Wales was hoping to arouse his mistress's waning sexual interest by making her jealous about what could have happened in his cabin, while reassuring Freda that she was the woman he *really* loved and wanted to marry. He still hoped she would leave her husband and obtain a divorce.

From Australia the HMS *Renown* went to Fiji, Samoa, Mexico and California and then headed for Britain.

Two years after Edward had left Australia, Mollee married her Australian admirer, the grazier Roy Chisholm. One year later she gave birth to David Anthony (Tony) and the Prince agreed to be godfather. Somehow, a myth went around that Mollee's son had been fathered by the Prince of Wales. Tony Chisholm was blonde and had regular features — a usual enough Anglo Saxon type and *did* look like the Prince of Wales. Rumours spread that Tony was the Prince's son.

Judy White, owner of Belltrees, (the celebrated rural White family property where the writer Patrick White was born), told me, 'It's a good story about a royal Australian love child. Unfortunately, the date of Tony's birth made this impossible — three years is a long time for anyone to be pregnant!' Judy White knew the truth as her mother and Mollee were good friends.

On Prince Edward's return to England George V and Queen Mary were disappointed to learn that his dependence on Mrs Dudley Ward had *not* waned. He confirmed he still had *no* intention of marrying a 'suitable' girl and providing them with grandchildren.

On 22 May 1921, the Prince spent several days with his parents and his siblings at Windsor. After another confrontation with his father, Edward confided in a letter to Freda, 'I loathe and despise my whole bloody family'. He regarded Windsor Castle as a prison, from which there would be no escape.

A familiar topic in the Prince's letters to Freda is how much he hated the formality of court life and his 'rotten' father, who exploded with temper when Edward refused to marry a suitable girl. George V could explode in rage over something relatively trivial, like the Prince of Wales wearing suede shoes, his son's use of American phrases in his speech and his choice of friends.

After his return from Windsor Castle, the Prince spent many afternoons at No 1, Cumberland Place, playing with Freda's daughters and their teddy bears or playing tennis with Freda and going dancing with her at night. In the evening he sometimes phoned her as many as three times. When visiting other parts of Britain or the Commonwealth his letters reveal his devotion.

> Fredie darling, beloved *á moi*. I feel ever so much better since our little talk on the phone this evening, sweet, you can't think what a huge comfort it was to your little David to hear your divine voice again. I'm terribly lonely tonight, my Fredie darling... It maddens me to be away from you'.[5]

In one of his letters the Prince expressed his delight that he might have made Freda pregnant. It was a false hope — there would be no royal love child for Freda. Edward continued to tell Freda that he loved her so much he could not continue his princely role without her. Calling Freda *'mon amour'*, he insisted he would never marry any woman but her. The Prince's words worried Freda as she had no intention of marrying him, due to their sexual problems and the fact that being a divorcee made her ineligible to become a royal consort. Kings of England had to swear an oath to uphold the tenets of the Church of England and the Anglican Church did not acknowledge the marriage of divorcees.

The Prince's infantile dependence on Freda continued. She remained 'My dear little Mummy' and he signed letters to her 'Your little David'. Clearly, he had not be able to overcome his sexual problems and saw Freda as a mother or Nanny Green substitute, as it seemed Freda bore a certain resemblance to his childhood memories of his nanny. In letters to Freda, he called himself an 'incompetent little boy', a revealing phrase from a young man suffering erectile dysfunction. At times he called himself 'your little puppy' referring to a game he had played with Nanny Green when he had to beg like a dog for something he wanted. He was grateful for Freda's forbearance over his sexual problems and repeatedly told her,

I love you beyond all understanding. All I can say is bless you for being so sweet and tender and *sympathetique* to your David last night, and for saving him, *mon amour*.[6]

By the mid 1920s, Freda was tired of acting as a counsellor for a young man with sexual problems. She had hoped to replace her elderly husband with a virile lover — not a neurotic one with suicidal feelings and sexual problems. She became desperate to end the affaire. In an attempt to discouge him, she joked about other admirers or cancelled meetings at short notice. When the Prince became angry, Freda claimed she had to spend more time with her daughters.

The more demanding the Prince became, the keener Freda was to end their relationship. She was weary of his limp performances as a lover and abject assurances that he was her 'devoted slave' and her 'little puppy dog'. She never enjoyed dressing up and acting the role of nanny to sexually arouse the Prince.

Freda attended parties without the Prince and flirted with other men. She met a handsome man, a Liberal Member of Parliament who was unhappily married. Freda hoped he would became her secret lover and gain a divorce at the same time as she did.

Careful not to hurt the Peter Pan Prince, Freda ended the relationship as tactfully as possible and somehow managed to remain good friends with him. Their mother-son relationship continued and several times a week they spoke to each other on the phone. The Prince still visited Freda and her daughters, Angie and Penelope, who regarded the Prince as their favourite uncle. Freda was an excellent tennis player and they still played games of tennis on the court in Regent's Park near her house but their bizarre sexual relationship was over.

Freda was the soul of discretion and never spoke in public about this extra-marital relationship. Not until many years later did she reveal what had worried her most in her long liaison with the heir to the throne was the masochistic side of his character. She was too kind to mention that the Prince's sexual problems had driven a wedge between them.

FREDA'S SECOND MARRIAGE

Freda had taken legal advice about divorcing her elderly husband. They had married in 1913 when William Dudley Ward was a celebrated oarsman who had rowed for his Cambridge College in the crew that had won the University Boat Race. He also won an Olympic medal for sailing. But life as a Party Whip in the House of Commons and working for the Royal Household aged him prematurely and the marriage broke down. Freda did not want a divorce until her daughters had left school and was relieved when the Prince of Wales started an affair with Lady Thelma Furness and encouraged it. Throughout the Prince's four year affair with Lady Furness, Freda Dudley Ward continued to be his confidante. She phoned the Prince at Fort Belvedere at least once a week and advised him how to proceed in his relationship with the flighty Thelma Furness, who was not nearly as intelligent and well-read as Freda.

Freda's Parliamentary lover died from tuberculosis in the early 1930s. Several years later she fell in love with a dashing Cuban aristocrat called Count Pedro (Peter) Jose de Casa Maury.

Freda remained close friends with the Prince of Wales and used to telephone him at least once a week. To her astonishment, when she made her usual weekly phone call to Edward — aware that Thelma had gone to America with her twin sister — she was shocked to be told by the telephonist her calls would no longer be accepted by the Prince of Wales. The woman who had instructed the telephonist not to put her calls through was Mrs Wallis Simpson, keen to increase her hold over the Prince of Wales.

Freda and her husband were finally divorced in 1937. William Dudley Ward moved between London and Calgary, where he had extensive investments. Freda married the handsome Pedro de Casa Maury who in World War Two became a pilot in the British Air Force. When the war was over they moved to Spain, but the Count de Casa Maury turned out to have a roving eye and Freda's second marriage ended also in divorce.

She returned to London, bought a house in Chelsea's King Road and for a time lived there with her married niece, Lady Bindy

Lambton, who had been left in a wheel chair after being involved in a car accident. Lady Lambton's unfaithful husband, Lord Tony Lambton, lived in a castle in Tuscany with his mistress so warm-hearted Freda helped her niece adjust to her new life.

Freda was always extremely discreet and never spoke to the press about her relationship with the Prince of Wales. When she died in London in 1983, aged 92, her obituary in *The Times* hinted at the liaison between her and the future Edward VIII. A cache of 313 miss-spelled love letters to Freda from the future King, who gave up his title to become the Duke of Windsor, were found in Freda's Chelsea home after her death. A previous batch of love letters, written on Edward's Antipodean tour in 1920, which had been found in a stamp collection in Canada, aroused great interest when sold at auction in 1970.

Thirty-three years later, in 2003, Freda's descendents decided to sell the remaining 313 letters, written by the lovesick Prince between 1921-1923 which once again reveal a disturbed selfish young man determined to avoid his royal role. In a letter dated 5 August 1922, long before he met Wallis Simpson, Edward confessed to Freda, 'What wouldn't I give to chuck the job of Prince of Wales. I'm so fed up with it!' In some letters he repeats the phrase I love you at least 20 times.

(Ten of Edward's letters, telling Freda how much he loved her, were purchased by Sydney's Mitchell Library in 2010. An excerpt from a letter written by the Prince of Wales from Government House Melbourne is reproduced on Page 425.)

But where were Freda's replies to the Prince? In answer to that question, Tilly Davies, one of Freda's granddaughters, said she suspected these replies were owned by the Royal Family.[7] She added that it was possible that many of Freda's letters, full of advice to Edward, had been destroyed by Wallis Simpson, the woman responsible for removing Freda from the position of confidante to Edward, Prince of Wales.

'My mother felt that Freda brought out the best in the Prince of Wales while Mrs Simpson brought out the worst', claimed Freda Dudley Ward's granddaughter.

The author's father, James Guthrie Adamson, was a cadet at Dartmouth Naval College at the same time as Edward David, Prince of Wales. The sixteen-year old Prince suffered a severe attack of mumps and still looks ill in this posed photo. Edward's mumps orchitis led to his severe sexual problems.

Freda Dudley Ward.　　　　　　Edward, Prince of Wales in his early twenties.

Freda with her daughters Penelope and Angela.

Freda and her husband, the Rt. Hon William Dudley Ward, MP.

Edward, Prince of Wales, on the observation platform of the royal train, during his 1920 Australian tour.

CHAPTER 8

Lady Thelma Morgan Furness (1905–1970)
and
Edward David, Prince of Wales
(King Edward VIII, later Duke of Windsor)

The Prince of Wales was extremely handsome but he disappointed me.
Lady Thelma Morgan Furness.

The Prince of Wales' mental and spiritual growth stopped dead in adolescence.
Sir Alan Lascelles, Private Secretary to Edward, Prince of Wales.

Women's autobiographies are filled with untruths and omissions.
Daphne du Maurier, novelist and descendent of royal mistress, Mary Ann Clarke, whose biography she wrote.

FROM DIPLOMAT'S DAUGHTER TO HOLLYWOOD STAR

Thelma Hays Morgan (pronounced Tel-mah in the Spanish way) and Gloria, her identical twin, were born in the Swiss city of Lucerne where their father had just been appointed American consul.[1] With their mother awaiting their move into the consular residence, the twins were born in a hotel suite overlooking a lake.

Harry Hays Morgan and his second wife, Laura Valdevieso Kilpatrick and their four children — Laura Consuelo, Harry, Thelma and Mercedes Gloria — lived in a series of consulates and embassies in Switzerland, Belgium, the United States, Argentina and Chile. The main language of the four Morgan children was Spanish but they spoke fluent English (with a slight Spanish accent) and excellent French. Their mother, Laura Delphine Valdevieso Kilpatrick Morgan, had been born and raised in Chile. Her maternal ancestors, were Spanish aristocrats from the ancient Kingdom of Navarre to whom the de Valdeviesos claimed kinship. Two younger sons of the Valdeviesos of Navarre had sailed across the world to settle in Chile in the seventeenth century.[2]

Mrs Morgan, although very attractive, was manipulative, unstable and temperamental. The workaholic Harry Morgan stayed late at his consulates or embassies in a bid to escape from the tears and tantrums of his volatile Chilean wife.

The three Morgan sisters and their elder brother were raised by a succession of nannies, none of whom lasted very long or showed the children much affection. Young Harry was his mother's favourite, but Laura Morgan showed little interest in her daughters, apart from the prospect of marrying them off to wealthy men. Laura Consuelo, the eldest daughter, known by her second name to distinguish her from her mother, was born in 1901, making her three years older than the twins.

Consuelo shared a Spanish-speaking governess with her brother Harry before he went away to boarding school. The twins had Spanish nursemaids and nannies, to whom they spoke in Spanish. The girls were taught ballet, ballroom dancing and riding as ladylike accomplishments. Consuelo took after her father and was clever and a keen reader. The twins never opened a book if they could help it and lacked their father's intelligence. However, they inherited their father's talent for learning foreign languages and his interest in foreign travel.

After Harry left school he decided to use his good looks to enter the world of silent films and departed for Hollywood.

In public Laura Kilpatrick Morgan was a charming hostess, but at home she was a domestic tyrant with a sadistic streak. On one occasion she insisted that, as punishment for a trifling offence, the twins' much loved pets — two baby pigeons — be served to the girls for lunch. The house servants were terrified of Senora Morgan, so they obeyed her and killed and roasted the pigeons at their employer's insistence. When their mother informed the twins what they had eaten, both of them were violently ill as a reaction to the horror of what they had done.

In her teens, Thelma suffered a bad fall when thrown from a bolting horse. As a result, she developed a pathological fear of horses and refused to go near one again. She longed to dance professionally, but her mother refused to countenance such an idea.

At 17, Consuelo left her convent school and, with her father away on government business, Laura Morgan negotiated a marriage for her under-age daughter with a elderly titled Frenchman who Mr Morgan believed to be an extremely wealthy well-connected widower with large estates in France.

Mrs Morgan was enjoying herself organising a large society wedding. Consuelo was never consulted about a marriage she dreaded. The Count had demanded a dowry from Mrs Morgan, claiming this was normal among French aristocrats. Keen to secure a wealthy titled son-in-law, Mrs Morgan paid the sum demanded.

On her wedding morning, Consuelo, in floods of tears, begged her mother to cancel the ceremony. Laura Morgan refused and dismissed Consuelo's tears as pre-wedding nerves, telling her she was ungrateful for all that had been done for her. Guests were arriving from all over Europe and America and it was too late — cancelling the wedding would shame her family and Consuelo *must* marry the Count de Maupas. Sick with nerves the unfortunate Consuelo donned her bridal gown and married her elderly groom, with Thelma and Gloria as bridesmaids. According to Consuelo's journal, her honeymoon was a nightmare.

A few weeks later, Mrs Morgan was mortified to learn that the title of Count de Maupas de Juglart was bogus — the Count had no money at all and expected the Morgans to provide for him and Consuelo. Mrs Morgan was furious to think she had been duped by a confidence trickster. Her attempts to have the marriage annulled by the Pope were unsuccessful. In spite of her professed

Catholicism, Laura Morgan engaged lawyers to obtain a divorce for her daughter. Meanwhile, Consuelo had returned to live with her family.

Under the circumstances, in a marriage arranged against the wishes of a minor, relatively quickly a divorce was granted to Consuelo. She never forgave her mother.

The twins were educated at convents in Barcelona and Montreux with a few terms at Strathalan House School in England to perfect their English. When their father was posted to New York, their mother remained in Chile and they were sent as boarders to a Convent of the Sacred Heart in New York where they showed aptitude for designing and making their own clothes.

At sixteen, Thelma and Gloria, according to the society photographer Cecil Beaton who took their pictures, resembled magnolia blossoms. They inherited their mother's good looks with long slim legs, curvaceous figures, doe-eyes and dark glossy hair. Their Spanish accent meant they lisped slightly when pronouncing certain English words, which sounded very attractive. Cecil Beaton was entranced by their exotic beauty, claiming the Morgan twins should be painted by John Singer Sargent, wearing white with a bowl of peonies beside them.

However, the twins had very poor examination results and no qualifications for anything apart from dressmaking. They had listened to their mother who claimed men did not like clever women and exams were unimportant — they would marry wealthy men and live in luxury. The twins believed her.

Once divorced, Consuelo fell in love with a young American diplomat, named Bernie Thaw, whose family had made their fortune from investing in railroads and were well-known philanthropists. Consuelo married Bernie, who was claimed to have a brilliant future as a diplomat. Bernie worked at the American Embassy in Brussels and was promoted to First Secretary at the American Embassy in Santiago, capital of Chile. Back home in her native land, Consuelo kept herself busy by researching and writing notes on her distinguished Chilean ancestors in a leather-bound journal. She continued this habit in London but after her husband fell ill and they returned to America the journal was lost, but resurfaced twenty years later in a second hand bookshop in London. I found the journal, purchased it and, being bilingual in Spanish, noted Consuelo's candid comments about the relationship between Thelma and the Prince of Wales.

※

Mrs Morgan announced she was leaving her husband in New York and returning to Chile to seek legal advice about a divorce. The twins left the Convent of the Sacred Heart and boarded at a finishing school, supposed to remain there until their mother could return to New York and arrange a coming-out ball and a debutante season for them.

With the dreadful example of Consuelo's first marriage arranged by their mother, Gloria and Thelma were reluctant to return to her control. They sought help from their father, who gave them a monthly allowance, so they could rent an elegant apartment at No 40 Fifth Avenue. The twins bought dress materials in sales and made themselves very stylish clothes.

Passing themselves off as 18, the attractive 16-year-olds obtained invitations to parties where, thanks to their good looks, they were known as 'the Magnificent Morgan twins.' Thelma and Gloria drank very little and, being virtually inseparable, protected each other from the predatory men who pursued them.

At 17, Thelma accepted a proposal of marriage from James Vail Converse, the grandson of the wealthy founder of the Bell Telephone Company and the American Telegraph Company. In her eagerness to escape from her mother's control, Thelma mistook the dissolute James Vail Converse, ten years older than herself, for a stable father figure. She did not realise that, in the Prohibition era, Vail Converse had spent his inheritance on illegal drinking and gambling. Her fiancé was living on money borrowed from relatives and hoped to marry a wealthy wife. Initially, Vail kept his drinking problem secret from Thelma.

Thelma and James Vail Converse were married in Washington DC on 16 February 1922. The large and expensive white wedding was organised by Mrs Laura Morgan. This was the *second* time the ambitious Mrs Morgan had married off a young daughter to a smooth-talking fortune hunter.

Thelma's honeymoon was almost as bad as that of her elder sister, Consuelo. Vail Converse drunkenly forced himself on his virginal bride.

Thelma endured three more years of physical abuse from the increasingly alcoholic Vail Converse. Mrs Morgan, not wanting the scandal of a second divorce in the family, insisted Thelma remain in the marriage.

Thelma's twin sister, Gloria, still under-age, had received a proposal of marriage from 42-year-old Reginald (Reggie) Claypole Vanderbilt, the playboy son of wealthy Cornelius Vanderbilt, Junior. Decades earlier Reggie had inherited ten million dollars from his father, whereupon he dropped out of college and spent much of his inheritance on wine, women and expensive cars. Reggie's first marriage had produced two children and ended in divorce.[3] By the time he met Gloria he had little money left and lived on an allowance from his wealthy mother.

Fortunately for Gloria, Reggie was much nicer and gentler than James Vail Converse. To protect the Vanderbilt image, the fact Reggie had squandered a sizeable amount of his inheritance on drink and his resulting health problems, were kept hidden. To provide security for the children of his first marriage, the remaining part of Reggie' huge inherited fortune had been tied up in a trust worth several million dollars to which he was denied access.

The Vanderbilt name was famous, so the story that the glamorous young Gloria Morgan was marrying Reggie Vanderbilt made headlines in March 1923.

Reggie's mother, Alice Claypole Vanderbilt, and his elder sister Mrs Gertrude Vanderbilt Whitney, acted as trustees to the Vanderbilt Trust. Gertrude, a talented sculptor, was married to the wealthy banker, Harry Payne Whitney. Alice Claypole Vanderbilt approved of Reggie's marriage to Gloria and saw the frivolous but sweet-natured girl as a good influence on her weak-willed son. She gave Reggie and Gloria a generous annual allowance, so they could live in the extravagant style associated with the Vanderbilt name.

In February 1924, by the time Gloria and Reggie's daughter, little Gloria Laura, was born, Reggie's liver was causing concern. His doctors had warned him that his prognosis was poor, but Reggie kept this information from his young wife. Under the terms of the Vanderbilt Trust Fund their baby daughter and the children from Reggie's first marriage, would inherit money held in the Vanderbilt Trust should Reggie die. The fact that Gloria was under-age when she married her husband would later become a bone of contention with the Vanderbilt Trustees.

By this time Thelma had enough of her abusive marriage. Consuelo, now married to the successful young diplomat, Bernie Thaw, was able to send her younger sister money to escape from her husband. Thelma joined her brother Harry, still a struggling actor, in Hollywood. Using money borrowed from Alice Claypole Vanderbilt, Gloria paid her twin's legal expenses to obtain her divorce on the understanding Thelma would refund them from her divorce settlement.

Living in Hollywood, Thelma as an aspiring actress and dancer, was struggling to climb the greasy pole of stardom. Studio publicists described Thelma in glowing terms as the new Mary Pickford. In reality she was a far better dancer than actress. Lecherous film directors promised young Thelma Morgan starring roles in their forthcoming movies but these never eventuated.

Working with Mary Pickford, Thelma became friends with the famous star and her dashing husband, Douglas Fairbanks senior, as well as Charlie Chaplin and other stars of the period. Her closest friends were Mary Pickford and Douglas Fairbanks. This glamorous couple, tired of the studio system, had established their own production company and were doing well.

In 1924, Metro-Goldwyn-Mayer contracted Thelma to appear in the silent film *So This is Marriage*, shot mainly in a new process, called Technicolor.

In 1925, Thelma turned 21 and finally received her divorce settlement of US$100,000 from Vail Converse. Because his wealthy family had been obliged to rescue him from bankruptcy Thelma's settlement was not nearly as large as her lawyers had expected. Nevertheless, the money was enough for her to establish 'Thelma Morgan Pictures' and allowed her to embark on a career as a Hollywood producer. This was a very courageous move for a young woman in an industry dominated by powerful aggressive male producers. Thelma, with the confidence of the young, relished the chance of running her own company.[4]

In the Golden Age of silent movies, Thelma engaged technicians, cameramen, a wardrobe mistress, props staff, a director and a film editor. The company produced films in which Thelma starred herself. In their first production Thelma employed major co-stars like Lionel Barrymore and Clara Bow.

However, Thelma's private life was still plagued by trouble. Courted by many actors, and with a weakness for older men who she hoped would prove to be surrogate fathers, she fell in love with the actor, Richard Bennett, a friend of her elder brother, who urged her to marry the actor. Richard Bennett was considerably older than Thelma. He had already been married, divorced twice and had three daughters from previous marriages.[5]

Like Thelma's previous husband, Richard Bennett drank like a fish. Thelma was unaware he wanted a big splashy wedding to gain publicity for his declining film career. Thelma realised that Richard Bennett had a severe alcohol problem and refused to seek treatment, no matter how she pleaded with him to do so. With her bitter experience of marriage to a violent alcoholic and all their fights, Thelma cancelled the wedding and returned Richard Bennett's engagement ring. Once again she was a free woman.

Thelma's divorce settlement from Vail Converse had financed some silent films which had received good reviews. But as Thelma's accountant pointed out to her, after deducting the costs of editing, producing and publicising or 'pitching' the films to distributors, most had broken even rather than made a profit. One had been deemed an 'art house' movie and so had lost her money.

Mrs Morgan tore herself away from living with Gloria and Reggie Vanderbilt and came to Hollywood. At this juncture Thelma's confidence was badly shaken. Her mother offered no words of praise for Thelma's courage in becoming a pioneer female film producer and told her she was stupid as silent films were a passing craze. She warned her daughter, if she continued to produce them, she was likely to end up in the bankruptcy court. Silent films and the dramatic style of acting that suited them, as practiced by Thelma and her friends Clara Bow and Mary Pickford, would be replaced by some new development like talking pictures. She should give up trying to be financially independent and find a wealthy husband, while she still had her looks. Discouraged by her mother, Thelma wound up her company, Thelma Morgan Pictures, sold the props and cameras for what she could get for them and left Hollywood for New York to stay with her twin.

Gloria and Reggie Vanderbilt were living in a New York brownstone mansion, bought for them by Reggie's mother, the wealthy generous Mrs Alice Vanderbilt. Because Gloria bore the magic 'Vanderbilt' name, the press assumed *both* the twins were wealthy. In reality Thelma was almost broke, but knew it was important to keep up appearances.

ENTERING THE BRITISH ARISTOCRACY

At one of Gloria's dinner parties, Thelma, wearing the fabulous black pearls her father had given her, was seated next to Lord Marmaduke Furness, the widowed chairman of Furness Withy Shipping Lines.

Gloria had done her homework. The company, founded by the Viscount's grandfather, owned shipyards and luxurious passenger liners and was in the process of purchasing an American subsidiary. This was why the papers announced that Lord Furness was spending over a month in New York. Marmaduke Furness had greatly increased his fortune during World War One through lucrative government contracts to build troop ships. His late wife, Daisy Hogg, had born him two children. She had died in 1921 on board her husband's sea-going yacht. Lord Furness, Britain's wealthiest man, was clearly in need of a second wife to act as his hostess.

Thelma, elegant in a bias cut satin evening dress that showed off her slim figure to good advantage, was seated at the right of Lord Furness. His well-cut dinner jacket emphasized his muscular physique, but his carefully combed auburn hair failed to hide the balding top of his head.

Lord Marmaduke Furness introduced himself to Thelma as 'Duke', short for his curiously old-fashioned Christian name. In the course of their conversation Thelma learned that not only was Viscount Marmaduke Furness the chairman of Furness Withy Lines and owner of several shipyards, he also owned an ocean-going yacht, a Mayfair mansion with a private gymnasium and indoor swimming pool, two private planes and a fleet of Rolls Royces — several in Britain and four more in Kenya, where he owned a private zoo.

Lord Furness was clearly a workaholic and business deals kept him constantly on the move. However, as he revealed to Thelma that evening, his pride and joy was his country estate near Melton Mowbray in Leicestershire, where he kept several hundred thoroughbred race horses and hunters and hunted with the famous Quorn hunt.

Disliking horses, Thelma attempted several times to change the subject from equestrianism and hunting foxes but with little success. She would rather have discussed Lord Furness's fleet of luxury liners, which were what she found most interesting about this aggressive businessman.

Thelma had lived in major European and South American cities and could talk knowledgeably about them. She also had many amusing stories about Hollywood actors and film producers. But Lord Furness wanted to talk rather than listen and kept returning to his pet topics — fox hunting and race horses, but Thelma could only feign polite interest.

Lord Furness was impressed by Thelma's looks and liked her slight Spanish lisp, which made her English sound charming. As a widower with two showgirl mistresses (a fact he did not mention to Thelma) he felt a former Hollywood star with a European background and family connections to the Vanderbilts would make an excellent second wife. She would be able to produce handsome sons to carry on the Furness shipping empire.

Unlike most English aristocrats, who had inherited stately homes and considered it bad manners to discuss money, Lord

Furness bragged about his wealth. His way of impressing women was to overwhelm them by boasting about his expensive possessions and then seduce them with lavish gifts.

Thelma, fresh from Hollywood, regarded him with awe — a English aristocrat who spoke with an upper-crust clipped accent. What she did not know was that the old-established British aristocracy regarded Marmaduke Furness with distaste as a *nouveau riche* war profiteer. She believed that a wealthy widower in his late forties would make a generous indulgent husband. Gloria had married a much older man and was happy — now she could do the same. Although the Morgan twins adored each other, there was an element of rivalry between them which was absent in the Thelma's relationship with Consuelo, who was older, more serious and less superficial than the twins. Thelma realised that, if she married a wealthy English aristocrat, she would be on an equal footing with her glamorous twin instead of being merely the poor relation.[6] She also liked the idea of being Lady Furness and having unlimited travel on luxurious passenger liners.

Lord Furness, who was more than twenty years older than Thelma, found her stunningly beautiful. To impress the warm-hearted Thelma, he played the role of the grieving widower and forbore from his usual swearing and cursing. During the evening, Lord Furness confided that, despite his wealth and possessions, he was lonely. He asked Thelma whether she would dine with him later in the week. She agreed.

Huge bouquets of flowers arrived daily at the Vanderbilt residence for Thelma Morgan, the name under which she had starred in films. Lord Furness wined and dined Thelma at the most expensive restaurants in New York. Although his conversations were normally larded with 'fucking this' and 'bloody that' he was careful to moderate his language in her presence.

Over their third candlelight dinner he told Thelma he loved her, wanted to marry her and would do everything to make her happy. Without making further inquiries, Thelma impulsively accepted his proposal.

Having seen many romantic movies in Hollywood, Thelma imagined that Lord Furness was offering love, status and wealth.

She convinced herself that in spite of their difference in age she was in love with Marmaduke Furness. But Thelma had little knowledge of English society or history. Her knowledge of England was gained from Hollywood films as she never read books and knew nothing of the arcane snobberies underpinning British high society and the reputation of Lord Furness.

Lord Furness, grandson of a coal merchant, turned ship owner, had been awarded his hereditary title of Viscount Furness of Grantley in 1918 for converting his transatlantic liners into troop ships. His father, Sir Christopher Furness, who began life delivering sacks of coal, had *purchased* his knighthood by donating large sums of money to charity. Consequently, Lord Furness was regarded as brash and vulgar by the old-established aristocracy.

As Lord Furness's only son showed no interest in entering the family business, what he wanted was a socially acceptable wife who would act as his hostess and bear him another son to take over the Furness Withy Shipping empire.

To impress Thelma and her twin, Lord Furness issued an invitation to Gloria and Reggie Vanderbilt to holiday in Paris as his guests, chaperoning Thelma. They were given state-rooms on one of his transatlantic liners. Taking their baby daughter and her nanny with them, Gloria and Reggie travelled to France and spent a fortnight in a luxurious Paris apartment near the Rue du Rivoli. After their holidays Gloria and Reggie returned to New York with their little daughter, but Thelma and her maid remained in Paris in a serviced apartment owned by Furness Withy Lines.

Lord Furness flew to Paris in his private plane to spend weekends with his fiancé and, aware how much Thelma enjoyed dancing, took her to spectacular shows at the Lido and the Folies Bergères. Against Thelma's better judgement they became lovers. She would later confide to Consuelo she found Lord Furness an inconsiderate lover, and sex with him was just as unsatisfying as it had been with Vail Converse.

As a divorced woman, Thelma knew she could not re-marry in a Catholic Church but was most surprised to learn that divorced people were not allowed to marry in the Anglican Church to which her future husband belonged. In the mid-1920s divorces were relatively rare in England while in the circles in which Thelma moved in Hollywood they scarcely raised an eyebrow.

***

Reggie Vanderbilt died on 4 September, 1925. His death meant Gloria became one of the trustees or administrators of the $2.5 million Vanderbilt Trust, which was created to benefit the children of Reggie's first marriage and his daughter, Gloria Laura.

Gloria soon became embroiled in a bitter dispute with her sister-in-law, Gertrude Vanderbilt Whitney, over the use of the trust money. Gloria had been under age when the Vanderbilt Trust was set up and this caused legal problems. Gloria's wealthy sister-in-law, claimed that Gloria was an unfit mother and demanded legal custody of little Gloria Laura, which Gloria contested.

Heavily involved with lawyers and hearings, Gloria was unable to be in London for Thelma's registry office wedding. Lord Furness had always been on his best behaviour in the presence of Thelma, so she hardly knew her future husband's real character and temperament but would soon find out.

LADY THELMA, WIFE OF BRITAIN'S WEALTHIEST MAN

Lord Furness and Thelma Morgan Converse, were married on 27 June 1926, at Chelsea Registry Office. Bernie Thaw took long leave from his Embassy position in Chile for the wedding and he and Consuelo acted as witnesses.

Thelma found it odd that neither of her new stepchildren — the Hon Christopher or the Hon Averill Furness — were present at the wedding. Nor did they attend the luncheon at which Consuelo and Bernie, several of Furness's elderly business colleagues and two of his hunting friends were the only guests.

What Thelma liked best was her new home in a quiet elegant street, called Lees Place, only a few minutes walk from the American Embassy in Grosvenor Square, where Bernie Thaw had been told he would soon be appointed First Secretary. She enjoyed the fact the house had been extensively modernised with luxurious bathrooms and a heated swimming pool in the basement.

By now Lord Furness had learned that his second wife had no private income but refused to give her a bank account of her own. He let Thelma shop wherever Furness Withy Lines had accounts and charge her purchases to the company. Refusing to give Thelma any cash or her own bank account was one way Lord Furness intended to control his beautiful young wife.

On the anniversary of the evening when they had met, Lord Furness gave his wife a red sports car as one of his kinder gestures. Furness Lines paid for her petrol and the car was serviced by the company's mechanics. Thelma loved escaping from London in her sports car, putting the hood down and driving fast. It was the only time she felt completely free.

Before World War Two the British aristocracy were the main travellers on luxury liners. To impress his clients Marmaduke Furness liked showing off his elegant young wife, so he made no complaint when Thelma bought expensive clothes. She wore Lady Daisy's jewels at dinner parties, including the famous Furness diamonds, a necklace so cleverly designed by Cartier that it would convert into a tiara should she have to attend a coronation or very grand ball. Thelma thought these beautiful jewels were a wedding gift from her husband, not realising that the company saw the jewels as theirs when they insured them.

To allow Thelma to take her place in British society, Lord Furness paid a titled lady, short of cash, to sponsor Thelma's presentation at court. Lady Furness wore a long white dress with a train to perform the regulation curtsey to Queen Mary. The fact that the second Lady Furness was a divorcee was kept hidden as divorcees were not welcomed at Buckingham Palace — Queen Mary and King George felt divorce was sinful.

Lord Furness spent a great deal of time away on business, but contrary to promises given in New York, did not ask Thelma to accompany him.

Although Thelma enjoyed London and all the luxury with which she was surrounded, she was shocked to discover her second husband, like her first, was a heavy drinker who could turn violent when he had consumed too much. Marmaduke Furness always had a slim silver hip flask of malt whisky in the inner pocket of his well-cut suits and, throughout the day, took swigs from it, refilling it frequently. But as he never *appeared* to be drunk no one realised the extent of his alcohol problem except Thelma and he refused to discuss it.

Apart from horse racing and hunting, the other passions of Viscount Furness were roulette and baccarat. Since gambling was illegal in England, he would get his private plane to take him to the casino at Le Touquet and gamble for high stakes. If he lost he would be in a foul mood for days and take it out on Thelma and his staff. Her husband was fastidious about his appearance to the extent that each morning a freshly ironed pair of shoe laces had to be inserted into his hand-made shoes or he would abuse his valet. He was a workaholic and his fortune was never enough. Each company had to increase its profits and he wanted more and more. A business deal that went wrong made him smash valuable ornaments or whatever else came to hand.

Lord Furness was a stickler for perfection — everything in his London residence and in his country house, Burrow Court, had to be just right. His dislike of children verged on the pathological, yet he insisted he wanted another son as he had such a poor relationship with his son from his previous marriage.

Young Christopher Furness, named after his paternal grandfather, disliked anything to do with Furness Withy Lines. He insisted on being called Dick to differentiate himself from his grandfather. About to leave Eton, Dick still refused to work for his father. In spite of bitter rows, he insisted he wanted to go to Sandhurst and serve as an artillery officer.

Lord Furness fought bitterly with his only son and despised his shy daughter, who he described as 'gawky, horse-mad and boring'. Averill, now 18, lived in her own apartment in a side wing of Burrough Court. She spent her time training her father's racehorses and exercised Dick's hunters which were stabled with those of Lord Furness. Thelma was shocked by the realisation that her husband disliked both his children who were scared of him and avoided him as much as possible.

One of Thelma's first tasks as the second Lady Furness was to organise a coming-out ball for Averill, her young and reclusive step-daughter. She chose the Dorchester Hotel in Park Lane for the venue, organised invitations, the dinner menu and the flower arrangements and attended teas with mothers of debutantes to obtain names of suitable young men to invite to the ball. The reclusive Averill showed no interest and left all the arrangements to her stepmother. Thelma found it worrying how few friends Averill had in comparison with all the friends she had had.

On the night of the ball, Thelma was wearing a hand-embroidered silk designer gown. As the new wife of Lord Furness, she attracted a great deal of attention from the 200 guests and the press. Averill, shy and gawky, in spite of a beautiful dress chosen by Thelma, failed to attract any suitors, which annoyed Lord Furness.

The next hurdle was meeting her new mother-in-law. Thelma wrote to Consuelo confiding that the widowed Lady Janet Furness resembled a barmaid with brassy hair and a strong Liverpudlian accent. Clearly, her mother-in-law doted on her only son and made it obvious to Thelma that she did not approve of his marriage to a American divorcee.

Lord Furness expected his second wife to act as his hostess at Lees Place and approve menus with the cook and supervise the flower arrangements which arrived twice a week from the firm Constance Spry, London's leading florist.

Thelma could cope well with life in London — what she hated was living in rural Leicestershire and everything to do with fox hunting. The hunting season started in earnest in November and Lord Furness moved his entire household to Burrough Court for the hunting season which did not end until April. He expected Thelma to run the annual Hunt Ball. At Burrough Court with its vast stable block and paddocks Lord Furness kept almost 200 hunters, racehorses and brood mares.

The household staff at Burrough Court wore uniforms in the Furness racing colours. Even the Rolls Royces, specially made for Lord Furness, were upholstered in maroon leather and on the bonnet of each one was a silver model of one of his racehorses. A cocktail cabinet was built into the partition that separated the chauffeur from the passengers.

Lord Furness had no shortage of staff as he paid well above average wages, but he was a demanding employer and did not hesitate to sack staff on the spot if something was amiss. A large team of gardeners, grooms and stable boys were employed to keep the formal gardens and grounds at his country estate tidy. Furness would fly into a rage and sack a stable boy or groom if he saw hoof prints or horse manure on his long white pebbled drive.

If a race horse consistently failed to win he would have the unfortunate animal shot and did the same with his hunters should they lose their nerve at fences. The tack room was filled with rosettes and silver cups won by horses Lord Furness had bred. Thelma told Consuelo she was beginning to feel like one of his brood mares. She joked that perhaps he would have her shot if she did not produce the required son to take over the shipping line.

Thelma had been forced to admit her fear of horses due her childhood riding accident. Her husband showed little sympathy, telling her she was being stupid. He expected her to get on a horse so that she could go out hunting with him, a command which made Thelma quail and she refused to obey, whereupon he called her a coward.

Thelma could cope with her husband's business colleagues who were well travelled so she had plenty of topics she could discuss with them at dinner parties. What she found so boring was the hearty hunting, shooting and fishing crowd her husband demanded she entertain at Burrough Court. She disliked attending hunt balls at which the guests drank too much and conversation revolved around who would administer the Hunt Wire Fund or become the next Master of Foxhounds.

⁂

Whenever her husband was away on business, Thelma spent time with Consuelo, who was living near her in Mayfair, as Bernie was now working as First Secretary at the American Embassy in Grosvenor Square. The sisters lunched at The Ritz each week with a group of wives from the American Embassy. They took one of the Rolls Royces to shop in Harrods, where the chauffeur waited for them at the side-door. Sometimes they walked to The White

House in Bond Street, where on the company account Thelma purchased silk nightdresses and swansdown trimmed negligees — the kind of clothes worn by Hollywood stars.

Consuelo showed her younger sister the account she had written of the Valdevieso family in Navarre and in Chile. She found writing easier in Spanish than in English. After arriving in London she wrote down her impressions of life in England and stated her amazement that so many English homes lacked central heating or showers in their chilly bathrooms.

Hating the cold after living in the warmth of California, Thelma was allowed to buy a mink coat and a glamorous white fox stole to wear when she accompanied her husband to social and business functions.

It soon became clear to Thelma that life with Marmaduke Furness was like living with a volcano that could erupt at any time. Surrounded by luxury, but kept short of ready cash, escape was difficult. She wished she were back in Hollywood running her own company and making her own decisions, but there was no going back.

To both her sisters Thelma confessed that her second marriage was not going well. She and her husband had almost nothing in common and, since he never took her on his numerous business trips, she was convinced that he had a mistress.

In the third year of her troubled marriage, Thelma was aware that her husband blamed her for failing to get pregnant with a much wanted second son. Whenever he was at home, Lord Furness enforced his conjugal rights. As her husband was an inconsiderate and sometimes brutal lover, marital sex had become an unpleasant duty for Thelma.

One day, Dick Furness arrived at Burrough Court to see his horses. Thelma, who found her husband's son very pleasant, attempted to arrange a reconciliation between him and his father. But her efforts failed — father and son again quarrelled over Dick's refusal to work for his father's shipping line. It was clear he loathed his father.

During a subsequent visit to Burrough Court, Dick confided to Thelma that he and Averill had severe misgivings over their mother's premature death and been haunted by it. Averill had never really recovered.

After his mother died at sea, Dick had been taunted by a bully at Eton who claimed his parents had told him that Lord Furness had got away with murder. Dick had hit out at him, but what was said confirmed his own worst fears as to what might have happened. Only in recent years had Dick learned that, as a result of his father's infidelity and brutal behaviour, his mother had sought consolation from a former boyfriend who became her lover. In one of his wild rages, Lord Furness, suspecting Dick was not his son, called him a bastard and his late mother a whore.

Using money left him by his mother, Dick managed to enter Sandhurst Military College and was hoping to become an infantry officer, determined to be totally independent from his father.

Thelma longed for financial independence but as the wife of one of the wealthiest men in the world could not return to acting or teaching ballroom dancing, two things she knew she was good at and enjoyed. Running her own company she had been financially independent and made her own decisions. Now she was the bird in the gilded cage, tied down by a controlling husband. She had no home of her own to escape to and felt trapped.

In desperation Thelma worked out a scheme which enabled her to accumulate some money. She bought expensive clothes at Harrods on the company account, returned the garments as unsuitable and pocketed the cash.

Aware that all telephone accounts were paid by Furness Lines, Thelma consoled herself by making expensive phone calls to Gloria, who was travelling around Europe with her little daughter and a nanny. Her twin had fallen in love with a German prince who owned a castle. He was charming and gentle and she hoped to marry him. Gertrude Vanderbilt was convinced the Prince was after the Vanderbilt money and did her best to ruin the romance.

MEETING THE PRINCE OF WALES
Thelma's first glimpse of the handsome Prince of Wales took place in 1926 at a ball held at Londonderry House, shortly after her

marriage to Lord Furness. The Prince noticed the attractive young wife of Lord Furness and observed how gracefully she danced. Seated at the far end of the ballroom, he had no chance to speak to her.

Near the end of the hunting season, Lord Furness, as patron of the Melton Mowbray agricultural show, attended an official lunch with his fellow members of the committee. Thelma found herself seated next to the Prince of Wales, who was the guest of honour, awarding rosettes to owners of prize cattle and listening to tedious speeches from elderly committee members.

Once the speeches were over, the handsome Prince started talking to Thelma. Learning she had worked in Hollywood, they discussed their favourite movies. In the course of conversation Thelma said she had heard Louis Armstrong play when Satchmo was recording sound tracks for silent movies. The Prince said he adored Louis Armstrong. Thelma showed genuine interest and clearly knew a lot about New Orleans jazz.

The Prince said Louis Armstrong was currently giving a few performances in Paris but would be in London for one single night. Would Lady Furness and her husband like to be his guests to hear him play? Lord Furness was flattered to be asked, but since he could not bear jazz he apologised to the Prince and said he had a business commitment in France on the date the Prince named, but was sure his wife would like to attend. Thelma was thrilled at the prospect.

On their return to London later that month Thelma found a note from the Prince with a ticket enclosed for the jazz session in the ballroom of a hotel in Soho.

After eating her solitary dinner, one of the chauffeurs drove Thelma to the hotel whose name and address was on the ticket. She told the chauffeur she had no idea when it would finish and she would call if she needed to be collected.

The ballroom was crowded with excited people. Thelma gave the name of the Prince of Wales and was shown to a secluded alcove where the Prince of Wales was seated with a bottle of champagne in an ice bucket in front of him. His Royal Highness apologised and said two couples had cancelled at the last moment due to that wretched flu epidemic. Once the music started, they beat time to their favourites like 'St Louis Blues' and 'When the Saints' and joined in the chorus.

The waiter kept topping up their glasses with champagne. The room was hot and they had almost finished their second bottle by the time a pianist playing dance music took over. The Prince led young Lady Furness onto the dance floor. He was an excellent dancer and it was as though she and the Prince had danced together for years.

Back at the table, the champagne had loosened their tongues and confidences were exchanged. Thelma confessed she missed America a great deal, all the more as her father was working in New York.

The Prince asked about her mother and Thelma told him her parents were divorcing and her mother was living in Chile. The Prince was interested and asked questions about South America as he was going on a tour of that vast continent the following year.

Next he wanted to know how, working in Hollywood, Thelma had met Lord Furness. She related the story and how he had proposed to her in New York. Perhaps it was all the champagne but talking about her marriage made Thelma's eyes brim with tears.

The Prince was kind and understanding. On the dance floor he held her close, they danced cheek to cheek and he kissed her softly on her forehead and then on her lips. They ended by spending the night in a suite at the hotel.

Thelma told Consuelo about her romantic evening with the Prince of Wales. She confided that nothing much happened, probably because they both had drunk a great deal.

Aware Lord Furness was still away, the Prince of Wales invited Thelma to spend the weekend at Fort Belvedere, his weekend retreat near Windsor Park. Thelma accepted. By now she knew her husband had a mistress. Surely she had a right to enjoy herself as well.

On Friday afternoon Thelma left London in her sports car, heading for Windsor Great Park. At the entrance to Fort Belvedere the gate keeper checked a list, found her name on it and allowed Thelma and her car to enter.

On her return to London, Thelma wrote to Consuelo telling her the whole weekend had been magical. They had listened to jazz records, swam in the Prince's heated pool and danced. In contrast to the brutal lovemaking of her husband, the Prince's demands were minimal. He was a very gentle lover. Having attended many Hollywood parties, Thelma was not shocked by some of Edward's more unusual demands. She reassured him that she enjoyed being with him. It was true. She had not been so happy since she arrived in England.

Whenever Lord Furness was away Thelma spent weekends at Fort Belvedere. Midweek she sometimes attended jazz sessions with the Prince and his friends or they made up a party and went dancing at a night club.

That winter, marooned at Burrough Court, which was a long way away from the nearest village or railway station, Thelma did her best to win the confidence of Averill. Her reclusive stepdaughter told her she much preferred animals to people. Thelma realised that how badly Averill had suffered from the shock of her mother's death. It was clear that she was terrified of her father and his violent outbursts of rage which also frightened Thelma.

Thelma learned that one of the reasons Averill feared her father was that, when she was nine, Lord Furness had punished her for a relatively trivial offence by having one of her beloved ponies shot.

Averill confided she was keen on a young man who worked for Furness Withy Lines in Kenya. She knew her father disapproved of staff becoming friendly with his family or their guests, so it was a secret. Thelma, afraid of provoking one of her husband's rages, did not tell Averill's story to him.

One evening when her husband was away on business, Thelma dined *en famille* with Consuelo and Bernie and confided in them she was scared of her husband's violence when he flew into one of his wild rages. Bernie looked worried. From a former Furness chauffeur, who now worked as a driver at the American

Embassy, Bernie had heard disturbing rumours about the sudden death of Lady Daisy Furness aboard the Furness yacht.

As Thelma pressed Bernie to tell her more, he related that the chauffeur had talked of foul play. Lord Furness always had showgirls as mistresses. Lady Daisy had discovered the truth and turned to a former boyfriend for comfort and had an affair with him. The chauffeur, who used to drive Lady Daisy, reported to Lord Furness that she made frequent visits to a certain address. In spite of his own infidelities, Lord Furness was a jealous husband. He engaged private detectives to follow his wife and learned she had a lover. To avoid a divorce and having to pay his wife large sums Lord Furness had poisoned her and ordered Lady Daisy's corpse to be buried at sea.

Thelma learned more of the story by questioning her maid and swearing her to secrecy. She was told that, in the summer of 1921, Lord Furness had sent young Christopher and Averill for a holiday to the South of France with their grandmother. He and Lady Daisy were to sail there on the yacht *Sapphire* and join them in Nice. When crossing the Bay of Biscay, Daisy Furness had died suddenly, aged 40 and in good health.

A footman, who doubled as a steward aboard the Furness yacht, told Thelma's maid he believed Lady Daisy had been poisoned. Before dinner Lord Furness had insisted on mixing the cocktails himself. Shortly after drinking her cocktail, his wife collapsed and died in her cabin. Lord Furness showed little emotion over his wife's death. He had been cool and calm, ordered the crew to sew up the corpse in a sheet and heave it overboard.

Later, Lord Furness had fired the footman, claiming he had stolen wine from the cellar. The footman was furious but not foolish enough to accuse England's wealthiest man, with access to the best lawyers in the country, of murdering his wife when he had no proof — only suspicions.

The death of her predecessor preyed on Thelma's mind. She brought the subject up again during her next family dinner with Bernie and Consuelo. Bernie thought that Lord Furness's decision to bury his wife at sea was suspicious. Even in heavy seas, like those in the Bay of Biscay, a large sea-going yacht would have been able to reach the nearest Spanish port. So why had Lady Daisy been buried at sea? Bernie's considered view was that this was done in case a Spanish doctor had asked for an autopsy to be carried out before issuing a death certificate for the deceased.[7]

∗∗∗

Lord Furness spent his weekends flying to Le Touquet by private plane to visit the casino. He did not offer to take Thelma as they were now living separate lives which suited her. She was careful to drive herself to Fort Belvedere and always checked no one was following her car. Lord Furness could not afford to have a second wife die a mysterious death. Scotland Yard would ask far too many awkward questions.

Lord Furness would have to buy her off if he wanted his freedom. Meanwhile she was living for the moment — enjoying weekends with the Prince at Fort Belvedere. Sometimes his equerry, Major Edward 'Fruity' Metcalfe, joined them and other guests. Fruity's wife, Lady Alexandra 'Baba' Metcalfe was involved in a love affair and rarely came to Fort Belvedere. Fruity told Thelma he and Baba stayed together for the sake of their children. Thelma realised this was how the English upper-classes behaved. Unlike Hollywood, where divorces were now very common, it seemed few British couples divorced as it was considered scandalous.

A shared passion for New Orleans jazz united Thelma and the Prince of Wales. Night-clubbing was the latest 'in thing'. A visit to the Embassy Club in Bond Street resembled being a guest at a well-organised private party. Members moved from table to table, danced with friends and listened to black American jazz musicians and singers.

The Prince loved taking parties of friends to this nightclub where a table was kept reserved for his exclusive use. Thelma was in her element, mingling with theatrical names like Noel Coward, Gertie Lawrence and Adele Astaire, who with her partner Fred had taken London by storm. The Prince had booked the entire front row of the theatre and taken them all to see Fred and Adele dance. Adele Astaire, born in Nebraska, was beautiful and talented and she and Thelma got on well. Adele joined their group, escorted by Lord Charles Cavendish, a son of the Duke of Devonshire. Consuelo, as Thelma's confidante warned her younger sister she must only be photographed as part of a group and never stand beside the Prince of Wales for photographs or it could give the newspapers ideas.

Edward's younger brother, Bertie, Duke of York, and his attractive wife, Duchess Elizabeth, often drove over from Windsor Castle to swim with Thelma and Edward in the heated pool he had built at Fort Belvedere. Sometimes Prince George, Duke of Kent, spent a weekend there with one of his many girlfriends.

Thelma realised that any permanent relationship between her and Edward was impossible. Not only was she a Catholic and non-royal but she was divorced. Sooner or later, the heir to the throne would have to follow tradition and marry a virginal princess. In the meantime they would enjoy themselves.

ON SAFARI IN EAST AFRICA

In October 1929, a few days before the Wall Street crash made headlines, various social columns announced that Lord and Lady Furness were embarking for East Africa and would stay in Nairobi where Lord Furness had business interests.

A few days later the Court Circular in *The Times* and *The Daily Telegraph* announced that the Prince of Wales was making an official tour of East Africa which would include a safari.

Before Thelma left London, the Prince threw a farewell party for her at the Embassy Club and gave her a small gold St Christopher medallion for luck. Dancing together, the Prince whispered that he had found a way of meeting her. He would invite her and her husband to join his personal safari. Thelma, dreading the prospect of weeks on end with her volatile husband, was delighted.

Consuelo accompanied her sister to the Army and Navy Stores, London's leading tropical outfitters, where Thelma was fitted for white linen jackets and trousers, a sun helmet with fly veiling and several pairs of elastic-sided boots.

As honoured guests aboard the Furness Withy liner bound for Mombassa, the chairman and his wife were given the largest stateroom with an adjacent sitting room hung with horse paintings by the chairman's favourite artist, Sir Alfred Munnings. Each night, standing at the reception line beside her husband, Lady Thelma Furness, elegant in slinky satin dresses and the Furness diamonds, hosted cocktail parties for the most important passengers.

Arriving at Nairobi, they spent the next ten days at the luxurious Norfolk Hotel and attended parties at the exclusive Muthaiga Club.

Thelma had to act as hostess on her husband's private safari. His twenty invited guests were to travel in a fleet of Rolls Royces, painted in the Furness racing colours of black and maroon. Each car had its own fully stocked bar fitted with unbreakable silver beakers, monogrammed with the Furness crest.

Lord Furness needed a constant supply of alcohol but never appeared to be drunk. His lavish expedition required mountains of baggage — tents and portable canvas baths for the guests, crates of tinned food from Fortnum and Masons, including tinned Beluga caviar, tinned *foie gras* and crates of vintage champagne. Lord Furness was known by his native bearers as 'Champagne Lordy' for the piles of empty Dom Perignon bottles that littered each campsite after the group departed.

What dismayed Thelma was her husband's passion for killing African wild life while all she wanted to do was to photograph these beautiful creatures. She was kept busy looking after their guests. In front of them her husband was careful to be very polite to his second wife, which was not the case when they were alone, where he either ignored Thelma or was rude to her.

On their return to the Norfolk Hotel, the receptionist handed Lord Furness a crested envelope containing an invitation from the Prince of Wales, inviting Lord and Lady Furness to join him on *his* private safari. The accompanying guest list contained the names of 40 aristocrats with vast landholdings in Kenya as well as the Governor of Kenya and his wife.

With reluctance Lord Furness had to refuse the invitation due previous business commitments, but was pleased to have been invited. In spite of his vast wealth, Lord Furness had never succeeded in penetrating the highest echelons of British society as apparently his American wife had done with ease. He told Thelma to join the royal safari and make friends with the Governor of Kenya and his wife. They could be useful to Furness Lines.

So, with her husband's encouragement Lady Furness joined the Prince of Wales on his safari. Fascinated by Africa's exotic wild animals Thelma enjoyed herself enormously. In the evenings native servants pitched a circle of tents around the main campfire and lit smaller fires in an outer ring to discourage lions and elephants from approaching too close.

Thelma and the Prince of Wales sat by one of the smaller campfires and talked under the stars before retiring to their respective tents. Under cover of darkness the Prince joined Thelma who was carried away by the romance of a starry African night. Her royal lover treated her with respect and a tenderness she had not experienced in either of her marriages or her broken engagement in Hollywood.

In her published memoirs Thelma gave no hint of sexual problems with the Prince of Wales. Her account of nights they spent together under the stars reads like a Mills and Boon romance. Thelma (or her ghost writer) related how 'This was our Eden and we were alone in it… I felt the Prince's arms about me… and the mounting tide of his ardour'.[8]

Whether the heir to the throne actually managed to maintain 'the mounting tide of his ardour' was not recorded. Nevertheless, Thelma did become anxious she could be pregnant, so possibly the romance of Africa overcame the Prince's sexual problems.

Just as Freda Dudley Ward had done, Thelma did her best to build up the Prince of Wales' ego, damaged in childhood by his father's constant criticism and his mother's lack of love.

The Prince's safari lasted seven days and nights before Thelma was due to join Lord Furness at the port of Mombasa. Once again they had the best stateroom on the Furness Withy liner, waited on by a personal butler. Worried she might be pregnant, Thelma was careful to initiate sex with her husband on the return voyage.

Meanwhile, the Prince of Wales travelled by private train around the vast area of the Belgian Congo and did his customary round of official functions and shaking hundreds of hands. Exhausted he returned to England on a naval vessel, arriving back early in April, 1930.

By now doctors had confirmed that Lady Furness *was* pregnant. Lord Furness was delighted, convinced the baby would be a boy. Thelma knew her husband would divorce her if he had any suspicions the child she was carrying might not be his.

What she needed was expert medical advice. Could the Prince of Wales' severe attack of mumps in his teens really have made him incapable of fathering children? If the Prince *was* the father of her child and if his sperm *had* been weakened by mumps could her baby be born damaged? It was all very worrying.

Consuelo recorded in her journal that her sister told her she had no idea what to do if her child had fair hair and blue eyes, like the Prince of Wales. Lord Furness's receding hair was reddish brown and all the Morgans had jet black hair.

Practical as ever, Consuelo suggested that, if her child would be fair-haired, Thelma should tell her husband the baby's features were a throw-back to Laura Morgan's Irish ancestors, the Kilpatricks, and get a copy of the family tree drawn up to prove it.

Thelma visited her Harley Street gynaecologist for a routine check up and used her acting skills to create a story which would provide answers to her queries. She told the gynaecologist she was worried about her brother, who, at seventeen had suffered a severe attack of mumps and had led a fairly wild life in Hollywood. She now feared he might be infertile, but should he decide to marry and *did* father a child what risk was there that the baby could be born damaged?

The gynaecologist opened a medical textbook and showed Lady Furness a diagram of a male sex organ as he explained that the testicular swelling known as a mumps orchitis narrowed and damaged the tiny passageways along which sperm was transferred. Were *both* testicles to be affected, the sufferer stood a high risk of being infertile. If the Leydig cells were effected any sperm that was produced would be low grade with lowered motility and there was a danger of premature ejaculation, a form of impotence.

Thelma started to realise the extent of the Prince of Wales' problems and feel sorry for him. Had Freda Dudley Ward known all this? She said nothing to her doctor, digesting what she had learned. The gynaecologist wrote down the name of an endocrinologist and suggested her brother visit him when he came to London.

Thelma realised it was unlikely the Prince of Wales was the father of her baby.[9]

***

The Honourable William Anthony Furness was born on 31 March, 1929. The doctor who delivered her baby told Lady Furness her son was perfect in every respect. What little hair Anthony had was dark like hers.

The birth of a son did not seem to make much difference to a marriage which was falling apart. Lord Furness spent a great deal of time away, allegedly on business and he and Thelma were leading separate lives.

In the 1930s very few affluent mothers cared for their own babies. Remembering the story of Queen Mary and the disturbed nanny, Thelma made enquiries and found that the Norland Training College in Chislehurst supplied the crème de la crème of the nanny world and checked all references very carefully.

Through an agency Thelma obtained a Norland nanny for her baby. Remembering Edward's stories of the miserable early years when his mother did not visit him and his brother for months, she visited the nursery daily to check on Anthony and his nanny.

Thelma resumed her former social life — shopping in Bond Street, visiting Elizabeth Arden's beauty salon, meeting Consuelo and her expatriate American friends for long gossipy lunches at The Ritz.

The Prince of Wales departed on a battleship for a six-month tour of South America. Thelma had taught Edward a few simple Spanish phrases to use in various speeches. She and Consuelo drove to Portsmouth to see Edward's ship depart.

From the ports he visited in Chile, the Cape Verde Islands and Argentina, the Prince wrote Thelma affectionate but very childish letters. Scared someone might discover them and tell her husband, Thelma burned all the letters after having shown them to Consuelo.

While the Prince was in South America, Consuelo introduced Wallis Warfield Simpson as a new member to their lunch group. Mrs Simpson came from a well-connected Baltimore family and had known Bernie's brother, Bill Thaw, in America. She was keen to join their lunch group as, having recently arrived in London, she knew very few people. Thelma thought Mrs Simpson had a harsh voice and hard features. Initially, Thelma did not take to her at all but Consuelo and the others found Wallis very amusing and accepted her as part of the group. Over time Thelma grew to like her more.

With Lord Furness away at Furness Lines offices in Marseilles, Thelma planned to host a dinner to welcome back the Prince on his return from South America.

His Royal Highness's arrival was a big social event for the local gentry. Looking forward to her 'welcome home' dinner for her lover, and having organised the seating plan, Thelma was upset to learn that, at the last minute, her sister had come down with influenza and she and Bernie had to cancel.

Consuelo suggested Thelma invite Wallis and her husband, Ernest Simpson, to make up the numbers. During the war Ernest had served in the Coldstream Guards and the Prince had been in the Grenadier Guards — this should give them something to talk about. Wallis was very entertaining and would keep her end of the table amused.

The Simpsons and other dinner guests were fetched from the station and installed at Burrough Court for the night. Everyone changed into full evening dress. At pre-dinner cocktails, Thelma introduced the Prince of Wales to Ernest Simpson, a tall and fair haired man with a clipped moustache and an equally clipped English accent. The Prince seemed to recall having met Ernest Simpson in the mess of the Coldstream Guards. At dinner the Simpsons were seated further down the table from the Prince of Wales who sat on Thelma's right.

His Royal Highness left the dinner table early, pleading he had to get up early to go out with the hunt the following morning. With the departure of the star guest, the party broke up.

Thelma received a polite note from Wallis Simpson, thanking her for such an enjoyable dinner and telling her how much the chance to meet the Prince had pleased her husband. Wallis realised that friendship with Thelma rather than with Consuelo was the way to meet the heir to the throne. Mrs Simpson worked hard at becoming friends with Lady Furness at their luncheons at the Ritz.

Thelma learned Wallis hoped to be presented at Buckingham Palace in order to gain admittance to London high society. Her sister-in-law, Maude Kerr-Smiley, had been presented at court but was not offering any help in that direction. In fact Maude Kerr-Smiley regarded Wallis as a gold digger who was after Ernest's money and wanted very little to do with her. Thelma suggested Wallis use the same titled English lady who had sponsored *her* presentation to Queen Mary when she arrived in London.

Thelma knew from her sister that Ernest Simpson's business was suffering and he had money worries. Ship broking was a tough world in an economic downturn and the creditors of Ernest's family firm were defaulting. The Simpsons had sold their Lagonda and sacked the chauffeur. Thelma, always warm hearted and generous said she would be happy to lend Wallis her court dress and ostrich feathers for the occasion. One of their chauffeurs could drive Mrs Simpson and her husband and herself to Buckingham Palace, wait for them and then take them home.

After the ceremony ended and Wallis had made her standard curtsey to Queen Mary, who was on the dais with the Prince of Wales beside her, refreshments were served. The Prince came over to see Thelma and commented politely how attractive she and Mrs Simpson looked tonight. Instead of smiling demurely as Thelma would have done, Wallis, who had overheard the Prince comment how unflattering the light was to female complexions, teasingly repeated his words back at him. There was an awkward pause. Would the Prince be cross at Wallis' impudence? Apparently not. He burst out laughing and talked animatedly to the Simpsons about America until the reception ended.

Thelma asked the Simpsons and the Prince of Wales back to Lees Place for a nightcap. Her cook rustled up some sandwiches to mop up the Dom Perignon they continued drinking. As usual Lord Furness was out. Thelma was pleased her impromptu party had gone so well, thanks to Wallis and her amusing stories. The Prince stayed late, clearly amused by Wallis. Having dismissed the chauffeur for the night, Thelma asked the Prince to drive the Simpsons back to their apartment, aware this would save them the cost of a taxi.

The following morning Wallis phoned to thank Thelma for the loan of the her court dress and the feathers. She asked her and the Prince to join her and Ernest for a typical American dinner — she would serve Chicken Maryland, her speciality. The Prince loved to come and left it to Thelma to fix a date.

At dinner the Prince seemed amused by Wallis's outrageous remarks and risqué stories, enjoyed talking to Ernest about the war and inspected Ernest's large library.

The economic downturn showed no sign of ending. Lord Furness was absent from London taking advantage of the recession to buy up ship yards and shipping lines at rock bottom prices. This suited Thelma who was to spend evenings with the Prince and his friends at the Embassy Club and weekends at Fort Belvedere.

The Prince of Wales suggested Thelma invite Wallis and Ernest Simpson to Fort Belvedere, as he found them so amusing. For the sake of propriety Thelma had her own bedroom at The Fort with a large double bed with a bright pink satin bedcover and three enormous Prince of Wales' feathers mounted symbolically over the bed head. The décor created by Thelma was pure 'Hollywood' and amused the Prince. He was also amused by Wallis's dry wit and the fact she was not afraid to contradict him if she felt he was wrong, something Thelma would never have done.

He told Thelma how much he enjoyed having the Simpsons as house guests. Thelma was grateful when Wallis took on the role of her chaperone.

Thelma, who adored her father, was shocked to find how much the Prince of Wales hated George V. He claimed his father had intimidated and thrashed him during his boyhood and his mother never intervened to protect him. Queen Mary's own childhood had been miserable and deprived so she had difficulty showing love to *her* children. Since Lord Furness also seemed to dislike children, he rarely visited Anthony. Thelma told Consuelo that the English upper-class seem to prefer their horses and dogs to their children.

In his early twenties the Prince of Wales had been in love with Freda Dudley Ward. After their sexual relationship ended Freda had remained fond of Edward and acted as his confidante and advisor. Freda, who approved of Thelma, sometimes talked to her on the phone. They both worried about the amount of brandy the heir to the throne consumed. To discourage the Prince of Wales from drinking so much, Thelma taught him to play patience. She also encouraged him to undertake delicate *petit point* needlework, a skill Thelma had learned from the nuns. She purchased wool and canvas from Harrods and long poles to act as embroidery frames. She transported these items to Fort Belvedere on hooks fitted to the sides of her sports car. As Ernest Simpson was away on business, Thelma took Wallis with her as a chaperone in case Marmaduke Furness was having her followed.

After dinner Thelma and the Prince sat side by side, each working on their own part of the needlework while Wallis read to them. Thelma claimed, 'The hand that holds the needle cannot hold a brandy snifter'.[10]

To celebrate the anniversary of the night they attended the Louis Amstrong concert, the Prince gave Thelma a diamond brooch in the form of three Prince of Wales feathers with his motto, *Ich Dien (I Serve)*, set in diamonds.

Wallis Simpson, who adored beautiful jewels, was green with envy. (Years later she would demand a similar brooch from Edward.) As Wallis was always talking about her prosperous Baltimore relatives and her wealthy school friends, Thelma had no idea that her friend's early years had been deprived. Wallis was jealous of those who she felt had done better in life that she had and Lady Thelma Furness seemed to have all the things Wallis wanted. She was an acknowledged beauty, owned wardrobes filled with designer clothes, fur coats, alligator and crocodile handbags and matching shoes and had her own sports car. She had jewels from the Prince *and* the Furness diamonds. Jewels spelled success to Wallis.

Thelma, unaware of Wallis's jealousy, liked having her at Fort Belvedere as it shed the load on her to provide constant amusement for Edward who, although in his late thirties, resembled an adolescent who was easily bored.

On 23 August 1929, Lord Furness was in France so Thelma spent her birthday with the Prince of Wales, who gave her an box market 'Cartier'. Opening the box Thelma found an elegant solid gold bracelet, engraved with her initials. She wore the bracelet at their next all girls' lunch at The Ritz. Wallis was green with envy.

'THE WIFE IS ALWAYS THE LAST TO KNOW'

It was clever Consuelo who discovered why Thelma's husband was spending so much time in the casino at Le Touquet. Thelma had suspected he went there to meet some showgirl or dancer from the floor show, but she was wrong. Lord Furness was besotted by Enid Lindeman Cavendish, a dazzlingly beautiful Australian. Her elderly husband had a holiday house at Le Touquet, but their main residence was near Lees Place and the American Embassy where Consuelo's husband worked.

Some of the American wives who lunched at the Ritz warned Thelma what was happening. Enid Lindeman Cavendish had acquired a reputation as a gold-digger in New York when she became the second wife of Roderick Cameron, a fabulously wealthy shipping tycoon from Staten Island, who was 24 years older than herself.

After a brief marriage of only twelve months, Roderick Cameron died, leaving his entire fortune to Enid. As the rest of the Cameron family loathed Enid for ending up with all the money, Enid Lindeman and her baby Rory moved to London where she met another wealthy widower, General 'Caviar' Cavendish, a much decorated war veteran with a large house off Grosvenor Square.

After a brief courtship Enid married General Cavendish. While they were staying in Le Touquet he suffered a heart attack. Enid did not stay at home to nurse her husband, but dressed up in evening dress and went off to the casino to play roulette, where Lord Furness saw her. Dazzled by her blonde good looks he asked her to dine with him.

Returning to Mayfair the elderly General Cavendish suffered a second and more severe heart attack, was comatose and had to be nursed round the clock. The gossips claimed Thelma's husband had become a very frequent visitor to the Cavendish home. He spent a few nights there with the beguiling Enid whose second husband was not yet in his grave.

'The wife is always he last to know', Consuelo warned her younger sister after telling Thelma the latest Mayfair gossip.

From the American wives in Consuelo's lunch group, Thelma learned more about Enid Lindeman. On her arrival in New York Enid had claimed to be an Australian wine heiress but had no money to speak of when she married a shipping tycoon old enough to be her father. She did the same thing in London when she married the wealthy elderly General 'Caviar' Cavendish and had two more children.

Consuelo advised her younger sister to leave this abusive marriage and settle for what she could get in the way of alimony. At least she would still be alive, unlike that poor Lady Daisy Furness.

Thelma did not believe Lord Furness could afford the scandal of a second wife dying under mysterious circumstances.

She did a little sleuthing and examined the monthly accounts from the company florist, Constance Spry. She saw that Lord Furness was also paying for regular deliveries of hot house blooms to Enid Lindeman Cavendish in her house on the far side of Grosvenor Square. She remembered those huge bouquets of flowers delivered daily to *her* at the home of Reggie and Gloria in New York and seethed with anger. This was her husband's standard ploy. How could she have been deceived so easily?

As usual, Thelma phoned Consuelo for advice. Her sister told her to keep calm and not to confront her husband. Thelma should take an early morning walk round Grosvenor Square and look at the competition. Enid Cavendish always took her morning exercise in the square between eight and eight-thirty.

'How will I recognise her?

'Easy! She'll be the only blonde walking a pet cheetah on a leash!'

Consuelo was right. It was hard to miss Enid Lindeman. She was much taller than Thelma and her ash blonde hair was clearly natural. Her figure was sensational and she had the face of a Botticelli Venus. Thelma could see why her husband was smitten.

Lord Furness's secretary must have told him Thelma had been looking at the Constance Spry accounts and seen the daily deliveries to Mrs Enid Cavendish. The following morning at breakfast, Lord Furness went on the attack and demanded why Thelma found it necessary to spend so many weekends at Fort Belvedere.

Thelma, a former actress, looked her husband straight in the eye and claimed she and Mrs Simpson went there to chaperone aristocratic girls being considered as potential wives for the Prince of Wales. She regarded being asked to do this as a great honour. Did he not agree? Lord Furness grunted and returned to his copy of *The Times*.

Later that day Thelma's husband paid a rare visit to the nursery to see Anthony. The next morning he commented that Anthony bore no resemblance to him and looked far more like the Prince of Wales. Thelma told her husband he was being ridiculous. Anthony had dark hair like the rest of her family. Marmaduke glared but said nothing more.

Another row erupted when Andrew Rattray, the animal trainer employed by Lord Furness, arrived. Andrew, a young Englishman with an educated Oxbridge accent and a Kenyan sun tan, arrived at Burrough Court in a van with two zebras who he had brought over from East Africa. He was to train them to pull in tandem a coach driven by Lord Furness, who intended to cause a sensation at the next local agricultural show.

Andrew Rattray, clearly from a 'good' family, was an employee so in the strictly regimented world of 'Upstairs-Downstairs' he was to sleep and eat downstairs in the staff quarters rather than in the dining room. Thelma found Andrew pleasant and well mannered and felt he *should* be invited to eat in the dining room but knew her husband would explode if she suggested this. She realised that Andrew must be the person with whom Averill had been corresponding and hoped things would work out. But as Averill was very secretive about it, Thelma found it wisest not to interfere.

A few days after Andrew's arrival at Burrough Court, he and Averill disappeared. By that time Lord Furness had gone to France for business. The local press ran a story saying the Hon Averill Furness had eloped with Lord Furness's animal trainer and the couple were on board a ship heading for East Africa. They planned to marry in Nairobi and find work running safaris.

On his return from France, Lord Furness read the story about his daughter at breakfast. Incandescent with rage he broke the back off one of the Chippendale dining chairs. He ripped a valuable horse painting by George Stubbs off the wall, put his clenched fist through it and threw the remains at Thelma, bruising her on the shoulder.

He yelled that it was her *duty* to have warned him Averill was involved with a servant. His daughter had disgraced the Furness name. He was cutting her of his will and hoped she *starved*.

Thelma retorted that Andrew's father was more respectable than *his* grandfather, who had very little schooling and had delivered sacks of coal before going into the shipping business.

Lord Furness threw a plate at his wife's head, missed and stormed out of the house.

On 15 February 1930, *Time* magazine reported that the Hon Averill Furness had married Andrew Rattray at the office of the District Commissioner in Nairobi and Lady Thelma Furness had defied her husband and cabled her congratulations to the happy couple.

On reading the story in *Time* magazine, Lord Furness smashed a valuable Oriental vase and called a press conference to announce that he had disinherited his daughter. He placed advertisements in the main newspapers saying neither Andrew Rattray nor his wife could charge anything to the accounts operated by Furness Lines. With satisfaction he told Thelma *no one* would dare to give Andrew Rattray a job. He hoped the couple *starved* to death. Thelma had defied him and Lord Furness wanted a divorce on the grounds of her affair with the Prince of Wales.[11]

Thelma took this threat very seriously and went to consult a divorce lawyer, accompanied by Consuelo, who recorded the consultation in her journal. In fact, Lord Furness was bluffing — to obtain a divorce on grounds of adultery he had to produce signed statements *to prove* Thelma had been found in a compromising position with the Prince. However, if she could get proof of adultery she could divorce Lord Furness as the innocent party.

Thelma decided the best course of action was attack. She paid a detective to obtain an affidavit from a housemaid in the Cavendish household, testifying that Lord Furness had spent several nights with Mrs Cavendish. The housemaid swore she had seen them together when she took morning tea into Mrs Cavendish's bedroom. General Cavendish was comatose in the room adjacent to Enid's bedroom where she and Lord Furness were disporting themselves.

Presented with the signed affidavit Lord Furness retaliated by repeating his threat to cite the Prince of Wales as a co-respondent, hoping this would silence his wife. However, his lawyers warned him *not* to get the Prince of Wales involved. The Prince was a very popular figure and there was a real risk that Furness passengers might be angry and switch to other shipping lines if Lord Furness cited the Prince in a divorce which would make headlines in the newspapers.

Not wanting to risk the same fate as Lady Daisy, Thelma moved out and leased a furnished apartment near Marble Arch. She filed a petition for divorce, citing adultery by her husband as the reason. As Lord Furness had never given her cash, she had to borrow money from Consuelo to pay her lawyers and would repay her sister once she received her divorce settlement.

Lord Furness now wanted a divorce as soon as possible. He knew that Enid had had other lovers, some of them younger and better-looking than him. He feared one of them might ask Enid to marry him before he was free.

He refused to involve Enid Cavendish in a divorce action as it would damage her reputation, although she was notorious for the number of lovers she took (a fact recorded by Enid's daughter in her memoirs). Lord Furness agreed to have a detective find him in a hotel bedroom with a woman who specialised in providing evidence for divorce cases. Enid Cavendish would not be named in the divorce and nor would the Prince of Wales.

In the 1930s, an era when most judges were male, not many women came off best in a divorce, even if they had children to support. The concept of splitting assets was not yet established even though Thelma Furness wanted custody of Anthony. She had also asked for the Lees Place house as part of her settlement, but did not receive it. Furness Withy accountants had been creative in their accounting and 'cooked the books'. The accountants were clever and made it appear the shipping line was losing money (The company was later broken up and sold for over a billion pounds).

In October 1933, the divorce of Furness versus Furness was finalised with no house for Thelma and a relatively small settlement for the wife of Britain's wealthiest man. Lord Furness had the money to pay top barristers, with the result that Thelma received less than half of what her lawyers had hoped for and did not get custody of Anthony. And, of course, there was no chance that the Prince of Wales would marry her.

The day after the decree absolute came through Lord Furness married Enid Lindeman Cavendish at a registry office and she became Lady Enid Lindeman Furness. Under British law Thelma retained the right to the title of Lady Thelma Furness for the rest of her life. Lord Furness's wedding presents to Enid were the Furness diamonds and a villa in the South of France.

It came as a shock when Thelma had to hand over the jewels of the late Lady Daisy Furness, which she had believed were a wedding gift but had never obtained a statement to that effect. Furness Withy lawyers asserted the jewels were part of the Furness estate. Lady Thelma Furness must hand them back or they would sue.

It was galling for Thelma to think that these valuable jewels would be worn by the third Lady Furness. Although she still had her beautiful clothes and her sports car, the rest of her lavish lifestyle had gone with the wind.

Lord Furness had managed to obtain custody of Anthony by bribing staff to say Thelma was an unfit mother. Bewildered, little three year old Anthony was joined at Burrough Court by Enid's young children, Pat and Caryll Cavendish. Lord Furness banished all three children and their nannies to a special nursery wing of Burrough Court. Pat Cavendish would later claim Lord Furness hated children and banned all three of them from the main house and the garden and called her third husband 'an ogre who did his best to make our lives miserable'.[12] The fact that little Anthony could not understand why he no longer saw his mother had a bad effect on their future relationship. Anthony perceived that his mother had abandoned him.

Lord Furness had said he hoped his daughter would starve to death and, in an ironic twist of fate, this actually happened. With very little money Averill and Andrew Rattray built themselves a bush shack and set up their own wildlife safaris.

In October 1933, on safari with wealthy Americans, Andrew caught a tropical infection and ran a high fever. Averill managed to get a plane to pick him up and Andrew was flown to Nairobi, but a few days later he died in hospital. This occurred in the same month Thelma and Lord Furness divorced.

Grief-stricken, the reclusive Averill remained in their bush shack, refused to eat and drank herself to death. Her emaciated corpse would not be found for another three months, but her father did not seem affected by the death of his only daughter.

The amount of alcohol Lord Furness consumed was taking effect and the former workaholic started to slow down. He spent time with Enid and her children at St Jean Cap Ferrat near Nice in one of the finest villas on the Cote d'Azur.

Villa la Fiorentina had magnificent gardens overlooking the Mediterranean. Lord and Lady Enid Furness spent a great deal of time there but returned to England for the hunting season. Enid had been raised on a property in New South Wales and was a crack shot and a brilliant horsewoman and greatly enjoyed fox hunting. She was wildly extravagant, spent money like water on clothes, jewels and superb décor for the villa. Lord Furness had found his match.

Enid Lindeman was not only very beautiful but highly intelligent and as determined to marry money as Thelma had been. Raised in the Australian bush, Enid was much smarter than Thelma. She enjoyed country life at Burrough Court where she kept a menagerie of rescued animals, including porcupines, stray dogs, her pet cheetah, three dozen poodles and horses that, without her intervention would have been shot or sent to the slaughter-house.

Lady Enid Lindeman Furness was wildly extravagant, knew she needed plenty of money in order to live the kind of life she wanted and educate her children well, so was determined to secure the Furness fortune for herself.

Thelma, on a relatively modest divorce settlement, split her time between staying with her twin in Paris and with the Prince of Wales at Fort Belvedere. As a divorcee she no longer needed a chaperone, but feeling sorry for Wallis left on her own in London, she drove her down for weekends at Fort Belvedere. At The Fort they swum, played jazz records and danced. Soon it became evident that the Prince of Wales wanted to dance with Wallis as much as he did with Thelma.

※

In January 1934, Thelma had long phone conversations with the widowed Gloria Vanderbilt who desperately needed her sisters' support at a forthcoming custody trial and begged her to come to New York.

Vanderbilt lawyers were demanding that Gertrude Vanderbilt Whitney took custody of little Gloria Laura Vanderbilt, the daughter of Thelma's twin sister. Mrs Morgan had switched sides, possibly thinking that a share of the Vanderbilt fortune might go to her when she claimed Gloria was an unfit mother and Gertrude Vanderbilt took charge of Gloria's little daughter. Thelma was appalled at her mother's duplicity and could not refuse her twin's request, even though she was loathe to leave England.

Since Reggie Vanderbilt's death, legal arguments over the custody of little Gloria, and allocation of the money held in the Vanderbilt Trust Fund, had dragged on for years of bitter conflict with Gloria's sister-in-law, Gertrude Vanderbilt Whitney, the main trustee of Reggie's money.

Gertrude Vanderbilt was a embittered woman who had never liked Gloria. She involved lawyers in what should be a family matter, determined to obtain custody of little Gloria Laura and insisted her niece must be raised in America.

At Fort Belvedere Thelma told the Prince of Wales of Gloria's problems. He did not want her to leave, but understood she must go to America to support her twin sister. He promised to drive down to Southampton to say goodbye.

Thelma had organised a farewell lunch with 'the girls' at The Ritz. At the lunch she trustingly asked Wallis Simpson to 'Look after the little man for me,' aware that the Prince of Wales had a roving eye. Thelma, being nominated in the press as one of the world's most beautiful women, feared no competition from Wallis, feeling that she would have little appeal for the Prince. (In *Double Exposure* Thelma described Wallis as 'not beautiful or even pretty, with large ugly hands — her blue eyes by far her best feature'.)

A week later Thelma's ship left for New York. The Prince was at the quayside with a farewell gift, an adorable miniature teddy bear, which Thelma kept in her handbag while she was in America (and forever after).

In New York, at an impromptu party thrown by Gloria, Thelma met Prince Aly Khan, a handsome playboy with a lean muscular body, a suntan and no problems with impotence.

Thelma flirted with the wealthy Aly Khan and was photographed dancing cheek to cheek with him in a New York night club. Later Thelma would confess to Consuelo that with the virile Prince Aly Khan, 'Things went further than I intended.'

In March 1934, as Thelma was leaving New York, Prince Aly Khan boarded the same transatlantic liner as Thelma, both of them bound for Europe. Aly Khan told her that he had decided to holiday in Nice. They spent evenings together on board ship and he invited Thelma to join him in his suite at the Negresco Hotel. Thelma rejected his offer, determined to return to London and try to gain custody of Anthony. She also wanted to see the Prince of Wales — in spite of his sexual problems, she was *genuinely* fond of him.

※

Meanwhile, Wallis used Thelma's absence in New York to move in on the Prince of Wales. She put doubts in Edward's mind about the fidelity of his mistress by showing him photographs of Thelma dancing cheek to cheek with Prince Aly Khan. While pretending to be Thelma's best friend, Wallis told Edward she was worried by gossip that Lady Furness was having an affair with one of Gloria's friends, Prince Aly Khan, son of the wealthy Aga Khan.

Wallis obtained more photos of the pair, dancing cheek to cheek on board ship and showed them to the jealous Prince. In response to seeing these photos he yelled, 'How dare that bitch betray me!'

Wallis comforted the heir to the throne, happy that her plan to discredit Thelma — her friend who had always been kind and generous to her — had succeeded. She was not in love with the Prince but at forty wanted to reassure herself that she was still attractive to men. One thing led to another and she employed her skills at oral sex on the 'little man' and from then on he was as putty in her hands.

On her return, Thelma telephoned Fort Belvedere saying she would be there very soon to see the Prince. Always a coward about personal relationships he replied coldly that he felt they should have some time apart. Bewildered by his response, Thelma phoned Wallis to ask her what was happening. Jokingly she asked Wallis, 'Has the Prince of Wales fallen in love with you?' Wallis denied this but admitted he had become 'fond of her'.

Thelma was shattered. She packed her suitcase with suitable clothes and drove to Fort Belvedere. After entering through the tall white gates she drove to the far end of the gravelled drive, parked her car and rang the bell. The butler let her in and showed her to one of the smaller guest rooms. He informed Thelma that the Prince of Wales and Mrs Simpson had gone for a walk.

Thelma noticed that Wallis had installed herself in the main guest room, which Thelma regarded as *her* room and, as a joke, had placed Prince of Wales feathers above the double bed.

Tired by the journey, Thelma slept before Wallis and Edward returned from their walk. She was woken by a knock on the door and told dinner was ready. As Thelma entered the dining room she found the Prince of Wales with Wallis sitting beside him at the head of the table, so she seated herself at the other end of it.

Thelma was amazed to see Wallis smack the Prince's hand in an intimate nanny-like gesture when he ate lettuce with his fingers rather than with a silver salad fork. Clearly Wallis had taken over the role of nanny-mistress more successfully than she had ever done.

After dinner Thelma picked up her bags and drove back to London and her small serviced flat near Marble Arch.

The following day she telephoned Wallis who, no doubt, was scared something might get into the papers, which would mean a showdown with Ernest. She tried to assure Thelma that the Prince was fond of her but that was all.

Thelma knew Wallis was lying. With a sinking heart she realised she had no wealthy husband and her romance with the Prince of Wales was over. She remembered Prince Aly Khan's invitation to join him in Nice, an offer she had turned down. She phoned the Hotel Negresco on the Promenade des Anglais and left a message for Prince Aly Khan, informing him that she was on her way. Thelma told her maid to pack a case with beach clothes, white trousers and her most glamorous evening gowns. She took a taxi to Victoria Station, caught the boat train, crossed the Channel by ferry and boarded the Blue Train to Nice.

At the Hotel Negresco, in a suite overlooking the Baie des Anges, Prince Aly Khan was delighted to see her. They swam from the beach below the Promenade des Anglais and made passionate love. The restaurants in the Old Town of Nice served the delicious food and wines of Provence. They drove to Vence and other picturesque hill villages where the air was scented with mimosa and orange blossom. By speedboat they went to Villefranche, then a small undiscovered fishing village and port.

They were like a honeymoon couple, but Thelma soon became aware that Prince Aly had no intention of marrying her or anyone else. One evening he admitted candidly that his motto in life was 'Flit from flower to flower'. Thelma returned to London, disillusioned by men and their egos.

SECRETS LEFT OUT OF THELMA'S MEMOIRS
Early in 1940, Captain Dick Furness died at Dunkirk leading a charge against a German gun post and was awarded a posthumous VC.

Once the German invasion of France took place, Lady Enid and Lord Furness were still at their villa in the south of France. Finally his high consumption of alcohol had caught up with Marmaduke and he was very ill, dying slowly from liver damage.

Lady Enid feared that the Italian Army were soon to invade, as Mussolini coveted the area around Nice which had once been part of Italy. Enid, her 12-year-old daughter Patricia and an English nurse took the ailing Lord Furness to Cannes by car seeking to return to Britain. But Marmaduke refused to board the filthy coal boat which had been sent by the British Government to take expatriates to England. He took one look at it, swore violently and insisted on returning to the Villa la Fiorentina on a stretcher.

Lord Furness had a will drawn up by Furness lawyers with a bequest of several million to Enid. In this will Furness lines, the ships and offices and other assets worth almost a billion pounds were to go to young Anthony Furness who his father hoped would eventually take control of the shipping line, to which Lord Furness had devoted his life.

As Thelma understood it, Lady Enid Furness was equally determined to obtain as much as possible of the Furness fortune for herself and her children. For some years Enid had given cocaine to her husband to calm his violent rages. When he was close to death, she gave him a large dose of cocaine to get him to write a new will with herself as the main beneficiary of Furness Lines. This will was witnessed by the English nurse who was caring for him. In many countries, including Australia, it is deemed illegal for a nurse to witness the will of a patient under her care.

Lady Enid Furness with the new will in her handbag and her young daughter left France on a train crowded with refugees. They crossed the Spanish border to Barcelona and from there took a boat back to wartime London and lived in the Lees Place house that Thelma had hoped would become hers under the divorce settlement.

In 1940, while being looked after by his third wife, Lord Marmaduke Furness died at the Villa la Fiorentina. Allegations by Thelma that Enid shortened Lord Furness's life by paying a nurse to inject him with cocaine and morphine, were never proved (although they may have been true).

The nurse who had looked after Lord Furness at the Villa la Fiorentina, managed to escape from France by a different route and eventually reached London. From there she contacted Lady Thelma Furness and told her what had transpired at the Villa La Fiorentina. She confirmed that Lord Furness had cut Anthony out of the will and she had been asked by Lady Enid to give her husband a large dose of cocaine and morphine to 'end his sufferings'. The nurse also swore that Lady Enid held the pen with which she made Lord Furness 'sign' the new will in which Lady Enid was the major beneficiary of the shipping line and other assets and made a very small bequest to Thelma's son Anthony.

Thelma paid the nurse to make a signed statement, claiming Lady Enid had rewarded her for killing Lord Furness by administering a lethal overdose of cocaine and morphine.[13]

Smarting from receiving a miserable divorce settlement, Thelma retaliated by making a legal objection to the new will on behalf of her young son Anthony Furness, who Lord Furness had intended to take over Furness Lines as well as inherit the title.

With over a billion pounds at stake in today's money Lord Furness's estate was worth fighting for. Thelma engaged the leading barrister Sir Walter Monckton, who she had known when he was a close friend of the former Prince of Wales, by now the Duke of Windsor.

On learning that the nurse had been *paid* to write the statement that Lord Furness had died from an overdose administered on the orders of by Lady Enid, Sir Walter Monckton withdrew from acting as Thelma's counsel, because the evidence (whether true or not) was deemed contaminated. And so Lady Thelma Furness's case against Lady Enid Lindeman Furness fell apart and she was not tried for murder.

Sir Walter Monckton's letter of apology, dated 13 July 1946, addressed to Lady Enid Furness's lawyer, Theodore Goddard, stated that Lady Thelma Furness had 'an entire misconception of the true facts of the case'. Walter Monckton, known for his honesty, added that there was not the slightest justification for the accusations and insinuations against Lady Enid Furness by his former client.[14] He further added that he wrote the letter with the authority of Lady Thelma Furness and had insisted she signed it.

Even though Thelma's wish to have Enid Lindeman Furness tried for murder had failed, she still contested her ex-husband's will on behalf of her son. She claimed Furness Withy Lines, its ships, docks and shipyards, offices, private planes and Rolls Royces and other assets should go to Anthony as Enid Furness was now married to a fourth elderly husband. It took five years for a judgement to be given on the validity of the second will brought back from France by Lady Enid Furness.

The judge decided that young Anthony Furness, the original main beneficiary should receive the major share in the Furness fortune, rather than Lady Enid, now Lady Kenmare, wife of the Earl of Kenmare

This decision made young Anthony Furness extremely wealthy and he was called by the press, 'the wealthiest little boy in Britain'. However, Thelma was not made a trustee for her son as she had hoped. Under the new judgement Lady Enid would still receive almost two million pounds. Lady Thelma Furness who had initiated the objection to the will, having received a relatively meagre divorce settlement in 1933, received nothing at all.

***

Thelma lived happily with Gloria in New York before moving to Beverley Hills. The Morgan twins' final move was to Culver City near the Hollywood studios. This was where, as an enterprising young woman, Thelma Morgan had produced and starred in her own films. Lady Thelma Furness died in New York on 19 January 1970, five years after the death of her twin.[15]

Thelma's niece, the fashion designer, Gloria Laura Vanderbilt, recalled that her aunt, Thelma Furness, dropped dead on Lexington Avenue on her way to see her doctor. In Thelma's handbag was the miniature teddy bear, that the Prince of Wales, gave her just before she sailed to America to support her twin in the Vanderbilt custody trial. The little teddy bear's head and arms were bald as she had carried it around with her for over thirty years.

The Morgan twins are buried side by side at the Holy Cross Catholic Cemetery in Culver City.[16]

Loyal friends like Mary Pickford and Douglas Fairbanks Senior, attended Thelma's modest funeral.[17] Needless to say, the Duchess of Windsor, did not send flowers.

The idea of writing a joint memoir telling the story of their marriages, relationships and law suits proved more complex than the Morgan twins had envisaged. What Thelma wrote about Wallis Simpson and her hated rival, Lady Enid Lindeman Furness, worried her publishers. After submitting the manuscript to lawyers they advised the twins to rewrite certain parts and remove others completely as they were libellous.

The subsequent rewrites and the onset of World War 2 delayed publication of *Double Exposure – A Twin Autobiography*. This joint memoir would not be published until 1955 in London and several years later with a different publisher in New York. Despite the suggestive title there was very little in the way of exposure and the title could easily have been changed to *Double Cover Up*.

By now the Prince of Wales as Edward VIII had abdicated the throne to marry the divorced Wallis, now the Duchess of Windsor. Lord Furness had died from a damaged liver as a result of his heavy consumption of alcohol. Not mentioned in *Double Exposure* was the fact that Thelma had done her best to have Enid Lindeman Furness tried for murder, bribed a witness but brought a legal objection to the will which finally succeeded. Thelma's son, Anthony, had regained the major share of the Furness fortune from Enid Lindeman Furness and Furness Withy lines had been broken up and sold for over a billion pounds.

There was enough material for many pages about the relationship of Thelma, the Prince of Wales and Wallis, but fears of libel actions prevented their publication in *Double Exposure*.

According to Consuelo's journal, Thelma gained some comfort by discussing the problems of the future king with Freda Dudley Ward, the woman who knew him best and who had received many hundreds of letters from him, laying bare his innermost feelings. Freda who never attempted to write or publish anything about her experiences, had a good knowledge of psychology. She tried to make Thelma understand how Wallis held Edward enthralled as a result of what had happened to him in the past.

Consuelo's journal contained observations on Thelma and the Prince, who had been frequent guests in the Thaws' London home. Bernie Thaw told Consuelo that in diplomatic circles it was known that Wallis had made visits to Shanghai brothels with her first husband. She would have seen prostitutes whipping or spanking men with cravings, similar to those of Prince Edward, as they needed to be hurt, humiliated and degraded in order to become sexually aroused. Thelma did not enjoy fulfilling these needs, but Wallis Simpson clearly did.

Wallis encouraged Edward's masochist tendencies, with the result he became obsessed by her domineering personality. This was why Edward found Wallis, who no one had ever called a beauty, more attractive than Thelma. Wallis's other attraction to the Prince was the fact she bore a strong physical resemblance to Nanny Green who had been his sole source of love from birth to when he was three years old.

Nanny Green's married name was Peters. After the death of their only son, Mr Peters left her for a younger woman. In a depressed state of mind, his wife went back to work under her maiden name of Nanny Green for Queen Mary. Her dead child had born a resemblance to little Prince Edward and, at times she hated him because *he* was alive while her son was dead. In that state of mind she spanked him savagely for minor misdeeds.[18] Then, softened by the little prince's tears she kissed and fondled him and ended up masturbating him to send him to sleep.[19]

Queen Mary who had a large family did not bother to visit her two eldest boys in their upstairs nursery, so had no idea what was going on. This sad state of affairs continued for three years. During that period, Prince Edward received no maternal love and was yelled at by his father. His disturbed nanny used to pinch him before he went into his father's office so he would cry and she would take him back to the nursery again. He was dependent on Nanny Green with her blend of cuddles and chastisement for love. So, in adult life, he continued to associate being humiliated in public and spanked in private with infantile feelings of comfort, security and love.

POST SCRIPTUM

Lady Enid Furness, having inherited her first fortune from her wealthy American husband and more money from her second husband, 'Caviar' Cavendish, under the contested will of Lord Furness became even richer. On marrying for the fourth time, Enid became Lady Kenmare.

The writer, Somerset Maugham, had been a neighbour of Lady Enid and Lord Furness at Cap Ferrat and was an acute observer of human nature. He liked Lady Enid Furness and had played bridge with her on her good days, but claimed that, at times, Enid drifted around the Villa La Fiorentina in a cocaine-induced haze. Sometimes she forgot she had invited guests to lunch or dinner until they arrived, which was embarrassing for them.

Somerset Maugham had as a joke referred to Enid as 'Lady Killmore', rather than Lady Kenmare. The name was used to good effect by Dominick Dunne in an article on Enid Lindeman in the March 1991 issue of *Vanity Fair*. The name stuck to her for the rest of her life.[20]

Dominick Dunne described Enid Lindeman-Cameron-Cavendish-Furness-Kenmare, as Australia's leading fortune hunter. Dunne claimed Enid Lindeman referred to herself as an Australian wine heiress, but this was an exaggeration. The family were land owners but the Lindeman vineyards, originally established in New South Wales, and Lindeman Island on the Barrier Reef had passed out of the hands of the Lindeman family before Enid was born.

After the death of the Earl of Kenmare, Enid Lindeman married her fifth husband, Lord Vincent Castlerosse, a charming and very amusing but far from wealthy Anglo-Irish aristocrat who she really *did* love.

Dominic Dunne was not only a journalist but a best-selling author in America and his article in *Vanity Fair* had wide readership and made Enid Lindeman appear like a fortune hunter *par excellence,* which was also the opinion of Thelma Morgan Furness.

It made Enid's daughter, Pat Cavendish, so angry that she wrote her own memoir (aided by a brilliant ghost writer) to refute the claims of Thelma Furness and Dominic Dunne that her mother married Lord Furness for his fortune and hastened his death.

Pat Cavendish, an engaging woman with several husbands and a passion for animals, claimed her mother genuinely loved Lord Furness. However she never quite managed to explain to readers how Enid Lindeman could have managed to love a man alleged to have murdered his first wife, who terrified Thelma and his own son with his violent rages, disinherited his daughter, leaving her to die alone and showed no remorse.

***

At the time of his father's death, Anthony was living with his nanny at Burrough Court. After Lord Furness's death, Thelma was granted custody of Anthony. He had been cared for by a changing succession of nannies and governesses.

In her memoirs, Lady Enid's daughter, Pat Cavendish, described Anthony, her step-brother, as 'a well-behaved but curiously silent child who seldom received love from anyone'.[21]

Anthony Furness became an introverted adolescent and a neurotic troubled adult who hated Lord Furness and refused to acknowledge him as his father, although he had inherited his vast fortune. Instead Anthony, now the third Viscount Furness told everyone he was the illegitimate son of the Duke of Windsor.

Due to his harsh treatment by 'the ogre' during his loveless childhood, Anthony vowed he would never give Lord Furness what he wanted — an heir to run his shipping line.

In his middle years, Viscount Anthony Furness became a tax exile in Switzerland.

Those with a vested interest in inheriting the Furness fortune managed to turn Anthony against his mother and he sought comfort in religion. His refusal to see his mother or answer her letters, caused Thelma much sadness in her final years.

For reasons explained earlier, it is highly unlikely Anthony was fathered by Edward, Prince of Wales. However, Viscount Anthony Furness remained *convinced* that the Duke of Windsor was his birth father. All Anthony's requests to meet the Duke of Windsor were ignored. When the Duke died, Anthony Furness was bitterly disappointed to learn he was not even acknowledged in his will.

As Viscount Anthony Furness aged he looked even less like the Duke of Windsor. Dark haired, always dressed in black, obese, suffering from diabetes, immensely wealthy and childless, he funded several theatrical productions, starring the actor Alan Badel and showed he had inherited Thelma's interest in the arts.

Later Anthony became involved with the ultra conservative Catholic Order of the Knights of Malta. As many of the Italians, who backed this religious order, were convinced that Viscount Anthony Furness *was* the natural son of the Duke of Windsor, he rapidly attained high office in the Order.

On Anthony's death in 1995 he left the bulk of the Furness fortune, worth many millions, to the Knights of Malta. The Furness title became extinct just as Anthony had wished. This was his ultimate revenge from beyond the grave on Lord Marmaduke Furness, the 'ogre' who had ruined his childhood.[22]

Thelma and Gloria as toddlers

Thelma and Gloria in New York

Lady Thelma Furness and her second husband, Lord Marmaduke Furness

Lady Thelma and Lord Furness with their three-year-old son Anthony at Burrough Court.

Above: His Royal Highness Edward Prince of Wales.

Left: Lady Thelma Furness and Edward, Prince of Wales at Burrough Court when her husband was absent.

Fort Belvedere, weekend retreat of Edward, Prince of Wales

Above: Burrough Court, the country estate of Lord Furness near Melton Mowbray, which burned down in World War 2.

Right: Australian born Enid Lindeman Cavendish who married Lord Furness, photographed attending the coronation of George VI.

Below: The Morgan twins in mid-life when living together in Hollywood.

CHAPTER 9

Wallis Warfield Simpson Duchess of Windsor (1895–1986)
and
Edward David, Prince of Wales
(King Edward VIII, later Duke of Windsor)

In a sado-masochistic relationship, Edward relished the contempt and bullying Wallis Simpson bestowed on him. Philip Ziegler. Edward VIII, The official biography, Alfred A. Knopf, 1991.

The Duchess of Windsor claims her husband is impotent: she was the only one to satisfy his passions. The former Duke Charles Alexander of Wurtemberg, cousin of the Duke of Windsor, in a 1951 statement to the FBI, obtained for President Roosevelt.

WALLIS WARFIELD, A 'CHARITY CHILD'

Wallis Warfield always claimed she was born in June 1896 at Blue Ridge Summit, a Pennsylvanian summer resort where her father was very ill with tuberculosis. Birth certificates were not mandatory at that time in Pennsylvania, but census figures reveal that Bessie Wallis, daughter of Teakle Wallis Warfield was born on 19 June 1895, a *year before* the birth date claimed by Wallis.[1]

The fact that Wallis had been conceived out of wedlock had to be concealed as her father came from a wealthy Baltimore family. He died when Wallis was five months old. His widow, Alice Montague Warfield, and her child were treated as charity cases by the snobbish Warfield family, who had always been opposed to the marriage. The Warfields had made their fortune from flour mills and other investments — Alice's family, the Montagues, had lost their money but both families claimed descent from younger sons of the English aristocracy who had settled in America in the seventeenth century and saw themselves as American aristocracy.

Alice and little Bessie Wallis, now the despised poor relations, were given a room in the Baltimore mansion owned by Teakle's widowed mother Anna. Her bachelor son, Solomon Warfield, who headed the family business lived with them. Grudgingly, Solomon Warfield agreed to pay his brother's widow a monthly allowance and to fund his niece's education at a private school.

In her memoirs Wallis hinted that her uncle became 'embarrassingly fond' of her mother who did not return his affections.[2] The situation became so difficult that Alice and her daughter left the Warfield residence and rented a room in a dingy private hotel. In retaliation for his rejection her wealthy brother-in-law often kept Alice waiting for her allowance so that she was reduced to asking local shopkeepers for credit until it was paid. Wallis never forgot the shame of being the poor relation — the humiliations, money worries and constant need for strict economy. Her mother tried to earn extra money by cooking dinners for the residents of her lodging house and taking in sewing to help make ends meet. Wallis hid this bleak part of her childhood from her wealthy school friends, but their lack of money would haunt her for the rest of her life, with the fear of returning to poverty.

Wallis and her mother were rescued from dingy rented rooms in cheap lodging houses by Aunt Bessie Merryman, the widowed sister of Alice's mother, who allowed them to live with her in her spacious Baltimore home. As Aunt Bessie had no children of her own, she became a second mother to Wallis.

In 1908, when Wallis turned 12, her mother married John Freeman Rasin, a man with an alcohol problem. Having been the focus of her mother's life, Wallis resented Rasin and out of spite destroyed the wedding cake just before the reception.

Alice and her new husband moved to Atlanta while Wallis chose to remain in Baltimore with Aunt Bessie Merryman. In 1912, when Wallis was 17, Uncle Solomon Warfield sent her to Oldfields, the most expensive finishing school in Maryland, hoping his niece might meet a wealthy suitor through her friends. Wallis became close friends with Mary Child Kirk, whose parents, Edith and Henry Child Kirk, were 'old money'. Mary's family was descended from the English banking dynasty whose stately home, Osterley Park House at Isleworth near London, was one of Robert Adam's masterpieces.[3]

Henry Kirk's family firm was a prestigious one — silversmiths who produced exquisite silver tableware in the tradition of the great English silversmiths.[4] The Kirk's home was furnished with beautiful antique furniture and silver and their refined home life strengthened Wallis's intention to marry for money. When she admitted this to Mr and Mrs Kirk they were shocked by such a mercenary ambition. Wallis envied her classmates — their clothes, pastimes and the European holidays they enjoyed. Like Becky Sharp she vowed that one day she too would have it all.

A photo of Wallis in her final year at Oldfields shows an angular young woman with a square jaw, large hands and a very flat chest. Her best features were her thick glossy dark hair, her piercing blue eyes and, when she wanted to impress, a magnetic personality. Wallis knew that she was no beauty but *was* an amusing story teller, an excellent ballroom dancer and an accomplished flirt. Wallis had no trouble attracting boys and was regarded as 'fast' by parents of several of her school friends.

In 1916, on leaving school, Wallis did not have a coming-out ball but attended those of other Baltimore debutantes. While staying with her wealthy cousin, Corinne Mustin, Wallis met a group of high spirited, daredevil naval pilots. She flirted with the handsome Lieutenant Winfield Spencer and wanted to marry him, believing that he would inherit a fortune from his wealthy grandfather. His inheritance plus the fortune she hoped to inherit from her childless Uncle Solomon Warfield would make them a wealthy couple. Sweet-natured Mary Kirk, who was to be Wallis's chief bridesmaid, had fallen in love with a handsome penniless Frenchman named Jules Raffray and would marry him.

A VIOLENT MARRIAGE AND A LATIN LOVER

Against her mother's wishes Wallis announced her engagement to Lieutenant Winfield Spencer. They were married in a church ceremony on 8 November 1916, just before America entered World War One. But Wallis had badly misjudged the situation. Win's grandfather had no intention of leaving his fortune to a wayward grandson who had already crashed one plane while drunk at the controls. Wallis and Win were provided with a small bungalow on the Pensacola Naval Base, where Lieutenant Spencer was an instructor in the U.S. Navy School of Aviation.

From the beginning there were problems in the marriage. Wallis had believed that Win's heavy drinking with his naval colleagues was due to youthful high spirits and did not recognise that her husband had an alcohol problem. Win Spencer's friends claimed that Wallis was frigid and refused to allow her husband to have penetrative sex. Win felt he had been tricked into marriage with a 'prick teaser' — a term used to describe flirtatious young women whose behaviour promised they would enjoy sex but in reality were frigid — and vented his anger and frustration on his wife.

Various theories have been proposed by doctors and psychiatrists for Wallis's behaviour. There have been suggestions that Wallis suffered from severe vaginismus, or muscular spasms which made sexual intercourse painful. These may have been psychological in origin or induced by physical problems. It has been suggested she had an abnormally short vagina, possibly the result of a chromosomal abnormality, known as a Disorder of Sexual Development (DSD). Another possibility was that Wallis, for one reason or another, had an oversupply of the male hormone testosterone. This theory is purely speculative, based on the fact Wallis had a square jaw, large hands and a domineering personality.[5]

Some psychiatrists and psychologists believe Wallis's flirtatious behaviour and her reliance on oral sex and masturbation were techniques she used to pleasure her lovers so she could avoid the penetrative sex she found painful.

When Wallis was a young woman, sex was not discussed openly. Few books for the general reader discussed sexual problems and there was no sex counselling for married couples. Friends of Win Spencer took his side, claiming Win had every right to be angry at his wife's refusal to give him his conjugal rights. In her memoirs *The Heart has its Reasons*, Wallis described how Win Spencer locked her overnight in the bathroom 'to teach her a lesson' but did not mention her refusal to have penetrative sex with her husband.

Eventually Lieutenant Spencer had enough of what he regarded as an unsatisfactory marriage, took a mistress and moved out of the matrimonial home. With no capital of her own, Wallis appealed to Uncle Solomon for money to divorce. Her uncle was shocked. He told Wallis that he did not want the disgrace of divorce in *his* family — she had made her bed and must lie on it.[6] Wallis, not wanting to offend an elderly relative from whom she hoped to receive a substantial bequest, dropped the idea of divorce. She had no job skills and refused to learn to type. She could have earned a modest income, but that would have meant a loss of status in the eyes of wealthy school friends. In those days girls from 'good families' did not work for money. Wallis chose to live with her mother and her despised step-father and be supported by them.

Eventually Lieutenant Spencer's mistress tired of his heavy drinking and left him. The American Navy failed to notice Win's alcohol problem and, with America about to enter the war, promoted him to the rank of captain and sent him to Washington.

Encouraged by her mother and Aunt Bessie, who were also horrified by the idea of divorce. Wallis rejoined her husband. But their reconciliation was brief. On the outbreak of war Captain

Spencer was posted to the Far East, promoted to the rank of Commander and given command of the aircraft carrier *Pampanga*.

Left alone in Washington, Wallis became a regular on the diplomatic party circuit. Here she met foreign diplomats, many of them bachelors or on unaccompanied postings to Washington. At a diplomatic party Wallis met the debonair Felipe Espil, First Secretary at the Argentine Embassy. What began as a flirtation resulted in Wallis losing her head and falling in love with Espil. He was good-looking, well-dressed, a wonderful dancer and in line to become an Ambassador. Wallis, who loved entertaining and parties, could see herself as a diplomatic hostess, living in an Embassy and waited on by well-trained servants. Without taking into consideration the fact Felipe's family were Catholic, so divorce was anathema to them as well as her own family, Wallis dreamed of divorcing Win and marrying Felipe Espil.

She was happy to be Felipe Espil's mistress, believing he would ask her to marry him. She was furious when Felipe announced his engagement to a wealthy Washington socialite whose money would further his career. When Espil suggested this should make no difference to their current relationship Wallis attacked Espil, clawing his face with her manicured fingernails. The whole experience was a salutary lesson which Wallis never forgot. Felipe Espil had been the great love of her life. Humiliated by him, Wallis would never allow herself to feel deeply about another man again. The thought of seeing Felipe Espil with his new wife at diplomatic parties was so painful she decided to leave Washington for good.

At this critical juncture she received a letter from her husband asking if they could make a fresh start. Would she join him in Shanghai? They would live in married quarters supplied by the American Navy who would pay her passage to the Far East. Encouraged by her mother and Aunt Bessie, who wanted her to be a respectable wife, Wallis agreed to join her husband.

With a group of American naval wives, Wallis departed for Shanghai. She found it an exciting cosmopolitan city with diplomatic and consular parties every night. White Russian aristocrats who had lost everything in the Bolshevik revolution worked as singers and dancers for a pittance in night clubs. Everything was for sale in the street markets and on Shanghai's famous thoroughfare, The Bund, including elegant silk dresses, French perfume, opium and women of many races and nationalities.

To improve their sex life, Win Spencer took his wife to visit some of the many Chinese brothels or 'sing song' houses he and his fellow naval officers patronised. Contrary to reports by the British Secret Service, who later maligned Wallis by claiming she had *worked* in Chinese brothels, Wallis only *visited* them to oblige her husband. However, she learned a great deal from her visits.

Commander Spencer had hoped that Wallis would learn what was needed to improve their marital life by observing the techniques used by Chinese prostitutes.[7] She looked at men with sexual problems, who took pleasure from being whipped and spanked by prostitutes.

Years later, a female friend of Wallis on hearing rumours that Wallis specialised in Chinese sexual techniques, including a vaginal one called 'the Shanghai clasp', burst out laughing. She said the rumours were wrong, Wallis specialised in *oral* sex which was scarcely exclusive to the Chinese.

However, Wallis's newly acquired skills did not save her marriage. Winfield Spencer reverted to his previous pattern of heavy drinking and once more became violent. When heavy drinking started to affect his work, the Navy posted Commander Spencer back to America and this marked the end of their troubled marriage. Wallis received a separation allowance from her husband, which enabled her to remain in Shanghai.

Shortly after Win's departure Wallis fell ill after drinking contaminated water. She was invited by a married classmate from Oldfields to stay in the diplomatic compound in Peking (as Beijing was known at that time). Kathleen Rogers and her husband Herman, an American diplomat and author, resided in Peking's diplomatic compound, which was famous for its lavish parties.

Wallis flirted with Herman Rogers, as she did with all handsome men. It was to Herman, after they had had a lot to drink, that

Wallis made the revealing comment, 'No man, not even my husband has been allowed to penetrate below my personal Mason-Dixon line' (the line which separated the northern states from the south in America).[8]

In Peking, Wallis supplemented her income with commissions from casino owners. She was paid to bring diplomats to their establishments and may have received commissions on drugs sold on the premises, though these allegations (made years later by MI5 when investigating Wallis) were never proved.

In the following years, despite the political and social turbulence in China Wallis travelled extensively with the Rogers as well as alone, acquiring beautiful pieces of Chinese porcelain and a fund of amusing stories. At another diplomatic party Wallis met the charismatic Count Galeazzo Ciano and may have had a brief fling with him. He would later marry Edda Mussolini, daughter of Italy's Fascist dictator and became Italy's Foreign Minister.[9] Wallis had an affair that went nowhere with a wealthy sophisticated Italian diplomat, Albert da Zara. Wallis was photographed attending race meetings with da Zara but he had no intention of angering his Catholic family by marrying a Protestant and one who would have to obtain a divorce. However they remained friends even after Wallis returned to America in 1925.[10]

When anti-European riots broke out in Peking Wallis was warned the situation could become dangerous and she must leave. Back in Washington, she decided the time had come to divorce Win Spencer. None of her romances in China had resulted in a proposal of marriage. Having turned 30, it was time to find a husband who could provide her with a home and financial security.

Wallis's mother and her Aunt Bessie, products of an older generation, were dismayed. They feared that, if Wallis did institute a divorce, no decent man would want to marry her and she might be cut out of Solomon Warfield's will. But Wallis did not listen, determined to regain her freedom.

Wallis moved to Virginia, where the divorce laws were such that she could sue for divorce as the innocent party. It was important to be seen as the innocent party if she was to have any hope of making a 'good' marriage. Fortunately Commander Spencer did not contest the divorce.

THE IMPORTANCE OF BEING ERNEST

In 1926, Wallis visited New York to help her former classmate, Mary Kirk prepare for her wedding to Jules Raffray. At a bridge evening at the Kirk home, Mary introduced Wallis to a wealthy shipbroker named Ernest Aldrich Simpson with whom she was partnered at the bridge table. Ernest Simpson with his military moustache and well-tailored suit seemed to be a typical upper-class Englishman, a type Wallis had met in China and found attractive.[11] Mary confided that Ernest felt trapped in an unhappy marriage.

Wallis and Ernest played bridge on several occasions and discovered they both enjoyed the theatre, opera, ballet and ballroom dancing. Wallis flattered Ernest while apparently teasing him, listened intently to his stories and laughed at his jokes. She was sympathetic to his business and family problems and made him feel he was the most intelligent, most desirable and important man in the room. Wallis played her usual flirtatious games and soon the pair of them became lovers.

Wallis Warfield Spencer, still smarting from being dumped by ambitious diplomats, saw Ernest Simpson as ideal husband material. He was good-looking and pleasant, did not have a vile temper like Win Spencer, did not gamble or drink to excess. Wallis listened to Ernest's stories about difficulties with his wife and encouraged him to file for divorce. This time she was considerably wiser and was careful to make extensive enquiries about Ernest's finances and his prospects and was reassured by her findings.

Ernest Simpson had attended Harvard, but did not graduate, leaving to join the British Army in World War One. He possessed dual American and British nationality but chose to travel with a British passport. Ernest had enlisted as a lieutenant in a prestigious English regiment — the Coldstream Guards and found he loved its regimental traditions and history. While Wallis rarely opened a book, he was a book lover with a passion for acquiring facts and had a keen interest in old buildings — one of the things Ernest loved about England.

Ernest was a considerate well-mannered man with a secure income. His father headed the prosperous ship-broking firm of Simpson & Spence in which Ernest was a partner. He was no rival to Felipe Espil in glamour or in looks but offered the stability and financial security Wallis wanted to secure her future. Ernest's wife, Dorothea Dechert Simpson, later claimed that Wallis had seduced her husband while she was ill in hospital and showed no compunction in 'stealing' him from her.[12] The couple had a young daughter named Audrey, who Wallis disliked and was determined would never live with them should she succeed in becoming the second Mrs Ernest Simpson.

Ernest talked fondly of his time in England where he had an older sister who was married to an Englishman. Ernest's sister, Maude Kerr-Smiley was many years old than her brother. Maude lived in a handsome house in Belgrave Square, was married to a member of Parliament and moved in aristocratic circles. Wallis who was a social climber hoped her future sister-in-law would introduce her to British high society. Wallis claimed she was from a wealthy Baltimore family and talked grandly of how the Warfield fortune of some US$5 million would one day be hers. She empasised her soft Southern drawl for her witticisms and funny stories, which enchanted Ernest Simpson.

Wallis was never 'in love' with Ernest but liked him and saw him as an undemanding man who she could control and who could provide generously for her. She admitted frankly to Aunt Bessie she was marrying Ernest Simpson for financial security and companionship in old age.

***

In 1927, aged 32, Wallis Warfield Spencer was entangled in two divorces — her own divorce from Winfield Spencer and the divorce of Ernest from Dorothy Simpson, in which she risked being cited for adultery.

Fearing the damage this would do to Wallis's reputation and the reactions of the conservative Solomon Warfield, Aunt Bessie took Wallis for a long holiday in Europe while both divorces were going through the courts.

In Europe Wallis learned that her childless Uncle Solomon Warfield had died. Angered by his niece's divorce he had cut her out of his will. He left over five million dollars to found a home for elderly women in memory of his dead mother.

Wallis was furious. She borrowed money from Aunt Bessie to pay lawyers to challenge the will. Eventually she obtained a small share of her late uncle's fortune but most of the money she obtained was eaten up in legal fees.[13] Her mother, whose second husband had died, received nothing. In 1925, following the death of John Raisin, Alice married for the third time — a bank clerk of modest means named Charles Allen — and invested her modest life savings in the booming stock market.

In the early 1920s, Ernest's firm, Simpson & Spence, were doing very well. Ernest's father regarded Wallis as a fortune hunter. In an attempt to remove his only son from her clutches, he sent Ernest to London to set up a British office for the ship-broking firm. But Wallis followed Ernest to London, determined to marry him.

On 15 July, 1928, she wrote to her mother telling her she was getting married. Her letter is revealing, as she never mentions the word 'love'. Wallis claimed to be tired of fighting the world alone on very little money. She pointed out how kind Ernest was, and how unlike her previous husband. She was 32 and worried about her future. She told her mother it was high time to settle down and the best thing she could do for herself was to marry Ernest Simpson.

Wallis had calculated that Ernest's share in the family business plus his salary would guarantee them a good life. Ernest's attractions for Wallis were his dependability, his secure income, his pleasant nature and the absence of the aggression she had learned to dread in her first husband. Significantly, Wallis made no mention of wanting children with Ernest, although she was still of child-bearing age.

On Saturday 21 July 1928, Ernest Simpson in spite of his father's and sister's intense disapproval of his bride as a 'fortune hunter' married Wallis Warfield Spencer in Chelsea's Registry Office. The newly-wed Mr and Mrs Ernest Simpson spent their honeymoon motoring through southern France and Spain, in a luxurious yellow Lagonda Ernest had just purchased. They spent a lot of time looking at ancient building and churches whose history Ernest relayed to Wallis with the aid of a guide book, something eventually she found tedious. Returning to London via Paris, Wallis treated herself to expensive couture clothes anticipating that her new sister-in-law would include them in her busy social life.

※

Ernest had purchased a short lease on an apartment in Bryanston Court in a quiet square to the north of Oxford Street. Under the system that prevailed in central London in addition to buying the lease he had to pay a substantial sum in rates and other outgoings to live in this tranquil but expensive residential district. Their comfortable apartment was ideal for a childless couple who enjoyed entertaining. Wallis had no intention of allowing Ernest's daughter to stay with them, claiming their apartment was too small for this.

Wallis bought antique and modern furniture, re-decorated the apartment with the aid of Syrie Maugham, wife of the author Somerset Maugham and entertained Ernest's clients. She proved to be a brilliant hostess, served excellent food and provided amusing conversation.

Soon Wallis became dismayed by the long hours her husband worked. Instead of an active social life and parties to meet high society, married life with Ernest was dull compared to the ceaseless rounds of parties, night clubs and race meetings she had enjoyed in Shanghai. Ernest, with his collection of rare books and his passion for reading, was essentially a home lover while Wallis loved to meet new people. To her annoyance she also discovered that Ernest demanded she keep accounts and each month would examine how much she had spent.

Ernest's sister, two decades older than Wallis, did not approve of Wallis still regarding her as a social climber.[14] To Wallis's chagrin Maude Kerr-Smiley made no attempt to introduce her into her social circle or invite her to parties in her elegant home.

Early in 1929, Wallis returned to Washington to see her mother who was suffering from cancer. Alice died on 2 November 1929, having lost all her savings in the Wall Street crash, which had taken place the previous month. The sad circumstances of her mother's death upset Wallis and increased her deep-seated insecurities about money. Wallis and Aunt Bessie exchanged long letters, trying to console each other for their loss.

The impact of the stock market crash of 1929 and the economic recession which followed badly affected Ernest's ship-broking business. Ernest urged Wallis to cut her spending and worked even longer hours than before including weekends. Wallis had married Ernest for financial security, now their changed finances led to arguments. Although Wallis was fond of Ernest, she had married him to live in luxury and resented the fact that Ernest's father did not provide them with financial assistance, so they had to economise. She was also aggrieved that her husband was paying alimony to his first wife to support and educate their daughter.

Because Wallis had to dismiss one of their maids and cut back on their expensive dinner parties, she insisted that Ernest must reduce the money he sent his former wife. Worst of all in Wallis's eyes, Ernest had to sell their glamorous car and dismiss the chauffeur. Getting a job to help her cash-strapped husband never occurred to Mrs Simpson.

Comparing herself with wealthy expatriate American friends with whom she lunched at the Ritz, like Consuelo Thaw and Thelma Furness, Wallis felt hard done by. She complained about the loss of their car to Consuelo and her sister Thelma but continued to meet them meet for expensive lunches at The Ritz. Wallis was annoyed because Ernest refused to let her go to Paris to buy more designer clothes. As a temporary measure she replaced French couturiers with a less expensive and very talented White

Russian dress designer, named Anna de Wolkoff, whose salon was in Conduit Street, Mayfair. Before the Revolution, Anna's father was the last White Russian Naval Attaché at the Russian Embassy in London and Anna knew several White Russian aristocrats Wallis had befriended in Shanghai.

A PRINCE WITH MONEY TO BURN

Wallis had read magazine articles about the handsome Prince of Wales and was keen to meet him. She already knew a great deal about the Prince of Wales and his younger brother, Bertie, Duke of York from Lady Thelma Furness, the Prince of Wales's current mistress. Aware of this fact Wallis ingratiated herself with Lady Furness at their weekly lunches at The Ritz.

Consuelo and her husband, Bernie had been invited to a dinner party by Lady Furness at which the Prince of Wales was to be present. Consuelo developed influenza and suggested to her younger sister Thelma she invite the Simpsons to make up the numbers at the dinner table at the Furness country mansion.

With some reluctance Wallis accepted Thelma's invitation as she had a bad head cold and a swollen nose. Wanting to make a good impression, Wallis spent the previous day having a facial and her hair and nails done before she and Ernest went by train to Melton Mowbray and were met by Lady Furness's chauffeur.

Thelma introduced Wallis and her husband to the Prince of Wales over pre-dinner cocktails.[15] Wallis found the Prince of Wales smaller than she had imagined, as she had previously only seen his photos in newspapers and magazines. The petite Prince, who watched his weight closely, had a muscular body, blonde hair and classic Anglo-Saxon good looks.

During dinner the Prince of Wales became bored with the conversation at his end of the table. He noticed that Mrs Simpson's neighbours were laughing at something she was saying. He was struck by Wallis's deep husky voice with its southern drawl, made even huskier by her sore throat. He left the party early and did not meet Wallis again for almost two years but did not forget her.

Wallis and the Prince next met at another party given by Thelma Furness to celebrate His Royal Highness's return from South America. Wallis was elegantly dressed as she had indulged herself in Paris and bought several couturier outfits in anticipation of another invitation to meet the Prince. She was thrilled that the Prince of Wales remembered her. Wallis's carefully crafted 'Southern belle' persona intrigued the Prince of Wales who was fascinated by anything and everything American.

On this occasion the Prince of Wales was accompanied by his friend and equerry, Major Edward 'Fruity' Metcalfe, a former Anglo-Irish Army officer engaged to care for the Prince's horses and polo ponies. Fruity Metcalfe later admitted that he disliked Wallis from the moment he met her. [16]

Now that she had penetrated the Prince's circle, part of the highest echelons of British society, Wallis became obsessed with impressing her American cousins with photographs of herself at Buckingham Palace. Thelma found her an aristocratic lady who, in return for a sum of money agreed to sponsor Wallis for presentation at Buckingham Palace, essential in those days to enter high society.

Thelma Furness, who by now had come to regard the scheming Wallis as a close friend, loaned her a sleeveless white satin dress with a long train, a head-dress and matching fan of ostrich feathers for her presentation. After the ceremony, Thelma invited the Simpsons and the Prince of Wales for a nightcap at her Mayfair home in Lees Place. The Prince of Wales, making polite conversation, told Wallis how attractive she and Thelma had looked at the ceremony. Wallis had overheard the Prince comment how the harsh lighting at Buckingham Palace made *all* the women look ghastly and he would have the lighting changed once he was in charge. Teasingly, Wallis repeated his words back to him.

The Prince found Wallis's frank approach refreshing. Thelma knew that the recession had forced the Simpsons to sell their car so she asked the Prince to drive Wallis and Ernest back to Bryanston Square, he did so with pleasure. En route the three of them laughed and chatted and the Prince of Wales accepted an invitation for himself and Thelma to join Wallis and Ernest for a typical 'American dinner' at Bryanston Court.

For her first royal dinner party Wallis served a 'deep South' menu — black bean soup, grilled lobster and her specialty, Chicken Maryland, followed by a raspberry soufflé. The Prince enjoyed the evening and laughed uproariously at Wallis's stories related in her Southern drawl.

Mr and Mrs Simpson soon became regular house guests at Fort Belvedere where Thelma played the role of hostess. The four of them and Fruity Metcalfe swam in the Prince's pool and helped clear the shrubbery in the garden the Prince was creating there. Ernest and the Prince reminisced about wartime experiences in the Brigade of Guards. To help a fellow officer in trouble the Prince loaned Ernest one of his cars and a chauffeur. A guest bedroom and dressing room were kept for the Simpson's frequent weekend visits.

The Prince had given Wallis a surprise birthday party at the elegant Quaglino's Restaurant. In return Wallis gave a lot of thought to the present they would give him for his 39th birthday. She gave Edward a silver matchbox holder, engraved with his personal emblem of three Prince of Wales feathers. The birthday card had a hand written message written by Wallis. It was addressed to 'David', the name the Prince of Wales had asked close friends to call him, rather than using his first name of Edward.

※※※

Thelma, 'David', the Simpsons and Fruity Metcalfe saw in the New Year of 1933 at the Embassy Club, dancing and drinking champagne until five in the morning. Ernest was pleased with Wallis and congratulated her for fitting so well into British 'high' society. He was a loyal monarchist and enjoyed the kudos of being seen as a close friend of the heir to the throne and found it a help in his business dealings.

The following night, the two couples dined at Bryanston Square before driving to the Chelsea Arts Ball, regarded as risqué because of the semi-naked art students, who made their own costumes, and mingled with the ticket holders.

The trusting Thelma was pleased that Wallis' gift for telling funny stories amused the Prince of Wales. 'David', the Peter Pan prince had a limited attention span and, if bored, could turn difficult and petulant. At times Thelma bored him while he found Wallis very amusing.

In spite of having mumps in his teenage years, which had caused certain problems, the Prince had a high libido. He had pursued many young women on his various long overseas tours. However, his emotional affairs with his two married mistresses — Freda Dudley Ward and Thelma Furness — had lasted longer than these purely transitory and unsatisfactory couplings. Although there were serious sexual problems in his four-year relationship with Thelma, she never breathed a word about Edward's sexual inadequacy to Wallis but did confide in her sister, Consuelo.

For the sake of propriety, Wallis chaperoned Thelma at Fort Belvedere and these two elegant American women often stayed there at weekends. Ernest was happy for Wallis to accompany Thelma as it distracted her from their difficult financial situation. Ernest, was working desperately hard to keep his company afloat in the 1930s depression and began to spend more and more time in Germany, one of the few countries expanding its shipping fleet. He and Wallis regarded Nazi Germany as the country which would save Simpson & Spence from going broke.

As Ernest had been forced to impose severe household economies Wallis bitterly resented the drop in their standard of living. She compared her life with that of Thelma Furness, Consuelo Thaw and other wealthy American friends and reproached Ernest for not providing her with a car, designer clothes and expensive holidays and cruises. Most of all she envied Thelma for her life of luxury and her jewels.

At the Kit-Kat Club, with the Prince of Wales, Wallis met tall good-looking Edward Fitzgerald, Duke of Leinster. The Duke was a war hero who had shown great courage commanding a platoon of Irish Guards in the trenches of Northern France. The deaths of so many of his platoon had taken a heavy psychological toll. The

Duke left his wife and the responsibilities of running his Irish estates, He moved to London where he frittered away what money was left in night clubs and illegal casinos. Wallis flirted with the Duke of Leinster, as she did with all handsome men and invited him to her cocktail hour at Bryanston Square. The Simpsons followed the American custom of keeping 'open house' for friends. In the evening the Prince of Wales would also drive across the park and 'drop in' on Wallis.

Against the wishes of the Prince of Wales, Thelma sailed for America in 1934 to support her twin sister, the widowed Gloria Vanderbilt, member of a wealthy dynasty now struggling with a harrowing court case with her sister-in-law for the custody of her little daughter.

The previous year Thelma had divorced Lord Furness, who, with some difficulty, had been prevailed upon *not* to cite the Prince of Wales in their divorce. Lord Furness, England's wealthiest man, arranged to be found with one of his mistresses in a hotel bedroom in order to fulfil the legal requirements for a divorce. The day after the divorce came through Lord Furness, married the fascinating Australian-born fortune hunter, Enid Lindeman Cavendish. As a result of machinations by clever lawyers and the skilful manipulation of her ex-husband's financial affairs by his accountants, Thelma's divorce settlement was not as large as she had expected. Now she was living in a small rented apartment in central London and desperate to gain access to her little son. Anthony was unhappy in the custody of Lord Furness who doubted the boy was his and neglected him. But Furness refused to let Thelma visit Anthony.

Wallis knew that Thelma needed the support of the Prince and her friends at this difficult time in her life. But this counted for little with Wallis, who was ruthless when she wanted something badly enough. She knew the Prince of Wales was attracted to her and was ready for a brief fling with a handsome wealthy prince and reckoned that Ernest would not mind.

Now that Thelma was in America the bachelor Prince often stayed on after the cocktail hour for one of Wallis's 'pot luck dinners'. After the meal, tired from a long day at the office, Ernest would retire to his study to work, desperate to prevent Simpson & Spence from sliding deeper into debt.

The Prince of Wales would talk for hours to Wallis about the changes he wanted to make to stifling royal routines and his plans to help the unemployed workers he had seen on his tours around England in the Great Depression. His informal easy-going manner made him very popular. Great things were expected of him when he came to the throne. Flattered by the Prince's confidences and his plans for future reforms, Wallis confided her worries about Ernest's ship-broking business and the downturn in their finances due to the recession.

WALLIS MOVES IN

According to Wallis, before departing for America in January 1934, Thelma had implored her to 'Look after the little man for me', as she was worried he might drink to much while she was away.

Thelma had her own version of this story and claimed that Wallis had told her she knew Edward would be lonely without her. Wallis, as Thelma's best friend, promised to ensure that the Prince remained faithful to Thelma while she was away. With Ernest and Thelma in America, Wallis spent an increasing amount of time at Fort Belvedere where she annoyed the staff by giving them orders and changing arrangements made by Freda Dudley Ward years earlier.

Wallis flattered the Prince of Wales with jokes about how he was a temptation to women, flirting with them knowing that he would not marry them. She had a fund of risqué stories and blue jokes from her time with Win Spencer and entertained 'David' with them. The Prince assumed that the worldly, twice married Mrs Simpson with her quick wit and sexual repartee knew about different sexual needs. Wallis had a particular type of *allure* which appealed to the Prince. There was a mounting sexual frisson between them, aided by the fact she reminded him physically of Nanny Greene, who had cared for him for the first three years of his life.

In the evenings they spent together, Wallis proved herself a far more attentive listener than Thelma. The Prince told Wallis that Thelma had never been interested in his schemes to help the unemployed. In fact Wallis had no more of a social conscience than Thelma but took the trouble to hide the fact, unlike Lady Furness.

The Prince confided in Wallis his intention when he became king to get rid of stuffy outdated customs at Buckingham Palace and Windsor Castle. As their relationship developed Edward confessed to Wallis what he had admitted in his letters to Freda Dudley Ward — he was bored with cutting ribbons, making speeches at civic functions and shaking endless hands.

Learning that Ernest had discontinued her dress allowance, he loaned Wallis money, a fact she did not disclose to Ernest, who she knew would not approve. Realising money and jewels were the way to please her, the Prince presented Wallis with valuable jewellery from Cartier. Wallis regarded 'David' with his income from the Duchy of Cornwall as incredibly wealthy and available. She wanted the excitement of a brief affair with royalty and the rewards that came with it.

Letters from a worried Aunt Bessie questioned Wallis about the propriety of seeing so much of the Prince of Wales while Ernest was away. Wallis reassured her aunt that the Prince was lonely and she only went to Bryanston Court to talk about Thelma, still in America, who he missed. She did not mention her unchaperoned weekends at Fort Belvedere. Wallis assured Aunt Bessie that she was 'not the kind of girl who would steal her friend's beau'.

In fact, Wallis believed the Prince's crush on her was only temporary and would soon be over. She confided to Aunt Bessie that she planned to enjoy the Prince's 'crush' while it lasted and extract whatever benefits she could until Thelma's return.[17]

Wallis continued to spend weekends at Fort Belvedere without Ernest and her increasing intimacy with the Prince was obvious to the household staff, who noticed lipstick stains on the Prince's shirt collar. A female member of the household staff mentioned to a fellow servant that she had seen the Prince of

Wales and Mrs Simpson in bed together. This gossip reached the household of the Duke and Duchess of York. The Duchess was fond of Thelma and disliked Mrs Simpson.

Becoming bolder in her ambitions and determined to supplant Thelma in the Prince's affections, Wallis deliberately planted newspaper photos of Thelma dancing cheek-to-cheek with Prince Aly Khan where Edward could not fail to see them. On seeing photos of his mistress with another man, the Prince's jealousy, coupled with his anxieties about his own sexual adequacy, erupted in a rage.

Prince Aly Khan was a notorious playboy, reputed to be a magnificent lover and well-endowed. Jealous Edward became incandescent, conveniently forgetting he was betraying Thelma with her alleged best friend. By the time Lady Furness returned to England in March 1934, the Prince was head over heels in love with Wallis.

Arriving in London, Thelma telephoned the Prince of Wales saying she needed to see him urgently and wanted advice from his lawyers about contesting her divorce settlement.[18] She was taken aback by the Prince's cool response but packed her weekend bag and drove to Fort Belvedere in her sports car.

At the Fort she found Wallis with the Prince. There was no sign of Ernest.[19] Thelma was shown to a small guest bedroom by an embarassed servant — not the large bedroom she usually occupied with the Prince which she had redecorated with the Prince of Wales' feathers over the double bed.

At dinner Thelma took her place as hostess facing the Prince. During a stressful meal, he absentmindedly picked up a lettuce leaf and popped it in his mouth with his fingers instead of using his silver salad fork. Wallis leaned across the table and slapped his hand, the intimate gesture of a wife or nanny. Thelma understood the significance of the gesture — Wallis had looked after the 'Little Man' *extremely* well.

Thelma accused the Prince of two-timing her with Wallis. The Prince of Wales countered by accusing Thelma of having an affair with Prince Aly Khan.

Lady Furness left Fort Belvedere and returned to her rented apartment. A few days later she telephoned Wallis at Bryanston Square demanding to know if the Prince of Wales was in love with her. Wallis denied this but admitted the Prince was 'fond' of her. Thelma recognised her treacherous friend was lying, and the Prince was lost to her. She packed her bags and joined Prince Aly Khan at a hotel in Nice for a holiday fling.

Hell has no fury like a woman scorned. Thelma felt she owned no further loyalty to 'David'. She told everyone she knew that 'the Little Man' was sexually inadequate, poorly endowed and suffered from premature ejaculation. To her sister Consuelo and several close American friends she described the heir to the throne as a limp lover. Consuelo noted down what Thelma had told her in her journal.

Thelma's comments on his lack of sexual prowess eventually reached the ears of the Prince of Wales. He flew into a terrible rage and called his former mistress 'a filthy witch'. His four-year liaison with Thelma was over. Wallis had her prize.

***

Anglo-American textile heiress Freda Dudley Ward, Edward's first married mistress, was now a trusted friend and confidante. He and Freda had known each other for 17 years and phoned each other regularly. Freda's daughters adored the Prince and since one of them had been very ill in hospital, Freda had lost touch with 'David' for some weeks.

Once her daughter had recovered, Freda Dudley Ward made her usual weekly phone call and asked to speak to the Prince of Wales. There was an awkward silence before the telephone operator confessed, 'I've something terrible to tell you, Mrs Dudley Ward. I've received orders *never* to put you through to His Royal Highness again.'[20] Stunned by this turn of events, Freda rang off.

These harsh orders came from Wallis Simpson whose word was now law at Fort Belvedere. Aware of the Prince's years of dependence on Freda, first as a mistress, then as a confidante, and the fact that Freda was friendly with Thelma, Wallis had decided to remove her. This rejection by 'David', whom she saw as a trusted friend, greatly distressed Freda who for decades she had 'mothered' the 'Peter Pan Prince,' the boy who refused to grow up. Now Wallis was determined to be the only woman in Edward's life.

Wallis believed her sexual fling with the Prince would not last. However, she was determined to block any possible competition and, while it lasted, enjoy the benefits of being a royal mistress. The dependable Ernest would be held in reserve in case things went wrong.

※

The Duke and Duchess of York, as friends of Thelma Furness, disliked Mrs Simpson, who they labelled an adventuress and a social climber, comments repeated back to Wallis.

The Duchess of York was plump and sensitive about her weight after bearing two daughters. Wallis was extremely thin because of her problems with stomach ulcers and had to be very careful what she ate. She laughed about the Duchess of York for being overweight and her nickname for the plump Duchess was 'Cookie'. Wallis also mocked the Duchess's dress sense. Elizabeth, Duchess of York, wore evening dresses with billowing crinoline skirts on formal occasions, which led Wallis to describe her as 'a meringue with an acid drop at the centre'. It was Wallis who coined the well known phrase, 'You can never be too rich or too thin'.

Wallis's unflattering remarks were relayed to the Yorks and turned their disapproval into loathing. Mrs Simpson's slim figure, simple but elegant clothes — a foil for the beautiful jewels she was acquiring from the Prince of Wales, put the Duchess of York at a disadvantage. Wallis's mockery of the Duke of York's wife created a coolness between the Prince of Wales and Bertie, his stammering younger brother, who had also suffered a childhood deprived of mother love.

Edward, the Prince Charming of his era, was something of a chameleon. He was enormously popular because of his visits to areas of high unemployment and making speeches that 'something must be done to help the unemployed'. He had led thousands of ex-servicemen from the Albert Hall to the Cenotaph in a torchlight parade to show his support for their demand for jobs, pensions and better benefits for the disabled. The Prince had a vast income from the Duchy of Cornwall and spent it indulging himself with expensive cars, aeroplanes, holidays and renovations to Fort Belvedere. He loved elegant clothes and insisted that his mistress dress in the height of fashion. Wallis now received gifts of couturier clothes, jewellery and a car.

With unlimited access to Edward's money, Wallis chose her clothes with great care — her favourite designer was Mainbocher, a young American working in Paris. Wallis also continued to buy a few outfits from Anna de Wolkoff, the talented White Russian couturier who had trained in Paris, who she regarded as a friend.

Wallis now appeared at parties and the theatre dressed in couture fashion, glittering with brooches, clips, necklaces and bracelets by the French house of Cartier. They had a branch in Bond Street where Edward commissioned the special pieces that he gave Mrs Simpson. She became famous for wearing jewellery with gems so large some people thought they must be cheap costume jewellery. When the writer, Marie Belloc Lowndes, criticised Mrs Simpson for wearing ostentatious imitation jewels, friends who moved in royal circles burst out laughing. They told her Mrs Simpson's jewels were *real*, given her by the besotted heir to the throne.[21]

By this time Wallis had taken over the management of Fort Belvedere and become the Prince's confidante, checking all incoming accounts from tradesmen to see whether the Prince was being cheated by his staff. The more Wallis did for him, the more the Prince of Wales became dependent on her and wanted those around him to acknowledge what a *wonderful* woman she was.

But his equerries and Alec Hardinge, the Prince's Personal Secretary, disapproved of the Prince's relationship and felt Mrs Simpson exercised far too much influence over the heir to the throne.

As well as catering to Edward's needs, Wallis mothered him and scolded him like a naughty child, admonished him for drinking and smoking too much. Many people including Winston

Churchill noticed the Prince of Wales was not drinking as much as before. The Prince seemed to relish being rebuked and ordered around by Wallis. The diplomat and author, Harold Nicholson, who accompanied the couple to the theatre, described Wallis as 'bejewelled, eyebrow plucked, virtuous and wise', having overheard Wallis forbidding the Prince of Wales to smoke during the interval. Harold Nicholson observed that Mrs Simpson was clearly out to help the Prince.[22] Others were less sympathetic, describing Mrs Simpson as having an evil influence on the heir to the throne.

Wallis was defended by a barrister friend of the Prince from his days at Oxford who was acting as legal advisor to the Duchy of Cornwall. Walter Monckton described Mrs Simpson as 'essential to the Prince of Wales' happiness and a companion of his mind and intellect'.[23] The use of the word 'intellect' was strange as neither Edward nor Wallis enjoyed reading books or could be termed intellectuals. Their passions were for parties, ballroom dancing, and buying clothes, jewels and antiques.

The subject of jewels was a sensitive point at Buckingham Palace. George V and Queen Mary were furious that the Prince's large revenues from the Duchy of Cornwall were being squandered on expensive gems for their son's mistress. The King and Queen made another fruitless attempt to persuade their eldest son to marry Princess Friedericke of Hanover, pointing out that his young German cousin had attended an English boarding school and spoke English fluently. Edward retorted that the German princess was *far* too young for him and he would only marry for love.

King George V expressed his fears about Mrs Simpson to Prime Minister Stanley Baldwin. They both decided that Mrs Simpson's mysterious past in the Far East needed investigating. Prime Minister Baldwin, with the support of George V, commissioned the British Secret Service to carry out investigations in China and had MI5 agents follow Mrs Simpson and report on who she met and what she did.

In the summer of 1934, Ernest Simpson was so short of money he could not afford a European holiday for Wallis and himself. The Prince had rented a large villa overlooking the sea at Biarritz and had invited a group of friends, including the Simpsons, to join him. Ernest was unable to attend as he was going to America on company business. With some reluctance Ernest agreed Wallis could accept the invitation provided she was chaperoned by Aunt Bessie. Other guests were Wallis's old friends Kathleen and Herman Rogers, Edward's equerry, the Hon John Aird and several other married couples.

Some evenings Edward and Wallis slipped away from the other guests and dined alone at a romantic little bistro on the sea front. Aunt Bessie was alarmed by the closeness she observed between her niece and the Prince of Wales and warned Wallis that she was putting her reputation and her marriage at risk. History had proved princes were notoriously fickle.

Again, Wallis reassured her aunt. She told her that she did not expect this exciting affair to last forever, but wanted to enjoy all that came with it while it lasted. She admitted that the Prince was very demanding and it was becoming increasingly difficult to keep 'dear Ernest' on side.

From Biarritz the Prince chartered the yacht *Rosaura* complete with a cook and crew for a cruise in Spanish waters, where they were caught in a wild storm in the Bay of Biscay. Wallis was always a nervous traveller and as the storm raged became hysterical, convinced they would all be drowned. She created such a scene and infected the Prince of Wales with her fears that Edward's equerry, John Aird, described her and the Prince as cowards at heart.

Back in French waters the sea was calm and the sun shone. The Prince was blissfully happy dressed only in shorts and sandals, something his father would have found most undignified. Wallis was also in her element, waited on hand and foot with the Prince anticipating her every whim. Wallis claimed in her unreliable memoir *The Heart has its Reasons*, that on that 1934 cruise she and the Prince of Wales 'crossed the line between friendship and love'.[24] She was lying — that line had been crossed much earlier.

On his return to Fort Belvedere the Prince of Wales told Major Fruity Metcalfe, that 'he had enjoyed the best and most relaxed holiday of his life' and that Wallis was 'the world's most wonderful woman'. Major Metcalfe was not convinced.

Wallis, with a wardrobe of new designer clothes and more jewels from Cartier bought with money from the Prince of Wales returned to Bryanston Square. Ernest Simpson had returned from America, but chose not to confront his wife, relieved that her expensive holiday had stopped her complaining about their financial problems.

On his next business trip to America, Ernest Simpson met up with Wallis's old school friend Mary Kirk Raffray. Over dinner in a quiet restaurant, Ernest confided his suspicions about Wallis to Mary, calling the spendthrift immature Edward 'Peter Pan in Never-Never Land'. As confidences were being exchanged, Mary confessed that her marriage was in trouble. She regretted marrying Jules Raffray, who had been unfaithful and was now an alcoholic. Ernest and Mary agreed to meet again on Ernest's next visit to America.

Back in London, Edward asked his mother to meet Mrs Simpson. Queen Mary, refused her son's request. Instead she reproached him for his unseemly infatuation with a married American divorcee. She urged him to give up 'that woman' for the good of the nation. Thousands of Englishman had died for their country in the Great War — surely, Edward should be prepared to make *some* sacrifice for his country and marry a suitable girl. Queen Mary held up the marriage of the Duke and Duchess of York as the example he should follow. The obsessed Edward listened to his mother, said nothing and returned to Wallis at Fort Belvedere.

The Duke and Duchesss of York refused to meet Wallis, aware that she was deceiving her husband with the Prince of Wales. One of the staff at Fort Belvedere had told a servant of the Duchess of York that she had seen the Prince and Mrs Simpson in bed together and this item of gossip had reached the ears of the Duchess of York who was shocked.[25]

※
※※

In November 1934, Edward's favourite brother, George, Duke of Kent, became engaged to Princess Marina of Greece.[26] The King and Queen were greatly relieved that their formerly wild son had reformed and was about to marry a beautiful and charming young woman.

Two days before the Duke of Kent's wedding, a large pre-wedding party took place at Buckingham Palace. The Prince of Wales horrified his parents by arriving at the celebration accompanied by Mr and Mrs Simpson. Queen Mary could not avoid having Mrs Simpson presented to her but received her coldly, aghast at the presence of a 'scarlet woman' covered in jewels. Wallis wore a diamond tiara and what the royal family called a vulgar violet lamé gown with an emerald sash whose colour matched her eye-catching necklace of emeralds and diamonds, another gift from the besotted Prince of Wales.

Just before Christmas 1934, the Prince of Wales invited Mr and Mrs Simpson to join him at the Tyrolean resort of Kitzbühel for a skiing holiday in mid-February. This was the last straw for Ernest. Normally even-tempered, he angrily told Wallis he had no interest in learning to ski and departed, slamming the door in her face.

Ernest was still a loyal monarchist. He wrote a polite refusal to the Prince of Wales, citing a prior business engagement in New York. In fact his wife's ski-ing holiday with the man he referred to as the 'Peter Pan Prince' suited Ernest, who was off to New York to meet Mary Raffray, with whom he was now romantically involved, in order to discuss their future. Wallis, totally absorbed in her affair with the Prince, had no idea what was afoot.

In February 1935, Wallis accompanied the Prince of Wales to Paris where they shopped together at the Rue de Rivoli for a mink coat. They travelled by train to the snow-covered Austrian Alps where they shared a suite at Kitzbühel's Grand Hotel. Wallis hated the cold. She took a few ski lessons but decided she did not like ski-ing and gave up. She wandered around the ski resort, conspicuous in her new mink coat and perilously high heels.

The Prince was an enthusiastic but mediocre skier. He wanted to show off to Wallis and wobbled dangerously down the steep slope on skis but she was not impressed. To placate his bored mistress, he presented her with a diamond brooch bought in the only jewellers in Kitzbühel. She wore the brooch in her dark hair for the après ski dancing at the Grand Hotel, which was more to her taste. From Kitzbühel the couple travelled by train to Vienna where in an exclusive jewellers on the Ringstrasse the Prince of Wales purchased more jewels for Wallis.

When they returned to London, society was abuzz with gossip about Mrs Simpson and the Prince of Wales but the British press, out of respect for the royals, *still* kept quiet. Ernest Simpson was in New York with Mary Raffray and Wallis spent her time at Fort Belvedere. The Prince of Wales' infatuation with Mrs Simpson had become an obsession and was so obvious it could no longer be ignored by the royal family. He had no interest in any other woman and it was clear from the way he spoke of Wallis that he intended to marry her.

Although the Prince of Wales rarely attended church, at his coronation he would become the titular head and Defender of the Church of England. As the Anglican Church did not acknowledge divorce if Edward insisted on marrying a twice divorced woman, this would pose a crisis. It was inconceivable that the Prince could believe that he would be able to *marry* Mrs Simpson.

On 1 May 1935, King George V's Silver Jubilee celebrations took place. The Prince of Wales was warned that his parents did not want Mrs Simpson to attend the Jubilee Ball. When Edward protested, the King replied that provided his son gave his word of honour that his friendship with Mrs Simpson was 'pure' she and her husband could attend. The Prince of Wales promised his father that their relationship was 'pure', possibly meaning that their sex was of the non-penetrative variety, owing to his sexual problems.

King George V had to accept his heir's word of honour and Mr and Mrs Ernest Simpson were permitted to attend the Jubilee Ball at Buckingham Palace. George V was now so frail he was unable to dance. It was left to the Prince of Wales to open the Jubilee Ball by waltzing with his mother, Queen Mary. The heir to the throne broke protocol by having the second dance with Mrs Simpson instead of with HRH Elizabeth, Duchess of York, the most senior royal lady present after Queen Mary. This was a public insult to the Duchess, whether intended or not.

Elizabeth, Duchess of York, looked plump and pretty in an ivory off-the-shoulder taffeta crinoline. In contrast, Mrs Simpson was sleek as a seal in a dark blue Paris ball gown worn with a diamond and sapphire tiara. It had been loaned by Cartier and was later purchased for Wallis by the lovesick Prince of Wales. Pinned to the neckline of her evening dress, Wallis wore a superb pair of diamond clips, her latest present from the besotted Prince of Wales.

Later that month, Wallis, without her husband, appeared on the Prince of Wales' arm at Royal Ascot, despite the fact divorcees were banned from entering the Royal Enclosure. To avoid a meeting with the Prince of Wales and his mistress, George V left Ascot early and returned to Sandringham House. The British press still maintained their silence and did not report this incident.

King George V was shocked by the contents of the Secret Service reports on Mrs Simpson's past in Shanghai. The King was convinced that Mrs Simpson was a fortune hunter with a sinister hold over the heir to the throne. Worst of all, she had pro-Nazi friends like ambassador Joachim von Ribbentrop and her White Russian couturier Anna de Wolkoff, who was already under surveillance for visiting Rudolph Hess and other Nazi leaders in Germany.

The ailing George V saw Mrs Simpson as an evil influence and gloomily predicted 'within a year that boy will ruin himself and the monarchy'.[27]

The Prime Minister was less worried by Mrs Simpsons' sexual prowess than by the fact the Prince of Wales was unsuited to the constitutional role of a king. Baldwin had noticed the Prince's immaturity and childishness, his limited attention span and lack of application. Although the handsome Prince of Wales performed brilliantly with crowds, he was clearly bored with planting trees and cutting ribbons at civic openings.

What concerned the Prime Minister most about Mrs Simpson were reports of her alleged pro-Nazi sympathies. MI5 agents noted she was sent carnations by Hitler's Ambassador, Joachim von Ribbentrop, allegedly an ex-lover, though this was never proved.

In contrast, Winston Churchill was one of few politicians to point out that the immediate danger was not so much from Stalin and Communism but from the *rise* of the Nazi Party. Hitler had been in power in Germany since January 1933. His avowed intention was to reverse the Treaty of Versailles which had inflicted heavy penalties on Germany after World War One. Many businessmen like Ernest Simpson, facing a recession in British and American markets, were making money from the booming German economy and they were convinced that the only way to avert economic and political catastrophe in Europe was to support Hitler.

'A SELFISH WOMAN INCAPABLE OF LOVE'

Bernard Rickatson-Hatt, Ernest's good friend who ran Reuters London office, was able to keep stories about Wallis and the Prince of Wales out of Reuters' press releases and put pressure on other media contacts to keep silent.

Rickatson-Hatt knew that Ernest was in love with Mary Kirk Raffray and favoured this new relationship. He had warned Ernest he could not see Wallis standing by him in poverty or misfortune as Mary would do. Ernest's closest friend claimed Wallis Simpson was 'incapable of being in love with any man and capable of extreme hardness and was selfish and self-absorbed'.[28]

In a revealing conversation with Walter Monckton, Rickatson-Hatt claimed that Mrs Simpson had employed the same techniques to ensnare Ernest Simpson as she was using on the Prince of Wales. Aided by her mocking wit she first entertained and then ridiculed and humiliated the men in her life, made them unsure of themselves before overwhelming them with kindness and care. Now the Prince had become dependent on her.

Bernard Rickatson-Hatt's next statement astonished Walter Monckton. Apparently the Prince of Wales had shocked Ernest Simpson by claiming he intended to marry Wallis. He could not live without her and intended to marry her as soon as she could obtain a divorce.

***

On the evening of 20 January 1936, the Prince of Wales was summoned to Buckingham Palace. Later the same evening, the King's physician Sir Bernard Dawson issued a press bulletin that read 'The King's life is moving peacefully to its close'. George V was dying of pulmonary obstruction. The royal physician gave the dying King two massive injections of morphine and cocaine in his jugular vein so the news of his death could appear in the next morning's papers.[29]

Once her husband had ceased to breathe, Queen Mary turned to the Prince of Wales, curtseyed, took his hand and kissed it, acknowledging him as king. Edward burst into hysterical tears a combination of grief and the realisation of the responsibilities he now carried.[30]

Two days later, on 22 January 1936, 'David' was proclaimed King Edward VIII. The coronation was scheduled for the following year as extensive preparations were required for the event.

Wallis Simpson watched her royal lover proclaimed King from St James's Palace. For the first time a photograph of her by the side of Edward VIII appeared in the English newspapers.[31] It was obvious to the Cabinet and the royal family that the new King's relationship with Mrs Simpson, now in residence at Fort Belvedere, was a political and constitutional issue that had to be faced.

At the reading of his father's will, Edward VIII was angry that his father had made bequests to his brothers of a million pounds each but had left him no money. He was given a life interest in the Sandringham and Balmoral estates which were expensive to maintain. In addition to paying for these estates he had to fund the upkeep of Fort Belvedere and its staff. Edward VIII's problem was that he had already spent a large part of the royalties from the Duchy of Cornwall (which his father had advised him to save for the time when he would become King) on fast cars, entertainment, jewels for Wallis and renting luxury yachts for Mediterranean cruises. Edward's legal advisor, Walter Monckton, tried to mollify the new king explaining that because he had received extensive royalties from the Duchy of Cornwall for so many years, this was why his father had not left him money and had warned Edward to save money against the day he would be king and needed to pay the upkeep of Sandringham and Balmoral.

Edward's distress at the financial provisions in the late King's will was apparent. What also became obvious was his lack of interest in performing the duties of a monarch as the prospect of endless years of royal tours and duties appalled him. One of the duties of a constitutional monarch was to be well-informed about current political developments and be consulted by his ministers. It soon became apparent that Edward VIII was not taking his responsibilities seriously. He failed to read all the documents sent each day in red leather despatch boxes from No 10 Downing Street. Edward had trouble concentrating, so asked Wallis or his Private Secretary to read the documents aloud to him.

Mrs Simpson was heard to tell the new King he must learn to digest the core information in these documents. Edward VIII attempted to follow her advice but his powers of concentration were poor and under stress seemed to have evaporated.

To the dismay of Prime Minister Baldwin important state papers were returned unread to Downing Street. Some papers were stained by rings which clearly came from wet cocktail glasses. The new King had no idea of security. On one occasion he asked the Scanlons, an American couple he and Wallis entertained to cocktails at Fort Belvedere, to drop off highly confidential dispatch boxes when the Scanlons returned to London.

The new King's lack of concern for security or any interest in matters of state horrified his Private Secretary, Sir Alan Lascelles, who described Edward VIII in his diary as 'half-man, half child'. Later, Sir Alan Lascelles would tell a trusted friend that England would be better off if Edward VIII broke his neck before being crowned.

The year 1936 was a critical one with far reaching implications for Britain and Europe. Recovery from the economic recession had stalled, except in Germany where Hitler had initiated major reconstruction programmes. German economic and political achievements were showcased in the 1936 Olympic Games, staged in Berlin.

What worried Britain was the fact that Nazi Germany was rebuilding its armed forces. That year Germany reinvaded the demilitarised Rhineland in breach of the Treaty of Versailles and more was to follow.

Amazing as it seems, King Edward VIII and Mrs Simpson were now *both* under surveillance by MI5 on the instructions of Prime Minister Stanley Baldwin.[32] The Foreign Office, the British and American Secret Service suspected Mrs Simpson of passing sensitive information to Count Ciano (which was unlikely) or to Joachim von Ribbentrop, the German Ambassador to London. Von Ribbentrop added substance to the suspicions by sending carnations to Mrs Simpson, another of her flirtations with handsome diplomats. In the interest of security, Prime Minister Baldwin eventually decided to send only documents to Edward VIII which required the royal signature.

Wallis, caught up in the excitement surrounding her relationship with the new King, enjoyed the deference shown to her. She was flooded with invitations to dinners and cocktail parties in the hope she would bring Edward VIII with her. In cooler moments Wallis knew that Edward would now be under intense pressure to marry and produce an heir, something she was unlikely to provide at the age of forty. Later Wallis wrote in her memoirs that, 'In the back of my mind I had always known that the dream would have to end — sometime, somehow'.[33] In fact, Wallis underestimated the depth of Edward's feelings for her. She was living partly at Fort Belvedere and partly at Bryanston Court and had no idea that Ernest and Mary Raffray were caught up in their own love affair. She had invited Mary to stay at Bryanston Court knowing that she got on well with Ernest and this would give Wallis freedom to spend more time with the new King.

Ernest Simpson had endured enough as an acquiescent husband and was planning a new life with Mary Raffray who was divorcing her alcoholic husband. He was waiting for Mary's arrival in London before making a final break with Wallis. Mary Raffray had no compunction about taking Ernest away from Wallis. Mary, like Berhard Rickatson-Hatt, believed Wallis had never truly loved Ernest and had only married him for his money. Mary intended to use her family money to invest in Ernest's failing shipping business and put him back on his feet financially. They were in love and wanted a child before it was too late.

In February 1936 Ernest Simpson requested a private meeting with the King accompanied by Rickatson-Hatt as a witness. Ernest confronted the King saying that finally Wallis had to choose between them. Edward VIII made it quite clear that he wanted Wallis to be his queen. Ernest agreed to let Wallis divorce him as long as the King 'looked after her financially' and asked Edward to deposit a large sum of money in Wallis's account.

Eventually it was agreed that Ernest Simpson would be cited as the guilty party in a divorce petition initiated by Wallis. Edward VIII would pay *all* the costs of both parties to the divorce. It was vital this illegal agreement be kept secret as any divorce action could be invalidated by a formal complaint of collusion to the King's Proctor.[34] Under today's divorce laws this agreement would be totally unnecessary, but in the 1930s collusion of any kind was illegal.

Ernest's insistence that the Edward VIII must look after Wallis financially resulted in the King settling almost a million pounds on Mrs Simpson, which was placed in her name in an overseas bank account. This considerable sum was not declared to Edward's brother, the future George VI, at the time of the abdication. It would become a bitter source of contention between the brothers.

Matters came to a head at Bryanston Court when Ernest told Wallis that he wanted a divorce so he could marry Mary Kirk Raffray. Wallis was initially stunned but, on reflection, acknowledged that her liaison with Edward had brought this about. This did not prevent Wallis from turning on her former best friend and accusing her of seducing Ernest.[35]

Mary packed her bags, left Bryanston Court and moved to a hotel. To preserve her reputation Mary could not live with Ernest while his divorce was going through the courts so she rented an apartment in central London.

Wallis was panic-stricken. She realised that Edward had to marry and sire an heir (or attempt to do so). She had always counted on returning to Ernest, the patient husband whose forbearance she had taken for granted. Years after their divorce she was still writing affectionate letters to Ernest recalling wistfully the good times they had shared at Bryanston Court, conveniently forgetting her boredom and reproaches to him for not providing her with the luxuries necessary for her happiness.

After her initial panic had passed, Wallis assessed her situation coldly and dispassionately. The fact that Ernest wanted a divorce to marry Mary, meant she could be the innocent party and marry Edward, who had made it clear marriage was what he wanted. All was not lost. Under the prevailing divorce laws in England, there had to be a guilty and an innocent party for a divorce to be granted on grounds of adultery.

Raised in America, Wallis had no idea about the laws and structure of British society. She assumed that Edward VIII could override any opposition because of his popularity with the people of Britain. He could marry a twice divorced woman, with two husbands still living, as long as she was the innocent party in a divorce (or in Wallis's case, in *both* divorces).

The usual procedure in a divorce was to pay someone of the opposite sex to be found in a bedroom with whoever was to be the guilty party. Evidence that adultery had taken place was provided to the court by a detective. Mary Raffray was prepared to be found with Ernest in a hotel bedroom, not wanting him to hire a prostitute for this. Ernest considered it fair that the King should pay his legal costs. He was prepared to be labelled the guilty party even though he was not the one who had broken up the marriage. Strict divorce laws meant any hint of collusion would invalidate the divorce.

Edward VIII was now in the grip of an obsession. He regarded Wallis as the most wonderful woman in the world, was determined to marry her and make her Queen of Great Britain. He and Wallis believed that such was Edward's popularity he would eventually get his own way although she realised she had been forced into a divorce she had not wanted.

※

In the months that followed, Edward VIII's private secretary and his equerries became increasingly concerned at the way the new King deferred to Wallis's opinions in everything, including important matters of State. Mrs Simpson definitely had the upperhand in this relationship.

With the stress over Wallis's divorce and whether or not they could marry, Edward's sexual problems increased, fearing he might lose Wallis to another more virile lover. As had happened with Freda Dudley Ward he became increasingly clinging and obsessive about Wallis who he regarded as his mistress and nanny rolled into one. Courtiers were horrified to see his self-abasement and how, in the presence of Mrs Simpson, the King was like a lovesick schoolboy.

Wallis found Edward VIII's abject dependence and desire to be humiliated stifling. Turning forty, a worrying time, she wanted reassurance that she still had the power to fascinate men.

MI5 agents, at the request of Prime Minister Baldwin, were still following Wallis and filing reports which claimed Mrs Simpson was having a sexual relationship with a Mayfair car dealer named Guy Trundle. They described Trundle as 'a cad' and 'a charming adventurer, good looking, well-bred and an excellent dancer'. The report continued 'Secret meetings are made when intimate relations take place'.

Zealous MI5 agents read the situation wrong. Wallis was unlikely to have had an affair with a car dealer. She was meeting handsome Edward Fitzgerald, Duke of Leinster, who was very attractive and lived in London's Portland Place. Wallis had previously met the Duke at the Kit-Kat and Embassy Clubs with Edward. In Shanghai Wallis had enjoyed gambling, now the Duke of Leinster was taking her to illegal gambling clubs in Mayfair. An MI5 agent recorded having seen Mrs Simpson with the Duke of Leinster, but the agent seems to have been inept as his report included only a brief note of this. Instead the agent concentrated his attentions on Trundle, who may have been used by the couple as a decoy to put MI5 off the scent.

Wallis badly needed a break from Edward's obsessive behaviour and had turned to the tall handsome Duke for amusement. The fact that the unhappily married Duke of Leinster owned three large Irish estates suggested that he had a great deal of money, but in reality he was on the verge of bankruptcy due to his heavy gambling losses.[36] Wallis was far too keen on money to exchange a wealthy King for a gambling addict who was losing large sums each night and had mortgaged his estates. In Shanghai Wallis had seen gamblers lose everything and live on the streets, so she swiftly ended the relationship. Wallis was correct — later that year, the Duke of Leinster went bankrupt. In the years that followed he divorced and married three more times, lost all his Irish estates and became known as 'the bed-sit Duke'.

A further confidential report by MI5, dated June 1936, given to Prime Minister Baldwin, claimed 'Mrs Simpson does not want to be treated like Lady Furness and is apprehensive of losing the affections of the King, which she is anxious to avoid for financial reasons, so she hides her lovers from the King'.

***

The uncrowned Edward VIII was severely stressed, fearing that his collusion in the Simpson divorce would be revealed thus invalidating the divorce. His second worry was that the Prime Minister and Cabinet were opposed to his marriage and Wallis becoming Queen or his morganatic wife. Without Wallis by his side the immature Edward was finding official engagements, many of whom he considered outdated, absolutely unbearable.

At his first official Buckingham Palace garden party, 600 debutantes were waiting to be presented. As the first group of debutants in their long white gowns and head-dresses of ostrich feathers filed past him, rain started to fall. Edward seized on the rain as an excuse to end the ceremony and return to the palace. He sent an equerry to tell the remaining debutantes they could take it that they had been presented to him. Their mothers and guests were told the ceremony was over and they could all go home. The King's off-hand behaviour offended mothers who had spent a great deal of money and effort on their daughters' debuts at Buckingham Palace, which marked their entrée into society. Edward VIII drove back to Fort Belvedere at top speed to see Wallis and discuss their future. At the Fort he refused to take any phone calls and closeted himself with his mistress.

THE KING SEES A PSYCHIATRIST

Wallis was worried that the King's collusion with Ernest over her divorce might be discovered. But Edward's mental state and heavy drinking were also of concern. Wallis had several American friends who had consulted psychiatrists, but helping the troubled King VIII was a more delicate matter. The King needed to see a specialist whose confidentiality could be trusted.

Wallis was having fittings with her White Russian couturier friend, Anna de Wolkoff, whose Mayfair salon advertised she was designing and making robes and ball gowns for the forthcoming coronation. In the course of their conversation Anna told Wallis about a friend of hers, a Harley Street psychiatrist, Dr Alexander Cannon, who had trained in Vienna and London and had several post-graduate degrees. Dr Cannon specialised in treating nervous disorders and sexual problems with hypnosis and a variety of other techniques. Wallis concluded that this well-trained psychiatrist could remedy the King's sexual and drinking problems.

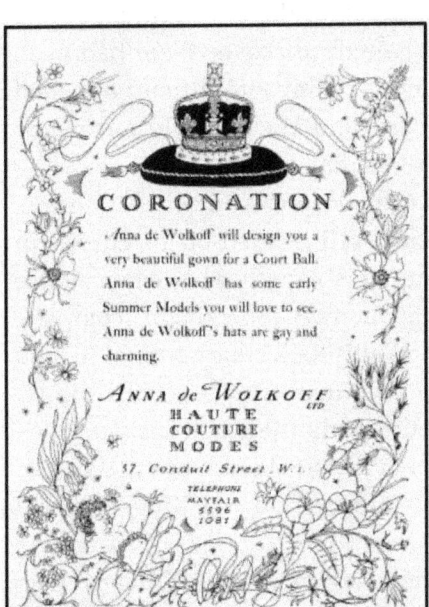

At Wallis's insistence the King reluctantly agreed to see the Harley Street psychiatrist and paid him several visits. Details of Edward VIII's treatment have never been revealed. While hypnosis may have relieved his problems with stress, treating sexual dysfunction and infantile paraphila takes a long time. As Edward's problems were deep-seated, the few sessions he was able to have with Dr Cannon before he left England would have had little effect.

THE CASE OF SIMPSON VERSUS SIMPSON

On 21 June 1936, Ernest Simpson and Mary Raffray provided the proof of adultery required to enable Wallis Simpson as 'the innocent party' to divorce her husband.

As arranged, a detective found Ernest Simpson in a bedroom at the fashionable Hotel de Paris at Bray-on-Thames with a woman who gave her name to the detective as 'Buttercup' Kennedy. This was a private joke dating back to their schooldays as Mary had worn a sun-hat decorated with buttercups. She hoped Wallis would remember this and realise it had been her in the hotel with Ernest rather than a prostitute.

Mary and Ernest were busy planning their wedding, in spite of the risk that the King's Proctor might discover there had been collusion between the King and Ernest Simpson. If that happened there would be no divorce, the King and Wallis could not marry and neither could Ernest and Mary Raffray.

Ignoring an admonition from the Prime Minister that he was derelict in his duties, King Edward VIII headed off to Europe in August 1936. He treated Mrs Simpson to another luxurious cruise on an expensive chartered yacht, named the *Nahilin*, complete with a swimming pool on board. Wallis took a lady's maid to look after her clothes, style her hair and manicure her nails. Secret Service men were posted at all the ports the yacht visited. They cruised along the Dalmatian coast and visited areas of the Balkans, despite fears of an assassination attempt on the King of Great Britain.

Wallis shared the yacht's main stateroom with Edward, who treated her as though she were already his queen and insisted all the crew did the same. However, Prince Paul of Yugoslavia was insulted that the King of Great Britain had brought his mistress to dinner and showed his contempt by being rude to Wallis. Edward VIII reacted by drinking far too much wine.

Photos of the inebriated King of England draped on Mrs Simpson appeared in the foreign press. The British press maintained its silence and did not print the photos out of respect for the monarchy. Guests on board were horrified when Wallis made Edward sit up on his haunches, beg like a dog for a cigarette and saw how he seemed to *enjoy* the humiliation.

Edward flew back to London while Mrs Simpson remained in Paris at the luxurious Hotel Meurice in order to have fittings for new outfits by Mainbocher. At the hotel Wallis received a pile of American press clippings from Aunt Bessie. Convinced she was living a great romance, Wallis was horrified that American papers referred to her as a `royal whore' and a `serial adulteress'. When Wallis saw that French newspapers carried similar stories she was even more distraught. With a shock she realised that this was the way the world perceived her.

Wallis took to her bed wracked by an attack of nerves and stomach pains. She was filled with foreboding about the future. For the first time she realised that it was unlikely that the British public would accept her as their queen, no matter how popular Edward VIII was. She phoned him and told him she would prefer to remain his 'secret' backstairs mistress and confirmed her change of heart in a letter.

Wallis hoped that by some miracle it might be possible, even at this late stage, to return to 'dear Ernest'. But when she arrived at Bryanston Court, she found the apartment had been let to a tenant — Ernest had moved out. As far as he was concerned the marriage was over, although, surprisingly enough, he bore Wallis no ill-feelings, being so happy with Mary Kirk.

On 16 September 1936, after receiving another package of American press clippings from Aunt Bessie, Wallis wrote to Edward repeating her 'misgivings' about her divorce and fears as to what the British press would print when they broke the story.

Edward tried to reassure Wallis. He told her he had rented her a comfortable house near Regents Park so she would be close to him and would rent another house at Felixstowe where the second hearing of Wallis's divorce was to be held. This was arranged deliberately as there would be far fewer journalists in rural Felixstowe than in London and there the court would be less congested, so a divorce was quicker to obtain.

Nerves were frayed to breaking point when finally British newspapers printed a story about the Prince's mistress. Mrs Simpson was vilified by protestors carrying blow-up photos of Wallis with captions calling her 'the American whore' and 'the woman who stole our King'

Hate mail and death threats made Wallis recognise the depth of public feeling against her in Britain. She telephoned King Edward VIII to tell him she would remain his mistress. He must *not* abdicate even if they could never marry as this would be a disaster for all of them.

Edward was so frantic that he sent Wallis a message threatening to cut his throat and kill himself if Wallis did not marry him. Alarmed by his talk of suicide Wallis agreed to attend a house party he was hosting at Balmoral for several dukes and duchesses including his brother Bertie and his wife, the Duchess of York.

It was Edward's first official house party as king and the Yorks had accepted the invitation on the understanding Mrs Simpson would *not* be present. The other house guests, apart from the Duke and Duchess of York, were members of the British and Scottish aristocracy. The Duchess of York, as the senior royal lady, believed she would be the hostess. Wallis, who had always acted as hostess for Edward at Fort Belvedere, believed *she* was to be the official hostess at Balmoral.

On 23 September 1936, Wallis took the train north to Aberdeen, the nearest station to Balmoral Castle. Instead of performing the official opening of Aberdeen's new hospital as planned, Edward drove the 100 kilometres to the station to fetch Wallis, leaving his brother, the Duke of York and his wife to deputise for him. They were furious. Bertie had a bad stammer and dreaded speaking in public, but somehow he managed to deliver his brother's speech. The Duke and Duchess of York took this as another sign of Edward's unfitness to occupy the throne.

The editor of the *Aberdeen Evening Express* was also outraged. He ran a front page story wondering how the King was too busy to open Aberdeen's new hospital but still had time to collect 'a female guest' from the station.

The house party was notable for difficult moments. Balmoral had been the favourite home of Queen Victoria and as such was held in reverential regard by the royal family. That Edward had brought his mistress there was offensive, but the fact he had installed her in Queen Victoria's bedroom was outrageous!

Leading a tour of inspection around the castle, Wallis made another *faux pas*. 'That tartan has to go,' Wallis announced, waving a manicured hand at the offending wallpaper as though she were already Queen. The fury of the Duchess of York can only be imagined.

There were two distinct dress codes. Elizabeth, Duchess of York, born and raised in Scotland, and other aristocratic ladies wore cashmere or lambs-wool sweaters, sensible walking shoes and kilts or tweed skirts, suitable for country life. Wallis Simpson in high heels and an elegant Parisian navy suit was dressed for a weekend in Paris.

That night the dinner guests included five dukes and their wives as well as Wallis's old friends Kathleen and Herman Rogers. When the Yorks arrived Wallis stepped forward to welcome them. The Duchess ignored Wallis, walked straight past her saying that she was the guest of the *King*.

Edward had unwisely placed Wallis in the position of honour on his right, which the Duchess of York felt was her due.[37] At the end of the meal Elizabeth, Duchess of York, asserted her precedence. Smiling pleasantly she rose from the table, leaving the men to enjoy their port and cigars, and led the assembled ladies out of the dining room, with Wallis trailing in her rear.

The relationship between the Yorks and Edward VIII was irreparably damaged. A week later, a worried Duke of York wrote to his mother, telling her he had tried to talk to his elder brother about Mrs Simpson and his threat of abdication, but Edward avoided the subject and fobbed him off.

The widowed Queen Mary regarded her eldest son's wish to marry his mistress as selfish and irresponsible. She and the Duchess of York realised how much the shy nervous Duke of York would suffer if he was called on to fill the role his elder brother was threatening to reject. No one in the royal family was happy with the situation, least of all the Duchess of York. She worried that the Duke's stammer was incurable as all doctors who had attempted to do so had failed.

After her long talk with Edward, Wallis left Balmoral for a rented house in Felixstowe to await the hearing of her divorce. Her lawyer hoped the divorce would attract less attention in the quiet market town of Ipswich than in a divorce court in central London.

***

By now the furore over 'Queen Wally' reached fever pitch in the United States. On 21 October 1936, *The Chicago Daily News* ran a front page headline, 'King Presents Valuable Gems to Wally — Necklace of Emeralds valued at $12,000'. The following week the American press claimed that valuable emeralds that had once belonged to Queen Alexandra had been reset by Cartier to designs approved by Mrs Simpson. In fact this was not true. These magnificent emeralds had been purchased by the King specially for Wallis.

The uncrowned Edward VIII finally realised he must choose between Wallis and the throne. Until then he and Wallis had been totally unrealistic in believing that if Edward abdicated he and Wallis could remain at Fort Belvedere, receive a handsome allowance from the Civil List and live there as private citizens. Edward and Wallis had expected to enjoy the perks of royalty without its responsibilities. They had hoped to taking long summer cruises in the Mediterranean while Bertie and Elizabeth shouldered the burden of kingship, cut ribbons and tour factories. At last Edward realised that if he abdicated, he would have to live abroad, at least until the fuss had died down.

With the coronation imminent, the British press finally ran headline stories about 'Queen Wally' and 'The Cutie who would be Queen'. Winston Churchill observed with dry humor that the British were traditionalists who did *not* want a 'Cutie' for their Queen.

Wallis was again deluged with sacks of hate mail and death threats. Never very brave, her nerves were shot to pieces. Too late she had visible proof that the British public, the Anglican Church, the British Government and all the Commonwealth countries would reject a twice-divorced American as Queen. Having little or no sense of religious obligation, Edward had failed to understand the insurmountable problems his proposed marriage to a twice-divorced woman would cause once he became the nominal Head and Defender of the Anglican Church.

At this late stage, King Edward VIII invited Mr and Mrs Baldwin to a dinner party hoping to enlist Prime Minister Baldwin on his side. He was convinced that if they met Wallis they would realize how wonderful she was.

Dinner was a frosty affair. Once the ladies had withdrawn leaving the men alone, Baldwin asked the King why he wanted to *marry* Mrs Simpson in view of the fact so many monarchs had had mistresses? He had no idea that much of Mrs Simpson's appeal was that she reminded the King of the nanny he had loved as a toddler rather than the mother he scarcely knew.

Edward VIII replied defiantly like a child, 'I *can't* do my job without her. I'm going to marry Mrs Simpson. And I *will*.'

The 69-year-old Prime Minister, reminded King Edward that neither the Church of England nor the governments of the Dominions (today's Commonwealth) were likely to approve of a divorced woman with two husbands still living as Queen of Great Britain. The Prime Minister was too tactful to mention that the British Secret Service was investigating Mrs Simpson for her alleged pro-German affiliations.

AN ILLEGAL DIVORCE?

Mrs Simpson was hissed by a hostile crowd as she arrived for the second hearing of her divorce from Ernest Simpson. Once the hearing was over, Wallis had to be smuggled out of a side door of the court to avoid a crowd of angry demonstrators and was almost reduced to hysterics.

In six months the divorce would be made absolute. Costs were awarded against Ernest Simpson, who was reimbursed by the King, according to their previous agreement. Edward was determined to marry Wallis even if he had to abdicate to do so. The decree absolute would be granted only a few weeks before the date set for the coronation.

After her divorce Mrs Simpson reverted to her maiden name Wallis Warfield by deed poll. Edward presented Wallis with a magnificent emerald engagement ring, weighing over 19 carats – one of the largest precious stones in the world. He had instructed Cartiers to engrave the inside of the ring with a coded message: *WE [Wallis and Edward] are ours now 27.10.36.* It showed his adoration of Wallis as well as his poor command of English grammar.

Wallis and Edward continued to worry that the King's Proctor might forbid the issue of her decree and leave her in legal limbo. She would be separated from her husband but unable to marry anyone else.[38] A complaint from a solicitor's clerk against the Simpson divorce, due to collusion, was mysteriously withdrawn. It has been alleged that the withdrawal was ordered by Prime Minister Baldwin who no longer wanted the King's Proctor to find fault with Wallis's divorce, hoping that Edward would abdicate, the country would be rid of an unsuitable King and the Duke of York would rule in his place.

In despair Edward VIII offered Prime Minister Baldwin a compromise – he was prepared to enter a morganatic marriage with Mrs Simpson once her decree absolute was through. Baldwin knew that this would be unacceptable, since there was no provision in the constitution for a morganatic Queen, so the laws of England would have to be changed to allow this to happen.[39]

Another complication was that Dr Alexander Cannon's psychiatric treatment of the King had been leaked to a member of the Anglican Church. A rural vicar, who learned about the King's sexual problems, felt it his duty to contact His Grace Cosmo Lang, Archbishop of Canterbury, who disliked the idea of crowning the irreligious Edward. However, it appeared that the Archbishop had already been advised that that the King was receiving treatment from a Harley Street psychiatrist for sexual problems.[40] The Prime Minister and the Cabinet also knew that something was amiss with the new King, and had grave concerns.

Wallis was horrified that Edward was considering abdicating. His wealth and status and the servants who attended to his every wish were what had attracted her in the first place. Life in exile with an immature ex-King with an uncertain income was not an attractive prospect. Wallis told Walter Monckton (previously the lawyer for the Duchy of Cornwall and now Edward's legal advisor) she would be prepared to stay on as the King's unofficial wife, code for Edward VIII's mistress.

The question that needed answering was whether the King would carry out his threat to abdicate if he could not marry Mrs Simpson? The coronation, a very expensive affair with so many crowned heads and politicians attending, had reached the final stages of planning.

A political crisis loomed. The *entire* British cabinet threatened to resign if the king married Mrs Simpson. The governments of Canada and South Africa were consulted. The Canadian and South African Prime Ministers vetoed the idea of a morganatic marriage to a double divorcee. The Rt. Hon Joseph Lyons, Prime Minister of Australia, a staunch Catholic, sent a message voicing strong disapproval of the proposed royal marriage.

The political instability had financial repercussions. Share prices, already low due to the recession, dropped even lower, which unsettled the business and financial institutions and the British Government feared a run on the banks. Prime Minister Baldwin knew that such a troubled, selfish and immature Prince could not make a good King. If, as Baldwin suspected, the new

King could not sire an heir, he must have thought it no great loss to the nation if Edward abdicated in favour of the dutiful happily married Duke of York. In London, dedicated monarchists paraded through the streets waving placards proclaiming 'Out with the American whore' and 'Wally, give us back our King!'

Journalists and angry demonstrators picketed Wallis's rented house in Cumberland Terrace, Regent's Park, ironically the same terrace where Freda Dudley Ward and her husband had once lived and where Edward had been a welcome guest. Surrounded by crowds shouting their distaste for Wallis. After receiving more death threats, Wallis was given security guards to escort her. She blamed Edward for not having warned her of the consequences of announcing he wanted to marry her.

Wallis, whose nervous stomach complaint had returned, told the King she had had enough, was scared and wanted to slip away quietly 'until all the fuss had died down'.

It was decided that the King's mistress must leave immediately for France. Edward asked his old friend, Peregrine Cust, Lord Brownlow, to drive Wallis to France. He was told to carry a pistol, and if necessary, to defend Mrs Simpson with his life.[41] Edward's parting words to Wallis were, 'Remember I will *never* give you up.' Wallis's friends, Kathleen and Herman Rogers, offered her hospitality at their villa near Cannes.

French papers were full of the abdication story and carried photographs of Wallis. She and Lord Brownlow crossed to France by the Channel Ferry and drove south through the night. Mrs Simpson was recognised at Lyons, mobbed by an angry crowd and had to lie on the floor of the car with a rug over her head. She insisted on stopping to use a public phone. From a village inn she called Edward at Fort Belvedere and implored him to make a broadcast informing the world he gave up the idea of their marriage, at least until all the fuss had blown over. But the line to London was so bad the King could not understand what she was saying.

Arriving at the Rogers' residence, Wallis and Lord Brownlow found the villa cold and bleak. Wallis had an unheated bedroom and shivered as she wrote to Edward telling him, 'I am so anxious for you not to abdicate'.¹⁴⁵ She sent the King a draft speech she had written for him to use as the basis of his radio broadcast. She hoped he would do what the American President had done — make his speech an intimate fireside 'chat' appealing to those who adored him so they would *refuse* to let him resign the throne.

Meanwhile, Prime Minister Baldwin had arranged for Wallis's divorce lawyer, Theodore Goddard, to fly to France to warn his client that a citizen's intervention (a complaint of collusion by one or other party) might still be made. This could prevent her divorce decree becoming absolute, in which case she could not hope to remarry.

Theodore Goddard, who was afraid of flying, took his doctor with him when he went to see Mrs Simpson. This sparked newspaper reports that Wallis Simpson was pregnant to the King — unlikely under the circumstances! On his return to London, Theodore Goddard rang Downing Street and told the Prime Minister that Mrs Simpson was prepared to abandon her divorce if it would settle the constitutional crisis. It has also been claimed that in a pencilled statement signed by Wallace, allegedly dictated by Lord Brownlow, she agreed to give up the idea of marrying Edward. However no trace of that document remains.⁴²

THE KING'S SPEECH AND HIS ABDICATION

Edward VIII, always a curious blend of weakness and stubbornness, refused to give up Wallis Simpson and continued to talk about abdicating in order to be with his beloved. His determination to abdicate over the marriage question was an excuse to abandon a post he had disliked since his relationship with Freda Dudley Ward.

Neville Chamberlain wrongly believed Wallis had persuaded Edward to abdicate so he could marry her because she 'wanted his money'. In his diary Chamberlain wrote that,

> Mrs Simpson is an entirely unscrupulous woman who is not in love with the King but is exploiting [him] for her own purposes. She has already ruined him in money and jewellery.

In fact, Wallis was desperate that Edward *remain* King, so he would have plenty of money, aware that if he abdicated he had no job skills. Due to his immaturity it was improbable Edward would have success in any other capacity. Wallis's deep-seated financial insecurity was so great, she was prepared to continue as Edward's mistress. Her notes for a speech for Edward, appealing to British supporters who wanted him to remain on the throne, were ignored. Walter Mockton, aided by Winston Churchill, wrote Edward's speech, stating he was abdicating — the first monarch in British history to do so voluntary.

The formalities of abdication took place when Edward VIII signed the Instrument of Abdication at Fort Belvedere on Thursday 10 December, 1936, with his brothers as witnesses. The following day Edward made his abdication speech over the relatively new medium of radio.

Sitting in front of the radio at the Rogers' villa in the south of France, Wallis listened to her royal lover and was mortified to hear him say,

> You must believe me when I tell you that I have found it impossible to carry the heavy burden of responsibility and to discharge my duties as King as I would wish to do without the help and support of the woman I love. And I want you to know that the decision I made has been mine and mine alone. The other person most nearly concerned has tried up to the last to persuade me to take a different course. I now quit altogether public affairs and lay down my burden. It may be some time before I return to my native land but I shall always follow the fortunes of the British race and the Empire with profound interest.

The Duke of York announced that Edward VIII would henceforth be known as His Royal Highness, the Duke of Windsor.

In her autobiography, *The Heart has its Reasons*, Wallis claimed she wept tears of joy as she listened to the King's abdication speech renouncing the throne for love of her. But Kathleen Rogers, Wallis's hostess and close friend, had a very different story to tell. Kathleen claimed that Wallis sobbed not with joy but with rage and vented her anger by smashing valuable ornaments, furious that the King had ignored her wishes. The *last* thing Wallis wanted was for Edward to abdicate as they now faced an uncertain financial future at a time of recession. Edward, now Duke of Windsor, had no job skills and expected to lead a life of leisure and live in luxury. But how would they do this? As the King's mistress she had become used to a life with servants, yachts and chauffeur-driven cars. Wallis had always been insecure about money and now she realised they would need much capital if they were to maintain a similar style of living.

Wallis's unhappiness increased when 'Slipper', her Cairn terrier, was bitten by an adder and died an agonizing death. The little dog, a present from Edward, was for Wallis like a child in a childless relationship.

Edward had been warned by his lawyers if he joined Wallis in France it could prejudice the outcome of her divorce. He realised he had to obey his legal advisors, so he kept away from Wallis for seven months and stayed in Austria, a German-speaking country where he had good friends and relations.

The Duke of Windsor stayed at Schloss Enzesfeld near Salzburg, loaned to him by the Rothschild family. He renewed contacts with relatives and professed admiration for the way Hitler was re-establishing the German economy and putting the country on a sound financial footing. Like many other aristocrats the Duke of Windsor regarded Nazi Germany as a bulwark against the risng tide of Communism, which had already killed his relatives, the Tsar and Tsarina and their entire family.

A QUIET WEDDING FOR A GLUM BRIDE

So not until the spring of 1937 did Wallis leave the gloomy Villa Lou Viei for the Loire Valley, where in a romantic fourteenth century chateau, complete with pepper-pot turrets, it had been arranged that the Duke and Duchess of Windsor to celebrate their marriage among friends and relations. Wallis was looking forward to a large and lavish celebration.

The Duke of Windsor had rented the Chateau de Candé from Charles Bedaux, a slippery character who had made millions in time and motion studies and owned an armaments factory in France which was selling arms to Nazi Germany. Wallis and Edward had decided to hire the fully renovated Chateau as their wedding venue, because it was very private and had excellent bathrooms. Fern Bedaux, the American wife of the immensely wealthy Charles Bedaux, insisted that every bedroom had the very latest modern bathrooms, which Wallis liked very much.

Wallis had planned a large and lavish wedding but had difficulty finding an Anglican clergyman prepared to officiate at it.

Finally an eccentric Northumberland village vicar agreed to defy the Archbishop of Canterbury and marry them. Wallis loathed the Archbishop, who, when speaking over the radio, claimed that Edward VIII 'had been *ruined* by his love for Mrs Simpson'.

Wallis and Edward were distressed and angered by a letter from Edward's brother, King George VI, which informed them that it was not possible for *any* members of the British royal family to attend the wedding. European royals followed his lead. They offered lame excuses why they could not attend as did Lord Mountbatten, who was to have been best man. To Edward's distress, it became obvious that none of his family or fellow royals would attend the ceremony.

The final blow came when Edward's legal advisor, Walter Monckton, brought a letter from King George VI, advising his elder brother that the title of Her Royal Highness could not be granted to his wife, the Duchess of Windsor. There would be no pension from the Civil List for the Duke of Windsor. Should he return to England within the next five years the small allowance he had been granted would be cancelled.

These terms angered Edward. He regarded the denial of the royal prefix HRH to Wallis as an insult implying that Wallis was unfit to be his wife. Without that prefix she would not be treated as a member of the royal family and would not entitled to a curtsey or to be treated as royal. Wallis always blamed the former Duchess of York, now Queen of Great Britain, for denying her the cherished status of being addressed as royal. George VI and his Queen believed that Wallis would not stay with the immature Edward, would soon tire of him and find another husband.

With no royal relatives at the ceremony, and with only ten guests present (instead of the more than hundred who had been invited) the Duke and Duchess of Windsor were married in the music room of the Chateau de Candé on 3 June 1937. Edward's friend and former equerry, Major 'Fruity' Metcalfe, was the best man, replacing Lord Mountbatten. Herman Rogers, Kathleen's husband, gave Wallis away.

Lady Alexandra Metcalfe, as the wife of the best man, was a guest and she recorded how surprised she was at how cold Wallis was to her new husband, who seemed so desperate to please her. Wallis refused to kiss or embrace Edward and kept him at arm's length through their wedding day, which clearly upset Edward.

Lady Alexandra Metcalfe could not bring herself to kiss Wallis because she had been so cold and unloving to Edward.[43] Lady Alexandra added that, had Wallis shown even a glimmer of softness towards the Duke of Windsor, clasped him by the arm or kissed him during the reception, she would have warmed towards her. But the bride showed no warmth at all.

In her romanticised memoir Wallis described her wedding as a 'supremely happy moment' in her 'great love affair' which does not agree with Lady Alexandra's description. Several wedding photographs show Wallis looking glum. She wore a tulle hat, intended to resemble a halo, a curious idea under the circumstances for a twice-divorced bride. Wallis's wedding outfit was a dress and matching jacket in pale blue satin with a long slim skirt, which emphasised her gaunt figure and flat chest. Her face was covered in a mask of heavy pancake make-up and for once her customary elegance had deserted her.

Walter Monckton was a guest at the wedding. Remembering Rickatson-Hatt's words that Wallis was so selfish she could never love anyone, he was very worried about the Duke of Windsor. In a private interview he made Wallis *promise* that she would do her utmost to make her husband happy. Wallis, always insecure about finance, replied brusquely that she expected that enough money would be forthcoming for them to live in the style to which the former king was accustomed.

The last six months of 1937 were an extended honeymoon for the couple, now homeless since Fort Belvedere was banned to them. The Windsors made lengthy stays in the Carinthian Mountains, Vienna, Salzburg, Budapest, Prague and Venice.

AN ILL-TIMED VISIT TO NAZI GERMANY

In October 1937, the Windsors were photographed on a visit to the Bavarian mountain chalet of Charles Bedaux and his American wife. Bedaux, wearing a jaunty Tyrolean hat, had arranged a German tour for the Windsors, culminating with a visit to Hitler.[44]

Bedaux was soon to be appointed economic advisor to the Third Reich and made responsible for the liquidation of Jewish businesses in occupied France, which helped to fill the coffers of the Nazi Party. Bedaux arranged for the Windsors to visit German factories and meet the Burgomeisters of several towns.

This visit gave Wallis an idea of what making a 'state' visit was like. Covered in jewels she did her best to look suitably royal. The Windsors were entertained by Edward's relatives, the Duke of Saxe-Coburg-Gotha and his family, and by Hermann Goering and Rudolf Hess. Anna de Wolkoff had visited Hess several times and kept in touch with him and with Wallis and may have acted as an intermediary.

When the Windsors' visited Hitler at his Bavarian mountain retreat, the 'Eagle's Nest' at Berchtesgarten the Fuhrer kissed Wallis's hand, a gallant gesture that flattered her. Photos show her smiling happily at Hitler. Nazi officials had been briefed to address the Duchess as Her Royal Highness which pleased the Windsors. Hitler claimed later that Wallis would have made an excellent Queen of England. Whether Hitler intended to make Edward a puppet king, had he succeeded in his plan to invade Britain, has never been substantiated but must have been included in the typed transcript the Nazis made of the Duke of Windsor's hour-long meeting with Hitler. The meeting did not include the Duchess, who sat in a different room talking to Hess.

With Teutonic thoroughness the Germans took minutes of everything discussed, typed up a transcript and made several copies. At the end of World War Two, British Intelligence found the transcript and sent copies to England where they went missing.

In *The War of the Windsors*, investigative journalists Lynn Picknett and Stephen Prior allege that the transcript contained material far too sensitive to be released.[45] A copy or the original may have been stored in the Royal Archives in Windsor Castle, but all enquiries about the missing transcript have been met with a firm denial of its existence. The Windsors' group of pro-Nazi friends worried Ml5 and the FBI, who were particularly concerned about Wallis and her contacts with von Ribbentrop.[46] The FBI prepared a dossier on the Duchess of Windsor to be shown to President Roosevelt. It claimed the Duke was impotent and Wallis made all their major decisions and favoured the Nazis.

Aware they could not return to England the Windsors rented a luxury villa in the South of France and had the furniture from Fort Belvedere transferred there.

At the start of World War Two the Duke of Windsor was created Field Marshall and worked as a Liaison Officer with the British Military Mission in Paris. Major Fruity Metcalfe and Lady Alexandra were now divorcing but remained friends. Rendered homeless by the divorce and with no regular income Major Metcalf returned to serve as the Duke's equerry on an unpaid basis. He knew that Edward and Wallis were mean about paying household staff but accepted the situation. Fruity regarded himself as a close friend of the former King and was keen to serve him.

While the Duchess was at their rented Villa de la Croe in the south of France, the Duke of Windsor received a phone call in the middle of the night, warning him that Hitler's forces were nearing Paris. Edward quickly packed his wife's clothes, jewels and other valuables into their car and fled into the night, leaving the faithful Major Metcalfe asleep in his bed. The Duke must have known that a serving British Army officer would be imprisoned by the invading German Army.[47] Lady Alexandra Metcalfe was scathing in her condemnation of Wallis and Edward's behaviour towards a loyal friend who had been best man at their wedding.

The Duke and Duchess of Windsor fled to Biarritz before continuing south to General Franco's Spain, where they were wooed by pro-Nazi groups. The British Foreign Office feared that Edward and Wallis would be kidnapped on Hitler's orders and installed as a puppet King and Queen, should the Nazis invade Britain. There were rumours that Wallis was still in touch with Joachim von Ribbentrop.

From Spain the Windsors moved to neutral Portugal and, unwisely, chose to stay in the villa of a banker with close contacts with the German Embassy. This sent the British Secret Service and the British Government into a state of high anxiety and renewed their fears of a German attempt to kidnap the Windsors.[48]

BOREDOM IN THE BAHAMAS AND THE OAKES MURDER

An alarmed Winston Churchill, worried about the Nazi affiliations of the Windsors, made certain that the Duke and Duchess left Europe. He arranged for the former King of Great Britain to be given the post of Governor of the Bahamas, where it was hoped the Windsors would be out of reach of the German Government and it would be easier to monitor any pro-Nazi activities.

The Duke and Duchess of Windsor saw Edward's appointment to such an insignificant post as an affront to their dignity and accepted it reluctantly. They were angered by a Foreign Office directive to the Bahaman authorities, informing them that as the Duchess lacked the title of Her Royal Highness, no one should curtsey to her. Wallis's lack of this title remained a bone of contention till the Duke's death. He repeatedly asked for this title to be granted, but his request was always refused — many thought unjustly as Wallis *was* his legal wife.

Princess Michael of Kent, not the most popular member of the royal family, was a divorcee and a Catholic when she married the Duke of Kent, but was given the title of Her Royal Highness.

Wallis's treatment was mainly the result of the personal antagonism between Wallis and the former Duchess of York. who was able to revenge those witty wounding remarks Wallis had made about her weight and lack of elegance.

Wallis hated the heat and humidity of the Bahamas. She told American friends it was a boring place and begged them to come and visit her there. In a letter to Aunt Bessie in the early stages of the war, Wallis defiantly insisted they would only return to England on their own terms. This meant acknowledgement of her as a royal wife and a return to their beloved Fort Belvedere once the war ended.

Wearing a specially designed and very flattering uniform, Wallis, with her usual efficiency undertook charity work on the small island and ran a canteen for troops in Nassau very effectively. But any credit Wallis might have earned for all her hard work was overshadowed by press reports that she flew to New York to have her hair cut and styled and have facials, while King George VI and the rest of the royal family were enduring German bombing raids on London.

Confined on a small island in constant company of the Duke Wallis felt trapped. Edward's slavish dependence and obsessive passion which irritated her. Feeling lonely she conjured up an idealised past with Ernest and continued to write to him.

The Windsors continued to be a worry to the British Government — a number of their friends were arrested for collaboration with the Germans.[49] On 20 May 1940, Wallis's Russian friend and couturier, Anna de Wolkoff, was arrested and charged with violating the Official Secrets Act and tried in secret. Anna was sentenced to ten years imprisonment as a Nazi spy for 'attempting to assist the enemy'.[50]

In 1942, the Windsors' friend and host in France and Germany, Charles Bedaux, was also arrested for pro-Nazi activities while supervising the construction of a pipeline for the Germans in Africa. Bedaux had dual American-French citizenship and was extradited to the United States where he was tried as a Nazi collaborator.[51]

The Windsors had previously aroused suspicions in Portugal for staying at the home of a banker with Nazi affiliations. Now they foolishly holidayed aboard the yacht of Axel Wenner-Gren, a wealthy Swedish businessman who owned the Bofors armaments factory which sold arms to Nazi Germany.

The Bahamas were seen as a sunny place for shady people including gun runners and armaments dealers. During the Duke of Windsor's governorship in 1943, Sir Harry Oakes, who had moved to the Bahamas to avoid paying taxes and had some very dubious friends, was found battered to death. When Government House needed renovation, the Windsors had stayed briefly in Sir Harry Oakes' residence.

As Governor of the Bahamas, the Duke of Windsor took personal charge of the investigation and mishandled it badly. Instead of calling in the local police and consulting with Scotland Yard, at Wallis's instigation the Duke called in police from Miami. A great many people disliked Sir Harry Oakes. Suspicion fell on Oakes's son-in-law Alfred de Marigny, a *louche* man who the Windsors particularly disliked. De Marigny was arrested for the murder, tried and acquitted. The police were accused of manufacturing evidence. The mysterious death of Sir Harry Oakes remained a *cause célèbre*, the topic of several books and films. The reputation of the Duke of Windsor suffered — he was seen as an incompetent bungler and was never offered another official post. In her biography of the Duchess of Windsor, Lady Diana Mosley (a close friend of Wallis) claimed the murder had been organised by Harold Christie, a business associate of Oakes who had brought in a Mafia hit-man to murder Oakes.

The Duke and Duchess were made to spend the rest of World War Two in the Bahamas, hosting cocktail parties and lunching with friends round swimming pools. Wallis remained deeply insecure, despite her jewels and the money Edward had deposited in foreign bank accounts. She continually worried whether they would have enough money to live in style once the war ended.

Anne Sebba, Wallis's biographer, discovered loving letters from Wallis to Ernest, written before and after her marriage to the Duke of Windsor, which throw new light on the triangle created by Edward VIII, Wallis and Ernest Simpson. In letters to 'dear' Ernest, Wallis referred disparagingly to the Duke by the private nickname she and Ernest used for him 'Peter Pan', the boy who refused to grow up. These letters suggest that Wallis idealised their former married life and was lonely.

In revealing letters to Ernest she expressed her regret for abandoning the 'simple life' they once led at Bryanston Court. Wallis chose to ignore she had been bored by this 'simple life', and had longed for parties, expensive clothes and jewels, everything she had achieved by her affair with Edward. She seemed to have forgotten her resentment at having to submit household and clothing expenses for Ernest's perusal and his long-winded talks on historic buildings. (Her affectionate letters exchanged over a period of years surprised everyone when they were featured in Anne Sebba's excellent biography of Wallis and in a television programme about the 'lost letters.')

Wallis never renewed her former close friendship with Mary Raffray. After two years of happy marriage to Ernest, to whom she bore a son, Mary died of cancer in 1941. Wallis felt genuinely sorry for Ernest and wrote him a loving letter of condolence.[52]

The war ended in 1945 with the invasion of Germany by the Allies. The Windsors hoped to return to their beloved Fort Belvedere as private citizens, albeit with some special priviledges. The Duke of Windsor's terms for his return included an HRH for Wallis. This request was refused, causing the Windsors much pain. In retaliation Wallis spoke unfavourably about England, a country which she saw as having rejected her and her husband.

Wallis's dislike of England and the English increased in 1946 when, as guests at the Berkshire home of the Earl and Countess of Dudley,some of her most valuable jewels were stolen. Wallis was distraught. She regarded the jewels given her by Edward as security for her old age and evidence of her excellent taste. For months she could talk about little else.

After some delay the Duke's insurance company paid up and he set about commissioning replacement jewellery for his wife.

With no job to occupy him, Edward spent much time and huge sums of money ordering designs approved by Wallis to be made up into distinctive pieces of jewellery by Cartier, as well as by Van Cleef and Arpels. Having been denied the coveted HRH prefix and had her wedding shunned by most of the invited guests, Edward was determined to make Wallis look as regal as possible.

A LUXURIOUS EXILE AND AN AMERICAN LOVER

What the Duke and Duchess of Windsor considered to be a meagre living allowance, granted them by George VI, was tax free. The Windsors persisted in thinking they had been badly treated. In contrast, King George VI believed Edward had deceived him over his financial position and was angry and not prepared to give his elder brother more money from royal funds.

Wallis's meanness became legendary. All her life she had worried about money and, even after earning a considerable sum from her ghosted autobiography which became a best-seller, it was never enough to alleviate her insecurity. The Duke and the Duchess became notorious for leaving their hosts with large unpaid bills for telephone calls, never tipping for services rendered and underpaying their household staff.

Unsavoury stories continued to swirl around Wallis. The Windsors became friendly with Jimmy Donahue and his wealthy mother Jessie, who, like the actress Barbara Hutton, was a Woolworth's heiress. Jessie Donahue invited Edward and Wallis on luxury cruises and basked in the reflected glory of having British royalty as her guests. Jessie's money paid for the best suites on cruise liners for the Windsors and she stuck to them like a leech. Jessie's bisexual son, Jimmy, was an excellent dancer and when sober, could be a very amusing companion and dance partner for Wallis.

By mid 1950s, the Duke was suffering from lumbago and could no longer take his wife onto the dance floor. It became apparent that the Duchess enjoyed mocking her husband and humiliating him in public. The Duke was always a perfect gentleman, never retaliated to her derisive wit and often looked sad when she left the room. In restaurants Wallis would embarrass her husband by passing notes to Jimmy Donahue if her bi-sexual lover was not seated next to her. When dinner ended, bored by the Duke, Wallis summoned a car, ordered the chauffeur to take her husband home and went night-clubbing with Jimmy Donahue, sometimes staying out all night with the bi-sexual playboy. Wallis enjoyed being seen with a youthful handsome dance partner which enabled her to show off her designer dresses on the dance floor. Noel Coward, always a source of gossip about other people's sex lives, told his gay chums that he knew Jimmy Donahue greatly appreciated Wallis's talent for oral sex.[53]

The Duke and Duchess of Windsor and Jimmy Donahue visited Australian-born Lady Enid Lindeman Furness (now re-married and known as Lady Kenmare) at her Villa La Fiorentina at St Jean Cap Ferrat. Wallis made an excuse she wanted to show Jimmy the view of the water from a first-floor guest room. The couple disappeared upstairs for a considerable time.

The Duke of Windsor sat at the lunch table, ignoring his wife's long absence, telling the other guest the same boring stories, always beginning, 'When I was monarch'. The guests were embarrassed, aware that, in the words of Enid's daughter Patricia Cavendish, 'the Duchess was having it off with Jimmy in one of the upstairs guest rooms'.[54]

In his cups, Jimmy had a fund of crude jokes and vulgar party tricks which even Wallis with her love of risqué jokes and blue stories began to find embarrassing. Their relationship ended when Jimmy, having had far too much to drink, quarrelled with Wallis.[155] Eventually, Donahue's drug-taking and love of alcohol escalated to such a point he became too hard to handle, even for Wallis. Christopher Wilson's book *Dancing with the Devil* claims that one evening Jimmy Donahue got so drunk he kicked the Duchess on the shins and drew blood. *Finis* to the friendship.

After six years of wandering, staying as guests in other people's homes and luxury hotels who offered free accommodation, the Windsors finally decided to settle in Paris. The French Government welcomed them with open arms, regarding them as a tourist drawcard and exempted them from paying French taxes. The Duke and Duchess were delighted, feeling that the royal family and the British Government had treated them badly.

In return for a nominal rent the French Government granted the Duke of Windsor a long lease on a three-storey mansion on the edge of the Bois de Boulogne. No 4, Route du Champ d'Entrainment would become the Windsors' permanent home in Paris.

Still angry that the world did not recognise Wallis as royal, since she had been denied the title of Her Royal Highness, Edward lavished his wife with expensive jewellery and elegant clothes in order to make her *appear* royal and compensate for the lack of the title of Royal Highness.

The Duke had no work and drank more than was good for him. Wallis did her best to limit her husband's consumption of alcohol and involved him in furnishing their new home, which he enjoyed. Together they produced colour schemes and visited antique shops in Paris in search for paintings, antiques, chandeliers and Baccarat crystal. The Duchess of Windsor was such a perfectionist that the decorators had to repaint her bedroom three times before she was happy with the colour, henceforth known as 'Wallis Blue'.

In spite of crying poor and making constant demands on his brother for more money, Edward and Wallis employed a butler, a chauffeur, footmen and housemaids, a chef and an under-chef, a scullery maid, a valet for the Duke, a personal maid for Wallis and each of them had a secretary. The Duchess used the services of a masseuse twice a week and her personal hairdresser came to the house every morning, often accompanied by a manicurist to make sure Wallis's nails were perfectly polished.

Couture houses, which Wallis patronised, sent projected designs for her clothes for her approval. Aware she was no beauty, Wallis made certain she was always elegantly dressed and changed her designer outfits at least three times a day. All her clothes and her alligator shoes and handbags were listed, catalogued and kept in perfect order by her personal maid.

The Windsors' male servants were given a distinctive uniform or livery, emblazoned with a ducal coronet. There were crowns and coronets everywhere, embroidered on their sheets and even on their bathmats and towels.

Twice a week the couple dined at Maxim's, one of Paris's most expensive restaurants. Wallis's dinner parties were famous for their elegance and the quality of the food and wines she served. However, her extravagance and desire to present the Duke of Windsor to the world as though he were still king, meant they were often short of ready cash.

Although Wallis read little, apart from fashion magazines, she became a brilliant promoter of her own highly selective autobiography, *The Heart has its Reasons*. She employed two ghost writers and earned over a million pounds from its publication. In this highly romanticised memoir, written to create the myth of a great love affair between herself and a king who abdicated for love of her Wallis established a legend. However her memoir concealed nearly as much as it revealed, including Edward's sexual problems and her anger and anxiety when he abdicated. It did not explain why Edward enjoyed being ordered about and humiliated in public and in their bedroom, where he liked her to act the role of the chastising and consoling nanny as part of his infantile *paraphilia*.

Feeling lonely, Wallis wrote to Ernest, seeing their married life through rose-coloured spectacles. But she forgot that in the Great Depression, when Ernest was economising and had annoyed her by selling their car, she was dreaming of owning fabulous jewels and designer clothes and cruises on luxury yachts.

What Wallis had desired was a brief sexual fling with the future king and being rewarded with jewels and lavish holidays. But her plans had backfired — he had become obsessed with her and Enrest had left her. She had been forced by threats of suicide to marry an immature ex-king with sexual problems who she neither loved or respected.

Nevertheless, Wallis did respect the enormous sacrifice Edward had made to be with her. She was telling the truth when she wrote about her 'duty' to Edward in her self-serving memoir.

> My husband gave up everything for me. My duty was to evoke for him the nearest equivalent to a kingly life that I could produce without a kingdom.[55]

Wallis liked living in cities but Edward missed the countryside and the garden he had created at Fort Belvedere. Though insisting they were short of money, the Windsors managed to find enough cash to buy a house near the village of Gif-sur-Yvette, south of Paris. They called it 'The Moulin' because it was built on the site of an old mill. To give her idle husband something to do, Wallis encouraged him to create a magnificent garden. Edward followed her advice. Creating and tending this garden kept the Duke occupied and made him feel happy.

Wallis's unrepentant Fascist friend, Lady Diana Mosely, also exiled in Paris, commented that the décor of The Moulin was 'more Florida than France'. In post-war Paris, Lady Diana Mosely became one of Wallis's closest friends and, like Wallis, was held in bad odour in Britain.[56] Hitler had been the guest of honour at Lady Diana's second wedding to Sir Oswald Mosely, held in Berlin in the home of their mutual friend Josef Goebbels.[57]

Diana Mosely was one of the fabled Mitford sisters and the most beautiful of the many daughters of Lord and Lady Redesdale. The Redesdales were members of the pro-Nazi Right Group, which held meetings at the South Kensington premises owned by the parents of Wallis's friend Anna de Wolkoff.

Lady Diana's continuing pro-Fascist stance was abhorrent to her sister Nancy Mitford, who was also residing in Paris. But rather than befriending Nancy Mitford, Wallis selected Lady Diana Mosley to write her biography. Diana Mosley described Wallis as 'an exceptional woman vilified by the Queen Mother.'[58]

Anna de Wolkoff had been jailed as a spy during World War Two and died in Spain under suspicious circumstances in a car accident, possibly because she knew too much.

⁂

Wallis, in the role of wife and nanny to Edward, often found him infuriating. The Duke of Windsor had never been a good conversationalist and whenever he was slow to understand a joke Wallis mocked him, calling her husband 'Lightning Brain.'[59]

As Duchess of Windsor, Wallis was surrounded by luxury but felt lonely and trapped in a marriage she had not wanted. However, she enjoyed giving elegant dinner parties for celebrities and the seriously wealthy. Her dining table was always set with the finest table silver, bone china and matching sets of embroidered linen mats for each china dinner service. Many small courses, exquisitely prepared and presented, were served by liveried staff. Wallis ate little and remained extremely thin.

The Duchess of Windsor hated the fact she had large ugly hands. To compensate she had hundreds of pairs of gloves in every colour imaginable — whenever possible she tried to be photographed wearing gloves. Edward, Duke of Windsor played golf, gardened at their country house and continued to regard Wallis as the perfect wife. Supervising the tiniest details of running her home, Wallis refused to economise. Fresh flowers were delivered daily from an expensive florist. She insisted that her linen sheets were changed every day and newspapers were ironed before being brought to the table. The Duchess of Windsor even sprayed perfume onto fresh flowers that had no scent and onto light bulbs just before a dinner party so her dining room would be perfumed.

Still insecure about money, Wallis bought very cheap presents for the Duke's godchildren and invested her own money carefully, but she spent a fortune on her couture clothes, her hairdresser and manicurist. She also spent a great deal of money on her beloved pugs — each one had a jewelled dog collar and at night they slept on her bed. The dogs were child substitutes. When asked why the Windsors were childless, the Duchess hid the fact the Duke was impotent and retorted with her usual wit, 'The Duke is not heir-conditioned!'

Any chance of reconciliation with the royal family seemed remote. The Duke of Windsor returned to England alone for the funeral of his younger brother, George VI, who died on 6 February 1952. Edward had some form of reconciliation with his mother but Queen Mary still refused to meet Wallis who she loathed.[60] A year later, again still alone, the Duke attended his mother's funeral.

In 1965, the Windsors paid a visit to London, so the Duke could consult an eye specialist. His eyesight had become so poor that he failed to see that Wallis's face had become rigid and masklike, due to frequent plastic surgery.

Two years later both Windsors went to Britain to attend the unveiling of a memorial to Queen Mary at Marlborough House. At the ceremony the Duchess of Windsor curtsied low to the Queen but not to her old enemy, Elizabeth, the Queen Mother.

Wallis and Edward were invited by Lord Mountbatten to stay with him at Broadlands. Mountbatten's ulterior motive was to secure Wallis's jewel collection for the British royal family and hoped to acquire the Windsors' letters and private papers, planning to have these stored in the Royal Archives at Windsor Castle, away from examination by the press or biographers.[61]

The last occasion when the Duke and Duchess returned to Britain together was for the funeral of Princess Marina, widow of the Duke of Kent. With age the Duke and Duchess had grown much closer. Wallis had accepted the limitations of her husband's immature personality and grew more affectionate towards him. She mellowed with the years and the mockery and sarcasm she had vented on Edward was replaced by genuine affection.

His doctors felt the Duke had become too frail to work in his beloved garden, so they decided to sell 'The Mill'. Like King George VI, the Duke of Windsor was a heavy smoker and eventually suffered from lung cancer, as did George VI.

The final six months of Edward's life were spent in great pain. The couple drew even closer as the Duke's death approached. The legend of a happy marriage which Wallis had created had finally come true.

On 28 May 1972, the Duke of Windsor, died. Wallis was devastated but was permitted to stay at Buckingham Palace for the funeral and the Duke was buried in the royal vault at Frogmore near Windsor Castle. At the funeral, Wallis claimed, 'He gave up so much for me. I can't begin to think what I shall do without him'. However, memory lapses made it apparent that the Duchess of Windsor was suffering from dementia. The Duke had bequeathed his widow £3,000,000, a *very* large sum in 1972. Fearing she might have difficulties coping with his estate, the Duke had entrusted its management to Mâitre Suzanne Blum, his French lawyer. She took control of the Duchess's life and ensured Wallis made a new will, leaving all her money and jewels to the Pasteur Institute.[62]

After the Duchess of Windsor suffered several bad falls, Mâitre Suzanne Blum blocked friends from visiting the Duchess, who was now completely under the control of the lawyer. Wallis ate very little and vascular dementia slowly blocked the blood supply to her brain. After suffering another serious fall Wallis was hospitalised.[63] On her return home, the heartless Suzanne Blum insisted that the Duchess of Windsor's beloved pugs must not lie on her bed for health reasons and had them put to sleep. This was the cruellest thing she could do to Wallis. Denied her pets' company, the Duchess of Windsor retreated into a world of darkness and misery for ten years, until she died in April 1986, aged 90.

Like her mother, Wallis had always feared dying in poverty. Instead she died very wealthy with a collection of magnificent jewels that would sell for more than $50,000,000 in a Sotheby's auction held in Geneva, rather than in London to avoid offending the royal family.[64]

Queen Elizabeth II had agreed that the Duchess of Windsor could be buried in the royal burial ground at Frogmore, near the graves of Edward's younger brothers, Prince George of Kent and Prince Henry of Gloucester. Royal in death, but not in life, the Duchess of Windsor was buried beside the dukes and duchesses who had refused to attend her wedding to a former King.

Wallis Simpson in France waiting for her decree nisi to come through with Slipper, a terrier given her by the Duke of Windsor.

Jewellery by Cartier given to Wallis by Edward and sold at Sotheby's in Geneva.

The 14th century Chateau de Candé rented by the Duke of Windsor for their wedding was owned by Charles Bedaux, imprisoned as a Nazi supporter.

Left:
Wallis and Edward on their wedding day. According to Lady Alexandra Metcalfe Wallis looked glum and refused to embrace Edward.

Below:
The Duke of Windsor seated at the feet of his domineering wife, gazes at her with adoration.

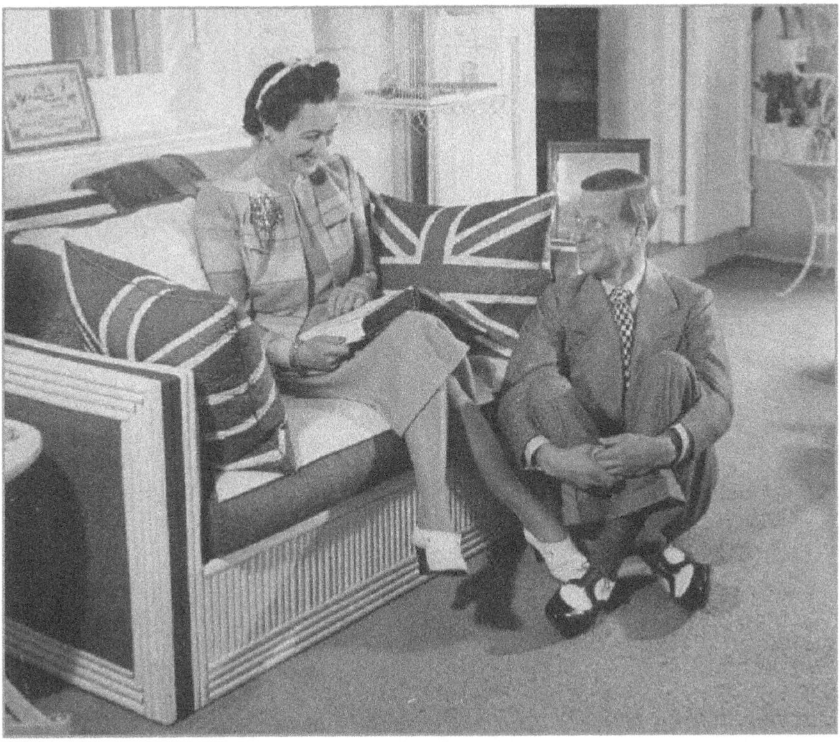

On the left of Wallis and Edward is Major 'Fruity' Metcalfe, best man at the wedding who the Duke abandoned in Paris when the Nazis invaded.

The Duke and Duchess of Windsor's residence in Paris

CHAPTER 10

Camilla Shand (Parker Bowles) Duchess of Cornwall (born 1947)
and
Charles, Prince of Wales

I'd suffer anything for you. That's the strength of love. Camilla to Charles, from the Camillagate tapes. Recorded 17 December, 1989.

The link between young girls, eating disorders and osteoporosis is a ticking time bomb. Camilla, Duchess of Cornwall, President of the National Osteoporosis Society, October, 2011.

A SECURE HAPPY CHILDHOOD BUILDS CONFIDENCE

Camilla Rosemary Shand was born on 17 July 1947, two years after the end of World War Two. After a distinguished military career, her father, Major Bruce Shand, left the British Army to become a partner in a London firm of wine merchants. Bruce Shand, child of a broken home, was determined to give his children Camilla, Mark and Annabel a happy and secure childhood.

Bruce Shand's father, Philip Moreton Shand, wrote excellent books on wine and architecture and was a colourful character with four wives and several mistresses. Bruce Shand wanted a more stable life for his children than his own childhood and made sure they had it. Major Shand's passion for hunting saw him become a popular Master of Fox Hounds and this passion was inherited by Camilla, his elder daughter. Major Shand was eventually honoured by being created Deputy-Lieutenant of East Sussex.

Camilla's maternal grandmother, Sonia Cubitt, was the second daughter of Alice Keppel, Edward VII's final mistress. Camilla's grandmother married Rolie Cubbitt, heir to the prosperous Cubitt construction empire and he eventually inherited the title Baron Ashcombe, but their marriage ended in divorce.

The Cubitt fortune (some of which would be inherited by Camilla) came from the hard work and enterprise of Tom Cubbitt, a humble carpenter-turned-builder who became the leading London property developer of his day.[1] Tom Cubbitt's son, George Cubbitt, attended Trinity College, Cambridge, and his success in business and his generous donations to charities saw him given the title of Baron Ashcombe. For a time George Cubbitt owned the magnificent Bodiam Castle in Kent.

Growing up in a happy home in the Sussex village of Plumpton, Camilla's childhood was funded by her mother's inherited money from the Cubitt side of the family and her father's success as a wine merchant. The Shands could afford a large three-storey home in South Kensington. They also rented a large country house in Sussex with nannies and ponies for the children.

Camilla was a happy confident child with two loving parents, unlike the unfortunate Lady Diana Spencer whose mother left her father for another man. This resulted in Diana's sense of loss and abandonment which had far-reaching effects when she felt Prince Charles had abandoned her.

In the late 1950s, Camilla attended the exclusive Queen's Gate School for Girls as a day-girl. School friends remember a confident child who boasted that her great-grandmother had been the last mistress of Edward VII.

Queen's Gate School occupied several large Victorian houses at the Cromwell Road end of Queen's Gate. The school prided itself on producing girls with a sound knowledge of household management and etiquette and emphasised the importance of good manners. Back in those days marriage was considered the only possible future for an upper-class girl — private schools like Queen's Gate prepared their pupils for marriage rather than for a career. As a teenager, Camilla flirted with boys and flouted the rules by smoking, a habit she continued in adult life but has done her best to give up.

Camilla left school with only one 'O' level — the lowest level of the school-leaving examinations in Britain — in the summer of 1964.[2] This does not mean that Camilla was stupid, but attending university was not the aim of private schools like Queensgate at that period. At the age of 16, Camilla was sent to Mon Fertile, in the French speaking part of Switzerland. It was the last Swiss finishing school to close its doors as increasing numbers of girls were entering university. Mon Fertile prided itself on preparing pupils for their debutante season where they would meet eligible young men and find a suitable husband.

Today Camilla's schooling seems bizarre but at that time it was regarded as perfectly normal for upper-class girls. (Attending a similar school at Ascot I was the only girl in my year to go to university rather than attending a finishing school or doing a secretarial course.)

Seen from today's perspective, Camilla and Princess Diana were both under-educated. But while Princess Diana read only romantic novels Camilla has always read widely and can talk knowledgeably on a broad range of topics.

In the 1960s, most girls from Camilla's kind of background expected to be married by the time they were in their early or mid-twenties. At her Swiss finishing school girls could learn ballroom dancing and skiing, as well as doing courses in flower arranging and French cooking.

At 18, after spending a year at finishing school, Camilla moved to Paris, where she attended the Institute Francais, learned French and enjoyed herself. She was a sporty fun-loving girl, brimming with confidence, who would eventually inherit a considerable sum of money from her grandmother, so had no money worries.

Camilla returned to her family in England and spent her time flirting with boys, riding horses and hunting foxes. The essential thing was to shine in the all-important debutante season. To 'launch' her into society, Camilla's mother, the Hon Rosalind Shand, hosted a large cocktail party in Searcey's premises in Pavilion Road, which runs parallel to Sloane Street.

There was gossip that Camilla had hosted a wild coming-out party, but she had done nothing of the sort. There were plenty of staff at the party and wild behaviour was firmly discouraged. I lived in a mews house in Pavilion Road with three others girls and attended parties there and Searcey's did not allow wild parties on their premises. By today's standards it was very sedate, no dope, no sex in bedrooms. The names of young men invited to Camilla's coming out party were on the 'debs delight' list and had all been vetted by mothers, including the Hon. Rosalind Shand.

By the time Camilla made her debut in the 1960s, it was not unusual for debutantes to lose their virginity during their debutante season. But most girls would have died rather than admit to their parents they were no longer virgins, because this was *not* an era of frankness about pre-marital sex.

Camilla left home and shared a London apartment with a female friend, who admitted that Camilla was untidy and had little enthusiasm for housework. She worked briefly as a secretary and 'Girl Friday' for Colefax and Fowler, an exclusive firm of interior decorators, and became involved in the activities of the polo playing set.

Camilla was popular with boys and dated several handsome young men, including Kevin Burke, son of Sir Aubrey Burke, the aircraft tycoon, and the dashing Andrew Parker Bowles, a protégé of the Queen Mother. When Camilla arrived unexpectedly at

Andrew's flat and discovered he was two-timing her with another girl, she left him with a few pithy remarks about his conduct.

As a sexually liberated girl in advance of her time, Camilla Shand wanted to enjoy herself before marrying Mr Right. Her ultimate aims were to live in the country with horses, dogs and raise her own children as she was raised in her happy childhood.

It was a myth that Miss Camilla Shand, when introduced to Prince Charles on the polo field, told him she was the great-granddaughter of Alice Keppel, the mistress of his great-grandfather, and that they should get together. This would have been dreamed up by the tabloids, because a girl of Camilla's class and background would not have made such a coarse remark on being first introduced to the heir to the throne.

Surely, this topic would have aroused much mirth by the time Camilla and the Prince knew each other better, as both of them have a good sense of humour. But it is unlikely to have been Camilla's opening gambit.

Prince Charles was a year younger than Camilla, (known to her friends as 'Milla'). Like most boys of his age he was immature and uncertain of himself. At Gordonstoun School he had tried desperately to win the approval of his father, Prince Philip, who had been a huge success at school and in the British Navy, achievements Charles feared he would never emulate.

When Charles met Camilla he had recently come down from Cambridge having attended an all-male school where he was teased and bullied, and was shy and gauche with women. It is claimed that it was Camilla who taught him a great deal about sex as Charles was a late developer, riddled with British upper-class inhibitions after attending an all-male private school where he was bullied. He found Camilla undemanding and great fun to be with. Her spontaneity and the fact she did not fuss over her looks or her clothes, made her appealing to the young heir to the throne.

In 1971, before Prince Charles was due to go away to sea, the couple spent an idyllic summer together. She watched him playing polo at Windsor and the pair of them often stayed with Charles' godfather, Lord Mountbatten, at his country house, Broadlands near Romsey in Hampshire. Prince Charles felt that with Camilla he had met his soul mate and did not want to lose her.

Prince Charles was nothing like his dissolute selfish Hanoverian ancestors He really did want to do the proper thing and marry a suitable girl who would make a good queen. But when the smitten Prince talked about making Camilla his wife, his godfather pointed out that, traditionally, Princes of Wales married aristocratic virgins or foreign princesses. Lord Mountbatten liked Camilla and found her intelligent and amusing, but while the Shands and the Cubbitts had aristocratic connections, both families were riddled with scandalous divorces.

In Lord Mountbatten's eyes divorce was shameful and this attitude prevailed in the 1970s. However, extra-marital bed-hopping — in which Mountbatten and his wife Edwina indulged a great deal during their turbulent marriage — was deemed better than divorce.

The ambitious Lord Mountbatten had hidden reasons for opposing Prince Charles' marriage to Camilla. He had high hopes the Prince might marry his attractive granddaughter, Amanda. Charles was influenced by his godfather, who was more like a surrogate father to him. Having listened to Mountbatten's warnings Prince Charles hesitated about proposing to Camilla, the girl he loved and found compatible.

As heir to the throne, mindful of his responsibilities, Prince Charles took his godfather's advice: he went away to sea without mentioning marriage to Camilla or asking her to wait for him until his return. And this was how Charles lost the love of his life to his friend Andrew Parker Bowles .

Blonde, long legged and athletic, Camilla had always had a very soft spot for her old flame, the dashing Andrew Parker Bowles. When Charles learned that Camilla had decided to marry Andrew Parker Bowles, he was devastated and shut himself away for days.

Prince Charles did not attend Camilla and Andrew's wedding which took place at the Guards Chapel, Wellington Barracks, on 4 July 1973. He excused himself by claiming that, as the Queen's representative, he had to attend certain Independence Day celebrations in the Bahamas. Several other members of the royal family *did* attend, including Princess Anne, who had previously dated Andrew Parker Bowles, a Catholic who Anne knew she could never marry as at the time Catholics *still* could not marry into the royal family, a restriction that has recently been removed.

Once he left the Navy Charles became a trusted family friend of the Parker Bowles. He enjoyed Camilla's large amusing dinner parties at their home, Bolyhyde Manor, near Chippenham in Wiltshire. Camilla, a country girl at heart was happiest at home, where she liked to wear old clothes, muck out the stables, create her garden and ride her beloved horses.

PRINCE CHARLES' FRIENDSHIP WITH AN AUSTRALIAN

Meanwhile, another effervescent blonde, who enjoyed watching polo at Smith's Lawn, captured the attention of Prince Charles. Melbourne-born Dale Harper, six months younger than Camilla Parker Bowles, was as blonde and vibrant as Camilla but more photogenic. The main difference between these two bubbly young women was that Camilla kept silent about her close friendship with Prince Charles, while Dale boasted that she had dated him. In his mid-twenties, Charles had considerable success with women but none had that special spark he found with Camilla and Dale.

Dale Harper first met Prince Charles in 1966 at a school dance while Charles was a pupil at Geelong Grammar. Dale was the daughter of a wealthy Melbourne publishing tycoon and was raised in luxury. However, she had the bad luck to be infected with a rare illness, called Perthes disease, a wasting condition that damaged the hip joint and the bones of one of Dale's legs, so she had to spent much of her childhood in leg irons.

In her teens her condition stabilised and she was able to live a more normal life and attend university.

Dale Harper was an intelligent young woman with an outgoing personality. She was an extroverted blonde with a beautiful smile and a curvaceous figure, who had inherited money, *chutzpah*, and social ambitions. After graduating, her first job was a brief stint as a reporter at the *Australian Women's Weekly*. In 1969, she went to work for the London office of that magazine.

Dale had many admirers, among them the Prince of Wales and his Old Etonian chum, Lord Anthony Tryon. Both men were fascinated by Dale's *joie de vivre* and both of them dated her. However, it was tall dark-haired Lord Anthony Tryon rather than Prince Charles who first gave Dale the nickname 'Kanga' although Dale, when wanting to publicise her 'Kanga' fashions claimed to the press that Prince Charles had done so.

Camilla realised that Dale was Charles 'type' and loathed her from the moment they were introduced to each other. It has been claimed that Dale initially entertained hopes that her *amitie amoureuse* with Prince Charles might lead to an engagement, but soon realised she lacked the combination of blue blood and virginity, necessary for a royal bride. However, Prince Charles was very fond of her and called her 'the only woman who really understands me'. This annoyed Camilla who saw herself as Prince Charles' special confidante.

Kanga enjoyed seeing her photo in the papers and knew it was good for her fashion business, so she 'fed' selected journalists stories in which she featured as the 'close friend' of Prince Charles. She became engaged to marry Lord Anthony Tryon, who was a merchant banker at Lazards, whose father had been keeper of the Royal Privy Purse and Anthony had been a page to the Queen.

The Tryon's 1973 wedding took place in the Chapel Royal at St James' Palace. Their first child, a daughter named Zoe, was born a year later, followed by a son named Charles, whose godfather is the Prince of Wales. Four years later Dale gave birth to twins.

Prince Charles remained a close friend and they went on fly fishing holidays together at Lord Tryon's fishing lodge in Iceland and Lord and Lady Tryon were invited to Balmoral to meet the Queen and her husband.

In December 1974, the Parker Bowles' son Tom was born and Charles agreed to act as his godfather. Encouraged by Camilla, Charles had purchased a Georgian period house with a run-down garden near Camilla's country home and Charles and Camilla enjoyed planning alterations and improvements to the property, known as Highgrove. Charles regarded Camilla as his closest friend and sometimes jokingly called her 'my manager'.

Charles admired Camilla and was fond of her as well as Kanga, both of whom were apparently happily married.

Camilla and her husband had decided that it was important to provide a stable home for their children and that she and the family would not accompany Andrew on various military postings. Unlike many military families, their children would not be shunted around from one military posting to another.

Camilla was certainly not a typical Army officers' wife. For a start she had more money than most and had no intention of living in Army quarters near military camps. She wanted to stay in her home with her beautiful garden and have her children grow up with their horses and dogs. Andrew Parker Bowles' career was going well and he received important postings which often took him away from home for long periods and, gradually, the Parker Bowles lives began to diverge.

When their son Tom was still a toddler and Laura a baby, Andrew Parker Bowles started to spend much time with other women so Camilla's close friendship with Charles became increasingly important to her.

Prince Charles on his Australian tour in 1974. Photograph Australian Information Service.

⁎⁎⁎

Lady 'Kanga' Tryon seemed to have it all — a beautiful home, four healthy happy children and a handsome peer of the realm as a husband. Dale was entrepreneurial and generous and donated a great deal of money and time to various charities. Helped by financial backing from her successful father — who was visited by Prince Charles on one of his Australian tours — Lady Tryon bought, refurbished and resold property at a profit before branching out into the fashion business with a label of her own.

Lady Tryon, like many creative people, had a vibrant and appealing personality which bordered on the manic depressive.[3] She enjoyed the challenge of work and established a successful fashion house, specialising in non-crushable clothes. Her experience in the field of public relations and her trips to and from Australia made her aware that women travelling by air wanted clothes that were easy to pack and did not crease. She catered for this emerging market with permanently pleated dresses in attractive colours, guaranteed not to crease.

Running and promoting 'Kanga' uncrushable dresses was very profitable. The success of the 'Kanga' label was helped by the fact that Lady Tryon told journalists that the name 'Kanga' came from the lips of His Royal Highness, the Prince of Wales. In fact, it had been Lord Tryon who had coined the name. Dale was a savvy promoter from her experience in publishing in Australia and London. She implied that there had been more than just friendship between her and Prince Charles, aware this would bring publicity to her fashion empire, which soon opened branches in Singapore, Dublin and Europe.

According to a Channel 4 documentary, *Prince Charles' Other Mistress*, put to air after Kanga's death, she and Charles had briefly been lovers before her marriage. When it was finally known that the Wales' marriage was crumbling, various tabloids alleged Charles had been 'consoled' in the homes of both Mrs Parker Bowles and Lady Kanga Tryon, both of whom were rivals for the Prince of Wales' affections.

THE TURNING POINT

When Prince Charles turned 30, he came under increasing pressure from his father and his godfather to marry. Conscious of his responsibility to produce an heir, he turned to Camilla and Kanga for advice on the prospective royal brides which his grandmother and other family members suggested as suitable.

In August 1979, the brutal murder of the Prince's godfather, 'Uncle Dickie' Mountbatten, came as a terrible shock to Charles who had regarded him as his surrogate father.

Lord Louis Mountbatten died under exceptionally brutal circumstances, being assassinated by members of the Irish Republican Army. A bomb, concealed aboard his fishing launch kept at his Irish holiday house, was blown up by remote control. Grief and shock sent Charles reeling into the arms of the woman he had known since his adolescence and who he trusted completely – Camilla Parker Bowles.

In hunting and polo playing circles it soon became obvious that Prince Charles and Camilla were an item. The passion that had united them years ago and the compatibility was still there. Camilla was certainly not going to let any other former girlfriends (and especially not the dazzling Lady Tryon) regain a foothold in Charles' affections.

Andrew Parker Bowles was now often away from home. He was posted to Rhodesia as Senior Military Liaison Officer to the Governor, Lord Christopher Soames, just before the Independence celebrations of Zimbabwe.

Charles and Camilla were able to spend time together, staying with discreet friends in large country houses surrounded by high walls, away from the prying lenses of the tabloid press.

In 1980, a year after Mountbatten's death, Prince Charles and the Parker Bowles were guests at the hunt ball at Cirencester. To the amazement of other dancers Camilla and Charles spent a long time on the dance floor, kissing passionately. A concerned friend drew Andrew Parker Bowles's attention to the behaviour of his wife and the Prince of Wales. Gazing at the pair of them, Camilla's husband is alleged to have replied with considerable *sang froid*,

'His Royal Highness is *very* fond of my wife'.[4] Charles and Camilla disappeared into the garden for a long time and came back with grass on their clothes, a fact confirmed later by Charles' valet, who revealed this to the press.

When news of what happened at the ball at Cirencester reached Buckingham Palace, the Queen was not amused. As a result, Camilla was code named 'The Problem' by Buckingham Palace staff and declared *persona non grata* in all royal residences by Her Majesty the Queen, who had grown up with the scandal of Wallis Simpson and her wayward uncle, Edward VIII.

In spite of his wife's behaviour, Andrew Parker Bowles remained a favourite of the Queen Mother and was invited to stay at her home on the Balmoral estate.

THE SEARCH FOR A VIRGINAL ROYAL BRIDE

The Cirencester ball incident gave the hunt for an aristocratic virgin bride for Prince Charles additional momentum. The pressure to find a suitable bride was also increased by the popular press who kept insisting the nation needed an heir.

Charles, about to turn 32, was understandably worried about marrying the wrong girl. His wife would have to fill a very public role as well as be his life companion. The sad fact was that in Camilla, the girl he let slip away he did believe he had found his ideal. As well as sharing his interests in hunting, polo, shooting, fishing and painting, she encouraged his work for environmental causes. His tragedy was to have listened to Lord Mountbatten, so Charles vacillated and did not propose to Camilla.

Now he had to make a decision about a wife. Prince Charles had first seen Lady Diana Spencer when she was a baby and he was a boy of twelve, when the Spencers had a house on the Sandringham estate. Some years later, Diana's father, succeeded to the title of Earl Spencer and inherited Althorp in Northamptonshire.

When Charles was 28, he noticed Diana on a visit to the Spencer family at Althorp, when dating Diana's elder sister, Lady Sarah Spencer. Charles found the sixteen-year-old Lady Diana very sweet so invited her to his birthday party. Diana was thrilled to be invited to a party attended by those she referred to as 'grown ups.' Later Diana admitted she had developed a crush on Prince Charles.

Lady Fermoy, Diana's maternal grandmother, was Lady-in-Waiting to Elizabeth, the Queen Mother. The pair of them discussed the virginal Lady Diana Spencer and agreed she would make an excellent princess — young and pliant she would do very well as a wife for Charles. Decades earlier, Lady Fermoy had married off her 18-year-old debutante daughter Frances to the much older 'Johnny' Spencer, a quick-tempered aristocrat from one of Britain's oldest and most noble families, but the marriage had ended in divorce.

Lady Fermoy kept quiet about the fact Diana had been raised without a mother, which had affected her badly. She did not mention the tantrums that Diana threw when she did not get her own way. Lady Fermoy was thrilled by the prospect of marrying off her teenage granddaughter to the 32-year-old heir to the throne. The Queen Mother believed that Lady Diana Spencer, coming from an aristocratic family with centuries of service to the royal family and known to love children, would be an ideal bride for Prince Charles. No one pointed out that Prince Charles's favourite pastimes were polo and fox hunting and Diana, having fallen off a horse as a child, was terrified of horses.

The subtle campaign for Charles to marry Lady Diana Spencer slowly gained momentum. Invitations to race meetings, house parties and dances, at which Lady Diana was present, were arranged for Prince Charles. To her surprise Diana noted that Camilla was usually present on these occasions and always seemed to know a great deal about Prince Charles' movements, his likes and dislikes.

Charles and everyone else found Lady Diana sweet and easy to please. At Balmoral she accompanied Charles when he went fishing and they made long romantic walks through the heather. Diana claimed she loved the Scottish countryside though later she would say she loathed it.

When the tabloids got wind of Charles' interest in Lady Diana Spencer, they pursued the young kindergarten teacher with telephoto lenses. Articles in the press and in women's magazines enthused that Lady Diana Spencer was a 'blue blood' from one of England's leading aristocratic families, just right for the heir to the throne.

Diana's childhood had not been a happy one, punctuated by a feeling of rejection, marred by deep misery over the departure of her mother, due to her parent's bitter divorce. Diana was only four when her mother left and under the terms of the divorce had little contact with her mother. In 1976, her divorced father, Earl Spencer, married again to Raine, Countess of Dartmouth, the daughter of romance novelist, Barbara Cartland. The Earl had not told Diana he was courting Raine, so Diana felt rejected when she found out her father had deceived her.

Only after marrying the Countess did Earl Spencer introduce her to his children. Diana and her siblings loathed their stepmother and christened her 'Acid Raine', as they disliked her for selling off family heirlooms and giving Althorp what they thought was a very vulgar make-over. Diana felt that those people supposedly closest to her had abandoned her, a feeling that would never leave her.

She had had left school with no exam results and disliking her finishing school in Switzerland had returned to Althorp. Initially she worked as a house cleaner for one of her married sisters and then as an untrained nanny. Diana's mother, Frances Shand Kydd, was able to buy her a small car and an apartment in The Boltons near the Brompton Road, which Diana shared with Sloane Ranger flatmates. Her life entered a new and happier phase when she was employed as an assistant kindergarten teacher.

The fact that Diana and Charles were so different in age, education and interests did not worry those who were pushing hard to bring about their marriage. At Cambridge Charles had gained a degree in Archaeology and Anthropology and developed wide interests He loved classical music and Georgian architecture and, like Camilla, was an avid reader on a wide range of topics.

Lady Diana was an immature teenager with a pretty face who loved pop music, dancing and swimming who had still to lose her puppy fat and was desperate to lose weight. Her favourite book was Barbara Cartland's sentimental romance, *Bride to a King*.

The 32-year-old Charles and 18-year-old Diana were so different in character that no computer dating agency would ever have linked them together as a potential married couple. Charles began to have doubts about the wisdom of the marriage everyone was so keen he made. He agonised over the question as to whether he should marry Lady Diana Spencer, supposedly filling all the criteria for a royal bride. The Prince of Wales wondered whether blue blood and virginity were enough to make the marriage work.

Prince Philip became irritated with Charles for his hesitation about marrying Lady Diana. He insisted Charles must propose without delay or stop seeing the little Spencer girl, otherwise her reputation would be damaged. Unkindly, Prince Philip added that if Charles did not marry very soon people would think he was gay. The Queen Mother, whom Charles adored, was also urging him to marry Lady Diana Spencer, saying she would make an excellent royal wife.

Of course, Charles consulted Camilla over such an important step in his life. She advised her lover that marrying Lady Diana Spencer was the right thing to do and genuinely hoped the marriage would work.

Diana, filled with romantic ideas about love still had her teenage 'crush' on Prince Charles. She refused to listen to those who warned her that he was very close to Mrs Parker Bowles. Looking in the mirror, Diana must have been reassured she was younger and prettier than Camilla and was sure that love would triumph as it did in romantic novels.

On 6 February 1981, Prince Charles proposed to Lady Diana Spencer at Windsor Castle. She replied 'Yes, yes', kissed him and rushed off to phone her mother, Frances Shand Kydd, with the news. Interestingly enough, during the stressful weeks leading up to the royal wedding Diana's mother was not there to support her teenage daughter at a time when Diana needed her most.

As the low achiever in a clever family, Diana was keen to shine at something. Her sisters had made good marriages and Diana knew that by becoming Princess of Wales and future Queen of England she would surpass her family's expectations for her.

Diana was convinced that once they were married, Prince Charles would forget Mrs Parker Bowles and they would be happy. She was unprepared for the realities of life with the Windsors at chilly Balmoral, where the conversation revolved around fishing, deer stalking and shooting, all things she disliked.

Charles began to realise just how little he and Diana had in common. Her sense of humour was totally different to that of Camilla and himself. In a television interview on 24 February 1981, when asked if the couple were in love, Charles hesitated as to what to say, looked embarrassed and answered lamely, 'Of course, whatever *love* is'. Diana was noticeably taken aback by this reply. What Camilla thought when she saw it televised no one knows.

Charles now began to notice that Diana was losing a lot of weight. He became concerned about his fiancée, because he knew that her older sister, Lady Sarah, had suffered from anorexia nervosa. Nevertheless, the Prince attributed Diana's weight loss to pre-wedding nerves. He was assured that brides usually lost weight before their wedding and afterwards things would settle down.

In 1981, bulimia had only just been categorised as a psychiatric disorder but very little was known about this eating and vomiting problem.

Diana had by now become uncomfortable with the depth of Camilla's friendship with Charles. Camilla had invited Diana and Charles to stay with her and her husband at Bolyhyde Manor many times. It seemed that she genuinely wished to befriend Diana but remain Charles' best friend.

One day, when Camilla had lunch with Diana, she asked her whether she planned to move to Highgrove and go fox hunting once she was married. Diana, knowing that Charles and Camilla often went hunting together, wondered what lay behind this question and why Camilla seemed relieved when she confessed to being afraid of horses, so would not be going fox hunting.

CAMILLA SHAND–DUCHESS OF CORNWALL

Diana resented Camilla's proprietary attitude to Charles and was puzzled that she knew so many details about him.

As a farewell gift for Camilla the Prince had ordered a solid gold bracelet engraved with the initials, 'G.F.', standing for 'Girl Friday'. The initials represented a joke between them, as Camilla had been a Girl Friday at the firm of interior decorators where she had worked for a year. The other meaning of these initials was 'Gladys' and 'Fred,' characters from the Goon Show, the programme that Charles and Camilla found hilarious, but bored Diana.

Finding the bracelet ready to be wrapped up with a card addressed to Camilla, only two weeks before her wedding, confirmed Diana's suspicions that the affair between Camilla and Charles was *not* over. Diana recalled how her father had deceived her over his relationship with 'Acid Raine' and then married her without any warning, now it seemed the man she loved was deceiving her with Camilla.

Diana attempted to have Camilla excluded from the wedding breakfast but Charles refused, telling his fiancée her suspicions of Camilla were ridiculous – she was his best friend.

The prospect of being the star of a televised wedding, that would be beamed around the world, was terrifying for a 19-year-old girl. For reasons of security Diana was living in Buckingham Palace, away from her Sloane Ranger friends in the apartment in the Boltons where she had been so happy. Diana wandered the corridors of Buckingham Palace by herself, eating comfort food and then, afraid of putting on weight and being unable to fit into her wedding dress, she would hide away in the toilet and stick two fingers down her throat to induce vomiting.

On 29 July 1981, the 'fairytale' marriage of Charles, Prince of Wales, and Lady Diana Spencer was celebrated in St Paul's Cathedral. Later, Diana told Andrew Morton, that, as she walked up the aisle of St Paul's Cathedral amid a sea of faces, she picked out Camilla dressed in pale grey with a matching pillbox hat, and her heart gave an involuntary lurch.

The teenage bride overcame her nerves and acquitted herself magnificently. Charles was proud of her and millions of television viewers worldwide fell in love with Diana, Princess of Wales. She looked so young, shy and vulnerable that the crowds roared their approval as what they saw as the Golden Couple appeared on the balcony of Buckingham Palace for their first televised kiss as husband and wife. It was obvious that Princess Diana had that indefinable thing known as 'star quality' largely missing from the royal family.

A newspaper report claimed that Charles and Diana had spent the night before the wedding in a luxurious sleeping compartment on the royal train. What the tabloids got wrong was the fact it was *not* Lady Diana who was with the Prince of Wales but Camilla. Diana had spent the night before her wedding alone, eating bowls of ice cream and throwing up.

In marked contrast, thirty years later, Kate Middleton spent the night before her wedding to Prince William surrounded by her loving family in a hotel.

Unfortunately, the fairy-tale wedding of Princess Diana and Prince Charles turned into a nightmare for both parties. On honeymoon on the royal yacht Charles phoned Camilla every day. There was a tearful scene when Diana saw a photograph of Camilla falling out of the Prince's diary. She could not believe that the physical affair between Camilla and Charles had ended.

During her honeymoon Diana continued to comfort herself with bowls of ice cream and her bulimia worsened. Jealousy and insecurity gnawed away at her and constantly she demanded affirmations of Charles' love. The smallest incident provoked the new bride's tears and tantrums.

Back in London after the honeymoon, it did not help that Diana was given little preparation for royal duties. Her mother was still not around to give her advice or comfort. Diana felt isolated, grew thinner and more and more miserable. Her jealous scenes, tears and bad breath (a side effect of bulimia) propelled her husband back into the arms of Camilla.

Diana's jealous scenes and bulimia repelled The Prince. Today, Charles, having had a long period of analysis would know far better how to deal with Diana, but at the time did not understand her problems and in those days far less was known about eating disorders.

Not surprisingly, daily phone calls between Charles and his Camilla, forced a wedge between Diana and her husband. Lonely and miserable, Diana reverted to childhood tantrums, beat the walls with her fists and even attempted to pummel Charles. In one row, Diana told Charles she hated *everything* he enjoyed most — holidays at Balmoral and Sandringham, fox hunting and horses. She also hated Highgrove, the house Charles and Camilla loved, whose garden Camilla had helped him plan and landscape. Diana demanded Charles sell Highgrove and buy a residence further away from the home of Mrs Parker Bowles. They looked further north at Belton House, which Diana liked but Charles reckoned was much too far from London.

✻

In 1982, Prince William was born. That same year the Prince and Princess of Wales made a visit to Australia and Diana insisted that her baby accompany them.

The Australian tour was a huge success, attracting record crowds, wanting to see the Princess of Wales. This was noticeable when the couple split up and those on Prince Charles' side of the road groaned with disappointment because they were unable to see Princess Diana properly. Charles joked about being eclipsed by his wife. It soon became obvious how painfully thin the Princess of Wales had grown.

PRINCESS DIANA VERSUS MRS PARKER BOWLES

Charles saw himself as a caring husband who tried to understand his difficult young wife. He was always prone to self-pity and turned for sympathy to Camilla — she was the only person who could help him. His grandmother, who he loved, was elderly and he could not confide his marital problems to her. Camilla was his confidante. Seated in her large comfortable kitchen at Bolyhyde Manor, sharing a glass of wine, the Prince could discuss problems in his marriage and other aspects of his life and know Camilla would not reveal them to anyone.

Charles' frequent phone calls to Camilla continued. Diana's bulimia worsened and she fainted on a tour of Canada in 1986.[5] Things went from bad to worse between the couple and Diana made an attempt at self-harm.

The Princess of Wales finally agreed to psychiatric treatment with Dr Alan McGlashan, an analytical psychiatrist who gave her twice-weekly sessions of Jungian analysis, Charles being a devotee of Jungian theories. However, Jungian analysis was not the right therapy for Diana — what she needed was specialist treatment for bulimia.

In an effort to help the Princess of Wales, Oliver Everett, her private secretary, gave her a biography of Princess Alexandra, hoping that reading about Alexandra's difficult marriage might help her adjust to the realities of life with a Prince of Wales.

'If he thinks I'm going to read those boring books he's got another think coming,' Diana yelled and threw the book into the corner of the room.[6]

Unknown to the public, who worshipped her, there were two sides to Princess Diana — sweet and charming normally but a screaming virago when really unhappy and with baggage from the past, it made it difficult for her to trust *anyone*. The darker side of Diana's personality was formed by feelings of loss and betrayal.

Due to Diana's unhappiness her bouts of bulimia became more frequent, which in turn affected her hormones, her brain chemistry and moods. Some of the Princess's personal staff resigned, claiming they could not put up with her tantrums. Their rows were terrible, leaving them both exhausted. In one of their arguments Charles made the comment he did not intend to be the only Prince of Wales *not* to have a mistress.

In spite of the fact the couple had two fine healthy sons, who they both loved, the marriage of the Prince and Princess of Wales had become the War of the Wales filled with anger.

THE 'CAMILLAGATE TAPES' AND PUBLIC CONFESSIONS

In December 1989 the cell phones of Prince Charles and Camilla were hacked while Charles was staying at the country house of Anne, Duchess of Westminster. He had telephoned Camilla at her home, aware that Andrew Parker Bowles was away.

His conversation with Camilla became known as the 'Camillagate tapes' which were published three years later in 1992 by Australia's *New Idea* magazine, and broadcast worldwide in one of the biggest royal scandals of all time.[7]

A few weeks after the broadcast Camilla was mocked on an American television show by Mick Jagger when the singer offered a tampon on a silver salver to a model dressed as Camilla, a reference in very poor taste to Prince Charles' wish, expressed in his phone conversation, to become a tampon and live inside Camilla.

Another humiliation was a press story, reporting that outraged housewives in Camilla's local supermarket had pelted her with bread rolls. One TV channel showed footage of Camilla running from the supermarket to her car. But Camilla's friend, the author Jilly Cooper, swore the bread rolls incident never happened. It became a legend, but like many legends, may be exaggerated.

In the same year the public was able to read Diana's version of Camilla's role in the breakdown of her marriage. Andrew Morton's book, *Diana, Her True Story*, was based on tapes the Princess of Wales gave to the author in which Diana revealed the depth of her anger and anguish over the invasive role of Camilla in her marriage.

On 9 December 1992, Prime Minister John Major announced in the House of Commons a statement that was only partly true 'The Prince and Princess of Wales have decided to separate. Their Royal Highnesses have no plans to divorce'.

Charles became the first Prince to confess to millions of viewers he had committed adultery.[8] Camilla had wisely warned Charles against doing this interview with Jonathan Dimbleby but he ignored her advice. In retaliation, Princess Diana appeared on the BBC's *Panorama* program and observed trenchantly, 'There are three of us in this marriage so it's a bit crowded'.

In fact, there were at least four of them in the marriage. Diana kept quiet about *her* complex love affairs which brought her very little happiness. The royal marriage was doomed. Tom Paine's famous remark that, 'Should the curtain that shelters the doings of the monarchy be drawn back, it will lose its mystery' was coming true.

In her running battle against Camilla, Diana enlisted the support of Lady Dale Tryon, who had also shared Prince Charles' confidences. Knowing that Camilla loathed Kanga Tryon, Princess Diana allowed herself to be used for publicity purposes for the House of Kanga. Princess Diana was photographed at a charity fund raising event, wearing one of Kanga's non-crushable miracle fabric dresses, just to annoy Camilla.

Lady Tryon was a very hard worker, but became ill and was diagnosed with uterine cancer. She became clinically depressed and, because of her agonising cancer treatments, became dependent on strong pain killers. She entered the private Farm Place Clinic and was given a new brand of anti-depressant, believed to be a wonder drug, but a side effect caused suicide in manic depressive patients, something not publicised at the time and only discovered later.

Lady Tryon, her mind clouded by the anti-depressant drug began to have delusions that Prince Charles was still in love with her and she made attempts to contact him. It was alleged Lady Tryon saved letters the Prince had sent her years earlier, which she read and re-read and reinforced her delusion.

Derek Harper, Dale Tryon's brother, confirmed that in the clinic Lady Tryon was given a strong anti-depressant drug which made her hear inner voices telling her to commit suicide.

In a fall from a balcony at Farm Place Clinic, Lady Tryon broke her back and became paralysed. Embarrassed and unwilling to admit she had attempted suicide, Lady Tryon, her mind clouded by pharmaceutical drugs, concocted stories about being pushed from the balcony of her psychiatric clinic.

Her behaviour continued erratic. At a sporting event Lady Tryon followed Prince Charles in her wheelchair, claiming she loved him. She became increasingly confused and was arrested while driving her car, interviewed by two psychiatrists and sectioned under the Mental Health Act. After she and Lord Tryon divorced, Dale spent her final months in Australia. During a trip to India she contracted an infection. Lady Tryon died aged 49 in England from uterine cancer, complicated by septic bedsores. Her Australian brother, her children and her former husband were at her bedside.

A Channel 4 television program, called *Prince Charles' Other Mistress*, tried to sensationalise what was essentially a very tragic story of mental illness and attempted suicide.

Dale's brother, Derek Harper, stated in his letter to *The Australian* newspaper that Prince Charles behaved in a distressing situation for everyone 'with compassion and humanity' and had been demonised for something that was scarcely his fault.

What Camilla felt about the demise of her rival is not known as she never gives interviews.

CRISIS FOR A MONARCHY SURROUNDED BY DIVORCEES

At the end of 1992, Queen Elizabeth II, arguably the most hard working and travelled monarch in British history, admitted she had endured an *annus horribilis* due to some members of her family and their broken marriages. Among the most scandalous royal couples were Prince Andrew and Sarah, Duchess of York, Princess Margaret and Tony Armstrong-Jones and Princess Anne and Captain Mark Phillips. Publication of Princess Diana's revelations in the 'Squidgygate Tapes' had caused more scandal when she commented about her royal in-laws, 'Bloody hell, after all I've done for this fucking family!'

Diana's appearance on television, questioning Charles' fitness to become King, made divorce imperative. The Queen hated the idea of divorce in the royal family but felt it wiser that the Prince and Princess of Wales separated, since the monarchy was being harmed by the 'War of the Wales'.

Camilla's response to Diana's attempt to destroy Charles' credibility as a future King was to call her 'that mad cow'. Mrs

Parker Bowles, slated by the tabloids as the cause of the breakdown of the marriage of the Prince and Princess of Wales, was pursued by journalists and photographers. The only press comment off the cuff Camilla ever made was misleading — 'I'm sorry if something has gone wrong but I know nothing more than the average man in the street', she claimed. [9]

In the stressful weeks that followed, Charles went into hiding at Sandringham while Camilla lost over a stone in weight. Besieged by the media she feared her phone was being tapped and had to crawl through a shrubbery to avoid journalists and received hate mail.

Looking haunted, Camilla hid away in Venice's luxurious Hotel Cipriani, located on an island in the lagoon which can only be reached by private launch. Camilla later took a long holiday in India.

As well as being vilified by sections of the media as a homewrecker for her role in the break-up of Prince Charles's semi-arranged marriage, Camilla was faced with problems of a different nature. She had invested the money inherited from her wealthy grandmother, Sonia Cubitt, with Lloyds. However, the two syndicates at Lloyds in which Camilla placed her inheritance crashed, causing her and others to suffer large losses, so her financial future looked uncertain.

Camilla's refusal to tell her side of the story to journalists and her discretion are good reasons why her relationship with Prince Charles has survived, as discretion is something he values highly.

Aware how Camilla's reputation had been damaged, Charles gave his godson, Tom Parker Bowles, and Tom's sister Laura a million pounds each, to be held in trust as compensation for the hurt they had suffered due to his relationship with their mother.

Camilla's father, Major Bruce Shand, paid Prince Charles a private visit to learn his intentions towards his eldest daughter. The Prince was quoted as telling Major Shand he would not marry Camilla but neither would he abandon the woman he had loved for more than 30 years.

In 1995 an amicable divorce between Andrew and Camilla Parker Bowles took place. Brigadier Parker Bowles subsequently married Mrs Rosemary Pitman. Camilla purchased Ray Mill House near Laycock in Wiltshire as her personal residence at a cost of £850,000.

The following year, Prince Charles divorced Princess Diana and gave her a generous divorce settlement. The Princess of Wales continued to live in her own apartment in Kensington Palace while Camilla lay low in Wiltshire and she and Charles took care never to be seen together in public.

At this stage, few people thought that Prince Charles and Camilla would ever marry. However, he bought Mrs Parker Bowles jewels and a designer wardrobe. His tax returns revealed he had paid many of Camilla's grocery bills.

***

Two years later, in July 1997 Charles hosted a large party at Highgrove for Camilla's 50th birthday. In a symbolic gesture he gave his mistress a magnificent pearl choker that his ancestor, Edward VII, had given to Camilla's great-grandmother, Alice Keppel, almost a century earlier.

Six weeks after Camilla's birthday party the situation changed completely. Princess Diana died in a car accident when the car in which she was travelling at high speed with her lover, Dodi Al-Fayed hit a post in a Paris road tunnel. The British nation went into mourning. Dying young at the height of her beauty turned Princess Diana into an iconic figure like Marilyn Monroe and Marie Antoinette. Mohamed Al-Fayed claimed the crash was the result of a conspiracy orchestrated by M16, a claim dismissed by a French judicial investigation and by Operation Paget, a Metropolitan police enquiry, which was not concluded until the year 2006.

After Diana's funeral Camilla kept a low profile aware many people hated her. Only in 1999 did she and Charles appear in public as a couple. The following year the Queen finally lifted her ban on Camilla, a royal mistress, entering any of the royal residences but was careful to keep her distance from her. At the Queen's Golden

Jubilee Camilla was seated ten rows away from Prince Charles rather than beside him.

In 2003, Camilla moved into Prince Charles' London home, Clarence House, where they lived as a couple. Clarence House was the former home of the deceased Queen Mother, who detested divorce and would have hated the idea of Prince Charles marrying a divorced mistress. There were worries that, should the Queen die, it would be very embarrassing with a new King as Head of the Anglican Church to be living 'in sin' with his mistress. Marrying the mistress seemed a better option.

'Like all the best families,' the Queen remarked 'we have had our share of eccentricities, of impetuous and wayward youngsters and family disagreements'. Her Majesty Queen Elizabeth finally acknowledged Camilla's presence by attending a luncheon at which Camilla and Charles were present. This made it clear that, at long last, Camilla had been accepted by the royal family.

By the time, Charles finally told his mother he wished to marry Mrs Parker Bowles — a precedent had already been set, as other divorced family members had married again.

FINALLY A ROYAL WEDDING FOR CAMILLA

On 10 February 2005, Clarence House announced that Camilla Parker Bowles and Prince Charles were engaged. Ironically, Camilla received an engagement ring that had once belonged to the late Queen Mother, a lady famous for hating divorce, who had opposed Princess Margaret's wish to marry the divorced man she loved — Group Captain, Peter Townsend.

The transformation of Camilla from adulteress to royal consort has been expertly stage managed but it has been a long journey. In 2001, Mrs Parker Bowles was voted into eighth position of the Worlds Worst Dressed Women's List and described as having 'the stylistic punch of a dilapidated Yorkshire pudding'.

By 2005, after an expensive make-over she was praised in newspapers in Milan, Paris, New York and London as being the 'epitome of graceful dignified style' having made an amazing transformation from a woman with scruffy hair who mucked out stables (albeit with a few servants) to her present soigné good looks.

On 9 April 2005, Charles and Camilla were married in a civil ceremony in a Windsor registry office, rather than in St George's Chapel at Windsor Castle. This was a royal marriage without precedent — unlike the secret illegal marriage of Maria and her Prince of Wales — this was the first time a Prince of Wales openly and legally married his mistress.

The low key civil wedding at a Windsor registry office in February 2005, between the divorced Mrs Camilla Parker Bowles (then living with Prince Charles at Marlborough House), *was* legal. The Queen, as Supreme Governor of the Anglican Church, felt it wiser not to attend the ceremony and nor did Prince Philip. For reasons of protocol Camilla's widowed father, Major Bruce Shand, also had to be absent.

Royal advisors who are famously snobbish had failed to realise that over the centuries the rules that royal brides must have royal blood and be virgins were totally outdated. Attitudes towards women have changed. In the 21st century divorce is no longer scandalous and a large proportion of the Prince of Wales' future subjects are divorcees.

Camilla's strong point has always been her discretion and her charm and her ability to get on well with many different types of people. While her intimate phone conversation with Charles, broadcast to the world as 'the Camillagate tapes' showed her as soothing and consoling the prince none of her love letters have ever come into the hands of the press.

However, intimate letters from Prince Charles to another English-born mistress, Janet Jenkins, written between 1976-1980 on notepaper headed Windsor Castle came into the hands of an American memorabilia business. In 2009, these letters were offered for sale on e-bay at a price of $7,500 each, authenticated by Janet Jenkins, who gave an interview to the *Sunday Mirror* about her former 'intimacy' with Prince Charles in Canada, in London and on one occasion at Highgrove. However by this time the public having had the Camillagate tapes scandal was not very shocked by the disclosure of more royal love letters from the past.

What was controversial in certain quarters was the marriage of the future Supreme Governor of the Anglican Church in church, and a civil marriage was deemed to be an acceptable alternative. Ironically, the Church of England had originally been created by Henry VIII so the King could divorce Katharine of Aragon and marry his young mistress, Ann Boleyn.

Camilla, having previously been slated by the press for her poor dress sense and untidy hair, now confounded her critics by looking stunning at her second wedding. Her outfit had been designed by Anna Valentine, a British designer, who would later design the attractive peach and blue coat-dress Camilla wore to the wedding of Prince William and Princess Catherine.

At her wedding to Prince Charles Camilla wore a flattering fitted oyster coloured, floor-length silk coat, embroidered with gold thread, over a silk chiffon dress in the same colour. Her hat by the Irish designer, Philip Treacy, was trimmed with a fountain of feathers that toned well with her blond hair and the total effect was stunning.

The media, who had delighted in pointing out the fact Camilla had twice appeared on lists of the World's Worst Dressed Women and claimed she had the fashion sense of 'a battered Yorkshire pudding', now changed their tune.

Charles and Diana's sons, Prince William, Prince Harry and Camilla's children acted as witnesses at the wedding.

A Service of Prayer and Dedication took place later in St George's Chapel at Windsor Castle, attended by the Queen, Prince Philip and Camilla's father. A special clause was inserted into the religious ceremony in which Camilla and Charles had to acknowledge their 'manifold sins and wickednesses', a phrase from the Anglican Book of Common Prayer. This was deemed by the powers that rule the Anglican Church to cover the sins of their adulterous relationship and to pacify angry members of Anglican congregations.

Camilla was given the title of Duchess of Cornwall. She also received the title of Her Royal Highness, which had been denied to the divorced Wallis Simpson and withdrawn from Princess Diana on her divorce. However it had been granted to Princess Michael, wife of Prince Michael, also a divorcee. Camilla had of course acquired the title of Princess of Wales, but aware that Diana had made it hers in the eyes of the populace, wisely chose *not* to use it.

※

Like the wives of newly appointed Presidents and Prime Ministers, Camilla, Duchess of Cornwall, had to overcome nerves about appearing in public and adjust to being surrounded by large crowds. She also had to take care not to become the focus of attention and steal the limelight from Prince Charles, as he used to complain Princess Diana had done.

Both Camilla's children were in favour of her second marriage. Her son Tom Parker Bowles claimed, 'My mother married the man she loved. We adore him, they're happy and my father is happily remarried.'

Camilla's first public test was the American tour she took after her marriage. There had been fears Americans might reject Camilla as Diana had been so popular. Besides, the publication of the Camillagate tapes had upset people in America's Bible belt. A carefully selected group of Americans met the newly created Duchess of Cornwall. They praised her warmth and keen sense of humour and commented on how easy it was to talk to her.

Camilla's rehabilitation was a slow process but friends who entertained them asserted that Prince Charles, who can be very tetchy at times, was easier to entertain with Camilla at his side.

THE DIANA MEMORIAL SERVICE AND CAMILLA

To mark the Duchess of Cornwall's sixtieth birthday in July 2007, over 150 guests attended the celebrations. That same year marked the tenth anniversary of Princess Diana's death and a memorial service was held to mark it. This caused a great stress and tension at Highgrove and reports from their staff Charles and Camilla argued fiercely over her attendance at the memorial service. It was to be held at the Guards Chapel in Wellington Barracks, on 30 August 2007, exactly 10 years after Diana's death.

Diana's sons as organisers of the memorial service had invited their stepmother to attend and Charles urged her to accept. When it became known that Camilla would be present there was such a public outcry that it was hurriedly announced that the Duchess of Cornwall would *not* be attending.

Just as she seemed to be achieving admiration for her own qualities, Camilla was caught in what could be described as a double bind situation – damned if you do and damned if you don't. A section of the public was outraged that Prince Charles' former mistress, the woman who had caused Princess Diana so much unhappiness, would dare to attend her memorial service. Camilla was damned by some if she attended the service or condemned by others if she decided to stay away. In the end she did not attend and spent the day alone.

What was interesting was the fact that against all odds she had finally managed to win the friendship of her two stepsons, William and Harry, who had been raised by their mother to think of Camilla as the intrusive 'Rottweiller' who had ruined their mother's marriage. Camilla, always very tactful, took things slowly with her step-sons and gradually seeing how happy she made their father they came to accept and like her.

Those lucky enough to be house guests at Highgrove confirm that Camilla is an excellent hostess. Well-known guests include the actor Stephen Fry, Rupert Everett and the popular author Alexander McCall Smith, who combined writing his Ladies' Detective series and other books with being Professor of Medical Law at the University of Edinburgh. Professor McCall Smith, with years of medical experience behind him, is an excellent judge of character. He told my close friend Dr Janet Irwin, who happened to be his aunt, that he found Camilla 'delightful, intelligent, easy to talk to and a considerate hostess. She is liked by her staff'.[10]

Years ago, at a Writer's Festival, fellow author Mary Wesley told me she had written a sympathetic letter to Camilla during the divorce of Charles and Diana, which was her darkest hour. Mary Wesley, having had a broken marriage herself, told me she had received a letter of thanks from Camilla, saying how much she appreciated her expression of sympathy and how much she enjoyed her novels.

Camilla is a hostess with a natural ability to put her guests at ease. Her equable nature enables her to take Prince Charles' grumpy moods and hot tempers (those famous 'Windsor gnashes') in her stride. She supports Prince Charles in his various aid schemes and acts as a sounding board for many of his ideas, which includes providing assistance to unemployed youth through his Prince's Trust. Like Prince Charles, Camilla sees the need to save listed buildings in Britain, such as Dumfries House and its collection of 18th century furniture, specially designed for the house. The house and its contents were due to be sold off at auction and Camilla backed Prince Charles who contributed a substantial sum to save it for posterity.

Charles and Camilla are keen on environmental projects such as preserving Dartmoor, the Lake District and other areas of scenic beauty. The beautiful gardens at Highgrove are a tribute to the skill and dedication of Charles and Camilla. In what was once a bleak area of lawn with a few stunted bushes and a pond, there are thyme-scented walkways, romantic arbours and colourful flowerbeds.

Meals prepared from organic vegetables, grown in Highgrove's gardens, are served to their guests. Several years ago, Charles and Camilla were ridiculed for their enthusiasm for organic farming, but in the era of climate change and decreasing food supplies their ideas are now regarded with new respect. Camilla has supported her husband in his efforts to grow crops without the use of chemicals and pesticides, a measure now widely acknowledged to be important in saving the planet.

Camilla and Charles enjoy the same kind of holidays, including sketching trips to Tuscany, a place they both love. Together they have visited Alice Keppel's former home at Bellosguardo with its magnificent view over Florence, which is no longer a private residence but a venue for society weddings. They have taken holidays in Turkey and Greece and cruised aboard the *Alexander*, one of the world's most luxurious private yachts, around the Greek coast. They have paid official visits together to many countries with links to Britain as well as to parts of the oil-rich Middle East.

However, two people of strong character, used to getting their own way and set in their opinions, are bound to have some difficulties when living together in marriage. Like all married couples, Prince Charles and Camilla have their differences. While Prince Charles is almost obsessively neat and tidy — even her closest friends admit Camilla has never been known for tidiness.

Camilla retreat to her own home when she finds the situation oppressively formal at Highgrove. Ray Mill House is situated in Wiltshire on the edge of Laycock some 25 kilometres from Highgrove. Wiltshire is one of the most beautiful and unspoiled villages in Britain. In this picture-book village no advertising signs are allowed — a village preserved by the National Trust who own many of its oak-beamed houses.

Ray Mill House, which dates from the Georigan era, is heritage listed under its original name of Ray Mell. This gabled house is where Camilla can play with her beloved grandchildren without disturbing Charles, which is important for both of them. Camilla held the wedding reception for her daughter Laura Parker Bowles at Ray Mill House. Camilla is fortunate that British tax payers foot a hefty bill to have her house guarded for security.

Camilla adores having her grandchildren around her. Charles, like many men of his age, does not appreciate the continual noise, clamour and mess made by small children. To solve this problem amicably, Camilla has converted the top floor of Ray Mill House into a nursery suite for her daughter's three children and those of her married son Tom Parker Bowles and his wife.

Camilla's daughter, Laura, with her little daughter Eliza and twin boys Gus and Louis, relies heavily on her mother and they all enjoy spending a great deal of time with Camilla at Ray Mill House. Camilla, a proud and devoted grandmother, loves being with her grandchildren in the privacy of her own home which she runs without the army of servants employed at Highgrove. On occasions she has been known to have cooked meals sent over to Ray Mill House from Highgrove.

Camilla has admitted to friends she sometimes finds the formality of royal life and the preoccupation with protocol irksome and craves a more simple life. After having a hysterectomy and again after breaking her leg in Scotland, it is significant that Camilla chose to recuperate at her own home rather than at Highgrove.

The current situation, where Charles and Camilla spend a fair amount of time apart, seems to suit both of them. In fact, they have never lived in each others' pockets. When they first met, Camilla's breezy informality and the fact she was mad about horses and hunting, charmed young Prince Charles. Camilla, not having been raised in royal palaces, at times has enough of rigid protocol. She dislikes the fact that her former school friends are expected to curtsey to her, a practice which Prince Charles feels must be observed. Ray Mill House has become Camilla's sanctuary. This is the place where she can relax, kick off her high-heeled shoes and be herself with close friends and family, rather than having to observe protocol.

QUEEN CAMILLA – OR DUCHESS OF CORNWALL?

Some members of the pro-Diana lobby continued to insist there would be a public outcry if an attempt were to be made to crown the Duchess of Cornwall as Queen Camilla, although their numbers are gradually waning.

Camilla, as the wife of Prince Charles rather than his mistress, was given a very public role at the Queen's Diamond Jubilee. As Prince Philip was ill in hospital, Prince Charles and Camilla were seated in the royal carriage beside the Queen. All three of them chatted away happily making it apparent that Queen Elizabeth II now approves of Camilla as a future Queen.

Things were very different ten years earlier at the Golden Jubilee, when Mrs Parker Bowles, the 'scarlet woman' , was seated ten rows behind Prince Charles. She was deliberately kept out of the limelight as Royal Household members and spin doctors knew there were strong feelings against her by a large section of the public which has gradually waned over the years.

At the time of Princess Diana's funeral, Alan Berry, co-founder of the American based Diana Appreciation Society, had said, 'What they did to Diana during her short lifetime is a dreadful indictment of Charles' lack of moral fibre and Camilla's ruthless ambition'.

'Ambitious' is not an apt description for Camilla who dislikes much of the pomp that goes with being royal and favours a more simple way of life and still a country woman at heart she enjoys being surrounded by horses, dogs and her own children and grandchildren and her sister and explorer brother, when he is back in England.

As Duchess of Cornwall she is always well-groomed. She can afford designer clothes and regular visits to a manicurist and a beauty therapist who provides her with $250 'bee sting' facials and $100 pots of a cream that are considered by many to be more effective than Botox injections or face lifts.[11]

Camilla's only mistake was to wear at a public function in Philadelphia a very heavy ruby and a diamond collar necklace with huge rubies the size of quails' eggs, which dropped into her cleavage. Critics claimed the necklace made Camilla resemble Imelda Marcos and that Her Majesty Queen Elizabeth II would never do anything as tasteless as wearing huge jewels on bare flesh. The tactful comment that such a large and heavy necklace was 'difficult to wear' was made by Ingrid Seward, editor of *Majesty* magazine.[12]

The disclosure that the necklace, worth over £2,000,000 was a gift from a Saudi prince aroused unfavourable comments. Buckingham Palace spin doctors refused to name the mystery donor who was later revealed as the ultra-wealthy Saudi Arabian Prince Al-Waleed bin Talal who had met Camilla in London as well as in the Persian Gulf and called her 'an exceptional woman.'

※

Camilla's role as a future Queen has been subject to contradictory statements. On her marriage, spin doctors employed by Prince

Charles, declared that when he acceded to the throne Camilla did not have to become Queen but could take the title 'Princess Consort' in a morganatic marriage.[13] This statement was intended to calm the anger from sections of the public at a well-known adulteress who had made Princess Diana's life unhappy becoming Queen of England.[14]

However, constitutional lawyers have always insisted that there can be no such thing as a morganatic marriage for British royals. In Parliament the Right Hon Christopher Leslie, at that time Britain's Minister for Constitutional Affairs, was forced to admit that Charles' and Camilla's marriage could *not* be a morganatic one. Eminent legal authorities have confirmed that a special Act of Parliament would be needed to *prevent* Camilla from becoming Queen. When finally Prince Charles mounts the throne of Great Britain, Camilla, as the wife of the King, will *automatically* become his Queen. This was clearly demonstrated by the fact that Camilla was seated with Prince Charles and Queen Elizabeth in the royal carriage at the Diamond Jubilee procession.

CAMILLA RAISES MONEY TO TREAT OSTEOPOROSIS

For many years Camilla has acted as President of the National Osteoporosis League. Until she saw her mother suffer terrible pain from this crippling disease, which made the bones of many elderly women brittle, Camilla had no idea of the extent of the problem. She watched her mother die slowly and in agony, loosing 20 cm in height with her spine so bent she had problems digesting her food.

Eventually, her mother could not breathe without oxygen or even walk aided by a Zimmer frame. Camilla subsequently learned that her grandmother, Sonia Keppel, the youngest daughter of Alice Keppel (see Chapter 6) also died from osteoporosis in the days when little was known about the disease of old age.

As President, Camilla works very hard for the National Osteoporosis League to raise funds and has made people aware of this insidious disease, as half of all women and one in five men will be affected during their lifetime.

Each year elderly women suffer more fractures from fragile bones than heart attacks. Nearing her mid-sixties, Camilla does not as yet suffer from this disease, but is aware of the need to publicise the importance of a good diet in childhood and to avoid crash diets, which can lead to serious eating disorders. She stresses the need for all older women to have bone scans.

The Duchess of Cornwall has also made several excellent speeches on topics such as the importance of soil conservation and the freedom of the press (a brave choice of topic for one who has had her share of suffering at the hands of the press). Although years ago Camilla was regarded by the press as a horse-mad socialite, she has over the past few years revealed a more serious side to her nature, which has gradually changed the public's perception of her character and personality. Camilla is no longer seen as the wicked 'Rottweiller', clinging to her lover, but as a supportive consort. She has won much praise for the kindness and empathy with which she has consoled widows and family members of dead soldiers.

The Duchess of Cornwall's grandmother, Sonia Keppel, died from the effects of osteoporosis.

Her work as the wife of Prince Charles was acknowledged in 2012 by the Queen who awarded Camilla her highest personal honour — Dame Grand Cross of the Royal Victorian Order.

AN END TO CENTURIES OF ARRANGED ROYAL MARRIAGES

In April 2011, when announcing his engagement to Miss Kate Middleton, Prince William, who has a strong will of his own, defied centuries of tradition and married a beautiful and talented young woman, lacking a title or royal blood, whom he had known and loved for many years. There were a few snide comments from courtiers at Buckingham Palace, many of whom are far more snobbish than the Queen, who over the years has adapted to changes in society and subtly changed the image of monarchy in many ways.

Queen Elizabeth II herself married for love and encouraged her grandson William to marry the girl he loved. However, some members of the Royal Household insisted that Kate Middleton and her family would not know how to behave on formal occasions. Private school and university-educated, discreet, charming and elegant, Princess Catherine, Duchess of Cambridge, proved these fuddy duddy aristocrats totally wrong. They and their snobbish children had expressed contempt one of Kate Middleton's distant ancestors had been a Durham coal miner. A few of Prince William's Old Etonian friends made a stupid attempt to embarrass Miss Kate Middleton in a restaurant. Because Kate's mother had worked as an air hostess, they tried to humiliate Kate by repeating in chorus the air hostess's call 'Doors to manual'.

In fact Mrs Carole Middleton, an intelligent elegant woman, was a great deal smarter than her detractors, having established a multi-million dollar business by hard work and initiative. The Middleton family had become wealthy enough to enable them to pay their share of a magical royal wedding, which, at a time of financial stringency, was something the British public greatly appreciated.

The wedding of Princess Catherine and Prince William was watched by billions of television viewers, who saw for themselves that the Middletons were a stylish family. Viewers all over the world warmed to Kate Middleton and her attractive sister who acted as her bridesmaid. Camilla won a great deal of praise for the kindness she showed to the new royal bride, helping ease Catherine into the difficult job of becoming 'royal' which royal men are not always good at explaining. Camilla had experienced for herself the difficulties of joining a royal family which has its share of difficult members, many of whom are preoccupied with status and the niceties of protocol. She her best to make the newly engaged Kate Middleton feel loved and wanted.

The newly created Princess Catherine chose to make her wedding vows to 'love, honour, comfort and keep' her husband, rather than using the word 'obey' as royal brides did in the past. Princess Catherine's choice of words showed a modern approach to royal marriage.

The welcome addition of Princess Catherine to the royal family has greatly broadened its appeal rather than diminishing it. In an internet survey, conducted after her wedding, 79% of Britons agreed strongly with the statement that 'William and Kate's marriage is good for the future of the monarchy'.

The Queen's highly successful celebrations for her Diamond Jubilee have also rekindled interest in the concept of hereditary monarchy. The Queen's Diamond Jubilee demonstrated in what high regard Queen Elizabeth is held worldwide.

Charles and Camilla were seated beside the Queen in her carriage, which demonstrated to the public that Camilla has finally won acceptance as a full member of the royal family and is no longer banished to the edge of the royal circle.

In November 2012 Camilla confounded her critics by making a very successful visit to Australia with her husband. Bestselling novelist, Thomas Keneally, the founding Chairman of the Australian Republican Movement appeared to have undergone a change of heart after meeting the Duchess of Cornwall.

Keneally admitted to The Australian newspaper that it had been a mistake to suggest Australians would not 'wear' Camilla as Queen Consort. The story indicates Camilla's excellent people skills are overcoming objections to her becoming Queen.

What is equally significant is that the old outdated restrictions have been abolished so princes can now marry for love rather than making arranged or semi-arranged marriages which, as this book shows, in past centuries created unhappiness for both partners.

DEDICATION AND THANKS

To Philippa (Pip) Lester-Wilson, friend of my schooldays when we read historical novels together and visited castles and stately homes. Due to her enthusiasm for this project, I dug out the unfinished typescript begun decades earlier and finally finished it.

Earlier this year my husband and I celebrated our silver wedding anniversary and over two decades of partnership in writing and creating books together. His is a labour of love and I can never repay Jake for all the work he has done on this book — designing the cover and layout, picture research, making pencil portraits and for doing a great deal of line editing. Many thanks also to graduate historian Marusia McCormick for acting as creative editor.

In hindsight it seems incredible that half a century ago I began this time-consuming project, sparked by the discovery of the journal of Consuelo Morgan Thaw, containing new information into the relationships of Thelma Morgan Furness, Wallis Simpson and Edward VIII. I was encouraged to research the topic by my late husband, Professor Larry Evans, DPM, MRC Psych and by his colleague the distinguished Professor Sir Martin Roth, then President of the Royal College of Psychiatrists of Great Britain. Thanks also for expert professional advice on the Duke of Windsor's impotence from my psychiatrist friend Dr Lilian Cameron and on his *infantile paraphilia* from the late Dr Janet Irwin, a child psychiatrist.

Thanks to my agent Selwa Anthony for her involvement with the creation of this book and selling it overseas. Thanks also to the staff of the London Library, to staff of the Pictures Library of the Royal Collection and for being allowed to undertake research in the Royal Library at Windsor Castle. This book is not only an account of royal mistresses but shows the progress women have made over the past three centuries.

One of the things that makes the British Commonwealth so unique is the monarchy — Her Majesty Queen Elizabeth II is an excellent example of a dedicated constitutional monarch. Raised in Britain and now an Australian, I trust that the monarchy will endure in Britain. Australia will make its own decision when the time comes to do so.

ENDNOTES

CHAPTER 1

1. The concealed story of Sophia Dorothea and the murder of Count von Königsmarck were first related in *Briefwechsel des Grafen Königsmarck and Sophia Dorothea von Celle*, W.F. Palblad, published in Leipzig, 1845 and then in W.H. Wilkins, *Secret Love of an Uncrowned Queen*, 1870 (reprinted 1909) and translated into French by le Vicompte de Beaucaire as *Une Mesalliance dans la maisin de Brunswick*. Paris, 1884. The story became a poignant but not always accurate film titled *Sarabande for Dead Lovers*.
2. The love letters between Count von Königsmarck and Princess Sophia Dorothea are archived in the University of Lund in Sweden.
3. Anna Louisa von der Schulenberg, (1692–1773), the eldest daughter of George I and Melusine married Ernest August von dem Bussche Ippenburg. George I's youngest daughter by Melusine, Margaret Gertrud 'Trüdchen' (1701 – 1728) was registered as the child of Melusine's brother and she married Count Albrecht Wolfgang of Schaumburg-Lippe. For details see P. Beaufort-Dewar and R. Powell, *Right Royal Bastards*. Burke's Peerage, London, 2009. It has been alleged that a civil marriage took place in Europe in mid-life between Melusine and George I but no wedding certificate for such a marriage has ever been found.
4. Alleged by Alan Hardy, author of *The King's Mistresses*, London 1980, to have amounted to £10,000, this would be worth at least fifty times that amount today.
5. Balen, Malcolm, *The Secret History of the South Sea Bubble, the World's First Great Financial Scandal*. Fourth Estate, London, 2004.
6. Walpole, Horace. *Memoirs of the Reign of George II*. London, 1846, reprinted McMillan, London, 1973. Vol 1, pp. 313-4 and Vol III, pp 315.
7. Walpole, Horace., *Memoirs of the Reign of George II*, London 1846.
8. Hardy, Alan. *The King's Mistresses, London, 1980, pp 73*.
9. Ditto

CHAPTER 2

1. Hibbert, Christopher. *George IV, Prince of Wales*. Penguin Books, 2002.
2. Robinson, Mary Darby and Robinson, Mary Elizabeth. *Memoirs of Mrs Robinson*, published posthumously, reprinted 2009 in paperback.

ENDNOTES

3   Grace Dalrymple and Lady Melbourne were alleged to have born illegitimate sons to the Prince of Wales. See Peter Beauclerk-Dewar and Roger Power. *Right Royal Bastards*. Burke's Peerage, London, 2009. These two ladies are also cited by Anthony J. Camp in *Royal Mistresses and Bastards*, available free on line at www.anthonyjcamp.

4   Other sources claim the Prince of Wales' bond was worth £20,000.

5   Alan Hardy in *The King's Mistresses (1980)* cites £5,000, estimated to be worth over forty times that sum today.

6   The Wallace Collection at Manchester House, Manchester Square, behind Oxford Street in London owns Gainsborough's portrait of Perdita Robinson where thanks to an enlightened policy it can be seen free of charge in this fascinating collection.

7   Entry under Mary Robinson in *The Feminist Companion to Literature in English*, Batsford, London, 1990, (ed) Blain and Clements. See also *The Green Dragoon, The Lives of Banastre Tarleton and Mary Robinson*, by Robert Bass, New York, Henry Holt, 1957 and Byrne, Paula, *Perdita, The Life of Mary Robinson*, London, 2004.

8   For the rest of her life Elizabeth Crole, mother of a royal bastard, received an annuity from the Privy Purse of £500 per annum.

CHAPTER 3

1   One version of the portrait miniature by Richard Cosway of Maria Fitzherbert is held in the Royal Collection at Windsor Castle, purchased by George, Prince of Wales. Cosway made several versions of this miniature for various clients including the Prince of Wales. Cosway's wife, also a portrait painter made a variant version, current whereabouts unknown. The Royal Collection also owns a portrait of Lady Hertford, commissioned by George IV, as Prince of Wales.

2   Swynnerton Hall is owned by Lord Stafford (Francis Melfort Fitzherbert) who is descended from Thomas Swynnerton.

3   See Christopher Hibbert, *The Gordon Riots*, Sutton History Classic, 1958, reprinted 2004.

4   Details of the original Brooke's Club are from Peter Cunningham, *Handbook of London*, 1850.

5   From Georgiana, Duchess of Devonshire's unpublished work, 'Anecdotes concerning the Prince of Wales', cited in Amanda Foreman, *Georgiana, Duchess of Devonshire*. London, 1998, page 79.

6. Amanda Foreman, *Georgiana, Duchess of Devonshire*, HarperCollins, London, 1999, pp 162-163, implies the young Duchess was not privy to the Prince's plot although Maria believed that she had been.

7. *Maria Fitzherbert, A Life from Unpublished Sources,* London 1939 by Sir John Leslie (writing as Shane Leslie), claimed Robert Burt was a prisoner in the Fleet prison when he agreed to officiate at the ceremony, subsequently proved untrue.

8. Steine House is located at 55 Old Steine, Brighton, (formerly known as The Steyne) near today's Brighton Pavilion, home of the Prince of Wales. Today Steine House is owned by the YMCA and used as a hostel for the homeless. There have been plans to buy the house and turn it into a house museum in memory of Mrs Fitzherbert but sufficient money has never been raised.

9. Dr Ida Hunter 'The 'insanity' of George III, a classic case of porphyria', *British Medical Journal*, 1966, Jan 8 pp 65-71; Drs Ida Macalpine and Richard Macalpine, *The 'Insanity' of King George III, a classic case of porphyria,* London 1996; Drs R Macalpine, I. Hunter and R. Rimington, C, Porphyria in the Royal Houses of Stuart, Hanover and Prussia, A follow up study of George III's illness. *British Medical Journal,* 1968, January 6, pp 7-18.

10. See John Derry, *The Regency Crisis 1788-89,* Cambridge, 1963 and Christopher Hibbert, *George IV, Prince of Wales,* London, 1972.

11. Georgiana, Duchess of Devonshire. (See Endnote 5).

12. Peter Beauclerk Dewar and Roger Powell, *Right Royal Bastards,* Burke's Peerage, London, 2007 and Anthony J. Camp in *Royal Mistresses and Bastards,* list the illegitimate children of George, Prince of Wales. None of these authorities believe that Minnie Seymour or Marianne Smythe was the daughter of Maria Fitzherbert and the Prince of Wales.

13. Susanna de Vries, 'London's Best Kept Secret, The Wallace Collection'. *The Collector and Connoisseur,* Sydney, 1985 written with the authority of the Wallace Collection contains the story of this portrait.

14. One of Mary Anne Clarke's daughters married a Frenchman named du Maurier. One of their descendants was the famous novelist Daphne du Maurier, who wrote a biography titled *Mary Anne* about her ancestor.

15. The Princess von Lieven's letters are in *Letters of Dorothea, Princess von Lieven during her residence in London, 1812-24,* published London 1902, reissued in paperback in 2001.

16. After Maria's death, the certificate of her illegal wedding, was transferred from the vaults of Coutts Bank to the Royal Archives in the

Round Tower of Windsor Castle. It can be seen on written application to the Royal Archivist at Windsor.

CHAPTER 4

1. According to Anita Leslie, author and descendent of Leonie Leslie, of Castle Leslie, an ancestor of Mrs Clarissa Jerome had Blackfoot Indian blood, as cited in Anita Leslie, *The Life of Lady Randolph Churchill*, Hutchinson, London 1960 and *The Fabulous Leonard Jerome*, Hutchinson, London, 1954. This claim is disputed by several Churchill descendents.

2. Financial details about Leonard Jerome from Anita Leslie *The Fabulous Leonard Jerome* and Celia Lee, author of *The Churchill Brothers*, London 2019, published the following year by Palgrave, New York.

3. Jerome Park racecourse no longer exits but Jerome Park in the Bronx remains.

4. Details from Anita Leslie, *The Fabulous Leonard Jerome*, Hutchinson, London and New York. 1945 and Seymour Leslie, *The Jerome Connection*, published John Murray, London 1964.

5. Letters cited by Anne Seba in *American Jennie, Winston's American Mother*, W. Norton, New York, 2007, page 52.

6. Some Churchill descendents insist that Winston was conceived in wedlock See Anne Sebba, *American Jennie*, pages 71-72. Lady Sarah Churchill told the author in the 1950s she believed her father had been conceived out of wedlock.

7. The small bedroom where Winston was born in Blenheim Palace is open to visitors. See www.blenheimpalace for opening hours.

8. Stanley Weintraub. *Edward the Confessor, the Playboy Prince who became Edward VII*. The Free Press, New York and London, 2001, pp 242, refer to threats to involve the Prince of Wales in the divorce actions of Lord Sefton and Sir Charles Mordaunt.

9. The Prince's heated exchanges with Lord Blandford and his brother Lord Randolph are recorded by Anita Leslie in *The Marlborough Set, 1964*.

10. Lord Blandford alleged Randolph caught syphilis from a prostitute.

11. Some family members argued that Lord Randolph did *not* suffer from syphilis but from a rare brain tumour, rendered worse by the strong medicines he was made to take The recently discovered notes of Lord Randolph's physician, Dr Thomas Buzzard in the library of St Thomas's Hospital state that his physician treated Lord Randolph with mercury by mouth, standard treatment for syphilis.

12   Ralph Martin, *Jennie: The Life of Lady Randolph Churchill*, Prentice Hall, London, 1969, and George Moore in *Memoirs of My Dead Life* (1921) claim Lady Jennie Churchill had 200 lovers. William Manchester in *The Last Lion, Winston Spencer Churchill, Visions of Glory*, 1984, claimed Lady Randolph Churchill had between 20-30 lovers, one of whom was the Prince of Wales.

13   Churchill, W.S. *My Early Life*, Macmillan 1930, p 19.

14   Cited in Elizabeth Kehoe *Fortune's Daughters page 77*, from Leslie Papers held by Richard Tarka King.

15   St George's Ascot is now a girls' boarding school attended by the author in the 1950s.

16   In January 1895, Count Karl Kinsky married Countess Elisabeth Wolff-Metternich zur Gracht, but their marriage was childless.

17   Kehoe, Elisabeth, *Fortune's Daughters*, page 103, states that the Princess of Wales, Lady Randolph Churchill and Mrs Gladstone were present at the first dinner. Anne Sebba, *American Jennie*, page 126, claims the dinner was for men only.

18   Stanley Weintraub in *Edward the Caresser* and Theo Arenson in *The Prince in Love* claim the Prince of Wales was addicted to sex but failed to explore the underlying reasons for this.

19   Anthony J. Camp in *Royal Mistresses and Bastards* (pages 25-29) lists many of the Prince of Wales's sexual liaisons. See www.anthonyjcamp.

20   Shane (Sir Jack) Leslie's papers held at Georgetown University USA and Leslie family archives are held at Castle Leslie, County Monaghan, Ireland. Some Leslie family letters are in the Tarka King papers; Tarka King being the son of Jennie's biographer Anita Leslie. Lady Randolph Churchill's papers are in the Churchill Archives, Churchill College, Cambridge.

21   The Prince of Wales' letter to Jennie Churchill, cited by Anita Leslie in *The Life of Lady Randolph Churchill*, page 176.

22   George Cornwallis-West, *Edwardian Hey-Days*, Putnam, London and New York, page 102.

23   Jenny Churchill to Daisy Warwick, cited in *Life's Ebb and Flow*, London, 1929, page 141.

24   George Cornwallis-West to Lady Randolph Churchill. His letter dated 2 May,1900 cited in *Edwardian Hey-days* by George Cornwallis-West. Elizabeth Kehoe in *Fortune's Daughters*, London, 2004, pp 204-5 has

ENDNOTES 403

Jennie and George meeting at Daisy Warwick's fancy dress ball, June 1898 held at Warwick Castle.

25 Elisabeth Kehoe, *Fortune's Daughters, The Extravagant Lives of the Jerome Sisters*, London, Grove Atlantic Books, 2005,page 207. Castle Leslie is now a luxury hotel and restaurant run by a Leslie descendent. For details see www.castleleslie .

26 Elisabeth Kehoe, *Fortune's Daughters*, pages 206-207.

27 Mrs George Cornwallis West, *Reminiscences of Lady Jennie Churchill*, published 1908 under what was then her married name.

28 From Emil Fuchs *With Pencil, Brush and Chisel: The Life of an Artist.* Putnam, New York, 1925.

29 Anita Leslie *Jennie: The Life of Lady Randolph Churchill*, London, 1969.

CHAPTER 5

1 Letters from Lord Brooke to the Hon Daisy Maynard 27 March, 1880 and Daisy Maynard to Lord Brooke, March, 1880 are owned by Daisy's great-granddaughter, Caroline Spurrier.

2 Lord Rosslyn to Lord Beaconsfield. 20 June, 1880 cited in Sushilla Anand, *Daisy, the Life and Loves of the Countess of Warwick*, Piatukus Press, London, 2008. p 20.

3 Frances 'Daisy' Warwick. *Life's Ebb and Flow*. Hutchinson, London, 1929. *Afterthoughts*, the sequel was published in 1932.

4 Sushilla Anand. *Daisy, The Life and Loves of the Countess of Warwick*. page 39.

5 The fact that Marjorie was the daughter of Lord Charles was a secret known only to William T Stead (W.T. Stead Papers, Churchill College, Cambridge) and Prime Minister Lord Salisbury , Salisbury Papers, Hatfield House.

6 Elinor Glynn, *Romantic Adventure*, London, 1898.

7 Stanley Weintraub, *Edward the Caresser, the Playboy Prince Who Became Edward VII*, The Free Press, New York, 2001, page 343.

8 G. Greenblatt, *Edward VII and his Jewish Court*. Oxford, 1986 and Niall Ferguson, *The History of the House of Rothschild*, London, 1998.

9 *The Clarion*, London, 16 February, 1895.

10 Cited in Sushila Anand,. *The Life and Loves of Daisy, Countess of Warwick*, Piatkus Books, 2007. page 82.

11   Peter Beauclerk-Dewar and Roger Powell *Right Royal Bastards*, suggests Maynard Greville was really fathered by the Prince of Wales. Anthony J. Camp in *Royal Mistresses and Bastards*, does not support this and Sushilla Anand's biography of Daisy Warwick has Joe Laycock as the father.

12   The Prince of Wales to Lady Warwick, 4 June, 1898. Caroline Spurrier Archive,

13   Sushila Anand, *The Lives and Loves of the Countess of Warwick*, Piatkus Books, 2009.

14   In that time the period of copyright was 50 years from the death of the writer of the letter.

15   Cited by Sushila Anand in *The Lives and Loves of the Countess of Warwick*, Piatukus Books, page 212.

16   Cited in Theo Lang, *My Darling Daisy*, London, 1966.

17   The final meeting between Lillie and Daisy, when both were elderly, is related by Daisy in the second volume *Afterthoughts* (1931). In 1928 Lillie Langtry died in Monaco and was buried in her birthplace Jersey.

18   My *Darling Daisy, the friendship of Edward VII and Frances, Countess of Warwick* exposed Daisy's love affairs and caused a great scandal when published in 1962. It describes Lang finding documents hidden in Switzerland about Frank Harris's failed attempt to sell Daisy's royal love letters in America and her failed attempt to extort money from the pious son of her royal lover, George V and how he thwarted it.

19   Easton Lodge was originally built by Daisy's ancestor, Sir Henry Maynard (1547-1610) for use as a hunting lodge. It was destroyed by fire in 1847 and replaced by a much larger Victorian Gothick mansion, which retained the old name of Easton Lodge. A second fire in 1918 destroyed part of Daisy Warwick's mansion. The main house of Easton Lodge has been demolished but the west wing still exsists and is now privately owned. The gardens, laid out by Harold Peto in 1902 for Daisy Warwick, are now restored and supported by the Gardens of Easton Lodge Preservation Trust. The gardens are open to the public. For opening times and location see www.eastonlodge.co.uk/content/.

20   Undated letter — Daisy Warwick to Jennie Churchill, Churchill Trust Archives, Churchill College, Cambridge.

CHAPTER 6

1   For details of Duntreath Castle, still owned by the Edmonstone family see www.duntreathcastle and the castle can now be hired for weddings.

2   Friedman, Dr Denis. *Ladies of the Bedchamber: the Role of the Royal Mistress.* Peter Owen, London, 2003, pp 118.

3   Giles St Aubyn, *Edward VII, Prince and King*, Atheneum Press, New York, 1979, page 378.

4   The pearl choker that Bertie gave Alice was recently re-purchased at auction by Prince Charles for Camilla, Duchess of Cornwall.

5   Souhami, Diana, *Mrs Keppel and her Daughters*, HarperCollins, London, 1992, pp 21.

6   Glendinning, Victoria, *Vita, The Life of Vita Sackville-West*, Penguin, London, 1983, pp 12.

7   In her diary for December 1908 Vita wrote 'The King was there,' Victoria Glendining, Vita, the Life of Vita Sackville West.

8   Souhami, Diana, *Mrs Keppel and Her Daughters*, HarperCollins, London, 1992, pp 21.

9   Polesden Lacey is now owned and run by the National Trust. For details and opening times see www.nationaltrust.org.uk/polesdenlacey.

10 Story of Alice and the King from Consuelo Vanderbilt, *The Glitter and the Gold*, George Mann Books, 1973.

11 Magnus, Philip, *Edward VII*, John Murray, London 1964 pp 260

12 Lamont Brown, *Alice Keppel and Agnes Keyser, Edward VII's Last Loves*, The History Press, UK, 2005.

13 Aronson, Theo. *The King in Love.* John Murray, London 1988, pp 251.

14 Stanley Weintraub, *Edward the Caresser*, The Free Press, New York, 2001, page 394

15 Professor Stanley Weintraub in *Edward the Caresser*, pp 394 bases his account on the words of royal physician Sir Francis Laking and Lord Esher who insisted that Edward VII was comatose and did not recognise Alice and records Alice's hysterics as to what will happen to her. This conflicts with Alice's account of the King's death which omits the hysterics and has the King recognising her.

16 Theo Aronson, *The King in Love, Edward VII's Mistresses*, London, 1989 takes the same viewpoint as Weintraub claiming Sir Francis Laking took Alice Keppel away from the dead King after Alice's hysterical outburst and kept her in Sir Frederick Ponsonby's office until she had calmed down. Lord Esher in *Journals and Letters*, claimed *he* led the hysterical Mrs Keppel out of the room following her outburst once she realised she would not receive the promised gift of money as the King was dead.

17 WS Blunt, *My Diaries, Being a Personal Narrative of Events 1888-1914*, M Secker, London, 1919, and A. A. Knopf, New York, 1921.

18 George V did not realise that the portrait of Alice Keppel, commissioned by Edward VII, remained in the Royal Collection. The Pictures Library staff of the Royal Collection confirm it is still in the collection.

19 Keppel, Sonia *Edwardian Daughter*. Hamish Hamilton, London, reprinted 1958, pp 83-4.

20 Vita Sackville-West's second son, Nigel, recorded Vita and Violet's love affair in *'Portrait of a Marriage'*, Weidenfeld and Nicholson, London 1992, based on his mother's diary.

21 Glendinning, Victoria, *Vita, The Life of Vita Sackville-West*, page 97.

22 Details of the affair between Violet and Vita from differing viewpoints are in Nigel Nicholson's *Portrait of a Marriage*; Souhami, Diane, *Mrs Keppel and Her Daughters* and Glendenning, Victoria, *Vita, The Life of Vita Sackville-West*.

23 Keppel, Sonia. *Edwardian Daughter*, page 199.

24 Details from *The Tatler and Bystander*, December 1920.

25 See *The Letters of Violet Trefusis to Vita Sackville-West 1910-1921* (ed) John Phillips and Philippe Julian, published London, 1976.

26 Villa dell'Ombrellino. Piazza di Bellosguardo,11-50124 Florence. For details contact them on info@villadellombrellino.it.

27 Villa dell'Ombrellino today has become a function centre for weddings and conferences run by Doney's Catering.

28 Related by Harold Acton in his classic reference work, *Tuscan Villas*, Thames and Hudson, 1958.

29 Diana Souhami, *Mrs Keppel and Her Daughters*, p 260.

30 Channon, Sir Henry. *The Diaries of Chips Channon* (ed) Robert Rhodes James, Weidenfeld and Nicholson, London, 1967.

CHAPTER 7

1 The eminent paediatrician and child psychiatrist Dr Donald Winnicot in his classic work *The Child, the Family and the Outside World* (Tavistock Press, London 1974) referred to nannies masturbating male toddlers to soothe them and send them to sleep. Dr Winnicott warned that in adult life these boys run the risk of remaining sexually 'imprinted' on their nannies as happened to Prince Edward. This condition has become a

recognised psychiatric syndrome classified as *paraphilia*, which can have various manifestations.

2 Prince Edward's mumps orchitis stunted his growth and caused sexual problems including erectile dysfunction and premature ejaculation.

3 In February 2012, a number of letters, written by Prince Edward to Freda on his 1920 tour of Australia, were purchased by the State Library of New South Wales. These poorly spelled, repetitive and anguished letters, addressed to Freda's home at No 1, Cumberland Place, Regent's Park, were sent from Australia to London in the diplomatic bag. To secure the contents of each envelope, the Prince used a gold seal, and imprinted their special seal on his envelopes, using blue sealing wax.

4 Letters from the Prince of Wales to Freda Dudley Ward appear in *Freda Dudley Ward: Letters from a Prince*, (ed) Rupert Godfrey, London, 1998.

5 Letter dated 18 November 1920, from *Letters from a Prince*, (ed.) Rupert Godfrey, 1998.

6 Cited in *Freda Dudley Ward, Letters from a Prince*, 1998. See also 'Fractured Fairy Tales: An Archive of Romance' *New York Times*, June 2003.

7 Mrs Tilly Davies quoted in Mitchell Owens, 'Fractured Fairy Tales: An Archive of a Royal Romance', *The New York Times*, June 8, 2003 just before Sotheby's New York auction of the second group of letters.

CHAPTER 8

1 At the time of writing Thelma's entry on Wikipaedia cites two different spellings of the family name, incorrectly spelt Hayes — Hays being the correct spelling.

2 The history of the Valdeviesos was told in a journal written in Spanish by Consuelo when living with her second husband in Chile in the 1920s. Purchased by the author from a second-hand bookshop in London in the 1950s, it was sold a few months later by a Barcelona dealer in rare books to a Chilean collector. The journal's current whereabouts are unknown.

3 The Vanderbilts became wealthy due to Cornelius Vanderbilt, Senior who made his fortune from investing in ferries and railroads.

4 The myth that Thelma formed her own film company aged 17 appears in her Wikipedia entry. Thelma did not receive her divorce settlement until 1925 by which time she was 21 and could then form her own film company. Silent films in which Thelma Morgan appeared include *The Young Diana* (1922)); *Enemies of Women*, (1923) with Lionel Barrymore and Clara Bow, *So This is Marriage*, (1924) and *Any Woman (1925)*.

5   One of Richard Bennett's daughters was Joan Bennett who starred with Spencer Tracey in *Father of the Bride* and other major films.

6   The Astors and the Rockefellers were 'old money' and regarded the Vanderbilts as *nouveau riche* upstarts.

7   Details about the mysterious death of Lady Daisy Furness aboard her husband's yacht at www.simontsler.com/macleans/daisyhogg, placed on the net by Simon Tesler, her cousin,

8   *Double Exposure: A Twin Autobiography,* London, 1955 and New York, 1958 page 266 is highly romanticised. Thelma claimed to friends and her sisters the Prince of Wales had been a ' limp lover' and Consuelo recorded this with the Spanish word *'debil'* or weak in her journal.

9   The effect on Leydig cells is to give impaired levels of testosterone to adolescent sufferers from a mumps orchitis. The biomedical term *infantile paraphilia* invented by a disciple of Freud, applies to Edward, Prince of Wales whose sole love object during his first three years was his nanny and rarely saw his mother, Queen Mary. As a result Nanny Green as a love object was imprinted' on him. She chastised and humiliated him and this had the effect of arousing him sexually which he craved in later life in order to become aroused. Fear he was unable to sire an heir and would be ridiculed as an impotent king may also have contributed to Edward's desire to abdicate.

10 Thelma Furness and Gloria Vanderbilt. *Double Exposure: A Twin Memoir* . London, 1955 and New York, 1958.

11 The Wikipedia entry on Lord Furness shows him divorcing Thelma Furness in 1933 citing Prince Aly Khan as co-respondent. However, they had not met by then and would not meet until after her divorce from Lord Furness was finalised.

12 Patricia Cavendish O'Neill. *A Lion in the Bedroom.* Park Street Press, Sydney, 2005.

13 Eventually most of the Furness fortune was awarded to Anthony, Thelma's son as Captain Dick Furness VC was killed at Dunkirk.

14 The letter signed by Thelma from Walter Monckton's papers in Oxford's Bodleian Library is illustrated on page 57 of Patricia Cavendish O'Neil *A Lion in the Bedroom.*

15 Consuelo moved to California after Bernie's death and after some years married again to Alfons Landa, a Californian lawyer and airline executive.

16 Grave No 2, Lot 176. Consuelo asked to be buried beside Bernie Thaw rather than beside her Alfons Landa, her third husband.

17 Pat Cavendish O'Neill, *A Lion in the Bedroom* (2005), pp 118-119. Pat Cavendish was only twelve at the time.

18 In her journal Consuelo related what Thelma confided about Edward's chastisement by his nanny, using the Spanish phrase *dar cachetazos* which translates as 'to give blows to the buttocks.

19 Jonathan Gathorne Hardy in *The Rise and Fall of the British Nanny London, 1989* stated that in Victorian England it was usual for nannies to masturbate little boys who had trouble in sleeping. Histories of prostitution relate that many London brothels had rooms dedicated to pleasuring male clients who associated spanking or whipping with sexual release.

20 Pat Cavendish O'Neill *A Lion in the Bedroom*, Park Street Press, Sydney

21 Patricia Cavendish, *A Lion in the Bedroom* stated that Enid, her mother genuinely loved Lord Furness, something Thelma always denied.

22 From the obituary of Anthony Furness in *The Times* dated 12.5.95.

CHAPTER 9

1 In the census records Wallis's first name is given as Bessiewallis. She dropped 'Bessie' (her aunt's name) and called herself 'Wallis' (the name of her dead father).

2 Wallis, Duchess of Windsor, *The Heart has its Reasons, Memoirs of the Duchess of Windsor*, Michael Joseph, London and New York, 1956. This romanticized and often incorrect memoir was mainly written by ghost writers.

3 Osterley House and the surrounding park, owned by the National Trust of Great Britain, are open to the public. For opening times see www.nationaltrust.osterleypark

4 Samuel Kirk and Sons made superb silver flatware for the table and ornaments using original patterns from the great English and American silversmiths of the past.

5 Michael Bloch and Anne Sebba suggest Wallis may have suffered from a Disorder of Sexual Development (DSD), a mild form of Androgen Insensitivity Syndrome (AIS). Her Parisian doctor examined the Duchess Windsor's body after her death, but found no genital mal-formation.

6 Wallis Windsor, *The Heart has its Reasons*, Michael Joseph, London, 1956, p 91.

7   British Secret Service reports on Mrs Simpson released to the public in 2003 contained false accounts of Wallis's working in Chinese brothels.
8   Ziegler, Philip, Windsor, Wallis, Duchess of, in an entry from *The Oxford Dictionary of National Biography*, Oxford University Press, 2004.
9   Mrs Milton Miles, a friend of Commander Win Spencer alleged Wallis had aborted a child by Count Ciano, an allegation which remains unproven and like many allegations about Wallis and her lovers seems unlikely.
10 Alberto Da Zara's memoir was titled *Pelle dell Amiraglio*, Milan, 1946.
11 Anne Sebba in *That Woman, The Life of Wallis Simpson, Duchess of Windsor*. Weidenfeld and Nicholson, London, 2011. pp 64-65 was the first to discover that Ernest's father was of Jewish origin and his family name was originally Solomon.
12 Anne Sebba *That Woman*, p 62.
13 Anne Sebba. *That Woman*, pages 59-60.
14 Edward, Prince of Wales met Freda Dudley Ward, sheltering under the porch of the Belgrave Square house belonging to Ernest Simpson's elder sister, years before Ernest and Wallis moved to London.
15 Vanderbilt, Gloria and Furness, Thelma, *Double Exposure, A Twin Autobiography*, David McKay, New York 1958 and London, Frederick Muller, 1959.
16 Lady Alexandra Metcalfe's unpublished diary, cited in Anne de Courcy, *The Viceroy's Daughters, Lives of the Curzon Sisters*, Weidenfeld and Nicholson, London, 2000.
17 Charles Higham, in *Mrs Simpson, Secret Lives of the Duchess of Windsor*, Sidgewick and Jackson, 1998, claimed Wallis acquired a variety of sexual techniques in Shanghai brothels, detailed in the 'China Dossier'. Many historians claim such a document never existed.
18 Recorded in Spanish in Consuelo Thaw's journal whose current whereabouts are unknown.
19 Anne Seba, *That Woman*, page 99, has Wallis claim that Ernest was with her at Fort Belvedere when Thelma arrived. Thelma contradicts this and she claimed Ernest was away on business.
20 Frances Donaldson. *Edward VIII. The Road to Abdication*, London, 1978, page 83. The late Frances Donaldson had access to the diaries of Lady Alexandra 'Baba' Metcalfe, wife of Major Edward 'Fruity' Metcalfe..

21 Lowndes, Marie Bellock. *Diaries and Letters of Marie Bellock Lowndes* edited by Susan Lowndes, Chatto and Windus, London, 1938 and 1971.

22 Frances Donaldson. *Edward VIII, The Road to Abdication*, p 84.

23 Personal Papers, Walter Monckton. Balliol College, Oxford.

24 Wallis Windsor, *The Heart has its Reasons*, Michael Joseph, 1956. p 197.

25 From the diary of Colonel Sir Clive Wigram, Assistant Private Secretary to George V cited in Sarah Bradford, *George V*, St Martins' Press, New York, 1990, p 173.

26 *Letters of Noel Coward* (ed) Barry Day, Methuen, London, 2007. p 691 and *The War of the Windsors*, Picknet, L, Prince, C. and Prior S., Hardie Grant Books, Sydney, 2002.

27 In 2002, the Public Record Office claimed that 'a dossier on Mrs Simpson's sexual exploits and her spying in the Far East would be held back by the Public Record Office for up to another 35 years'. No reason for this prolongation of the time limit of papers normally available under Freedom of Information legislation was cited.

28 Frances Donaldson, *Edward VIII, The Road to Abdication*, London, 1978 pp 102-103 cites the full conversation between Rickatson-Hatt and Monckton.

29 Picknett L, Prince C, Prior S, *War of the Windsors*, Hardie Grant Books, 2005, p 128. As the authors point out, this was euthanasia, illegal for the general public but permissible for monarchs.

30 Information from King George V's Private Secretary, later Keeper of the Archives, Colonel Sir Clive Wigram, cited in Sarah Bradford, *George V*, 1990, p 174.

31 Frances Donaldson, *Edward VIII, The Road to Abdication*, London, 1978, p 96.

32 See Sarah Bradford, *George V, 1990*, p 165.

33 Wallis, Duchess of Windsor, *The Heart has its Reasons*, p 222.

34 Noted in Higham, Charles, *Mrs Simpson, Secret lives of The Duchess of Windsor*, Sidgwick and Jackson, 1998 and Bloch, Michael, (ed) Wallis and Edward, *Letters 1931-1937*. Weidenfeld and Nicholson, London, 1987.

35 Anne Seba, *That Woman – The Life of the Duchess of Windsor* contains the full story of the broken friendship between Mary Raffray and Wallis Simpson, Mary's marriage to Ernest and Wallis's subsequent letters to Ernest as Duchess of Windsor in which she often tells him how lonely she was when married to the Duke.

36   Information from my father's cousin, the late Sir Tyrone Guthrie of Annaghmakerrig House, County Monaghan, who was related to the Fitzgeralds. A report from an M15 agent mentions Edward Fitzgerald m as one of the Duchess of Windsor's lovers but gives no further details. He appeared before the House of Lords as a bankrupt at the end of 1936.

37   Guests included the Dukes of Buccleuch and Queensberry, the Duke and Duchess of Sutherland, the Duke and Duchess of Marlborough, the Duke and Duchess of Kent and Lord and Lady Mountbatten.

38   Bradford, Sarah. *George V*, p 175.

39   The wife and the children of a morganatic marriage do not have the same status as the husband and cannot inherit his possessions.

40   Ben Fenton in the *Daily Telegraph*, reprinted in *The Sydney Morning Herald* on 2 December, 2006, p 13.

41   Wallis's description in her memoir, *The Heart has its Reasons (1956)*..

42   Theodore Goddard's papers were burned when his office was bombed during the London blitz.

43   See Anne de Courcy, *The Viceroy's Daughters*.

44   Jim, Christy, *The Price of Power: A Biography of Charles Eugene Bedaux*, Doubleday, New York, 1984.

45   Lynn Picknett and Stephen Prior. *The War of the Windsors*, Mainstream Press, London 2003 and Hardie Grant, Melbourne, 2007.

46   The FBI presented a report on the Duchess of Windsor's pro-Nazi activities to President Roosevelt in 1941 and American Ambassador in London Joseph Kennedy was also informed by MI5. One of Edward's cousins, a German duke turned monk assured the FBI that the Duke of Windsor was impotent and Wallis was the only woman able to help him with his problems.

47   Major Metcalfe managed to escape from Paris before the German Army were able to capture and imprison him.

48   Information from Sir John Ward, British Ambassador to the Argentine in the 1950s to the author, his niece, related in 1958 at The Mill House, Farningham, Kent where he had retired.

49   Madonna's film *W.E.* while good on details of costumes and jewels presents a romanticised view of Wallis and Edward and at one point suggests that Wallis did not have Nazi friends or affiliations. Lack of research has a news vendor announcing the death of George III rather than the death of George V.

50 Leaving jail in Britain in 1947, Anna de Wolkoff, friend of many members of the pro-Nazi Right Club whose membership list has recently been published as 'The Red Book' and includes several British dukes, Lord and Lady Redesdale, parents of Diana Mosely and several wealthy g businessmen died in a mysterious car accident in Spain. Wolkoff may have been killed to silence her because she knew too much about Hess's mysterious flight to Scotland. The Spanish file on her car accident has since disappeared.

51 Jim Christie and Charles Higham have both written biographies of Charles Bedaux. He was arrested by the Free French in Africa in World War 2, extradited by the Americans and committed suicide in jail.

52 Wallis's letters to Ernest Simpson discovered by Anne Sebba are quoted in *That Woman, The Life of Wallis Simpson*.

53 Bloch, Michael. *Wallis and Edward, Letter 1934 – 1937*, p 191.

54 Patricia Cavendish O'Neill, *A Lion the Bedroom*, p 298.

55 The Duchess of Windsor, *The Heart has its Reasons*, Michael Joseph, published London, 1956 went into several editions.

56 During the war Sir Oswald Mosley and Lady Mosley, had been arrested and jailed in Britain.

57 Diana Mosley, *The Duchess of Windsor*, Sidgwick and Jackson, London, 1980.

58 Diana Mosley, *The Duchess of Windsor. 1980*.

59 Details from Charles Higham, *The Duchess of Windsor, the Secret Life*, London, 1998.

60 Charles Higham, *The Duchess of Windsor, the Secret Life*, p 434-5.

61 Personal papers including correspondence between the Duke of Windsor and his brothers were removed from the Windsor's Paris house in an unmarked lorry without Wallis' permission after the Duke died when she was too ill to protest. The lorry was allegedly sent by Lord Mountbatten and the whereabouts of the papers are unknown. The letters of Freda Dudley Ward to Edward may have been among them. Edward warned Wallis to beware that Mountbatten who might try to obtain their personal papers. L. Picknett, C. Prince and S. Prior. *The War of the Windsors*, 2007, pp 224-291.

62 The lease of Windsors Paris house was purchased by Mahommed al Fayed, whose son Dodi would take Princess Diana to see the house shortly before he and Diana died in a road accident in Paris, a death which leaves many questions unanswered. A film funded by al Fayed

forbidden a showing in England voices his views. It is interesting that a film of the Windsors' wedding was forbidden to be shown in England in 1936 as it was regarded as subversive.

63 The Duke of Windsor told Wallis to beware of his cousin, Dieckie Mountbatten, who had been his friend when they were young but felt he had become 'power-crazy, avaricious liar'. See Picknett, C. Prince and S. Prior. *War of the Windsors, 2007, pp 224-291.*

64 The two-day sale of the jewels of the Duchess of Windsor took place a year after Wallis's death, on 2 April 1987 in Geneva. Sotheby's were warned it would be offensive to the British royal family to sell the jewels in London. Elizabeth Taylor bought the diamond brooch of Prince of Wales's feathers given to Wallis by the Duke which Prince Charles had contemplated buying for Camilla. After Elizabeth Taylor died in 2011 and the same diamond brooch made over $1 million at a Christie's sale.

CHAPTER 10

1 Details on George Cubbit from Wikipedia, and in Gyles Brandreth's *Charles and Camilla, Portrait of a Love Affair*, Century, London, 2005, pp 55-56. The Cubbit building empire no longer exists and has become part of the building conglomerate known as 'Tarmac.'

2 Gyles Brandreth, *Charles and Camilla, Portrait of a Love Affair*, pp 107-8.

3 Dale Tryon claimed to have had had an affair with Prince Charles to several journalists but no evidence in the form of letters has ever been produced to confirm this. Dale's brother Derek Harper confirmed in a letter to *The Australian* newspaper that allegations her husband had something to do with her fall from a balcony were untrue. He claimed his sister's depressive illness was aggravated by the antidepressant drug Prozac which made it worse, leading to her attempted suicide in a private psychiatric clinic.

4 'HRH is very fond of my wife', Holden, Anthony, *Charles a Biography*, Bantam Press, London, 1998, pp 139.

5 When Diana's bulimia reached crisis point, a close female friend feared she was suicidal, and insisted she see the psychiatrist Dr Maurice Liversedge, who specializes in the treatment of bulimia who was able to help her.

6 Benson, Ross, *Charles the Untold Story*, Gollancz, London, 1993. page 143

7 The Camillagate tapes originally had their own Google website, now removed.

8   In 1995 Jonathan Dimbleby wrote about the love affair between Camilla and Prince Charles in *The Prince of Wales* in which Charles annoyed many people for blaming his father for much of his predicament.

9   Cited by Gyles Brandreth, *Charles and Camilla*, page 274, source not provided.

10 The late Dr Janet Irwin was the aunt of Alexander McCall Smith and related his account of a weekend spent at Highgrove to the author who was a close friend.

11 This skin cream contains a percentage of bee-venom which increases blood flow to the skin and aids the elasticity of the skin by mimicking the effects of a bee sting.

12 Ingrid Seward's comments in the *Australian Women's Weekly*, February, 2007, *Stories everyone's talking about* by William Langley. Several internet sites contained scathing references to Camilla's ample cleavage adorned with huge jewels as 'tacky'.

13 The term 'morganatic' as defined by the Shorter Oxford Dictionary is 'A marriage between a man of exalted rank and a woman of lower station in which neither the wife nor her children share the dignity or inherit the possessions of the husband'.

14 The TV program *Queen Camilla*, shown on Channel 4, 31 May, 2007, produced by Blakewell Productions featured 'a nameless source close to the royal family; saying 'The statement by Clarence House that Camilla would be Princess Consort was only a smoke screen. *We* all know that Charles wants Camilla as his Queen. But, to look good Charles has to deny this, since it's constitutionally inappropriate for the Prince to say his real aim is to have Camilla as Queen beside him. Another staff member of the Royal Household claimed on the TV programmed, 'You can win the public round to *anything* as long as you do it *slowly* enough.' which is probably true.

INDEX

A

Abercorn, Duke of, 97
Acton, Sir Harold, 203
Adelaide, Queen, 2, 89
Aga Khan, Prince, 276
Ahlden Castle, 9
Aird, John, 314
Albert Edward, (Bertie) Prince of Wales (see Edward {VII} Prince of Wales
Albert, Prince (husband of Queen Victoria), 140, 180
Alexandra of Denmark, Princess of Wales, 7, 96, 100, 102, 103, 113, 122, 141, 147, 149, 150, 152, 158
Alexandra, Queen, 171, 181, 183, 184, 185, 187, 188, 191, 192, 193, 194, 207
Alington, Lord Henry, 178, 181
Althorp, 370, 372
Al-Waleed bin Talal, Prince, 392
Aly Khan, Prince, 275-277, 309, 310
Ancaster, Duke of, 48
Andrew, Prince, 381
Anne, Princess (later Queen Anne), 5, 7, 13, 14, 17, 73
Arbuthnot, Lady Harriet, 89
Armistead, Lizzie, 43
Armstrong, Louis, 253
Armstrong-Jones, Tony, 381
Ashcombe, Lord, 200
Augustus, Duke of Sussex, Prince, 75
Augustus, Elector of Hanover, 12
Aylesford, Earl of, 102
Aylesford, Lady Edith, 102, 103

B

Bagehot, Walter, 53
Baldwin, Stanley, Prime Minister, 313, 318, 322, 333, 334, 337
Balmoral Castle, 320, 330, 366, 370, 371, 374, 377
Barnard, Lady Anne, 80
Beaton, Cecil, 237
Beckett, William, 176-178, 189
Bedaux, Charles, 338, 340, 342, 345
Bellosguardo, 389
Benckendorf, General Alexander von, 88
Bennett, Richard, 241
Beresford, Lady Minna, 143-150
Beresford, Lord Charles, 103, 143, 144, 155
Bernhardt, Sarah, 128, 182, 190
Bertie, Susan, 48
Birkin, Charles Wilfred, 217
Blandford, Lord George, 97
Blatchford, Robert, 154, 155
Blenheim Palace, 16, 98-100, 107, 245
Blunt, John, 17
Blunt, Wilfred Scawen, 180, 184, 195
Bodiam Castle, 360
Bolyhyde Manor, 365, 374, 378
Bowes-Lyon, Lady Elizabeth, 3
Brambridge House, 54
Brett, Lady Anne, 14, 15
Brett, Reginald , 2nd Viscount Esher, 189
Bridgeman, Lord Orlando, 68
Brighton Pavilion (see Royal Brighton Pavilion)
British South Seas Company, 17-19
Brook's Club, 33, 34, 38, 39, 45, 46, 58, 60, 70
Brooke, Lady Daisy, 105, 137-166, 172, 178, 181, 182, 195, 394
Brooke, Lady Daisy, marriage of, 141
Brooke, Lady Daisy, death of, 166

Brooke, Guy, 147, 165
Brooke, Leonie, 117
Brooke, Lord Francis Greville 'Brookie', 139-141, 144, 145, 148, 150, 151, 153, 157, 159, 164, 165
Brooke, Marjorie, 143, 153
Brooke, Maynard Greville, 158
Bruce, Robert the, 172
Brunswick, Duke of, 7
Bryanston Court, 300, 304, 308, 322-324, 329, 347
Brydges, Henry James, Duke of Chandon, 15
Buckingham House, 34, 35, 38, 42, 71
Buckingham Palace, 34, 86, 114, 122, 174, 191, 192, 199, 219, 221, 247, 264, 303, 308, 313, 316, 317, 320, 326, 354, 369, 370, 375, 376, 387, 392, 395
Burke, Kevin, 362
Burke, Reverend Robert, 67
Burke, Sir Aubrey, 362
Burrough Court, 248-251, 255, 263, 269, 270, 273, 274
Buzzard, Dr Thomas, 104

C

Cameron, Roderick, 267
Camillagate tapes, 359, 387
Camp, Anthony J., 121
Campbell, Mrs Pat, 129
Cannon, Dr Alexander, 327, 334
Carioccolo, Duchess di, 129, 182
Carlton House, 34, 38, 44, 45, 60, 62, 64, 65, 66, 69-73, 79, 80, 82
Carol, King, 205
Caroline of Brunswick-Wolfenbuttel, Princess, 76-78
Caroline, Princess of Wales, 6, 13, 16
Cartland, Barbara, 372

Casa Maury, Count Pedro (Peter) Jose de, 230
Cassel, Sir Ernest, 121, 128, 151, 180, 181, 189, 190, 192-194
Castle Leslie, 117
Castlerosse, Vincent, 284
Caswall, George, 17
Catherine, Duchess of Cambridge, 376, 378, 385-387, 393-396
Cavendish O'Neill, Patricia, 284
Cavendish, Caryll, 273
Cavendish, Enid, (see Lindeman, Cavendish Enid)
Cavendish, Lord Charles, 258
Cavendish, Patricia, 273, 284
Chamberlain, Neville, 337
Chandos, Duke of, 15, 17, 19
Charles, Prince of Wales, 187, 363-374, 377-384, 387-395
Charlotte, Princess, 79, 80, 83, 84
Charlotte, Queen, 1, 33, 74, 75
Chesterfield, Earl of, 14
Child Kirk, Mary, 291
Chisholm, David Anthony, 227
Chisholm, Roy, 225, 227
Christie, Harold, 346
Churchill John (Jack), 121, 126
Churchill, Clementine, 181
Churchill, General John, 98
Churchill, John Strange Spencer, 105
Churchill, Lady Jennie, 93-132, 152, 154, 165, 166, 179, 186
Churchill, Lady Jennie, third marriage of, 131
Churchill, Lady Jennie, death of, 132
Churchill, Lady Randolph, (see Churchill, Lady Jennie)
Churchill, Lord Randolph, 96-107, 110, 111, 116-118, 127

Churchill, Winston, 107, 100, 110, 127, 128, 130, 181, 183, 313, 319, 332, 344
Churchill, Winston Leonard Spencer, (see Churchill, Winston)
Ciano, Count Galeazzo, 296
Clarence House, 384, 393
Clarke, Mary Anne, 84, 85, 234, 394
Clarke, Sir Edward, 149
Clifden, Nellie, 141
Clingendaal House, 197
Cole, Mrs, 81
Coleridge, Samuel Taylor, 45, 48
Connaught, Duke of, 128
Conyngham, Lady Elizabeth, 2, 87, 88
Conyngham, Lord, 87
Cornwall, Duchy of, 34, 35, 217, 221
Cornwallis-West, George, 123, 124, 129
Cornwallis-West, Patsy, 123, 130
Cosway, Richard, 60
Countess of Warwick, Daisy, (see Brooke, Lady Daisy)
Coutts Bank, 36, 77
Covent Garden, 27, 58, 67, 72, 192
Coward, Noel, 257, 349
Crole, Elizabeth, 49, 50
Crole, George, 49
Cros, Arthur du, 161
Cubbitt, George, 360
Cubbitt, Rolie (Baron Ashcombe), 200, 201, 206, 360
Cubitt, Rosalind, 360
Cubitt, Sonia, 201, 205, 206, 360, 382 (see also Keppel, Sonia)
Cubitt, Thomas, 200
Curzon, Lady Mary, 178

D

d'Abernon, Lord, 105
Dalrymple Elliott, Grace, 40
Darby, Captain John, 25, 26
Darby, Hester, 25-28
Dawson, Sir Bernard, 320
Devonshire, Duke of, 100
Devonshire, Georgiana, Duchess of, 30, 58-60, 63-65, 74
Devonshire House, 59, 64, 65
Diana, Her True Story, 379
Diana, Princess of Wales, 84, 361, 370-373, 375-383, 385-389
Dimbleby, Jonathan, 379
Disraeli, Prime Minister, 103, 139
Dominguez, 'Buster', 213
Donahue, Jessie, 348
Donahue, Jimmy, 348, 349
Double Exposure, 275, 281, 282
Downshire, Kitty, Marchioness of, 158
Drury Lane Theatre, 31, 32, 35, 37, 72
Duchess of Cornwall, Camilla, (see Parker Bowles, Camilla)
Duchy of Cornwall, 308, 311, 313, 320, 335
Dudley Ward, Angela (Angie), 217, 292
Dudley Ward, Freda, 213-231, 394, 396
Dudley Ward, Freda, death of, 231
Dudley Ward, Freda, first marriage of, 217
Dudley Ward, Freda, second marriage of, 230
Dudley Ward, Penelope, 217, 231
Dudley Ward, William, 217, 230
Dunmore, Lord, 75
Dunne, Dominic, 283
Duntreath Castle, 172-174

INDEX

E

Easton Lodge, 115, 140, 142, 143, 146, 147, 150, 162-165
Edmonstone, Archie, 183
Edmonstone, Lady Alice, 172-174
Edmonstone, Sir William, 174
Edward (VII), Prince of Wales, 3, 96, 100, 102, 106, 109, 111, 114, 119, 141, 145-149, 151, 171, 178
Edward (VIII), Prince of Wales, 213, 243, 252-254, 257-267, 269, 271, 272, 274, 275, 281, 302, 303, 306, 308, 311, 314
Edward VII, King, 93, 127, 128, 129, 130, 137, 163, 171, 178, 182, 183, 192
Edward VIII, King, 289, 320-325, 327-333, 335, 337, 338, 340, 346
Edward VIII, King, abdication of, 338
Edward, Duke of Windsor, 289, 338-347, 353, 354
Edward, Duke of Windsor, death of, 354
Edward, Prince, Duke of Kent (son of Queen Victoria), 2, 81, 90
Egremont, Lord, 81
Elizabeth, Duchess of York, 258, 317, 330, 331, 334, 335, 339
Elizabeth II, Her Majesty the Queen, 370, 381,384, 392
Errington, Henry, 58, 67, 68
Errington, Mary, 54
Esher, Lord, 181, 183, 189, 192-194, 217
Espil, Felipe, 294, 298
Eugenie, Empress, 95
Everest, Nanny, 107, 116

F

Fairbanks Senior, Douglas, 240, 281
Falmouth, Viscount, 105
Fermoy, Lady, 370, 371
Fitzgerald, Edward, 305, 325
Fitzherbert, Maria, 53-90, 385
Fitzherbert, Maria, first marriage of, 53
Fitzherbert, Maria, second marriage of, 55
Fitzherbert, Maria, death of, 90
Fitzherbert, Thomas, 54-57
Fort Belvedere, 220, 230, 254, 257, 265, 266, 271, 275, 276, 304, 305, 307, 308-310, 312, 314-317, 320-322, 327, 330, 332, 336, 338, 345, 347
Fox, Charles James, 43, 53, 60, 68, 69
Frederick, Prince of Wales, 34
Frederick, Prince, Duke of York, 34, 67, 84
Fredericka Charlotte, Princess of Prussia, 84
Frewin, Moreton, 110, 154
Friedericke, Princess, 313
Furness, the Hon Anthony, 279, 280, 284, 285
Furness, the Hon Averill, 242, 248, 249, 251, 270, 273, 278
Furness, the Hon Christopher 'Dick', 242, 245, 248, 278
Furness, Lady Daisy, 256, 271, 272,
Furness, Lady Enid, (see Lindeman Cavendish, Enid)
Furness, Lady Janet, 249
Furness, Lady Thelma, 230, 234-286, 280, 284, 302, 303, 305
Furness, Lady Thelma, marriage to Marmaduke Furness (second marriage), 246
Furness, Lady Thelma, death of, 281

Furness, Lord Marmaduke, 242-249, 251-263, 265, 266, 268-273, 278, 279, 281, 283-285, 306
Furness, William Anthony, 262

G
Gainsborough, Thomas, 44
Garrick, David, 27, 28, 30, 31
George Augustus, Prince of Wales 'Prinny', 6, 8, 9, 13, 25, 32-36, 38-41, 53, 56, 60-66, 70-72, 75, 81, 83
George I, King, 5-7, 10-22,
George II, King, 20-22, 61,
George III, King, 1, 33, 34, 41-43, 50, 63, 66, 69, 72-75, 84, 86, 88
George IV, King, 2, 25, 53, 84, 86-89, 172, 228, 418
George Ludwig of Hanover, Prince, 5
George Ludwig, Prince, 6
George V, King, 3, 130, 158, 160-163, 195, 216, 222, 228, 313, 317, 318, 320
George VI, King, 3, 323, 340, 345, 348, 354
George, Duke of Kent, 315
Gillray, James, 50, 61, 65, 83
Goddard, Theodore, 280, 337
Goebbels, Josef, 352
Goering, Hermann, 342
Gordon, Lord George, 56
Gordon-Cummings, Sir William, 149
Green, Nanny, 215, 218, 219, 282, 283
Greville, Hon Ronnie, 186
Greville, Maggie, 186, 205
Greville, Sir Charles, 25
Grimthorpe (see Becket, William),
Guelph, 4, 10

H
Haggerston, Lady Frances, 56, 59
Hamilton, Lady Bertha, 97
Hardinge, Alec, 312
Harper, Dale (see Tryon, Dale)
Harper, Derek, 380, 381
Harris, Frank, 160-164
Harry, Prince (son of Prince Charles and Princess Diana), 386
Hartington, Lord, 100
Hays Morgan, Harry, 235
Hays Morgan, Thelma, (see Furness, Lady Thelma)
Henry VIII, King, 386
Henry, Duke of Gloucester, Prince, 229
Herrenhausen Palace, 8, 9, 21
Hertford House, 82
Hertford, Lady Isabella, 75, 82, 83
Hertford, Lord, 45
Hess, Rudolf, 342
Highgrove, 367, 374, 377, 383, 389-391
Hitler, Adolf, 318, 319, 321, 339, 342-344, 352
Hogarth, William, 18
Hogg, Daisy, 242
Holland, Henry, 62, 71
Hoppner, John, 32, 44
House of Kanga, 380
Howard, Henrietta, 22, 61

I
Irwin, Dr Janet, 390

J
Jenkins, Janet, 385
Jerome, Clara, 93
Jerome, Jennie, (see Churchill, Lady Jennie)

Jerome, Leonard, 93-99, 108, 123
Jersey, Lady Frances, 75-79
Jocelyn, Colonel John Strange, 105
Jordan, Dorothea 'Dora', 70, 77, 86, 89

K

'Kanga', 366, 368 (see Tryon, Dale)
Keate, Mr, 64
Keith, Dr Thomas, 119
Kenmare, Lady Enid, 283, 284 (see also Lindeman Cavendish, Enid)
Kensington Gardens, 16
Kensington Palace, 10, 12-16, 81, 90, 383
Keppel, Alice, 127, 128, 130, 171-206, 360, 363, 383, 391
Keppel, Alice, marriage of, 175
Keppel, Alice, death of, 207
Keppel, Hon George, 174-178, 183, 186, 196, 197, 202, 203
Keppel, Joost van, 175
Keppel, Sonia, 177, 187, 199, 200,
Keppel, Violet, 176-178, 184, 188, 196, 199
Kerr-Smiley, Maude, 214, 298, 301
Keyser, Agnes, 192
Kielmansegg, Baron von, 13
Kielmansegg, Baroness Sophie von, 12, 13
King of New York, The, 94
King's Bench Debtor's prison, 30
Kinsky, Count Charles (Karl), 109, 110, 119
Kirk Raffray, Mary, 315, 319
Kirk, Mary, 292, 297
Knole House, 176, 182
Knopf, Alfred A., 289
Königsmarck, Count Philip Christoph von, 9, 13, 14, 19

L

Laking, Sir Francis, 192, 193
Lamballe, Princesse de, 74
Lambton, Lady Bindy, 231
Lang, Cosmo, Archbishop of Canterbury, 335
Langbein, Theodore, 165
Langtry, Lillie, 121, 129, 150, 152, 164
Lascelles, Sir Alan, 213, 321, 234
Lawrence, Gertie, 257
Laycock, Joseph 'Joe', 153, 156, 157, 158, 163
Leicester House, 16
Leinster, Duke of, 305, 306, 325, 326
Leopold of Saxe-Coburg, Prince, 84
Leopold, Prince, 138, 139, 141
Leslie, Anita, 115
Leslie, Christopher, 393
Leslie, Jack, 117, 129
Leslie, Shane, 115
Lewis, George, 144, 145
Lewis, Rosa, 114
Lieven, Princess Dorothea von, 88
Lindeman Cavendish, Enid, 267, 272, 273, 278, 280, 283, 306, 349,
Lindesay, Lady Anne, 63, 65
Lipton, Sir Thomas, 183, 196
Little, Mollee, 225-227
Lord Brownlow, 336
Louis XIV, King of France, 74, 153
Lowndes, Mrs Belloc, 312
Lupescu, Magda, 205
Lyons, Joseph, Prime Minister of Australia, 335
Lyttleton, Lord, 29

M

Macclesfield, Countess of, 14
Major, John, Prime Minister, 379
Makepiece Thackeray, William, 21
Malden, Lord, 33-36, 40, 42-46

Malmesbury, Lord, 78
Marble Hill House, 22, 61
Margaret Gertrude, Countess von Schaumberg-Lippe 12
Margaret, Princess, 381, 384
Marie Antoinette, Queen, 74, 153
Marigny, Alfred de, 346
Marina of Greece, Princess, 315
Marlborough House, 100-102, 106, 111, 114, 120, 142, 145, 149, 151, 152, 180, 182, 354
Marlborough House set, 100, 101, 114, 142, 147, 149
Marlborough, Duchess of, 97, 99, 100, 105, 108, 109, 116, 120 (see also Churchill, Lady Jennie)
Marlborough, Duke of, 96, 97, 102, 104, 105, 108, 109 (see also Churchill, Lord Randolph)
Married Woman's Property Act, 26, 31
Mary, Queen, 130, 195, 199, 215, 216, 222, 247, 264, 266, 283, 313, 315, 317, 320, 332, 354
Maugham, Somerset, 283
Maurier, Daphne du, 234
Mayer, Baroness de, 128
Maynard, Blanche Fitzroy, 137
Maynard, Daisy, (see Brooke, Lady Daisy)
Maynard, Frances Evelyn, 137, 138
Maynard, Viscount, 137, 138
McCall Smith, Alexander, 390
McEwan, Sir William, 186
McGlashan, Dr Alan, 378
Melba, Dame Nellie, 198
Melbourne, Lady, 39, 40
Melusine, Duchess of Kendal, 1, 5-21
Merryman, Bessie (Aunt Bessie), 290, 291, 293-296, 298, 299, 301, 308, 314, 329, 345

Metcalfe, Lady Alexandra, 341, 343, 344
Metcalfe, Major Edward 'Fruity', 303, 304, 314, 343
Metternich, Countess Elizabeth, 119
Michael, Princess, 387
Middleton, Kate, (see Catherine, Duchess of Cambridge)
Middleton, Mrs Carole, 395
Mitford, Diana, 352
Mitford, Nancy, 352
Monckton, Sir Walter, 279, 280, 313, 319, 320, 335, 340, 341
Morgan, Laura Consuelo (see Thaw, Consuelo)
Morgan, Laura Delphine, 237
Morgan, Laura Kilpatrick, 235, 238
Morgan, Thelma, (see Furness, Lady Thelma)
Morgan, Thelma, first marriage, 238
Morris, William, 160
Morton, Andrew, 375, 379
Mosley, Lady Diana, 346, 352
Mountbatten, Lord Louis, 3, 222, 340, 353, 363, 364, 369, 370
mumps orchitis, 215, 261
Murray, Hon Augusta, 75

N

Napoleon III, Emperor, 95
Nicholson, Harold, 197, 313
North, Lord John, 42

O

Oakes, Sir Harry, 346
Onslow, Lord, 64, 65
Orleans, Duke of, 66
Osterley Park House, 291

INDEX

P
Paget, Mrs Gerald, 150
Paine, Tom, 380
Palace of St James, 13, 14, 15, 78
Parker Bowles, Andrew, 362, 364, 365, 367, 369, 370, 379
Parker Bowles, Camilla, 3, 187, 200, 201, 207, 359-396
Parker Bowles, Camilla, marriage to Andrew Parker Bowles, 364
Parker Bowles, Camilla, divorce from Andrew Parker Bowles, 383
Parker Bowles, Camilla, marriage to Prince Charles, 385
Parker Bowles, Laura, 367, 382
Parker Bowles, Tom, 382, 366, 387
Payne, Captain Willet, 38, 40
Perdita, (see Robinson, Mary Darby)
Pergami, Bartolemeo, 81
Petronilla Melusina, Countess of Walsingham, 10, 12, 14
Philip, Prince, 3, 363, 373, 385, 386
Pickford, Mary, 240, 242, 281
Piggott, Miss Isabella, 61, 64, 79, 89
Pitman, Rosemary, 383
Pitt, William, Prime Minister, 73
Platen, Countess Clara, 12
Polesden Lacy, 186
Porch, Montagu (Porchy), 131
Pordon, William, 72
porphyria, 17, 83
Prince Charles' Other Mistress, 368
Prinny (see George Augustus, Prince of Wales)

R
Raffray, Jules, 292, 297, 315
Raffray, Mary, 316, 317, 322, 328, 347
Ragley Hall, 82
Raine, Countess of Dartmouth, 372
Ramsden, Captain Caryl Harry, 122
Rasin, John Freeman, 291
Rattray, Andrew, 269-271, 273
Ray Mill House, 383, 390, 391
Ribbentrop, Joachim von, 322
Rickatson-Hatt, Bernard, 319
Robinson, Maria Elizabeth, 30, 31, 35, 36, 43, 50
Robinson, Mary Darby 'Perdita', 25-50, 60, 394
Robinson, Mary Elizabeth, 29, 418
Robinson, Thomas, 27-31, 36, 44
Rogers, Herman, 295, 314, 336, 341
Rogers, Kathleen, 295, 338
Rosalind Cubitt, 204, 207
Rosslyn, Earl of, 138
Rosslyn, Lady, 138, 139, 140
Rothschild, Alfred, 123, 151
Royal (Brighton) Pavilion, 72, 81

S
Sackville, Lionel, 176
Sackville-West, Lady Victoria 'Vita', 176, 177, 182, 184, 196, 201
Sagan, Princess de, 190
Salisbury, Prime Minister, 146
Sandringham, 113, 116, 151, 183, 191, 318, 320, 354, 370, 377, 382
Sarah, Duchess of York, 381
Sargent, Singer, 237
Sassoon, Reuben, 128
Saxe-Coburg-Gotha, Duke of, 342
Schloss Enzesfeld, 339
Schulenburg, Petronilla Melusina von (see Petronilla Melusina, Countess of Walsingham)
Sebba, Anne, 346
Sefton House, 54, 55
Sefton, Earl of, 54, 58
Sefton, Lady Isabella, 54, 55, 57, 59
Seymour, Lady Anne Horatia, 81

Seymour, Lord Hugh, 81
Seymour, Mary Georgina, 81
Seymour, Minnie, 81, 82
Shand Kydd, Frances, 372, 373
Shand, Annabel, 359
Shand, Camilla Rosemary (see Parker Bowles, Camilla)
Shand, Major Bruce, 201, 207, 359, 382, 385
Shand, Mark, 359
Shand, Philip Moreton, 360
Shand, Rosalind, 362
Sharp, Becky, 291
Shaw, George Bernard, 156
Sheridan, Richard Brinsley, 31, 39
Simpson, Dorothea Dechert, 298,
Simpson, Ernest Aldrich, 263, 297-300, 313, 315, 317, 319, 322, 323, 328, 333, 334, 346
Simpson, Wallis Warfield, 230, 263, 274-276, 370, 385, 388, 289-354
Simpson, Wallis, marriage to the Duke of Windsor, 341
Sitwell, Osbert, 202
Slane Castle, 87
Smythe, John, 67, 68, 82
Smythe, Maria, 53
Smythe, Maria, first marriage of, 53
Smythe, Marianne, 82
Soames, Lord Christopher, 369
Sophia Dorothea, Princess of Celle, 7-9, 16, 19, 20, 418
Sophia, Electress of Hanover, 8
South Sea Bubble, 17
Southampton, Lord, 64, 65
Spencer, Lady Diana (see Diana, Princess of Wales)
Spencer, Earl, 372
Spencer, Lieutenant Winfield 'Win', 291-293, 295-297, 307
'Squidgygate Tapes', 381
St Aubyn, Giles, 179

St Laurent, Julie de, 2, 81, 90
Stamfordham, Lord, 161, 162, 163
Stavordale, Lord, 178, 204
Stead, William T., 155, 156
Steine House, 72, 74
Swift, Dean Jonathan, 11
Swynnerton Hall, 54, 55, 57

T

Tarleton, Captain (later Colonel) Banestre 'Ban', 45, 46, 48
Tate Gallery, 18
Thaw, Bernie, 237, 246, 302
Thaw, Consuelo, 235-237, 244-246, 249, 254-256, 262-264, 266, 301, 305
The Heart has its Reasons, 290, 293, 338
'The King's Loosebox', 183
The Mill (home of the Duchess of Windsor), 354
Tilbert, Philip, 165, 166
Townsend, Peter, 384
Tranby Croft, 148, 149
Tranby Croft affair, 148
Treacy, Philip, 385
Trefusis, Major Denys, 198-200
Trefusis, Violet (see Keppel Violet)
Trundle, Guy, 325
Tryon, Charles, 366
Tryon, Lady Dale, 365, 366, 380, 381
Tryon, Lord Anthony, 366
Tryon, Zoe, 366

V

Vail Converse, James, 238-241, 245
Vanderbilt Whitney, Gertrude, 275
Vanderbilt, Gloria, 234, 235, 238-242, 244-246, 274-276, 283, 306
Vanderbilt, Gloria Laura (daughter of Gloria and Reginald Vanderbilt), 274, 275, 281

Vanderbilt, Reginald 'Reggie' Claypole, 239-242, 245, 275
Victoria of Saxe-Coburg-Saalfeld, Princess, 90
Victoria, Queen, 90, 111, 114, 118, 122, 128, 138-140, 149, 152, 160, 172, 175, 180, 187, 188
Villa dell'Ombrellino, 202-204, 206, 207
Villa Eugenie, 190, 191
Villa la Fiorentina, 273, 278, 349
Villa Rosetta, 95, 96

W

Wallmoden, Sophie von, 1, 22
Walpole, Horace, 5, 15, 19, 21
Walpole, Sir Robert, 11, 19
Walters, Catherine 'Skittler', 179, 182, 184, 191, 195
Warfield, Alice, 289, 301
Warfield, Solomon, 290-292, 296, 299
Warfield, Wallis, 289-299 (see also Simpson, Wallis Warfield)
Warfield, Wallis, first marriage of, 292
Warfield, Wallis, marriage to Ernest Simpson, 300
'War of the Wales', 381
Warwick Castle, 123, 139, 140, 150, 151, 153, 155, 156, 159, 160, 163, 165
Warwick, Daisy (see Brooke, Lady Daisy)
Warwick, Daisy, death of, 166
Warwick, Earl of, 139, 140, 150, 153, 159, 163
Wayman, Henry, 28

Webb, Beatrice, 156
Webb, Sydney, 156
Wellington, Duke of, 89
Wells, H.G., 156
Wenner-Gren, Axel, 346
Wesley, Mary, 388
Westminster Abbey, 10, 20, 50, 86, 87, 183, 228
White, Judy, 227
Willett-Payne, Captain Jack, 40, 77
William III, King, 175
William, Prince, Duke of Clarence, 2, 70, 77, 86, 89
William, Prince (son of Charles and Diana), 376, 386, 395, 396
Wilson, Christopher, 349
Wilson, Lady Sarah, 197
Wilson, Sir Arthur, 149
Wilton Crescent, 175, 180
Windsor Castle, 2, 80, 83, 87-89, 115, 138, 141, 149, 221, 227, 228, 258, 308, 354, 355
Wolkoff, Anna de (also known as Anne Wolkova), 302, 312, 327, 342, 345
Wollstonecraft, Mary, 49
Worth, Charles, 95
Wurtemberg, Duke Charles Alexander of, 289

Y

Yarmouth, Lord, 82

Z

Zara, Albert da, 296
Ziegler, Philip, 289

ADDENDA

Excerpt from a letter written by Edward, Prince of Wales, to Freda Dudley Ward during the Prince's 1920 visit to Australia. The complete letter is held by the State Library of New South Wales (Mitchell Library).

> (Letter No 15.)
>
> GOVERNMENT HOUSE
> 3rd June 1920. (6.00.P.M.) MELBOURNE
>
> Fredie darling darling precious beloved a moi
>
> The mail has gone sweetheart tho. I must anyway just begun my next letter as I'm sleeping in the train to-night before another day in the interior & I may not be able to write much as I've got to go to another dance & I wont get to the train before midnight!! Its been a fairly strenuous day tho. things are easing up a bit now; I got a game of squash before lunching with the executive of the "R.S.S.I.L. of A" (the Australian returned men's ——) rather an important stunt needless to say as it was important to impress them favourably tho. I think it was all right!! Then a conferring of a silly hon. degree at the university — waste of time followed by a gov't. garden party from which I've only just got back!! What a life angel but then its nearly over anyway for a week only 2 more days stunting here!! I'll wire to-morrow to let you know about staying on here next week & postponing Sydney & the rest of the Australasian program a whole week in case you see any mad press cables about it all; its all as good as fixed now tho. I'll be more certain to-morrow beloved!! The people here are still very enthusiastic & I still get crowds in the streets when I drive around stunting which really is amazing & frightfully touching after a whole week!! And I feel more or less at home in Australia now at least I feel I understand the people & the general spirit tho. its taken me longer than it did in Canada; but I must say I like these diggers & their women better than I thought I was going to as I liked the canadians much the most during the war!! But comparisons are odious

www.ingramcontent.com/pod-product-compliance
Lightning Source LLC
Chambersburg PA
CBHW032029150426
43194CB00006B/204